DE CONTROVERSIIS
CHRISTIANAE FIDEI
ADVERSUS HUIUS TEMPORIS
HAERETICOS

ON THE CONTROVERSIES OF
THE CHRISTIAN FAITH
AGAINST THE HERETICS
OF THIS TIME

ST. ROBERT BELLARMINE
OF THE SOCIETY OF JESUS
DOCTOR OF THE CHURCH

TRANSLATED FROM
THE ORIGINAL LATIN BY

RYAN GRANT

MEDIATRIX PRESS

De Controversiis Fidei Christianae

ON THE MOST HOLY SACRIFICE OF THE MASS

St. Robert Bellarmine, S.J.

Translated by Ryan Grant

Mediatrix Press
MMXX

ISBN: 978-1-953746-60-3

Translated from:
Disputationes de Controversiis Fidei Christianae, Tomus III, Prague, 1721, *De Eucharistia*, libri V-VI.

©Ryan Grant, 2020

All rights reserved. No part of this work may be reproduced in electronic or printed formats except for quotations in journals, periodicals, blogs and classroom use without the express permission of the publisher.

Cover art: *The Last Supper*, Peter Paul Rubens, St. Rombout, Mechlen. Sculpture of St. Robert Bellarmine: Gian Lorenzo Bernini, Chiesa di Gesu, Rome.

Mediatrix Press
607 E. 6th Ave.
Post Falls, ID 83854
www.mediatrixpress.com

TABLE OF CONTENTS

Translator's Preface ... 7

ON THE MOST HOLY SACRIFICE OF THE MASS: BOOK I

CHAPTER I: *On the word "Mass"* ... 13
CHAPTER II: *On the definition of a sacrifice* ... 20
CHAPTER III: *The death of Christ is a sacrifice properly speaking* ... 31
CHAPTER IV: *On the partition of sacrifice* ... 34
CHAPTER V: *Is the Mass a sacrifice? The state of the controversy is explained, and the positions of Catholics and heretics related* ... 36
CHAPTER VI: *That in the Mass a true sacrifice is offered: Proven firstly from the testimony of scripture and the priesthood of Melchisedech.* ... 39
CHAPTER VII: *The sacrifice of the Mass is proven from the figure of the Paschal Lamb* ... 61
CHAPTER VIII: *The sacrifice of the Mass is proven from the figures of different sacrifices of the Old Testament* ... 70
CHAPTER IX: *The sacrifice of the Mass is proven from predictions of the prophets* ... 74
CHAPTER X: *That the Mass is a sacrifice is proven from Malachi* ... 77
CHAPTER XI: *The sacrifice of the Mass is proven from John 4* ... 89
CHAPTER XII: *The sacrifice of the Mass is proven from the Words of Institution* ... 92
CHAPTER XIII: *The sacrifice of the Mass is proven from Acts 13* ... 100
CHAPTER XIV: *The sacrifice of the Mass is proven from 1 Corinthians 10* ... 101
CHAPTER XV: *The sacrifice of the Mass is proved from the tradition of the Fathers, and first from the terms Sacrifice, Oblation and Immolation* ... 105
CHAPTER XVI: *The sacrifice of the Mass, properly speaking, is proven from the rite of Altars* ... 118
CHAPTER XVII: *The sacrifice of the Mass is proven from the word "Priest".* ... 120
CHAPTER XVIII: *The sacrifice of the Mass is proven from the Liturgies* ... 123
CHAPTER XIX: *The same is proven from those for whom the sacrifice of the Mass is offered* ... 124
CHAPTER XX: *The sacrifice of the Mass is proven from the union of Law and Sacrifice* ... 125
CHAPTER XXI: *The sacrifice of the Mass is proven from the comparison of the Christian law to the Mosaic* ... 129
CHAPTER XXII: *The same is proven from the difference between the Sacrament and the Sacrifice* ... 131
CHAPTER XXIII: *The same is proven from the consensus of the Church* ... 132
CHAPTER XXIV: *The objections of Luther are answered* ... 134
CHAPTER XXV: *The arguments of John Calvin are answered* ... 138

Chapter XXVI: *The objections of Chemnitz are answered*   148
Chapter XXVII: *The last objection is answered, and it is explained in what part of the Mass the essence of the sacrifice properly consists*   150

ON THE MOST HOLY SACRIFICE OF THE MASS: BOOK II

Chapter I: *We lay down the first controversy: Whether the Mass is a propitiatory sacrifice*   161
Chapter II: *That the Mass is a propitiatory sacrifice is proven*   163
Chapter III: *The sacrifice of the Mass is also impetratory*   169
Chapter IV: *The proper efficacy of the sacrifice of the Mass is explained*   171
Chapter V: *We answer the objections of our adversaries*   178
Chapter VI: *The sacrifice of the Mass benefits all the living*   180
Chapter VII: *The sacrifice of the Mass is duly offered for the dead abiding in Purgatory*   183
Chapter VIII: *The sacrifice of the Mass is rightly celebrated in honor of the Saints*   190
Chapter IX: *On Private Masses*   200
Chapter X: *The arguments against Private Masses are answered*   208
Chapter XI: *On the kind of language*   217
Chapter XII: *Not everything in Mass must necessarily be said in a loud voice*   219
Chapter XIII: *What the heretics suppose regarding the ceremonies of the Mass*   225
Chapter XIV: *The ceremonies which precede Mass are ancient and pious*   230
Chapter XV: *On the ceremonies which are done in the Mass, and in the action in which they consist.*   240
Chapter XVI: *On what is recited in the Mass of the Catechumens*   246
Chapter XVII: *On the Offertory, and the Preface*   256
Chapter XVIII: *On the word "Canon"*   259
Chapter XIX: *On the author of the Canon*   262
Chapter XX: *On the antiquity of the Canon*   266
Chapter XXI: *On the truth of the First Prayer of the Canon*   269
Chapter XXII: *On the Truth of the Second Prayer of the Canon*   279
Chapter XXIII: *On the Truth of the Third Prayer of the Canon*   281
Chapter XXIV: *On the Truth of the Fourth Prayer of the Canon*   283
Chapter XXV: *On the Truth of the Fifth Prayer of the Canon*   290
Chapter XXVI: *On the Sixth Prayer of the Canon*   291
Chapter XXVII: *On the Lord's Prayer, and the following prayers*   294
APPENDIX A: *The Text of the Canon*   300

TRANSLATOR'S PREFACE

Those already familiar with our series of translations of St. Robert Bellarmine will not need a repetition of what we have written elsewhere, in our prefaces to the translation of *On the Roman Pontiff*, or *On the Church*, etc. We have instead determined on making some general notes about this volume and the translation.

This work is excerpted from the larger treatise on the Eucharist, which comprises six books altogether, these last two being specifically devoted to the Mass. In the first four, St. Robert takes up all the questions concerning the Real Presence of Christ in the Eucharist against the Protestants of the 16th century. Then follows the chapters on the Mass which represent this volume.

St. Robert here takes up the argument in two books: On whether the Mass is a sacrifice, and in the second, the nature of that sacrifice and the place for ceremonies within it. Thus, in the first book, he labors at great length to show what a sacrifice is, properly speaking, a phrase he employs rather frequently. This was necessary for Bellarmine to meet the arguments of the Protestants of his day who argued that a sacrifice was merely prayers and almsgiving or the like. It is in the second book that he takes on questions such as the propitiatory nature of the Mass, its benefits to the living and the dead, and above all, the ceremonies of the Mass.

Those familiar with St. Robert's argumentation will see his familiar *modus operandi*; to fight the Protestant authors on their own ground, in Scripture and its interpretation, then to add the understanding of the Fathers on those verses of Scripture, and again, the teaching of the Fathers in general, and then reason.

The work is not as strictly technical as a scholastic treatise might be, given that he is arguing primarily to individuals who reject the scholastics altogether, so a simpler mode of argument had to be chosen. Nevertheless, that does not mean there are no theological technical terms employed, and these have been left in Latin with an explanatory footnote, or else their customary formula has been used.

At times, because Bellarmine or his interlocutors are making specific arguments from the Vulgate, and then arguing according to the propriety of these terms in Latin, it has been necessary in a few places to render an excessively literal translation, which again, has explanations provided in the footnotes.

Next, for those who are unfamiliar with the liturgical tradition of the Church, we must point out that the Mass in St. Robert's time is virtually the same as what can today be found in the 1962 Missal, give or take a few changes. The reader should attempt to look up the text of the Mass, which can be found in many places. Because there are many arguments on the Canon (the Eucharistic Prayer) at the end of the treatise, and we left many of these prayers in the Latin, we have provided the text of the Canon in the Appendix with our own translation for reference to assist in understanding various arguments.

Finally, I want to thank all of those who assisted in the proofreading of the work, and the many suggestions given to improve it. In this regard, I must gratefully thank Mr. Ashton Wilkins, who provided so much assistance to the revision of Book I. Next, I must thank all of those who have donated to the Bellarmine translation project, for their patience as I have had many delays and have worked through many difficulties to persevere in this work.

I also want to thank my family, which has suffered much from the death of our youngest daughter Emma, who being below the age of reason, is certainly now in heaven. Without their love and support, as well as Emma's intercesion, this work would not be possible, and I would perhaps have given up altogether.

Post Falls ID
January, 2020

❦ Ad Meam Carissimam Emmam ❦

Citius nos reliquisti ut appropinquares
tuam domum cœlestiam.
Hoc tamen brevi tempore, gaudium nobis dedisti;
Quam pulchra fuisti, sicut angelus,
Sed parva teneraque.
Satis tempus non habuimus, ita poscimus,
Cur diliculo vitae profecta es?
Quam nemo scit, obscura providentia Dei.
Cum laetemur quod in meliori terrâ ades,
Abes a nobis, et non possumus te complecti oscularique;
liberata es a lacrimarum valle, sed non liberati sumus,
et te desidero.

Utinam Stygos transirem et blandirer Charon,
Sed tu ultra velamen mortale,
Sic necesse est nobis hic degere,
Usque ad horam appositam Deo,
Ut juctim cum sanctis ejus eum laudemus,
Et turba nullum locum habeat.

Emma Josephine-Marie Julia Serissima Grant
28 May 2018 - 8 September 2019
Ora pro nobis!

ON THE MOST HOLY SACRIFICE OF THE MASS
BOOK I

ON THE MOST HOLY SACRIFICE OF THE MASS
BOOK I.

CHAPTER I
On the word "Mass"

LET US begin the argument on the "Mass" from the terms, of which there are four, whether it is ancient, what are the etymologies, what are the significations, and in what sense it should be received by a Catholic when they say the Mass is a sacrifice.

There can be no doubt that this word is the most used and ancient in the Latin Church. St. Ambrose uses it (lib, 5, epist. 33), "I remained in my duty, I began to do Mass, to pray in sacrifice to God that he might bring assistance." St. Augustine uses it (Serm. 91 *de tempore*), "In the reading, which is going to be read for us at Mass, we are going to hear, etc." The same word is used by Victor of Utica (lib. 2 *hist. de persecutione Wandalica*). It is found in Cassian (*de canonica divinarum oratinum et psalmorum ordine*, lib. 3). It is found in Leo the Great (Epist. 81 *ad Dioscorum*, & 88 *ad Episcopos Germaniae, & Galliae*); cited by Felix IV (Epist. 1); in St. Benedict (*Regula*, cap. 17); Gregory I (lib. 1 epist. 12 & lib 4 epist. 10) and in many other places. At length, in the most ancient Councils, as we have in the Roman Council under Sylvester I, in the second Council of Carthage (can. 3), in the fourth Council of Carthage (can. 84), Ilerdensis (can. 4), Valencia (can. 1) Agathensis (can. 47) the first council of Arles (can. 28). These testimonies were written nearly a thousand years ago or more.

Now, what attains to the etymology. The Lutherans, from their customary impudence, deduce it from the Hebrew word מָעֻזִּים *Mahuzim* which is found in Daniel 11, where we read about Antichrist: "He worshiped the god Mahuzim in his place." Our adversaries would have it that this is the case, and in the first place Chemnitz (*Examination of the Council of Trent*, par. 2), in the very beginning of the disputation of the Sacrifice of the Mass, says the Mass is a god, or the ark and stronghold of the Roman Antichrist, *i.e.* the Pope; and he tries to show it because it seems to have happened that by divine providence, the word for Mass would agree with that god of Antichrist.

But we prove from that very passage of Scripture that Mahuzim has nothing in common with *Missa*, and is rather more some idol of the Lutherans, if one may be allowed to play with the Scriptures. For in the same chapter we read that the king who worshiped the god Mahuzim, is the king of the North, and the king of the south was going to come against him in battle, namely the Romans were going to fight against the same king. For, in his commentary, St. Jerome witnesses that those Hebrew words זִיִּים *ziim* and כִּתִּים *Chitthim* are shown by the Jews to mean the Romans and the Italians. But if the people of the south, namely the Romans, fight with the king who worships the god Mahuzim, certainly the god Mahuzim is not the god of the Romans, nor is it the Mass, unless they would have it now that the Mass is attacked by the Romans, and defended by the people of the north.

Besides, that king who worshiped the God Mahuzim, as we read in the same chapter, did not worship any other gods, nor the gods of his fathers, but rose up against all divinities.[1] Moreover, our adversaries assert that the Romans worship innumerable gods, and a great many idols, namely all the saints, and their relics as well as images. Yet, our very adversaries clearly rise up against images, relics and even the saints themselves, therefore they should, if they would speak consistently, declare frankly that the god Mahuzim is their god and not the god of the papists.

For this purpose, if the god Mahuzim is a god made and set up by antichrist, and antichrist was born in the six hundredth year of our Lord, as the Lutherans commonly teach, how can that god Mahuzim be the Mass, which is by far more ancient, as we have already shown from Ambrose, Augustine, and other more ancient Fathers?

Lastly, Antichrist will not only worship the god Mahuzim, but do so publicly. For the words of the same prophet are reconciled which at first glance appear to be opposed to each other. When he says that Antichrist is going to scorn all gods so that he alone (as the Apostle declares to the Thessalonians), will be held as a God, and in the same chapter he adds, "He will venerate the god Mahuzim in his place," these words are not opposed to each other, because Antichrist will publicly oppose all gods. Yet, secretly in his citadel (for that is what Mahuzim properly means), he will worship the devil as a god, by whose crafts he will obtain that power to be believed to be God, and carry out his signs and lying miracles. So, if the god Mahuzim is going to be worshiped in a most hidden and secret place, who cannot see how far from the truth they wander, who say Daniel is interpreted on the Mass, when the Mass is celebrated publicly throughout all the world, in churches with the people present?

---

1 Translator's note: For more of St. Robert Bellarmine's thought on this subject, see *On Antichrist*, which constitutes book 3 of *On the Roman Pontiff*.

Book I, Ch. 1: On the word "Mass"

Now that I have left behind these trifles, I shall come to the teaching of Catholics. Most try to show that the word *Missa* is Hebrew and means a voluntary offering, since the word מסח *misach*, which we find in Deuteronomy 16:10, has this meaning. Not only Catholics, but even Philip Melanchthon in his *Apology for the Augsburg Confession* (disputation on the word *Mass*), acknowledges this etymology and meaning, and also tries to twist it to his own teaching.

But this Hebrew term did not seem to be in use among the Apostles, and the opinion of those who teach that the word *missa* is Latin and was first taken up by Latins in the celebration of the mystery of the Eucharist, is much more probable. For, if that Hebrew word were in use among the Apostles, the Greeks and the Syrians would most certainly have retained it, as well as all other nations, just as they retain other similar terms such as *Amen, Alleluja, Sabaoth, Osanna, Satan, Sabbath, Pascha*, etc. These Hebrew terms come to us through the Greeks, seeing that the Apostles themselves and the first doctors of the Church wrote in Greek. Moreover, the Greeks never use the word *Mass*, rather, they use λειτουργίαν. Moreover, the λειτουργίαν is a *munus* (office), or public *ministerium* (ministry), and although the Greeks only take it up to mean the ministry of offering the sacrifice of the Eucharist, nevertheless, of itself this word is much broader in meaning. Demosthenes, in his *Oration against Leptines*, very frequently uses this word for a public office, and Paul himself in Philippians 2:25, calling Epaphroditus the τὸν λειτουργὸν (the minister) of his necessity.

Additionally, the Syrians, such as the Maronites, who celebrate the divine Sacrifice in the Aramaic language, do not have the term Mass, rather they use קודשׁה *kodesihah* in its place, which means holy, or sacred. And still, if the Hebrew word ought to be preserved in use by anyone, it would in fact be those who always use that language, although it would be a little corrupted. Furthermore, the fact that men learned in the Hebrew language such as Origen, Epiphanius, Justin, and Jerome never used it would be rather surprising if *missa* were a Hebrew word. Lastly, if it was a Hebrew word, it would not be *Missa*, rather it would have to be rendered *Missah*, yet nobody writes or speaks of it in that way.

Now, those authors that would have it that it is a Latin term do not explain it the same way. Some say that *missa* is said because it is an oblation, and prayers sent to God. So thought Hugh of St. Victor (*de Sacramentis*, lib. 2 part. 8). Others, less probably, that the Angel sent by God who assists at the Sacrifice, brings it to God, such as St. Peter

Lombard (in 4 dist. 13) and St. Thomas (III, q. 83, art. 4).

Others, as well as a great many heretics, would have it that *Missa* was named by the ancients from the sending and conveying of offerings into the midst, like a certain symbol, from where the sacred dinner and drink would be given to the poor; wherefore they would also have it that the Greeks called this same Mass ἀγάπην (agape). Thus, John Calvin (*Instit.* Lib. 4 cap. 18 § 18), Peter Martyr (in chapter 5 on 1 Cor.), and Philipp Melanchthon more profusely in his *Apologia for the Augsburg Confession* in the disputation on the word Mass. Such an exposition has no testimony in antiquity, and is altogether false insofar as it confounds *missa* with *agape*. The agape was a meal of Christians devised particularly as a consolation for the poor, as we can gather from Tertullian (*Apologeticus*, cap. 39) and St. Augustine (*contra Faustum*, lib. 20, cap. 21). It was sober, and mixed, but still a human and secular action. On the other hand, Ambrose, Augustine, Leo and the others that we cited always take up the word *Missa* for a sacred and mystical action, in which a special part of our religion consists.

The most probable opinion is of those who would have it that *Missa* comes from *missio*, or the dismissal of the people, so that *missa* is the same as *missio*, just as among the ancients *collecta* forms from *collectio*, and among the Greeks συλλογή from σύλλεξις, and *remissa peccati* (remission for sin) from *remissio*. We also find that Cyprian uses *remissa* (lib. 3 epist. 8; *de bono patientiae*, in epist. Ad Jubajanum, and other places). This is the opinion of St. Isidore (*Originum*, lib. 6); Rabanus (*de institute. Clericorum*, lib. 1 cap. 32); of Alcuin (*de Ecclesiasticis*, cap. *de celebration Missae*); Hugh of St. Victor (*loc. cit.*) and other more recent authors admit this etymology.

Now, although *missa* comes from *missio*, nevertheless, it does not only mean dismissal, rather it is a word drawn from it to mean other things. Therefore, there are accepted uses of *missa* among ecclesiastical writers.

1) *First*, it is received simply for *missio* (dismissal). It is received in this way in the Fourth Council of Carthage (canon 84), "The bishop shall not forbid anyone from entering the Church and hearing the word of God even to the *Mass of the Catechumens* (*Missam catechumenorum*), whether he be a heretic, or a Jew, or a pagan." In that place, Mass cannot be received for the Sacrifice, or the Lord's Supper, since that was not for the Catechumens, but only the *faithful*. Nor can it be received for the Gospel and the readings, which were recited while the Catechumens

were present, for the Council willed for them to be heard even by infidels. This is why in that place, *missa* cannot be received except for the *dismissal of the Catechumens.* This word is received in the same way in the Council of Ilderda (can. 4), where it is forbidden for the incestuous to remain in Church, except that it be until the end of the Mass of the Catechumens. St. Augustine receives it this way and in the same sense (serm. 237 de tempore). "Behold," he says, "after the sermon the Mass of the Catechumens (*missa catechumenis*) takes place, and only the faithful remain, etc." St. John Cassian receives *missa* in the same sense (*de canonia orationum et psalmorum*, 2, 7; *in titulo*, cap. 15), where he calls the Mass of Prayer (*Missa Orationis*) the dismissal at the end of the prayer. And elsewhere (lib. 3 cap. 7) he calls it the *Mass of the Congregation* (*Missa Congregationis*), and in chapter 8 he calls the *Mass of vigils* (*Missa Vigiliarum*) the dismissal after vigils. St. Benedict also takes us *Masses* in this way in his rule (cap. 17), where he bids these "Masses", namely dismissals, to be made after each nocturn. Lastly, even in our liturgy it is received in this manner when the Deacon sings, "Ite missa est", as Alcuin rightly explains (*loc. cit.*). The sense is: Now it is the dismissal of the congregation, everyone is allowed to leave.

2) *Secondly*, Mass is received for the *divine office* of readings, prayers and every other kind of thing celebrated in a Church where the dismissal of the Catechumens takes place. And rightly, these words of the most ancient Council of Valencia (cap. 1) should be noted: "We have decreed that this must be observed, that after the most holy Gospels are read, before the conclusion of the offices in the Mass of the Catechumens, in the order of readings, etc." Here, it cannot be understood on the dismissal of catechumens, but the divine office, at which they were present.

3) *Thirdly*, it is received for that part of the Liturgy which is from the Offertory even to the end, properly called the Mass of the Faithful (*Missa fidelium*), as Alcuin witnesses (*loc. cit.*). It is also received in this way by St. Ambrose (Epist. 5, 33), "I remained in the office, I began to do the Mass, to pray over the offering, etc."

4) *Fourthly*, it is received for the celebration of the Divine Office, wherein the Eucharist is consecrated, as it includes the Mass of the Catechumens and the Faithful together. So, it is received in Leo, Gregory, Felix IV, and the Council of Agde and Arles (*loc. cit.*), and this is the common reception found in all later authors.

5) *Fifthly*, it is received for the *collects* themselves, that is the prayers which are said in the Liturgy. It is received in this way by the Council of

Milevis, can. 12.

But the fourth meaning is, how is the word "Mass" received when we ask, "is the Mass a Sacrifice?" This is the sense of the question: Whether that sacred action, in which the Eucharist is confected, with many prayers and ceremonies preceding and following, is a sacrifice? We do not understand in this question whether this or that individual rite pertains to the essence of the sacrifice, but only, whether among those rites there is something which should properly be called a sacrifice, to which all the rest refer.

Now that the question has been defined properly, we can refute the deception of Chemnitz. In *Examination of the Council of Trent* (2 part. Pg. 717), he proposes to explain what the Mass is which the Popes properly understand to be a sacrifice, and he says that it is clearly explained by John of Eck (*de Sacrificio Missae*, 1, 10), and at length, after citing some words from Eck, he so concludes: "The sacrifice of the Mass, for which the Popes make war, consists in this, a sacrificing priest that uses certain ornaments and instruments, over bread and wine of the Eucharist with various gestures, motions, actions, dances, to bow with hands together, then to extend them, then to lower the arms, repeatedly turning himself, here to shout, there to murmur in great silence, to lift himself up, and to lie prostrate, to stand in one place, then to move to the right of the altar, then to the left, etc."

But this is a marvelous deception from this new Evangelist. For John of Eck, a very learned man, who always triumphed over Luther and his followers, says that the passion of Christ is represented in the Mass, with various actions, gestures, ornaments and rites. But Chemnitz impudently lies, as Eck does not say the essence of the sacrifice (which we are talking about) consists in that representation, and in those gestures. Rather, he teaches that the Sacrifice properly consists in the oblation of the body and blood of the Lord, which the priest makes to God. In the tenth chapter of that work cited by Chemnitz, he makes a fourfold division. The certain action of Sacrifice, and a representation that is not a sacrifice; the certain representation, and a sacrifice that is not a representation. And this is twofold: for there is one type of simple representation, customarily when something painted is discerned, or recited from a book of history; another type of representation is brought to life by various actions, such as when a battle or a triumph is represented on stage by actors, where masks, costumes and weapons, as well as the actions themselves are discerned, and words are heard.

Lastly, a certain sacrifice, and a representation of a sacrifice.

The death of Christ on the true cross pertains to the first division; for that was a sacrifice and not a representation of some sacrifice. To the second division, the consumption of the Eucharist pertains, as those who do it simply commemorate the passion of Christ, but they do not properly offer the Sacrifice, nor even represent the sacrifice of the Christ to the living. To the third division pertains the divine office, which is carried out in the Church on Good Friday; in that the passion of Christ is accurately represented with various gestures, movements, words, garments, instruments, etc.; there is not any action in that whole office which is properly a sacrifice. The Mass pertains to the fourth division, in which the Sacrifice of the Cross is represented with various gestures, actions, the sacrifice of the Cross and at the same time the true and proper sacrifice of the body of the Lord is offered to God.

This is the doctrine of Eck, and of all Catholics, from which it is absolutely certain that the Sacrifice does not properly consist in those different gestures and motions, for otherwise on Good Friday the true Sacrifice would be offered, since a great many different gestures and motions of this sort are made in that office, but still Eck clearly rejects this.

Add that Eck, when he means to prove the Sacrifice of the Mass, in that whole work directs his argumentation to prove that in the Mass a sacrifice is made to God, not to prove it should be done with different gestures and motions. Therefore, he does not understand the Sacrifice to be made through gestures and motions, according to the calumnies of Chemnitz, but the sacrifice of the body and blood of the Lord.

CHAPTER II
On the Definition of a Sacrifice

Now that we have explained the term *Mass*, we will explain the term *sacrifice*, so that the state of the controversy would be plainly understood, namely whether the Mass is a sacrifice. Hence, in the word *sacrifice* there is no need to look for etymologies, or some common meaning because it is known to all; rather, what a Sacrifice properly is, or what is its nature and definition. In this matter many persons are deceived.

1) The *first* is Philipp Melanchthon (*Apologia for the Augsburg Confession*, in the article on the Mass), who so defines a sacrifice, "A sacrifice is a ceremony or work, which we render to God and uphold his honor." Then, he divides sacrifice into two species, into a Sacrifice of Propitiation, and a Sacrifice of thanksgiving (εὐχαριστικὸν). He says that a propitiatory sacrifice is that which is made in satisfaction for sin, and to appease God; whereas he would have it a sacrifice of thanksgiving, which does not reconcile man to God, is an action of thanksgiving which those that have been reconciled to God show him for the benefits they have received. He then says that faith, preaching of the Gospel, prayers, castigation of the flesh and briefly all goods are contained in the latter kind of sacrifice for which praise rises unto God. And also, from these foundations he gathers that the Mass can be called a Sacrifice in this second mode, because the reception of the Eucharist can be made in praise of God, just as other good works, but not as a sacrifice of the first kind.

It seems the opinion of a certain modern doctor, who is otherwise very erudite and pious is not far off from the opinion of Melanchthon, which teaches that a sacrifice properly so called is every good work which is done so that we might adhere to God in holy society, or of itself is a work of virtue, or not, so that the castigation of the flesh, taken on for God's sake, is no less a sacrifice than the Sacrifice of the Eucharist (Gaspar Cassiensus, *de Sacrificio*, cap. 5). The same opinion divides sacrifice properly speaking into two species, namely into a figurative sacrifice, and one that is not figurative. The figurative describes those things which are done for another meaning; such as were the sacrifices of the old law, and such as are all the sacraments of the new law. The non-figurative describes those works of virtue, which although they will signify nothing, still are pleasing to God.

This opinion is false and can be refuted by many clear arguments. Firstly, Sacred Scripture opposes many works of virtue to sacrifices, as when it says in Hosea 6:6, "I desire mercy and not sacrifice," and 1 Kings [Samuel] 15:22, "Obedience is better than holocausts," and Psalm 50 [51]:17, "If you desired sacrifice, I would have indeed given it, but in holocausts you take no delight. A sacrifice to God is a humbled spirit; a contrite and humbled heart God will not despise." But if all works of virtue were sacrifices properly speaking, certainly obedience, mercy, and works of penance would also properly be sacrifices, and these teachings of the Scriptures we cited would not be true. How would God mean mercy and not sacrifice, if mercy itself is a true sacrifice properly speaking? Or again, how would obedience be better than holocausts, if obedience itself were truly and properly a holocaust? Just the same, would God not want sacrifice and holocausts but a contrite and humbled heart if this is a true sacrifice?

The *second argument*: In every sacrifice properly speaking, some sensible matter is required to be offered, since sacrifice cannot consist in action alone. But if a sacrifice were some ceremonies, or a work done for God's honor, there is no reason why an action alone could not constitute a sacrifice, and he that sings psalms, and genuflects, or does some other thing of this sort, he would be properly said to sacrifice. Therefore, certain ceremonies or a work done for God's honor are not a sacrifice. The major is proven from Gen. 22:7, when Isaac says to his father, "Here is the fire and the wood, where is the victim for the holocaust?" And in Hebrews 8:3, "Every priest is constituted to offer gifts and holocausts, so it is necessary that he also has something to offer." Here, the Apostle gathers from the common notion of sacrifices, that Christ could not truly be said to be a priest unless he had a victim which he might offer.

The *third argument*: It cannot be denied that to sacrifice is an act more properly called forth by religion, and apart from the Scholastic Doctors, St. Augustine teaches this (*Contra Faustum*, 20, 21). Moreover, the same act cannot properly be called forth by different virtues, therefore, one's own works of mercy, temperance, and other virtues cannot properly be called sacrifices, except through a certain participation. For although one and the same act could be more properly called forth by diverse virtues, still, it can be called forth by one thing, and commanded by another, in the same way it pertains properly to one thing, and by participation to another. Just the same, to take food soberly, is an act called forth by temperance; nevertheless, if it were commanded by fortitude, so that a man would be more suited to fight, he will participate in fortitude. If by justice, namely that he would have the means to pay monetary debts, he will participate in justice. So, in this way, the works of any virtues you like can be commanded by religion, and called sacrifices after the manner of participation, but not absolutely and properly, seeing as they are not called forth by religion. Consequently, this is why in Scripture works of virtue are not absolutely called sacrifices, but something added, such as *sacrifice of praise, spiritual hosts, burnt offerings of the lips*, etc., according to the same mode. But those works which are properly sacrifices are called such simply and absolutely, just as in those passages brought in the first argument: "I demand mercy and not sacrifice...".

The *fourth argument:* In the Church of Christ there is properly only one true Sacrifice; therefore, all the Sacraments, or all good works which are done to worship God, are not properly sacrifices. The preceding is from St. Augustine, and all of the holy authors. In *City of God* (8, 27), Augustine, meaning to show that those food offerings which certain people placed over the tombs of the martyrs are not sacrifices, he says, "He that knows there is one sacrifice of Christians offered to God knows that these are not sacrifices to the martyrs." He says in other places the one and singular sacrifice of the Eucharist succeeded all the sacrifices of the ancients (*de Baptismo contra Donatistas*, 1, ult; *contra advers. Legis, et Prophetarum*, c. 20). In *de spiritu et littera*, c. 11, he calls it the most true and singular Sacrifice of the Eucharist; and in *Contra Cresconium*, 1, 25, he calls it the only one. St. Leo the Great declares, "Now too, the variety of fleshly sacrifices has ceased, and the one offering of your body and blood fulfills all those different victims" (Serm. 59,7). St. John Chrysostom says, "The number of Sacrifices in the law was great and without measure, which in the new [law] a supervenient grace embraces in one sacrifice, constituting a one true offering" (in Psalm. 95).

The *fifth argument:* Sacrifice and priesthood are relative, so that a priesthood, is properly called by a sacrifice, properly speaking; a priesthood improperly speaking by a sacrifice improperly speaking. But not all those who do good works for the honor of God are priests properly speaking; therefore, such works are altogether not sacrifices properly speaking.

The major is most certain. For a priesthood, inasmuch as its proper office is to offer sacrifice (Heb. 5:1), and Justin Martyr, (*Dialogue with Trypho*) says God does not receive sacrifice except from priests. St.

Book I, Ch. 2: The Meaning of a Sacrifice

Augustine always adds these two words, sacrifice, and priesthood, as if they are inseparable (epist. 49, q. 3; *City of God* 3, 31; 22, 10). The terms themselves also teach this. In Latin, *sacerdos* and *sacrificus* are taken as one in the same. In Greek, θύειν, which is to sacrifice, comes from θυσία, sacrifice, and θύτης, priest; ἱερεύειν, to sacrifice, ἱερεῖον, sacrifice, and ἱερεὺς, priest. Next, there is no other reason the Lutherans do not acknowledge a true priesthood, properly speaking, in the Church than that they do not recognize a true sacrifice properly speaking.

Now the assumption is proven. For in the Old Testament it is common knowledge that one could not be properly called a priest unless he was among the sons, grandsons or other posterity of Aaron. We see this when King Ozia violently usurped the priesthood from Azariah the high priest (2 Chronicles 26:18), and still all the sons of Israel ought to have done good works. But in the Church of Christ, whether the Lutherans will or no, never was anyone properly called a priest except for bishops and presbyters. Moreover, Dionysius the Areopagate (*de Eccles. Hier.*, 1, 1, 3 and 5) uses this word, as well as Justin (*loc. cit.*), and Tertullian (*de praescript.*; *de velandis virginibus*). St. Cyprian (*Epist.* 1;4) and all later writers. The Apostle himself, speaking about the priesthood says, "Neither does any man take the honor to himself, but he that is called by God, as Aaron was" (Heb. 5:4). And this is so true that in the same place Paul says that even Christ himself did not take up the priesthood on his own, but received it from the Father. Lastly (here I pass over the rest of the argument), the Council of Nicaea in can. 14, and the Council of Trent, which Catholics cannot reject (sess. 33 can. 1 & 7), clearly teach that in the Church, not everyone, but *certain men* are priests. This is why it necessarily follows that either the rest of the faithful should not do good works, which would be completely absurd, or those who do good works are not all properly priests, which is very true.

The *sixth argument*. Altar and sacrifice are relative; moreover, an altar properly speaking is not necessary for every good work, nor all ceremonies with which we worship God. Thus, every ceremony or good work of this sort is not a sacrifice. The major proposition is clear. In the first place, both Hebrew and Greek deduce the words *sacrifice*, and *altar*, from the root. From זָבַח *zabach*, he sacrificed, comes זֶבַח *zebach*, sacrifice; and from מִזְבֵּחַ *mizbeach*, altar; from θύειν, which is to sacrifice, comes from θυσία, sacrifice, and θυσιαστήριον, altar. Latins prefer to deduce the terms from the form and the rite. They say *altare* as it were, comes from *altum*, and *ara* from *ansa* (handle), as Varro interprets it, because the priest holds the altar while he offers sacrifice. Thus, the poet: *Talibus orantem dictis, arasque tenentem.*[2]

Then, in Gen. 8:20, where we read the first altar was erected, we read that it was erected for the sake of sacrifice, and in every nation and religion, altars were always raised for sacrifice. And just as the sacrifice can be offered rightly to God alone, so also an altar can rightly be raised for God alone, as St. Augustine teaches (*Contra Faustum*, 20;21). Hence, the assumption of this argument requires no proof. For who does not see that a great many good works and ceremonies can be done for the honor of God without any altar?

Consequently, what Melanchthon writes is not true, that every ceremony or work, which we render to God so that we might fasten honors to him, is a sacrifice. John Calvin (*Institutes*, 4, 18 §13) rebukes this definition, though omitting the name of the author: "I do not see how, by any reasoning, those who extend the term sacrifice to all ceremonies and religious actions do so."

There is one argument to the contrary, and particularly of that Catholic teacher we mentioned above. St. Augustine (*City of God*, 10, 6), defines a sacrifice in this way: "A true sacrifice is every work which is done that we might cleave to God in holy society, and are able to be carried to that end, whereby we shall be blessed."

But the answer is easy. For St. Augustine does not define a sacrifice in general, nor a sacrifice properly speaking, but only a sacrifice which is particularly internal and opposed to legal and merely external sacrifices. And he calls it a sacrifice by reason *of the dignity* and effect, not by reason of the form and essence of the sacrifice properly speaking. For, he does not mean to say that internal sacrifices are more properly called sacrifices than external ones, since that would be contrary to the truth; but they are more excellent and pleasing to God, and it is easier to placate God. There is a similar teaching in John 15:1, "I am the true vine." In that passage, the Lord does not mean to show he is more properly a vine, because he attains to the form and essence of a real vine which is planted in vineyards; rather, only a more noble vine and to produce more excellent effects, as Euthymius explains in his commentary on this passage.

2) Now, let us spend some time on the definition of Calvin. He rebukes others, but he does not advance a better definition. For he so writes (*loc. cit.*), "We know that a sacrifice, in the perpetual use of

---

[2] Praying with such words and holding altars. *Aeneid* IV, 219.

Book I, Ch. 2: The Meaning of a Sacrifice

Scripture, is sometimes called in Greek θυσίαν, sometimes προσφοραν, and sometimes λετὴν, which is generally received as something altogether offered to God." Thus he. He clearly teaches that a sacrifice is the same thing as some oblation made to God. And then, he partitions a sacrifice into two species, in the same way as Melanchthon did, except that sacrifice which is not propitiatory, he contends can not only be called εὐχαριστικὸν, but even λατρευτικὸν, and σεβασικὸν, that is, the sacrifice of cult and veneration.

But after the partition has been omitted, on which there is no great controversy, certainly the definition advanced by Calvin cannot be admitted. For, although according to the use of Scripture, every sacrifice is a type of oblation, nevertheless, not every oblation is a sacrifice. Sacrifice, apart from oblation, requires a change and consumption of the thing which is offered, which a simple oblation does not require.

Firstly, it is proved from the word *sacrifice*. In Hebrew *zebach* (זֶבַח), comes from *zabach* (זָבַח) which is to slaughter. So also, in Matthew 22:4, Ταῦροι μου καὶ τὰ σιτιστά τεθυμένα, bulls and fatlings were slaughtered, as it is said from the word θυμίασις, i.e. death, as Porphyry contends (cited by Eusebius, *Preparation for the Gospel*, 1,6). He wanted sacrifices to be dedicated by death and the smoke which ascends from the burning of the sacrifice. This is why even Chrysostom and Theophylactus (commenting on Hebrews 10), note the difference between the words θυσίαν, and προσφοράν, i.e. sacrifice and oblation, because those things which are killed should be called θυσία, or otherwise consumed. It pertains to this that the term τελετὴ comes from the word τελέω, which is "I consume". Thereby it is gathered that Calvin did not correctly unite these words; προσφοράν which means a simple oblation, and θυσίαν and τελετὴν which add consumption on top of the oblation.

Secondly, it is proven from the use of the Scriptures. For in the Scriptures many things are said to be offered to God, which cannot be said about a sacrifice in the use of the divine Scripture, nor the common manner of speech. In Exodus 25:4 and 35:6, gold, silver, bronze, wood, precious stones, flax, scarlet, goat hair, and similar things were offered to God, which it would be utterly absurd to call a sacrifice. In Numbers 8:21, Aaron offers the Levites in an offering to the Lord from the sons of Israel, and still Scripture does not say that those men were sacrificed, nor could it be said, except very improperly, since these men were not killed, but merely assigned to ministry. On the other hand, Isaac truly and properly was about to be sacrificed by his father when he was led up to be killed and burned to the Lord (Genesis 22:9). And altogether everything which is called a sacrifice in Scripture necessarily had to be destroyed; if living through slaughter, if lifeless, such as salt and frankincense, through burning, if liquid, such as blood, wine and water, through effusion (Lev. 1 & 2).

Some might argue that this is opposed to the example of Melchisedech, who was a priest of the most high God and offered bread and wine. But in reality, it is in no way opposed seeing as it is read that the oblation was consumed (Gen. 14:18). For, Scripture does not explain the manner of this sacrifice; but from those passages we can gather that he sacrificed in the customary manner, to the extent that he consumed bread and wine for the honor of God. As a result, it is certain that a sacrifice is not anything offered to God, as Calvin says, rather something else must be added.

Then *thirdly*, we may add arguments introduced from the words *priesthood* and *altar*, which we already spoke of a little while before against Melanchthon. The oblation, taken up generally, requires neither priesthood nor altar. The widow in the gospel truly and properly offered up two insignificant farthings, although she was neither a priest nor had an altar.

3) I come now to Martin Chemnitz. In the first place he advances the meaning of the word *sacrifice*, which he says are three kinds. *Firstly*, he would have it that it be received for an external and ceremonial sacrifice, such as he says only existed in the Old Testament; and in this kind he numbers holocausts, burnt offerings, peace offerings, and burnt offerings for sin, and lastly a sacrifice of profession, such as a tithe and the first fruits. *Secondly*, he says it means the death of Christ, which is called the sacrifice of the Cross. *Thirdly*, for an inward, invisible, and spiritual sacrifice of the faithful, and to this kind he reduces preaching of the Gospel, sermons, almsgiving, praises of God, mortification and similar good works (*Examination of the Council of Trent*, 2 part, pg. 712). He also adds in another place (*loc. cit.* pg. 717), *fourthly*, the meaning for a commemorative sacrifice, *i.e.* for that thing which is recalled at the sacrifice of the Cross, although he affirms this reception is not held in the Scriptures. After he concludes all of these, on account of so many different meanings of the word sacrifice, that St. Augustine defined it well in general, "Every good work which is done that we might cleave to God in holy society. (*City of God*, 10, 5&6).

But there are many errors in this doctrine of Chemnitz. *First*, tithing and the first fruits are not properly numbered with the sacrifices of the Old Law, properly speaking. Tithing and first fruits are never called sacrifices in Scripture, nor does the word sacrifice, or its very notion suit them, as we showed above. Add to that the fact that sacrifice can be offered to God alone, as everyone upholds, but the tithe was offered without a medium and to the priests, not to God.

Next, when Chemnitz says that outward and ceremonial sacrifices were in the Old Law, but now they have altogether ceased, he contradicts himself, because the same Chemnitz says that every good work done to the honor of God in this time is a sacrifice. For certainly Baptism, and to confect, give and consume the Sacrament of the Eucharist are good works done to the honor of God, and yet they are outward and ceremonial. Nay more, the same Chemnitz, a little later in that citation, proves that the consecration and consumption of the Eucharist can be called a sacrifice in many ways. Just the same, nobody can deny that it is external and ceremonial.

Thirdly, it is a wonder why Chemnitz admits a fourth meaning of Sacrifice since he affirms it cannot be gathered from Scripture, yet he appears to admit the meaning so that he could elude the passages of the Fathers in which Mass is called a sacrifice. Moreover, this meaning is plainly arbitrary and fabricated, for neither Scripture nor the Fathers call what is only a type or commemoration of a sacrifice an actual sacrifice.

Then, Chemnitz falsely concludes that a sacrifice is defined in general by St. Augustine. For, in no way did Augustine mean to define a sacrifice in general in that place, rather he expressly excluded from his definition all the sacrifices of the Old Law, which consisted in the slaughter of sheep and oxen, which very properly retain the name and notion of a sacrifice. This is why Chemnitz cannot obtain what he desires by dividing or by defining so as to properly explain what a sacrifice is.

So, now that these have been rejected, this can be the true definition of a sacrifice in general, properly so called: *A sacrifice is an outward oblation made to God alone, whereby for a profession of human weakness and a profession of the divine majesty, some sensible and permanent matter is consecrated and changed by a legitimate minister in a mystical rite.* This definition ought to be a little longer to properly embrace all the conditions of a sacrifice properly so called.

Firstly, we say it is an *oblation*, so that we might show the kind of sacrifice. In this place we receive a sacrifice *for an action of sacrificing*, not for the victim itself, which is sacrificed, even though it is also customarily called a sacrifice. Therefore, a sacrifice received for the action is a species of oblation; it is a sacrifice which properly and per se, pertains to the action of a priest. Hence, the proper office of a priest is to offer sacrifice. "Every priest taken from men is constituted for men in these matters which are to God, that he might offer gifts, etc." Among Scriptural and ecclesiastical authors to offer (*offerre*) and to sacrifice (*sacrificare*) are received for the same thing. In Gen. 4:4, where the first mention of sacrifice is made, it is said that Abel offered from the first fruits of his flock. In Genesis 8:20, Noah offered holocausts and Scripture speaks everywhere in the same manner. Among the Fathers, Tertullian says there are three offices of the priests of the New law, to wash, offer and teach, *i.e.* to baptize, sacrifice, and preach. Then, the same author reveals the same word which the Greeks everywhere use, since when they speak about sacrifice, they use προσφορὰ, that is, oblation, which even Calvin notes as we saw above.

Secondly, we say that sacrifice is an *external* oblation. An oblation is twofold, and broadly speaking, we can distinguish two types of sacrifice, just as St. Augustine distinguishes it (*loc. cit.*), as invisible (internal), and visible (external). Invisible is a pious will, which offers itself and all of its things to the divine majesty, whereas a visible sacrifice is a solemn external demonstration of an inward inclination. This is why in the same passage, when Augustine is defining a visible sacrifice, he speaks of an invisible Sacrament of sacrifice, namely the sacred sign. Although an invisible oblation may be nobler and better than a visible one, and an invisible oblation might please God without a visible one, a visible oblation without an invisible one would not please him. Just the same, the name and notion of a sacrifice does not properly suit an invisible oblation, rather, only a visible and outward one, as we have posited in our definition. For an invisible oblation is always secret and private, whereas by the word sacrifice, everyone properly understands a public and manifest honor shown to God by a common and public minister. Therefore, for a sacrifice properly so called, it is necessarily required that is an outward oblation.

Thirdly, we said in our definition: "made to God alone". For an outward oblation can also be made to man, or to man and God, such as when alms are given to the poor for God's sake; for these are offered to men, and at the same time to God, when Christ says, "As often as you did it to one of the least of my brethren, you did it to me" (Matt. 25:40). But sacrifices of this sort are not oblations; for a sacrifice properly pertains to the cult of *latria*, which can be shown to God alone. For, as it is a certain interior cult which we show to God, when we acknowledge him as first, and the supreme God, the efficient and final cause of all things, and to such as he we prostrate our heart most dejectedly, so also there ought to be some outward sign whereby we testify that this cult is due to God alone. Moreover, there is no such sign apart from a sacrifice, for every other external reverence, which we show to God, whether it is a bow of the head or a genuflection, or prostrating the whole body, or even supplication and invocation, customarily may also be shown to men. We see this in Exodus 22:19, where we read, "Let he who sacrifices to gods, apart from the Lord alone, be slain." Not only does Scripture teach this, but all the gentiles acknowledge this by the natural light of reason. St. Augustine says, "What man ever thought of sacrificing unless it were to one whom he knew, supposed or feigned to be a god?" (*City of God*, 10, 4). And again, he says, "A demon would not demand sacrifice be offered to him unless he knew it should be offered to God. For, the remaining obsequies, which are shown to divinity, men dared to arrogate to themselves in the scorn of pride. However, it only rarely happened that they would command sacrifice to be offered to themselves, when they could do so with royal power. Still, whoever dared to do this, willed themselves to be held as gods" (*Contra adversarium legis et prophetarum*, 1, 18).

We said *fourthly*, "for the recognition of human weakness and the profession of divine majesty." Because this is the general purpose of all sacrifices; for there are, as if they were allotted, those things which are rendered to God in recognition of his supreme lordship, and our subjection. And this is also the reason why the action of sacrificing has praise, and is a work of virtue. Of themselves works are indifferent, such as to kill and burn animals, and like things; but when these are to show that all things proceed from God, and must be consumed in his honor, now they are works of religion, and hence good and praiseworthy.

Fifthly, we said "by a legitimate minister." It is not for anyone to offer sacrifice, but a *public and certain* man, who completes it by a common name. In the law of nature there were priests, or heads of households such as Noah, Abraham and those in whom God inspired it. In the written law, only the sons of Aaron. In the law of grace only bishops and priests properly ordained, as all the Councils, fathers and the custom of every Church teaches. Furthermore, as a consequence, the many oblations of private men which are made to God alone are excluded by the notion of sacrifice properly so called, acts such as when the faithful light candles and that are consumed in the Church for God's honor.

Sixthly, we said, "Some sensible and permanent matter", so that without a doubt transitory actions made for God's honor would be excluded by the notion of sacrifice properly so called. Acts such as psalmody, prayers, genuflections, and other things which are done by priests in an external act to honor God, and nevertheless are not properly sacrifices.

Seventhly, we said, "consecrated in a mystical rite." That matter which is offered to God should be made sacred from the profane, and dedicated to him. That is the very thing *sacrifice* means (*sacrificare*), to make something holy, as St. Thomas rightly teaches us (II IIae, q. 85 art. 3). Moreover, this very consecration and dedication was always done in the Old Law with a certain rite, and the ceremony contained a mystery, such as in the imposition of hands upon the victim, or in the elevation of the oblation on high. And in this sacrifice is distinguished from a simple oblation, which does not require of itself a mystical consecration of this sort.

Eighthly, we said: "And it is changed". For a true sacrifice it is required that what is offered to God in sacrifice be completely destroyed, *i.e.* it will be so changed that it will cease to be what it was. And in this it especially differs from a simple oblation, which for a short time was elevated in the presence of God with a mystical rite, but was not destroyed except when it was truly sacrificed. On such a condition we said many things a little while ago in refutation of the definition of Calvin. Moreover, the notion of this thing seems to be twofold. 1) On account of the meaning of the death of Christ. For God, who without any doubt first inspired Abel, and other holy men in the use of sacrifices, meant through these sacrifices to emphasize the most excellent sacrifice of all: that it consists in the death and destruction of the thing offered. 2) The other reason is, because a sacrifice is the supreme protestation of our subjection to God, and the supreme external cult, which could be shown. Moreover, that supreme protestation requires that not only the use of the thing is offered to God, but its very substance also: and therefore, not only the use but *the substance* is consumed.

CHAPTER III
The Death of Christ Is a Sacrifice Properly Speaking

Now, we run into one uncertainty in regard to the definition of a sacrifice. The Sacrifice of the Cross, *i.e.*, the passion and death of Christ was a most perfect and true sacrifice, as St. Augustine teaches (*Contra adv. Leg. Et prophet.*, 1, 18); yet it does not seem to suit the definition we have assigned. For (that I might pass over other things), the notion of sacrifice that we described requires that it not be an action of some virtue, apart from religion. The death of Christ, however, was an action of charity, patience, fortitude, humility, and obedience, as St. Paul says (Romans 5:8; Philipp. 2:8; Hebr. 12:2, and other places).

I respond: The sacrifice of the cross was properly an act of religion. For, Christ offered himself in death that he would be an oblation, and sacrifice to God for the expiation of the sins of the whole world, as the sacred writers teach, especially St. Paul in Ephesians 5:2, Hebrews 7:27, 8:3, 9:14, and 10:12. Just the same, it is in no way opposed that an act of religion could also participate in many other virtues; just as on the other hand, the acts of all other virtues (as we said above) participate in the notion of religion, and are termed sacrifices in a certain mode. For, if anyone furnishes obedience to a superior on account of the honor of God, that obedience will be a sacrifice; so also, if anyone would offer a true sacrifice to God, because a superior had commanded him, that action could be called obedience. And just the same, when almsgiving has been given to the poor on account of God, it is a type of sacrifice; so also, a sacrifice offered for sin is mercy.

Now someone will say, if the matter so stands, then truly the passions of the martyrs could also properly be called a sacrifice, although they seem to pertain chiefly to charity and fortitude.

I respond: The passions of the martyrs can be called sacrifices broadly speaking, just as all other good works, but not properly and strictly, as the passion of Christ. The passion of Christ differs from the passion of the martyrs in four ways, by the concept of the person, act, form and end.

By the concept of the person, because Christ was truly and properly a priest, "You are a priest forever," (Psalm 109 [110]:5), and he was a great priest (Heb. 10:21), nay more, clearly the supreme and greatest priest, who could offer any sacrifice, and therefore, even his own body. The holy martyrs also, either were not priests or certainly not such who can choose the victim prescribed in law.

By the concept of the act, because Christ properly sacrificed himself, since it was in his power to die and not to die. "He was offered because he willed" (Isaiah 53:7); "I lay down my life, that I might take it up again; no man takes it from me" (John 10:18), that is, I offer myself as a sacrifice, as St. John Chrysostom (*hom. 81 in Joan*). and Cyril (*in Joan*, 11, 25) explain it. The martyrs, however, could neither die nor impede their passion and death when they wanted.

By the concept of the *form*, because Christ was truly sanctified in a mystic rite. It did not happen by chance, but by election, so that on the day of the Paschal feast, and on the altar of the Cross, while extending his hands, he suffered outside the gate of the city, as St. Leo notes (*in epist. 83 ad Monachos Palaestinos*). And John the Evangelist writes, "Jesus, knowing that his hour had come" (John 13:1), and Paul, "For the bodies of those beasts, whose blood is brought into the holy of holies by the high priest for sin, are burned outside the camp. This is why Jesus also, that he might sanctify the people by his own blood, suffered outside the gate" (Heb. 13:11).

By the concept *of the end:* because it was the proximate and principal purpose for the death of Christ, to appease God in regard to the human race, which is the purpose of a true sacrifice, "Making peace through the blood of the cross, etc." (Coloss. 1:20), and all the Scriptures proclaim the same thing. This is why all sacrifices of the Old Law were a figure, and a type of this most true and supreme propitiatory sacrifice, as St. Augustine witnesses (*loc. cit.*). Moreover, the purpose of the death of martyrs was more properly not to appease God, but "to show testimony to the truth," and of its nature the death of a martyr is an act of fortitude, because he chose to lose life rather than deny the faith. This is why St. Leo says in Epistle 83 (*loc. cit.*), "Although the death of many of his saints are precious in the sight of God, yet the death of any of those innocent persons was not the propitiation of the world. Righteous men receive crowns; they do not give them. And from the courage of the faithful, examples of patience arise, not the gifts of the righteousness. For their deaths were all single deaths, neither did any of them pay another man's debt by his end." And that concludes the topic of the definition.

CHAPTER IV
On the Partition of Sacrifice

A Few things must be said on the partition. A sacrifice, properly speaking, is customarily divided into two parts: by the concept of the *matter*, and by the concept of the *form* and *end*. By the concept of *the matter*, it is divided into three kinds: victims, or hosts, immolations, and libations. Victims, or hosts are sacrifices made from animals, namely sheep, goats, oxen, doves, sparrows, turtledoves, etc.; no other living thing could be sacrificed. And although these names are general, nevertheless, among the Latins they derived from those sacrifices which were offered after victory over enemies had been reported. For the word *victima* comes from *Victoria*, and *hostia* comes from *hostes* (enemy), according to what Ovid says in *Fasti*, lib. 1:

> *Victima quae cecidit dextra victrices, vocatur,*
> *Hostibus a victis hostia nomen habet.*[3]

By the concept of *the form and end*, it is divided into three kinds: holocaust, hosts for sin, and hosts for a peace offering. Holocausts are offered properly in reverence for the divine majesty, and therefore are completely burnt so that after it is dispersed in vaper the whole of it ascends on high, in a sign that whatever we have is of God. Hosts offered for sin are said to be those offered for the expiation of sin; and these are partly burned and partly eaten by the priests in the holy place. There were, however, many kinds of hosts for sin, they even differed for a variety of sin, and for a variety of persons. One was offered for perjury, another for other sins, and in similar fashion, one for the priest, another for the king, another for the Synagogue, another for private men. Peace offerings were partly burnt and partly eaten by the priests, and partly by those who donated it. Moreover, there were two species of peace offering. Some were offered for a benefit which was received, and some to receive a benefit, which differs from the others because these offerings could also be eaten on the next day, while the others had to be consumed on the very day of sacrifice.

---

[3] The *victim* is so called because it is felled by a *victorious* right hand;
The *hostia* takes its name from the conquered *foes* [*hostes*].

From that St. Thomas rightly gathered, when he wonderfully disputes on this whole matter (I IIae, q. 102, a 3), that a holocaust was the most excellent sacrifice, sacrifice for sin obtained the second place of dignity, and sacrifice as a peace offering for a benefit received is the third, while the last was a peace offering to obtain a benefit. We are especially obliged to give honor to God on account of his infinite majesty, therefore, secondly on account of an offense committed against him, thirdly on account of a benefit received, and lastly on account of a benefit hoped for.

Next, he gathers three states of the faithful from these three kinds of sacrifices. For the holocaust signifies the state of the perfect, those who dedicate their whole lives in service to God. The peace-making sacrifice, the state of the proficient, who give thanks to God for justification received from their sins, and seek perseverance in good; and therefore, their sacrifices are made in three parts, one is burned for God, the other eaten by the priest, and the third by the one offering; because the grace of God is acquired by perseverance in good, the ministry of the priests and rightly even for their own good works. Lastly, sacrifice for sin signifies the state of beginners, or the penitents, who seek forgiveness of sins from God. And because justification from sins cannot be acquired by one's own merits, but only by the grace of God through the ministry of the priests, for that reason, one part of his sacrifice is offered to God, the other of the priest, but none falls to the one offering.

CHAPTER V
Is the Mass a Sacrifice? The State of the controversy is explained, and the positions of Catholics and heretics related

SINCE we have explained the terms Mass and Sacrifice, it follows that the question itself should now receive some treatment: Is the Mass a Sacrifice? Moreover, the principal question with the heretics of this time is not whether it is a spiritual or improper sacrifice. Melanchthon (*Apology for the Augsburg Confession*), Chemnitz (*Examination of the Council of Trent*), and Brenz (*on the Würtemberg Confession*) and others, affirm that the Mass, or the Lord's Supper, can be called a sacrifice in many ways. Rather, the issue rests upon the question of an external, visible sacrifice truly and properly so called, eminently on that kind of sacrifice, on a visible oblation made to God by the ministry of the priests.

Therefore, the state of the controversy will be this: whether in the Mass, or in the action of the Lord's Supper, if it is duly celebrated, the Eucharist should be offered to God. This is the true state of the question, and can easily be proven from the testimony of our adversaries, as well as those on our side. First, the *formulae* that they have published for the celebration of the Lord's Supper sufficiently demonstrate what displeases them in our Mass.

The formula for Mass in the Church of Wittenberg, published by Luther in 1523, admits 1) the Introit with a Psalm; 2) the *Kyrie eleison* with the Angelic hymn, the *Gloria in excelsis Deo*; 3) The *collect*, or the prayer with a reading to follow it; 4) The Gradual with the Alleluia; 5) A few sequences, such as on the Holy Spirit and the Nativity of the Lord; 6) The Gospel; 7) The Creed. Then it so adds: 8) "Now that whole abomination follows, which one is compelled to serve, everything that precedes in the Mass, which is why it is called the Offertory, and from here everything sounds and smells like an oblation." And again, it says, "Hence, all of these things which express oblation have been repudiated, along with the whole Canon, while we retain what is pure and holy." He then very briefly prescribes the consecration of the Eucharist by the words of the Lord, and Communion.

The formula of administration of the Sacraments of Calvin for the Church of Geneva, and all the others that I could examine, most diligently

Book I, Ch. V: Is the Mass a Sacrifice? 37

take care lest any mention of oblation should be made.

In addition, Luther, in all of his books, many of which he wrote on this very question, argues this one thing, to teach that in the action of the Lord's Supper, or the Mass, we offer nothing to God apart from prayers, but rather more conversely, we offer the Sacrament of the Eucharist to God in testimony of the promise. In 1520, he published a little book on the *Babylonian Captivity of the Church*, where he profusely argues this in the chapter on the Eucharist, near the end. In 1521 he published his book *On the Abrogation of Private Mass*, where he more profusely and furiously argues the same thing. In 1522, he published a book against the King of England in which he repeats the same. In 1523 he published a book against the Canon of the Mass. In 1527, in a book on the words of the Lord's Supper against Zwingli's followers, he holds the same thing. In like fashion, in his *Confession*, which he published in 1528, he says that he holds the Mass above all abominations, and is sorry for nothing more than that he had celebrated Mass as a Catholic for 15 years. In 1534 he published a book on private Mass and the anointing of priests, in which he was not ashamed to confess that the devil taught and persuaded him that the Mass is the chief abomination, and that this took place not in a dream but while he was awake.

All the heretics of this time teach the same thing. Melanchthon (*de Locis*, tit. *De Sacrificio*), Brenz (*On the Würtemberg Confession*, cap. *de Eucharistia*, Illyricus (in his *Apologia pro Confessione Antwerpiensi*, cap. 15), Chemnitz (*Examination of the Council of Trent*, 2 part), John Calvin (*Instit.* Lib. 4 cap. 18 §1 and 2 et seqq.), Peter Martyr (In 1 Cor. 4 & 10), and Theodore Beza (*Confessione*, cap. 7 §3), along with others, deny the Eucharist can or should be offered to God.

On the other hand, Catholic writers that have written in our age on the Sacrifice of the Mass, all labor chiefly in this: to show that in the Mass the body and blood of the Lord is truly and properly offered to God, under the visible species of bread and wine: John Eck, in three books on the Sacrifice of the Mass, Clictoven, in *Propugnaculo Ecclesiae*, lib. 1; Caspar Schazgerum, *Tract. De Missa*; John Faber *de Missa et Eucharistia*, books 2, 4 and 5; John Fisher in his book *On the Defence of the Catholic Priesthood*; Cajetan in his treatise on the Sacrifice of the Mass, which is tomus 3 tr. 10; Martin Persius *de Traditionibus*, part. 3 consideration 4; John Driedo, *De Scripturis et dogmatibus Ecclesiasticis*, lib. 4 cap. 5 part. 4; Ambrose Catharinus in *de Veritate Incruenti Sacrificii Novi et Aeterni Testamenti*; Domingo del Soto in 4 *Sent.* Dist. 13, q. 2; Tiletanus in his defense of the Council of Trent against Chemnitz; Rudyard Tapper in his explanation of art. 16, Lovaniensum; Albert Pighius *hierarch. Eccles.* Lib. 2 cap. 5; and contr. 5 &6; Anthony Democharis in his four books on the Sacrifice of the Mass; Alonso de Castro *contra haeresesi,* lib. 10; Cardinal Hosius in the *Confessione Polonica,* cap. 41; Wilhelm Lindanus, *Panopliae,* lib. 4, cap. 37, et. Seqq.; Melchior Cano *De Locis Theologicis,* lib. 12, cap. 13; Wilhelm Alanus, *de Eucharistia,* lib. 2; Gregory de Valentia, *tract. Et Apologia de Sacrificio Missae,* among many others.

We gather from these that Melanchthon and Chemnitz have incorrectly explained the state of this question. Melanchthon, both in *de Locis* (tit. De Sacraficio), and in his *Apology for the Augsburg Confession* (cap. de Missa), does not correctly define nor correctly divide a sacrifice, he places the whole controversy on one point—whether in the Mass a propitiatory sacrifice is offered. But there is another controversy that comes before that, whether a sacrifice is both truly and properly offered. For, the truest sacrifices are those which still are not propitiatory, as we showed above.

Chemnitz, however, does not only speak ignorantly, but also rather impudently in his *Examination,* where on several pages he asserts the state of the question to be whether that representation through various gestures and vestments which are seen in the Catholic Church, is a sacrifice instituted by Christ (pp. 739, 744, 761, 766, & 777). Furthermore, in the last place we cited, he dares to say that the panoply of words, rites, gestures, actions, ornaments and vestments, which were added later to the simple institution of Christ, are the very sinews and substance of the Popish Mass, although no Catholic has ever written that! For they all teach, in a supreme consensus, that all of these things which are added to the institution of Christ, are accidental ornaments. For more on this and his objection from the book of John Eck, see what we refuted above in chapter 1.

CHAPTER VI
That in the Mass a True Sacrifice is Offered: Proven Firstly from the Testimony of Scripture and the Priesthood of Melchisedech.

Now at last, we have come to arguments for the truth. First, we will advance the testimonies of the Scriptures, then of the Fathers, and lastly from reason. Moreover, when we examine the Scriptures, the figures of the Old Testament will occupy the *first* point; what was foretold by the Prophets *second*; the testimony of the Gospel *third*, the Acts of the Apostles *fourth*, and *fifth* and last shall be the Epistles of St. Paul.

1) The *first* testimony of Scripture is that of Genesis 14:18, "Melchisedech, the king of Salem, brought forth bread and wine; for he was a priest of the most high God." David (in Psalm 109 [110]:5), and Paul (in Hebrews 9:7) so relate this passage to Christ that they do not say Melchisedech merely bore the figure of Christ, which could also be said of Aaron, but that Christ was a priest according to the order of Melchisedech, and not according to the order of Aaron, as Paul clearly writes.

Moreover, there are two differences between those two priesthoods, from which we may advance two arguments. The first and most principal difference is placed in the external species of sacrifice. Even if all the sacrifices of the Old Law come together in a thing that has been signified, since they signify the same Christ crucified, still, they were different in their signs. The Aaronic sacrifices were bloody, and under the species of slain animals they represented the death of Christ; but the sacrifice of Melchisedech was unbloody, and under the species of bread and wine it prefigured the body and blood of the same Christ. This is why if Christ is a priest according to the order of Melchisedech, and not of Aaron, he should have instituted an unbloody sacrifice under the species of bread and wine, just as the Catholic Church rightly sings at Vespers for the feast of Corpus Christi: "Christ the Lord, the priest forever according to the order of Melchisedech offered bread and wine." But if from the force of the priesthood according to the order of Melchisedech it were not gathered for certain (although it certainly is) that Christ should sacrifice a host under the species of bread and wine, it could still be gathered from the force of the type and the figure. In that ceremony of bread and wine, Melchisedech is a very manifest figure of Christ establishing the sacrament of the Eucharist in bread and wine by the consensus of the Fathers, whom we will advance shortly. But Melchisedech offered bread and wine as a priest of the most high God, and hence, he truly sacrificed. Therefore, Christ also offered sacrifice in the institution of the Eucharist, as a priest does, otherwise he would not have exactly fulfilled the figure.

The second difference between the priesthood of Melchisedech and Aaron is the former was only of one man who was not succeeded by another, and to whom no other succeeded; the latter, however, was of many who succeeded each other through death. The Apostle follows up this difference in Hebrews 7:3, where he says Melchisedech was without father, without mother and without a lineage, nor beginning of days, having no end of life. Applying all these characteristics to Christ, he says that he was a priest forever, namely one that no man succeeded, and no one should succeed him, since he always lives, seeing that God swore there would be no change to that priesthood, or a transference upon another, as happened to the Levitical priesthood. Paul proves it from the words of Psalm 109 [110]:5, "The Lord swore an oath and will not change, you are a priest forever, etc." But if the priesthood of Christ endures to the end of the world, (for Scripture says "eternal" in this passage, as Anselm and Theophylactus explain it), certainly, the rite of sacrifice should endure, unless perhaps Christ were not employed in the priesthood. But the Sacrifice of the Cross was only carried out once, since Christ cannot die again. Consequently, there should be another sacrifice which is continuously offered; for one cannot be called a priest when he offers no sacrifice. Therefore, it is necessary to admit that in the Church the true action of sacrificing, which is attributed to Christ the High Priest through its ministers is such that certainly it will be no action if the Sacrifice of the Mass were abolished.

Besides, before the Incarnation of Christ, because Christ was really not yet a priest (for the priesthood is suited to Christ as one lesser than the Father, and hence as a man, not as God, as Augustine also notes on Psalm 109 on the verse, *Tu es sacerdos in aeternum*), he could not offer sacrifice by himself, still, that it could also be said he was a priest at the same time, and really was, that one high priest from the beginning of the world, even to the end in that manner whereby he could offer sacrifice, namely by types and figures. For, as all the old sacrifices were figures of the sacrifice of the Cross, and in all those victims the immaculate lamb itself was slaughtered under a type, this is why in Apocalypse 13:8, the

Book I, Ch. VI: The Priesthood of Melchisedech

lamb is said to be slain from the beginning of the world. So, all those priests were types of Christ and in all their sacrifices *he* was sacrificed. Now, if on account of the eternity of the priesthood, Christ also exercised it in the manner which he could before the incarnation, how much more after the Incarnation, when he really was called a priest by the Father, and a priest without a successor, ought he not cease to offer sacrifice by that office until the end of the world? What sort of person remains a priest if he should never again offer sacrifice?

Our adversaries do try to respond to these arguments. Calvin (*Instit.* 4, cap. 18, §2) and Marin Chemnitz (*Examination of the Council of Trent*, 2. Part, pg. 740 &747), other authors on Genesis, and Peter Martyr (on 1 Cor. 5), all admit that Melchisedech was a priest and a type of Christ. But they all reject that he offered bread and wine to God as a sacrifice. From there, they gather that the priesthood of Christ does not consist in the oblation of bread and wine, while still it is according to the order of Melchisedech. They also argue that the eternity of the same priesthood of Christ is not placed in the fact that sacrifice will be offered in the Church to God under the species of bread and wine.

The answer, so that we might accurately give a refutation, will be found *firstly* by explaining the text in question from the book of Genesis. *Secondly*, we shall adduce the consensus of the Fathers who clearly wrote that Melchisedech offered bread and wine to God, and who place in that action the eternity of the priesthood of Christ, as well as the similitude of the sacrifice which is offered in the Church under the species of bread and wine to that of the priesthood of Melchisedech. *Thirdly*, we shall refute what they offer conversely in objection.

a) Now, for the *first* point, these are the words of Scripture in the Vulgate edition:

Now Melchisedech, the king of Salem, bringing forth bread and wine; (for he was a priest of the most high God), blessed them, etc. (Genesis 14:18).[4]

Right away Chemnitz asks in regard to what is read in the vulgate: Why do we read, "Melchisedech offered bread and wine," when the Hebrew, Aramaic, and Greek do not have the sacrificial word, *obtulit* [he offered], but a word which simply means to bring out, namely *protulit*, which is also how St. Cyprian read it.

But we might more truly ask of Chemnitz why he makes such an

---

[4] *At vero Melchisedech Rex salem proferens panem et vinum; (erat enim Sacerdos Dei altissimi) benedixit ei, etc.*

obvious lie about our edition. There is no edition of the Latin that has ever had "obtulit", rather I continuously see they all have *proferens* [bringing forth]. Nevertheless, that word, although of itself it means nothing other than to bring something out or add to something, still, it is often taken up for the bringing out of a host to immolate it, such as in Judges 6:18-19, where the same word *hotsi* הצא is added twice, and it is the same word we have in this passage of Genesis, and it clearly means to bring out a host. We see the same thing with the word הביא (*hebi*), which properly means to add, and still everywhere in Scripture it is restricted to sacrifice, so that it is the same thing as to offer, as in Genesis 4:4 where it is used to describe the sacrifice of Cain and Abel.

Now follows the next part of the sentence we cited above: *bread and wine*. Here Calvin and Chemnitz contend that he brought forth bread and wine as refreshment for Abraham and his companions who were tired and returning from battle.

While we do not deny that they were given as food to Abraham and his companions, we say that they were first *offered and consecrated to God*, and then given to the men, so that they might participate in the sacrifice. In the first place, there was no reason why Melchisedech should offer bodily refreshment to Abraham. As the Scripture holds in the same place, Abraham returned from battle with great spoils, among which were food as it is said there; nay more at the end of the chapter it is added that the soldiers of Abraham had taken food before Melchisedech met them. So why was bread and wine necessary for those who abounded in spoils and had just ate and drank? Besides, when Scripture describes the priesthood of Melchisedech in so many places, as distinct from the Aaronic priesthood while similar to the priesthood of Christ, should it not hand down in some place what the sacrifice of Melchisedech actually was? Accordingly, a priesthood is ordered to sacrifice, and if a sacrifice were unknown, it is necessary that the priesthood also be unknown. There is no mention anywhere of precisely what sacrifice Melchisedech offered except in this passage. Consequently, it is fitting to understand by bread and wine not profane foods, but consecrated ones first offered to God. Lastly, it is most efficaciously proven from the following words that Scripture adds: "For he was a priest of the most high God." The reason given by the Holy Spirit himself as to why Melchisedech brought forth bread and wine altogether compels us to understand that the bread and wine was brought forth in sacrifice.

Nevertheless, Chemnitz appears again to accuse the Latin Vulgate

Book I, Ch. VI: The Priesthood of Melchisedech

because it places a causal particle for a conjunction; for in Hebrew *chi* is causal, whereas *vau* is a conjunction. This is why he followed Calvin when he translated it: "He was a priest of the most high God and blessed it", etc. And so he distinguishes the actions of Melchisedech himself as a king and as a priest, so that the bringing forth of bread and wine would pertain to his munificence as a king, whereas the blessing to his priesthood.

But in vain does Chemnitz flog the vulgate edition. Although the Hebrew is not literally, *Erat enim Sacerdos*, rather, *Et erat sacerdos*, nevertheless, the conjunction is very frequently employed by the Jews to mean something causal, and it should be translated by *enim*, if the sentence were to be elegantly expressed in Latin prose, which St. Jerome customarily did. Many examples come to mind:

Genesis 20:3. En morieris propter mulierem, quam tulisti, habet enim virum. In Hebrew, it is *vehi behhulath bahhal*, and she has a husband. *Genesis 30:27*. Experimento didici, et benedixit mihi Dominus. *Isaiah 64:5*. Tu iratus es et peccavimus. Namely, you are angry because we have sinned, where very clearly a *vau* is placed for a *chi*, that is a conjunction for a causal particle.

Next, our adversaries overturn the whole distinction of speech to accommodate the words of Scripture to their interpretation. But if this were allowed, we would interpret the entire Scripture wrongly. For, in the Hebrew text, after those words, "And he was a priest of the most high God," an accent is found, which the Jews call *soph pasuch*, which indicates that there a period ends. This is why "and he was a priest of the most high God" cannot be joined with: "And he blessed," but rather, is connected with what came before, "He brought forth bread and wine." We find the same distinction in the Aramaic, Greek, and Latin text. When we have posited this true and common interpretation, and the punctuation of speech, even if there is no causal particle, the part of speech itself declares that bread and wine were brought forth for sacrifice. Why ever would "and he was a priest of God," be joined with the words "he brought forth bread and wine," except for us to understand that Melchisedech the priest brought forth bread and wine to offer unto God?

Moreover, our adversaries do not rightly say that Melchisedech, as a priest, blessed Abraham, and hence interpret Scripture poorly when they say "He was a priest and blessed him," or, (as Calvin would have it), "Seeing that he was a priest of God he blessed Abraham." For, Abraham was also a priest (as is clear from the many sacrifices which he offered), so Melchisedech did not bless Abraham as a priest, or because he was a priest, but because he was a *greater* priest or because he was without question greater, since he was both priest and king. For it is not of a priest alone to bless, but every superior. King Solomon, who was not a priest, blessed the people (3 Kings 8:55) and David did the same (2 Kings 6:18), and before them Joshua did the same thing (Joshua 8:33; 22:6), although he was not a priest, but a head of state. And Jacob (Genesis 48:16) asked the Angel to bless the sons of Joseph. This is why in Hebrews 7:7, St. Paul did not gather from the fact that Melchisedech blessed Abraham that Melchisedech was a priest, as he would have were he to follow Calvin and Chemnitz, but rather that he was a *greater* priest than Abraham, since, as he says (*ibid.*), an inferior is blessed by a superior without any controversy.

b) Now we add, so as to come to the second point, the consensus of the ancient Fathers, which certainly should suffice by itself to confound the temerity of these new interpreters. *First*, the whole Church witnesses this in the Canon of the Mass, when it says, "Supra quae propitio ac sereno vultu respicere digneris, et accepta habere, sicuti accepta habere dignatus es munera pueri tui justi Abel, et sacrificium Patriarchae nostril Abrahae, et quod tibi obtulit summus sacerdos tuus Melchisedech, sanctum sacrificium immaculatam hostiam." St. Ambrose expressly mentions this part of the Canon (*de Sacramentis*, 4, 6), which shows that this is a most ancient and public teaching of the whole Church.

Additionally, we will add the testimonies of individual Greek and Latin Fathers, in order of time. Clement of Alexandria (*Stromata*, 4) says, "Melchisedech, the King of Salem and priest of God most high, who gave wine and bread sanctified as nourishment as a type of the Eucharist." Observe in this place that he does not speak of profane bread as refreshment for the stomach, the way our adversaries would have it, but calls what was given by Melchisedech *sanctified*. Hence you see for this purpose, the bread and wine given by Melchisedech, as a priest of the most high God, hence it was already offered to God and in that manner sanctified. Lastly, the bread and wine of the priesthood of Melchisedech are a type of the Eucharist, from which it follows that the priesthood of Christ is called "according to the order of Melchisedech," because it consists in the species of bread and wine.

St. Cyprian (Epistles, 2, 3 *ad Caecilium*), after he recites the words of the Psalm: "You are a priest forever, according to the order of Melchisedech," he so adds: "At any rate, what is this order, concerning

Book I, Ch. VI: The Priesthood of Melchisedech 45

that sacrifice coming and thence descending, because Melchisedech was a priest of God on high, because he offered bread and wine, because he blessed Abraham. For, what greater priesthood of God on high is there than our Lord Jesus Christ? Who offered sacrifice to God the Father, and offered this same thing which Melchisedech had offered, *i.e.* bread and wine, namely his own body and blood?" Here we can clearly see that Melchisedech offered the bread and wine to God in sacrifice, and on account of the imitation of this sacrifice, the priesthood of Christ and Christians is called according to the order of Melchisedech. The same Cyprian, or whoever was the author of the sermon *De Coena Domini*, says: "The sacraments, in times past, prefigured from the time of Melchisedech do come forth. And the most high priest did bring forth bread and wine unto the children of Abraham who were doing his works. This is, Christ says, my body." And further on the same author places the eternity of the priesthood of Christ in the fact that the sacrifice of the Eucharist is continually offered. "This sacrifice is perpetual, and the holocaust remaining forever." And above he had said that religion would come to ruin if the body of the Lord were to be consumed in the Eucharist, because no victim would remain, without which there could be no religion.

Eusebius of Caesarea (*Demonst. Evang.* 5, 3) says, "He rightly said that he forsook the priesthood after Aaron's type, and to be a priest after the order of Melchisedech. And the fulfillment of the oracle is truly marvelous, to one who recognizes the way in which our Savior, Jesus, the Christ of God, even now performs through his ministers even in our day the sacrifices after the manner of Melchisedech. For, just as he, who was a priest of the gentiles, is not represented as offering outward sacrifices, but as blessing Abraham only with wine and bread, in exactly the same way our Lord and Savior himself first, and then all his priests among all nations, perform the spiritual sacrifice according to the customs of the Church, and with wine and bread darkly express the mysteries of His body and saving Blood. Melchisedech foresaw this by the Holy Spirit, and used the figures of what was to come." And here you see that Melchisedech used bread and wine in his only sacrifice, and both Christ and his ministers throughout the world offer sacrifice under the species of bread and wine and in this manner (if I may say it) the priesthood of Christ according to the order of Melchisedech is perpetuated.

St. Ambrose, (*de Sacram.* 5,1) says, "We know the figure of these very Sacraments preceded in the time of Abraham, when holy Melchisedech offered sacrifice. ... We have said that the chalice is placed upon the altar, as well as the bread, and that wine is poured into the chalice, and what else? Water. But you ask me, how, therefore, did Melchisedech offer bread and wine; why did he wish for himself the mixture of water?" You can see similar things in his works (*de Sacrament.* 4, 3 & 6; *de Initiandis Myst.*, cap. 8). Ambrose also, commenting on Hebrews 5, explaining the verse, "you are a priest forever," says, "It is certain that the animal sacrifices which were in the order of Aaron perished, while what Melchisedech established remains, and that is celebrated in the distribution of the Sacraments throughout the world."

St. Epiphanius (*Panarion*, haeres. 55 which is of the Melchisedechiani), teaches that the Aaronic priesthood was translated through Christ to the priesthood of Melchisedech: "What rightly now flourishes in the Church from Christ to this very day, no longer allots it by seed or succession, rather, the form is sought according to a power."

St. Jerome (*Epist. Ad marcellam*), says: "Run back to Genesis and you will discover Melchisedech, the King of Salem, the ruler of this city, who as a type of Christ offered bread and wine, and consecrated the Christian mystery in the body and blood of the Savior." And in another Epistle (*Ad Evagrium de Melchisedech*), he writes on the opinion of the more ancient Fathers, Irenaeus, Hippolytus, Eusebius of Caesarea, then of the Emissenus, Apollinarus, Eustachius, that the order of Melchisedech consisted in the fact that he did not immolate bloody victims, but simple bread and wine, and consecrated the sacrament in the pure sacrifice of Christ. He says the same thing in *Questions on Genesis*, explaining chapter 14: "Our mystery is prefigured in the word 'order', by no means through Aaron with the immolation of irrational victims, but by the oblation of bread and wine, i.e. the body and blood of the Lord Jesus." In his commentary on Matthew 22, he says the same thing, that Melchisedech offered bread and wine for Abraham, and in chapter 26 he says that Melchisedech, as a priest of the most high God, in offering bread and wine prefigured the mystery of the Eucharist.

St. John Chrysostom (*In Genesis*, Homily 35), says: "Seeing the type, I pray you also think to admire the truth." And in *Homily 36*, "After Melchisedech, the king of Salem brought forth bread and wine (for he was a priest of God most high) Abraham received the oblations from him."

St. Augustine (*Epist. 95 to Pope Innocent*), which he writes in the name of many other bishops, says: "Melchisedech, after he brought forth

Book I, Ch. VI: The Priesthood of Melchisedech

the Sacrament of the Lord's table knew that he prefigured an eternal priesthood." Here, in a few very clear words, Augustine teaches that the oblation of Melchisedech was a figure of the Eucharist, and that the eternal priesthood of Christ consists in offering the Eucharist. In *City of God* (16, 22), speaking on the oblation of Melchisedech, he says, "There, the sacrifice which Christians now offer to God throughout the whole word, first appeared." In other places (*ibid* 17,17; 18, 35; *on Psalm 109*) he very clearly says that the priesthood of Christ is perpetual according to the order of Melchisedech, which now flourishes in the Church by the oblation that is on the altar. In *Contra avers. Leg. et prophet.* (1, 20), he follows up the same thought: There, it was certainly said, 'The Lord swore an oath and he will not repent, you are a priest forever according to the order of Melchisedech.' Those who read this knew what Melchisedech had brought forth to Abraham, and now they are partakers of it; they see such a sacrifice is now offered throughout the world. Moreover, the oath of God is a rebuke to unbelievers, and that God will not repent is a sign that he will not change this priesthood, as he clearly changed the priesthood according to the order of Aaron." Then, in *Sermon 11*, on the saints, which is the fourth on the Innocents, treating on the relics of the Martyrs that rest under the altar, he says: "What can be said that is more reverent and honorable than that they rest under that altar, upon which the sacrifice is celebrated for God, in which hosts are offered, in which the Lord is the priest, as it was written, "You are a priest forever, according to the order of Melchisedech?"

Theodoret, in his commentary on *Psalm 109*, says: "We have found Melchisedech is a king and priest, offering to God not the sacrifices without reason, but bread and wine. ... Christ is now a priest, not himself offering something, rather, he is called the head of those who offer, seeing that he calls the Church his body." And before that citation he had said that Christ began the priesthood according to Melchisedech at the Last Supper, when he consecrated bread and wine. See the same thing in *Question 63 on Genesis*.

St. Leo I (*Serm. 2 de anniversario assumptionis suae ad Pontificatum*), says: "You are a priest forever, according to the order of Melchisedech; this is not according to the order of Aaron, whose priesthood descended along the line of his own offspring and was a temporal ministry, and ceased with the law of the Old Testament; but after the order of Melchisedech, in whom was prefigured the eternal high Priest. And no reference is made to his parentage because in him it is understood that he was portrayed, whose generation cannot be declared. And finally, now that the mystery of the Divine priesthood has descended to human agency, it runs not in the line of birth, nor is that which flesh and blood created, chosen, but without regard to the privilege of paternity and succession by inheritance, those men are received by the Church as its rulers whom the Holy Spirit prepared."

Eusebius Emissenus (or whoever was the author of *Sermon 5 on Easter*), says: "Melchisedech prefigured the sacrifice of Christ with this oblation of bread and wine (namely which is celebrated in the Eucharist)." He also said that this oblation is going to be eternal in the Church.

Arnobius, commenting on Psalm 109, says, "Christ, through the mystery of bread and wine has become a priest forever."

Eucherius (*in Gen.* 2, 18), says: "Melchisedech, a priest of the most high God, offering bread and wine in sacrifice. ... without some priestly genealogy, Christ the man existed from men, inasmuch as he was not from the tribe of Levi, but from the tribe of Judah, from such a tribe he receives nothing in regard to a priestly precept: at any rate, on account of the mystery of the Sacrament, which Christians are commanded to celebrate, that we might offer the sacrament of his body and blood in sacrifice not by animal sacrifices according to Aaron, but the oblation of bread and wine."

Primasius (in his commentary *on Hebrews 5*), says: "This is why, he is said to be a priest according to the order of Melchisedech, and not according to the order of Aaron, and there are different reasons. The first is that Melchisedech was not a priest according to legal commands, but according to the dignity of a certain singular priesthood, offering bread to God, not the blood of brute animals; Christ became a priest in the order of such a priesthood, not a temporal one, but an eternal one; not offering legal victims, but the equal form of it; bread and wine, namely his own body and blood. ... This is why it is clear that the sacrifice of animals perished, because it was of the order of Aaron, while on the other hand, the former remains, which was of the order of Melchisedech, because Christ fortified it and taught the Church to hold it."

Cassiodorus (in Psalm 109), says: "The most just king, Melchisedech, established such an order through a mystical similitude, when he offered to the Lord the fruits of bread and wine. It is certain that animal victims perished, which were of the order of Aaron, and what Melchisedech established remained instead, which is celebrated throughout the world in the distribution of the Sacraments."

Book I, Ch. VI: The Priesthood of Melchisedech

Remigius Antisiodorensis and Euthymius Zigabenus write the same things in their commentaries on Psalm 109.

St. John Damascene (*De Fide*, 4, 14), says: "That table prefigured this mystical table, just as that priest was a type and image of Christ, the true high priest."

Oecumenius, in his commentary on Hebrews 5, says: "Melchisedech was the first to offer a bloodless host, to offer bread and wine. ... He did not say eternally that the host and offering that was made once to God, but looking to the priests of our time by which Christ sacrifices himself and is a sacrifice, and handed down the model of this priesthood in this mystical feast and supper."

Theophylactus, commenting on Hebrews 5, while explaining the verse, "You are a priest forever," etc., says, "Clearly, what was said is about Christ. For he and Melchisedech alone, offered sacrifice in that manner, with bread and wine. ... He said forever, because it is offered daily, the oblation is offered forever by the ministers of God, having Christ as Lord and priest, and he breaks and distributes the sacrifice who sanctifies himself for our sake."

St. Anselm, also commenting on Hebrews 5, says, "You are a priest, *i.e.* giving sacred things through you and your own, forever, *i.e.* as long as the world will last, because the priesthood of Christ does not pass away, as he succeeded the other, as the Levitical passed away."

It would be a marvel if these testimonies did not suffice to rebuke the boldness of these new men. Still, let us add the testimonies of the ancient Jews which are recalled in the *Bereishit Rabbah*.[5] For, among others contained there are the words of Rabbi Samuel on chapter 14 of Genesis: "He hands down the acts of priesthood, for he sacrificed bread and wine to the holy and blessed God." Rabbi Phineas, on Numbers 28 says, "In the time of the Messiah all the sacrifices will cease, but the sacrifice of bread and wine will not cease, for it was thus said in Genesis 14:18, 'Melchisedech the King of Salem brought forth bread and wine.' For Melchisedech, that is the Messiah King, will begin, from the cessation of the sacrifices, the sacrifice of bread and wine, just as it is said in Psalm 109:5, "you are a priest forever, according to the order of Melchisedech."

It remains, that we see what our adversaries make in objection to our argument on their behalf. Firstly Calvin (*Instit.* 4, 18 §2) objects in this way: "They wrongly apply these words to bread and wine, 'And he was a

---

[5] Translator's note: The *Bereishit Rabbah* (Great Genesis) is a collection of rabbinical interpretations of the book of Genesis from the Midrash.

priest of the most high God,' which Paul relates to the blessing. For Paul (Hebrews 7:7) gathers its excellence, because the lesser was blessed by the greater.

I respond: It is false to say that Paul refers those words, "And he was a priest of the most High God," to the blessing. Paul does not even cite those words, rather he only briefly writes that Melchisedech, the King of Salem, a priest of the most high God met Abraham while he was returning from the battle of the kings, and blessed him, all of which are true; but it does not follow from this that the words, "And he was a priest of the most high God," in the Mosaic text, are joined with, "he blessed", and not rather with what comes before it, "He brought forth bread and wine." Moreover, the fact that the Apostle adds the lesser was blessed by the greater does not prove Melchisedech was a priest of God, but that he was a *greater priest than Abraham*, as we deduced above.

Secondly, Calvin (*ibid.*) objects in this way: "What if the oblation of Melchisedech were a figure of the missal sacrifice, would the Apostle, I ask, who scrutinizes the least detail, have forgotten of a matter so serious and grave?

I respond: The reason why the Apostle does not call to mind the sacrifice of bread and wine is primarily known in that it did not fit his purpose. The Apostle meant to show from Melchisedech the excellence of Christ over the Levitical Priests. For the Jews, to whom he wrote, were exceedingly proud on account of the Aaronic priesthood. Therefore, Paul calls attention to the fact that Melchisedech, according to whose order Christ was a priest, blessed Abraham, and in the former was Aaron, hence he was greater than Aaron. Likewise, the fact that they received the tithe from Abraham, and in him from Aaron, who then was a twinkling in the eye of Abraham, and by this he was greater than Aaron. For the high priest received the tithe from lower priests. Consequently, because Melchisedech was in a certain measure eternal, seeing that his beginning and end are not written in the scriptures, all of which pertain to the excellence of Christ, and thus were called to mind. The fact that he offered bread and wine does not especially make an excellence, neither of Melchisedech, nor of Christ himself, and therefore it is no marvel if Paul would have omitted it.

Besides, it happened that the Apostle, after spending so much time on the subject, omitted the oblation of bread and wine lest he would be compelled to explain the mystery of the Eucharist, which was loftier than his readers could understand. For Paul himself says, "Of whom [Christ

Book I, Ch. VI: The Priesthood of Melchisedech

as priest] we have much to say, and it is hard for it to be said intelligibly, because you have become weak to hear" (Hebrews 5:11). And rightly, seeing that the Apostle clearly explained everything else which is said on Melchisedech in Genesis, with the exception of the oblation of bread and wine, it does not appear that it could be denied that the mystery of the Eucharist should be understood in a discussion that is hard to say intelligibly, for which the Jews were not suited.

Furthermore, the Greek Fathers, such as Jerome, relate (in epist. Ad Evagrium) that Paul omitted a certain sacrament of Melchisedech, and this he called a discussion that is hard to say intelligibly, because it was written to the unfaithful Jews. It is certain that the Sacrament, which could not be revealed to unbelievers could hardly be other than the Eucharist.

Now, this is not opposed to what Chrysostom and Theophylactus say in their argument on this Epistle, that it was written for the faithful Jews. Really it was written to both, or certainly so written to the faithful Jews that it should also be shared with those who were unbelievers; for on that account the Apostle labors much in a great part of the epistle to prove that Christ is the Son of God, and the sole teacher of the world.

Chemnitz (*loc. cit.*, pg. 750), after he badly attempts to effect an argument from the Hebrew text, that Melchisedech did not offer a sacrifice of bread and wine to God (which we refuted above), adds that even if it were certain that Melchisedech offered the aforesaid sacrifice to God, nevertheless, it could not be effected from this point that Christ offered a similar sacrifice. He tries to show it with a twofold argument.

The *third* argument, which is Chemnitz's first, is of this sort: "Dogmas must not be fabricated from types, unless these types are clearly explained in the Scriptures. Hence, David explains that Melchisedech was a type of Christ when he says in Psalm 109 [110]:5, 'You are a priest forever, according to the order of Melchisedech'. But he does not explain in precisely what this similitude between Melchisedech and Christ actually is. Moreover, the Apostle, in Hebrews 5 and 7, explains in what it consists; he says many things, but he does not touch upon the oblation of bread and wine. Therefore, it must not be affirmed that Melchisedech bore a type of Christ when he offered bread and wine in sacrifice to God."

I respond: Dogmas can be forged from types when the explication is gathered from the Scriptures according to the common consensus of the Fathers. So it is not necessary, that the Scripture must always explicitly say something, rather, it is enough if it speaks in such a way that we, following the common interpretation of the Fathers, might obtain its teaching; otherwise very few things, or rather nearly none would be certain dogmas in the Church. Now truly Scripture, in Psalm 109:5 (or 110 according to the Hebrew numbering) witness that Christ is a priest according to the order of Melchisedech. The Apostle often repeats this fact in his epistle to the Hebrews. Moreover, Scripture does not clearly explain in what this order of Melchisedech consists. Paul, as we said, does not treat on what the order of Melchisedech was, rather he only showed the excellence of Christ above Aaron. Now, although Scripture does not clearly say in what the order of Melchisedech consists, and the figure of the priesthood of Christ, nevertheless, it so insinuates it that the Fathers fall into a supreme consensus in the same exposition, as we showed above.

And besides, reason manifestly teaches that this exposition is true. For if Christ is a priest according to the order of Melchisedech, consequently he should agree in this priesthood with Melchisedech, namely in what is proper for that priesthood, except the form of such a sacrifice. What Melchisedech blessed and what he received as a tithe, is not proper to that priesthood, since it is in common with the Levitical priesthood. That Melchisedech was not anointed with sensible oil, nor succeeded by another, nor did any man succeed him, is not proper to Melchisedech, since it is in common with Abel and with several others. Lastly, because his lineage is unwritten, and thence was a type of the eternity of the priesthood of Christ, besides what is something intrinsic to the priesthood, is not proper to Melchisedech, but is in common with Job, Heli, and others, who were both priests and do not have their lineage described (as Epiphanius shows, *Panarion, haer. 55*). But to offer bread and wine, is proper to Melchisedech and especially pertains to the priesthood since it is his proper act. Therefore, no doubt remains on the explanation of this figure, though among prudent Christians, even without this notion, so many authorities of the Fathers ought to suffice seeing that on the other hand, no man could be advanced who would deny it.

The *fourth* argument, which is the second of Chemnitz, opposes this very answer. He speaks in this way: "The type of the priesthood of Melchisedech consists in these things, which are not in common with the Aaronic priesthood, but in which Melchisedech and Aaron are discerned. But a sacrifice of bread and wine was a daily offering in the Aaronic priesthood, as we see in Exodus 29:32 and Numbers 28:2.

Book I, Ch. VI: The Priesthood of Melchisedech

I respond: First, in the Aaronic priesthood there was indeed a sacrifice of bread and wine, but as a certain part and tempering quality of the other sacrifice. Then, bread, the loaves which were offered in the Aaronic sacrifice with animals, as we said, were always mixed with oil, and much of the time from this they became a cake. But the sacrifice of Melchisedech was simple bread. Then, it could also be said that the difference between those priesthoods was that Aaron offered sacrifices of all kinds, *i.e.* both bloody and unbloody. Melchisedech, on the other hand, only used an unbloody, pure, and simple sacrifice, as we taught above from the citations of Jerome, Eusebius and all the Fathers.

But against this answer is the *fifth* argument. If the priesthood of Melchisedech has this difference from the Aaronic, in that nothing bloody was offered in sacrifice, then it follows that Christ cannot be said to be a priest according to the order of Melchisedech, since the sacrifice of Christ was especially bloody, namely the sacrifice of the Cross.

I respond: The sacrifice of the cross, if it is considered by itself, is not according to the order of Aaron, nor according to the order of Melchisedech. That it was not according to the order of Aaron should be absolutely certain for the faithful; for Christ was not a priest according to the order of Aaron, as the Apostle clearly teaches in Hebrews 7:17, and it is also manifestly clear from the fact that he was not from the tribe of Levi, but from the tribe of Judah. How would a priest not according to the order of Aaron offer an Aaronic sacrifice? Next, the sacrifice of the Cross is the most perfect of all sacrifices, and is even more excellent than the sacrifice of the Mass, insofar as in that place a distinction is made between them. But who would advance that the Aaronic sacrifice should be said to be more excellent than all sacrifices and even the Mass itself, which is according to the order of Melchisedech? Besides, the Apostle teaches very clearly in Hebrews 7:19 that the sacrifice of Aaron was imperfect, nor could it bring those sanctified by it to perfection. But the sacrifice of the cross was most perfect, and brought those sanctified by it to perfection forever, as it is said in the same place, and therefore, the sacrifice of the cross cannot pertain to the order of Aaron. Then, the sacrifice of Aaron necessarily required two conditions: one that it was bloody, the other that it was a type, or representative. But the sacrifice of the cross, even if it was bloody, nevertheless was not a type, for no types are needed where the truth itself is present.

From such reasoning it is also gathered that the sacrifice of the cross, if it is considered by itself, was not according to the order of Melchisedech.

The sacrifice of Melchisedech was a type, though an unbloody one. Thus it agrees with the Aaronic in this, that both were types; nay more a type of this same thing, or a figure, that is of the passion of Christ. Rather, they differed in the species of types, because the type of Aaron was bloody and in the form of animals, whereas the type of Melchisedech was unbloody and in the form of bread. From which it follows by the notion of the sacrifice of the cross that Christ was not a priest either according to the order of Melchisedech, nor according to the order of Aaron, because he did not offer himself on the cross under the form of bread, nor under the form of a lamb or calf, but under his very own human form. Again, it follows from this, that Christ cannot be said to be a priest according to the order of Melchisedech, as it is nevertheless said everywhere in Scripture, except that he established a sacrifice, or offered one under the form of bread. Just the same, he cannot be called a priest according to the order of Aaron, because he did not establish a sacrifice of himself under the form of a calf or lamb, or of any other type in a bloody manner according to the Aaronic rite. For the paschal lamb, as we will say, he did not offer according to the rite of Aaron, nor did he establish it, but rather more abrogated it.

But someone will say: If Christ offered a bloody sacrifice, even if he did not offer that according to the order of Melchisedech, nevertheless, such a sacrifice as he offered prevents that Christ could be called a priest according to the order of Melchisedech, seeing that it is proper for that order not to have any bloody sacrifice.

I respond: Christ is called a priest according to the order of Melchisedech not for a little while, but forever, *i.e.* in respect to that sacrifice which is going to endure forever, *i.e.* it was going to be repeated perpetually, after the sacrifices of the law were abrogated, and because he was going to be the sacrifice of the Christian religion. And because Christ did not establish, nor offer a sacrifice to be celebrated perpetually, and of his own religion apart from an unbloody one, therefore, he is truly and properly a priest according to the order of Melchisedech. Here it must still be observed, that although Christ was not a priest according to the order of Melchisedech by reason of the sacrifice of the cross (rather only by reason of the sacrifice of the Eucharist), nevertheless, the sacrifice of the cross can be said to be according to the order of Melchisedech by reason of the very priesthood of Christ, by which it was offered; for he absolutely was a priest according to the order of Melchisedech. This is why the Apostle, in Hebrews 5:10, also calls Christ a priest according to

Book I, Ch. VI: The Priesthood of Melchisedech 55

the order of Melchisedech while he was on the cross.

The *sixth* argument: Matthias Illyricus (*Apologia Confessionis Antwerpiensis*, cap. 25) takes up the dissimilarity between the sacrifice of Melchisedech and our Mass. For, if Melchisedech offered anything, he offered bread and wine. But in the Eucharist the bread and wine do not remain apart from the accidents, as Catholics themselves teach.

I respond: The sacrifice of the Mass is truly according to the order of Melchisedech, both because it is unbloody (for it was the proper sacrifice of Melchisedech), and also, that which represents Christ in the Mass in the species of bread and wine, as it also represented him in the sacrifice of Melchisedech, clearly agrees in this way with the outward symbol. Moreover, that the inward substance is different is of no importance, because the meaning (as we said above), or the representation is in the accidents not in the substance. I add that necessarily the substance of the sacrifice of the Mass should be different than the sacrifice of Melchisedech seeing that it should be more excellent and divine, in which truth itself is with the symbol, than that in which the symbol is contained.

The seventh argument they take from the Fathers. Peter Martyr, commenting on 1 Cor. 5, tries to show that Melchisedech did not offer bread and wine to God, because several authorities say that Melchisedech gave the bread and wine to Abraham (Rabbi Solomon on Genesis 14; Ambrose *de Sacramentis*; Augustine in *Questions on the Old and New Testament*). In the same opinion he cites Chemnitz (*loc. cit.*), Josephus and Chrysostom.

But these citations make altogether nothing at all. In the first place, Rabbi Solomon was not only a Jew, but in no way can be pitted against so many holy Fathers whom we have cited; nay more he was an enemy of the Christian religion. Besides, he shows (*ibid.*), as even Peter Martyr affirms, that oblation that Melchisedech prefigured was later going to be that sacrifice of bread and wine that would be offered in Jerusalem. But how could that oblation prefigure a future sacrifice if it was merely a profane meal and not, rather, a sacred meal from the participation of a thing first offered to God? Therefore, although Rabbi Solomon says that Melchisedech offered bread and wine to Abraham's refreshment, as well of his companions, still he does not deny, nay more he shows in addition that it was first offered to God. The ancient rabbis clearly taught this, as we have already shown.

St. Ambrose is wholly on our side, as we showed above, and therefore perhaps Peter Martyr, as he is careful in matters of this sort, refused to annotate a certain book and chapter.

The passage of Augustine he cites is neither of Augustine, nor does it make the argument for our adversaries, but rather for our side. The author of those questions holds many errors which are refuted by Augustine, and in the first part of question 109, which Peter Martyr adduces in his own favor, that author contends that Melchisedech is the Holy Spirit, which is an error that Jerome expressly refutes in his epistle to Evagrius about Melchisedech. Moreover, the fact that this author, whoever he was, writes on the oblation of Melchisedech, argues for us against our adversaries; for he says that Melchisedech offered the Eucharist of the body and blood of the Lord to Abraham. From there we understand that for this author, Melchisedech did not show some common and profane dinner, but a *sacred type of the Eucharist*, which our adversaries now pertinaciously deny.

Next, Josephus, whom Chemnitz cites, writes that the bread was given to Abraham (which we do not deny), but that author does not deny that it was first offered to God, which we affirm.

Next, Chrysostom is on our side, as we proved above.

The *eighth* argument is opposed to another part of our argument, on the eternity of the priesthood according to the order of Melchisedech. Moreover, the argument is put in this way: For Christ to be a priest forever, it is not necessary to have a daily offering made through the ministers; therefore, that argument does not conclude the matter. Chemnitz tries to prove the antecedent (*Examination of the Council of Trent*, 2 par. pag. 745), where he shows from Paul (Hebrews 7&9) both negatively and in the affirmative, as he says, the measure whereby Christ is and is not a priest forever. In the first place, he says that Christ is not a priest forever because he offers himself many times; for Paul repeats it more than once. Then, he adds five reasons why it can be said that Christ is a priest forever. *First*, because he lives forever. *Second*, because the power of his unique oblation endures and is efficacious forever. *Third*, because he always intercedes for us in heaven. *Fourthly*, because through him, as priest, we shall always have access to the Father. *Fifth*, because he can and will always save those who come to God through him.

I respond: In respect to the negative part of this argument, when Paul says that there was no need for Christ to offer himself many times, he clearly speaks about the *bloody* oblation, which was completely sufficient, nay more, of infinite price and value; the other oblations were and are repeated because they are of finite value. Moreover, what

Book I, Ch. VI: The Priesthood of Melchisedech 57

is necessary for the eternal priesthood of Christ, that he would offer frequently by himself or through his ministers, not in a bloody manner but in some other way, is the same as what Paul teaches in Hebrews 8, as St. Thomas nobly explains in his commentary on that verse. For, when the Apostle said Christ is the high priest, and minister of the saints and the tabernacle, what God established and not man, *i.e.* he is the high priest of the Church, not the synagogue. He also adds, in verse 8, "Every priest is constituted to offer gifts and hosts, wherefore it is necessary that even he should have something to offer." There you see, Paul gathers by the necessary consequent that Christ ought, if he is truly a priest, to have something to offer, and consequently ought to offer because every priest is constituted to offer something. This is why, according to Paul's teaching, Christ is not a priest forever except that he continually offers; nor is it sufficient that he once offered himself in a bloody manner. Next, the same Apostle added in verse 4, declaring the victim which Christ now continually offers, is not something earthly, like sheep and oxen, but something heavenly, namely the most holy Eucharist: "If, he were on earth, he would not be a priest, seeing that there would be others to offer gifts according to the law; those who serve the example and shadow of heavenly things" (Hebrews 8:4). This is the teaching of such words: If hosts must be immolated upon the earth, *i.e.* if it were something earthly, and mortal, such as sheep and oxen, etc., Christ would not be a priest, because there would not be any necessity for the new priesthood, seeing that many would frequently offer earthly gifts of this sort according to the law without him. Next, Paul continues, and shows Christ is the priest of a better Covenant than the ancient, and from which it follows he now offers hosts that are better than the ancient sacrifices were.

Furthermore, from that it becomes clear that the five arguments which Chemnitz brings forward do not sufficiently show why Christ should be called a priest forever. The *first*, that he lives forever, is not sufficient: Eternal life is truly required in one who should have an eternal priesthood, but *it does not suffice*; otherwise every Levite priest after the final resurrection might be said to be a priest forever, because they have a priesthood and will live forever. Therefore, as a living man it is required that *he would exercise the priesthood forever.* Just the same, someone cannot rightly be called a King for thirty years if he neither did, nor could reign except for a day. This is especially important for the opinion of our adversaries, because they think the priesthood, or Ecclesiastical ministry, is a mere office. Next, as we showed above, St. Paul clearly requires it when he says that it was fitting for Christ to have something to offer, if he is a priest. For Paul, in Hebrews 7:24, where he posits this argument of Chemnitz, "Christ, in the fact that he remains forever, has an eternal priesthood", does not therefore prove Christ only has a priesthood because he remains forever, rather, he thereby proves that since he remains forever, he can perpetually exercise the priesthood. Nor is it fitting that someone would succeed him in a continual succession as in the Levitical priesthood, because none of them could minister perpetually owing to the fact that death would prevent them from so doing.

The *second* argument, that the power of the sacrifice of the cross is perpetual, is also not sufficient. For that shows the effect of the sacrifice of the cross is perpetual, and hence that sacrifice is improperly called perpetual. Nevertheless, it is not properly called an eternal sacrifice because it happened once; nor is it called an eternal priesthood when it does not sacrifice continually; otherwise the priesthood and sacrifice of Noah could be called eternal (as we gather from Genesis 8:21), because the effects of the sacrifice offered by Noah after the flood will always remain. He asked lest a flood of water would ever return again upon the earth. For equal reasoning, the birth of Christ from his mother, his passion and death can be called eternal, and Christ could be said always to be born, suffer and die because the effect of these things always remains.

The *third* argument, that Christ always intercedes for us in heaven, either does not prove he is a priest, or proves he now offers [sacrifice] through ministers. For, if our adversaries would have it that Christ intercedes for us by prayer alone, then they do not hold him properly to be a priest, for any man you like, even a layman, can intercede for another through prayer. But if they contend that he intercedes as a priest, *i.e.* by the medium of the oblation of a victim, then it is necessary for Christ to always offer sacrifice; and hence the Eucharist is a sacrifice, which is continuously offered by Christ through human ministry.

They will say Christ offers himself in heaven while he continually represents his passion to the Father, and reconciles us through it. Calvin seems to think this in the *Institutes* (4, 18 §2), where he says that there is no longer any priest on earth, because it was translated into heaven, and there Christ is a priest forever.

I respond: Either they mean the oblation which is in heaven is true and properly called a sacrifice, or only improperly and figuratively. If the first, a great many things follow against our adversaries, and some of these also against the truth. *Firstly*, the Christian religion and law would no longer be on earth, but translated into heaven; for when the priesthood was translated, it is necessary that the translation of the law would also happen (Hebrews 7:12). *Secondly*, in heaven there is no bare truth, but also shadows and figures and ceremonies; for all sacrifices properly speaking should be representative of the sacrifice of the cross, and certain ceremonies of religion. *Thirdly*, it will behoove our adversaries to concede that the oblation of Christ is frequently repeated, which they do not wish to concede in any manner.

If the second, then it will be necessary to confess the true sacrifice of Christ is offered on earth, which is what we contend; or certainly Christ is not truly and properly a priest, which is most absurd and against the clarity of Scripture. Moreover, it is evident that it would follow that he cannot truly and properly be a priest who cannot offer a true and proper sacrifice.

The *fourth* argument of Chemnitz is similar to the third, for thence Christ as a priest intercedes for us, and we through Christ the priest have an entrance to the Father, which was the *fourth*.

The *fifth* argument, that he could save forever, proves that he is a *savior*, but not a priest. For is this argument is similar to the second and third; hence it is refuted in the same way. This is why Chemnitz did not prove Christ is called an eternal priest without oblation of a victim through the ministers of the Church. Moreover, in this passage it must be admitted that we do not deny the priesthood of Christ is absolutely going to be eternal by reason of the effect, just as the virtue of this oblation completes the sanctified forever, as St. Thomas teaches from the Apostle (III Q. 22 art. 5). Because Christ, in whom the supreme sacerdotal dignity will always reside, truly remains eternal, and always immolates a sacrifice of praise and thanksgiving to God; just the same, by reason of the priestly office properly so called, and according to the prophecy in Psalm 109:5, we argue the priesthood of Christ is called eternal, not because he is going to endure until the end of time, but because *no one shall ever succeed him as priest*. David did not only say, "You are a priest forever," but added, "according to the order of Melchisedech, *i.e.* as we have shown from the Fathers: You are a priest forever, offering through your ministers in your Church the sacrifice of your body and blood in the species of bread and wine. Moreover, the sacrifice in the species of bread and wine will not endure for an infinite period of time, and still, it will endure forever, because it will always endure as long as the aforesaid sacrifice will be necessary, *i.e.* even to the *end of the world*. For the Lord swore and will not repent, this is, he will never change this priesthood with another priesthood, just as he changed the priesthood according to Aaron with the priesthood according to the order of Melchisedech.

CHAPTER VII
The Sacrifice of the Mass is proven from the figure of the Paschal Lamb

ANOTHER testimony for the sacrifice of the Mass is taken from Exodus 12:3, and similar passages, where it is argued in regard to the Paschal Lamb. Moreover, there is this argument: The celebration of the Paschal Lamb was an express figure of the celebration of the Eucharist. Yet, that was a certain immolation of the victim offered to God; so the celebration of the Eucharist ought to be an immolation of a victim offered to God, that the figure would correspond to what had prefigured it. Now, seeing that some, such as Chemnitz, deny the proposition while others the assumption, both will have to be proved and then the arguments of Chemnitz will be washed away, whereby he attempts to strengthen his reasoning.

The fact that the celebration of the Paschal Lamb was a figure of the celebration of the Eucharist is proven firstly from Scripture. 1 Corinthians 5:7, "Christ our Pasch has been immolated, let us feast ... on the unleavened bread of sincerity and truth." From this passage we can constitute for certain that the Paschal Lamb which is called the Pasch in the Gospel, was a figure of the immolation of Christ. When, however, it was fulfilled cannot be constituted as certainly from this passage.

For, our adversaries will say that the Apostle speaks on the immolation made on the Cross, and on the spiritual eating, which is through faith. But we will prove from the Gospel that this figure was properly fulfilled in the institution and celebration of the Eucharist. In the first place, it is certain from the Gospel that before the passion of Christ the Apostles ate the flesh of Christ in the Last Supper, and hence ate the true Paschal Lamb, the feasting upon which the Apostle exhorts us to when he says, "Therefore let us feast on the unleavened bread of sincerity and truth." But the feast follows the immolation; for first, the lamb had to be immolated, then eaten, not the other way around. So, the immolation of Christ should precede that eating of the Last Supper which the Apostles did before the passion of the Lord. Therefore, not only is the passion the immolation about which Paul is speaking, but also the consecration and oblation of the Eucharist prefigured by the immolation of the Paschal Lamb.

Besides, as is certain from the same Gospel, immediately after the ceremony of the Paschal Lamb, the Lord added the celebration of the Eucharist; and he did not delay it for another time or place, seeing that he clearly showed that with this new ceremony he put an end to the old ceremony.

Next, if we were to consider the circumstances of each celebration, we will see that no figure was more manifestly fulfilled by Christ than this one. The Paschal Lamb was to be immolated on the fourteenth day of the first month in the evening (Exodus 12:3), and this was the necessary circumstance, as can be shown from many places of Scripture. As we know, Christ established the Eucharist at this very time. *Secondly*, the lamb is immolated in memory of the passing of the Lord and the liberation of the people from Egypt; the Eucharist is celebrated in memory of the Lord's passing from this world to the Father by the passion, and of our liberation from the power of Satan, which was done by the very death of Christ. *Thirdly*, the lamb was immolated so that it could be eaten and was like a viaticum for wayfarers; thus, it was eaten by the Jews, the habit of wayfarers carrying before themselves with staffs, chalices, etc. And what else is the Eucharist but a refreshment and viaticum for wayfarers to the true and heavenly homeland? *Fourthly*, the lamb could not be eaten except by the circumcised, and the clean, and in Jerusalem; so the Eucharist cannot be taken except by those who have been Baptized, cleansed, and are within the Catholic Church.

So, if Christ did not fulfill the figure in the institution of the Eucharist, let our adversaries tell us when he fulfilled it; for when Paul witnesses that it was a figure, necessarily it should be fulfilled.

Perhaps they will say that Christ fulfilled the figure either when he ate the Paschal Lamb, or certainly when he was crucified, for nothing else occurred which could be said to have the appearance of truth.

In response to the first: There is no reason to defend it. When the Lord ate the Paschal Lamb, he *observed the law*, which he had always done while he lived on earth, but he did not fulfill the figure. Accordingly, to fulfill the figure is not to do the very thing which the law prescribes one to do, but to substitute something else more excellent for it, to signify the very thing which the figure foreshadowed. In the same way, the figure of Circumcision was not fulfilled when Christ received Circumcision, but when he substituted Baptism for it. This is why in Coloss. 2:11, Paul calls Baptism the Circumcision of Christ "not done by hand".

Moreover, that second argument on the Lord's passion is indeed something, but not the kind that would suffice. For the immolation of

Book I, Ch. VII: The Paschal Lamb

the Paschal Lamb can indeed be said to be a figure of the passion of Christ. If that lamb is a figure of the Eucharist, and the Eucharist is a representation of the passion, who would also deny that lamb was a figure and representation of the passion? This is why in John 19:36 we see the Evangelist render the reason why the legs of Christ were not broken during the passion: because it was said on the Paschal Lamb, "You shall not break a bone of him." Just the same, the ceremonies of the Paschal Lamb were more immediately and principally a figure of the Eucharist than the passion, as is clear from the circumstances we explained a little before. For the passion did not fall on the fourteenth day, nor in the evening, but about noon on the fifteenth. And Christ was not crucified in memory of some passing or liberation. Nor was he crucified that he should be eaten, nor was there any then who ate him so immolated. And he was not immolated in the house, or Jerusalem, but outside the gate in in the open ground. Next, not only the baptized and clean, but even others can and should eat Christ, as he was immolated on the cross, by faith, for faith comes first, then baptism and justification.

Now we prove from the common consensus of the Fathers that the Paschal Lamb prefigured the Eucharist. Tertullian (*in Marcionem* 4), gives an exposition of the Eucharist from the verse in Luke 22:15, *With longing I have desired to eat this Pasch with you.* "He professed that with desire he longed to eat the Pasch, as his own (for it would be unworthy that God would desire something else), received bread, made his body, etc." And a little before that he had said Christ had not desired the castrated lamb of the Jews, when he said he desired to eat the Pasch. Why would Tertullian understand the Eucharist, not the Paschal Lamb? He would not understand the Eucharist by the Pasch unless he believed the Eucharist was prefigured by the Paschal Lamb.

St. Cyprian (*de Unitate Ecclesiae*) proves that the Eucharist cannot be eaten with any benefit outside the Church, because it is written about the Paschal Lamb: "it shall be eaten in one house." And in his sermon on the Lord's Supper, he says: "After the Supper was administered, among the sacramental meals instituted for himself the ancient and the new came together; and after the lamb was consumed, which the ancient tradition proposed, the master placed before the disciples a food which could not be consumed."

Ambrose, on Luke 1, says: "when we sacrifice, Christ is present, Christ is immolated, and indeed Christ our Pasch has been immolated for us."

Gregory Nazianzen (*De Pascha*, orat. 2), explaining the ceremonies of the Paschal Lamb, says that God asked that it be immolated in the evening because it was then that Christ gave the sacrament of his body to the disciples.

Gaudentius (*in Exodum*, tract. 2) explains the whole celebration of the lamb in regard to the Eucharist: "In a shadow of that Pasch of the law, not one lamb was killed, but a great many; for individually they were slaughtered in homes, for one could not be sufficient for all. ... The same through individual houses of Churches in the mystery of bread and wine, being immolated he refreshes, being believed he brings life, being consecrated he sanctifies the consecrators; this is the flesh of the lamb, here is his blood."

Jerome, commenting on Matthew 26, says: "After the type of the Pasch was fulfilled and he had eaten the flesh of the lamb with the Apostles, he that strengthens the heart of man took bread, and the sacrament changed to the true Pasch."

John Chrysostom (*Homil. On the Betrayal of Judas*, tomo 3), says: "On that very table, each Pasch, both the type and the truth, were celebrated. ... It was indeed at some point the Jewish Pasch, but it was emptied and removed for the arrival of the spiritual Pasch which Christ gave. For when they ate and drank, he took bread and broke it, and said, 'This is my body, etc.'" And in Homily 83 on Matthew, speaking on the institution of the Sacrament he adds: "He joined the truth to the figure. ... If the figure freed from servitude, how much more will the truth claim the whole world?"

Augustine, (*Contra Literas Petil.* 2, 37), says: "They celebrate one thing from that sheep, we receive the other in the body and blood of the Lord."

Leo I (serm. 7 *de passione Domini*), speaking about the Pasch, says: "That the shadow would yield to the body, and the images would cease under the presence of truth, the ancient observance was abolished by the new Sacrament, host passed to host, blood excluded blood, and while the festivity of the law is changed, it is fulfilled." Later, speaking on the institution of the Sacrament, he says, "He completed the Old Testament and composed a new Pasch while his disciples were reclining with him."

Isichius (*in Leviticus*, 2, 8), says: "Earlier, the Lord dined on the prefigured sheep with the Apostles, then he offered his own sacrifice." See also 6,23, and Procopius Gazaeus on Exodus 12 who holds the same.

Gregory the Great (*Hom. 22 in Evangelica*), while explaining the whole ceremony of the Paschal Lamb suited to the Eucharist: "You have learned what the blood of the lamb is not by listening, but by drinking," etc.

Bede (*in Luke 22*) and from him Anselm (*on Matt. 26*), say, "After the solemnities of the old Pasch were finished, which were carried out in commemoration of the ancient liberation of the people of God from Egypt, he passed to the new, which he willed the Church to repeat in memory of his redemption, that he might establish in place of the flesh and blood of the lamb, the sacrament of his body and blood."

Rupert (*in Exodum* 2,6), says: "At length, on the fourteenth day at evening, after he ate the lamb of the old Pasch with his disciples, then he, the lamb of the new sacrifice, was taken and led to be immolated, but already, agonizing in the meanness of his passion, he had already immolated himself to God the father with his own hands when he received bread and wine, and with marvelous and ineffable power of sanctification transferred these things into the sacrament of his body and blood."

From these testimonies the proposition of our argument seems sufficiently confirmed; but the assumption, that the celebration of the Paschal Lamb was a certain sacrifice must still be borne out though it is a lesser business. For we read in Exodus 12:21, "And Moses called all the ancients of the children of Israel, and said to them: Go take a lamb for your families, and sacrifice the Paschal feast." and in verse 27, "It is the victim of the passage of the Lord, when he passed over the houses of the children of Israel". In Numbers 9:6, "But behold, some who were unclean by occasion of the soul of a man, who could not make the Paschal sacrifice on that day, coming to Moses and Aaron, said to them: We are unclean by occasion of the soul of a man. Why are we kept back that we may not offer in its season the offering to the Lord among the children of Israel?" And again, in verse 13, "But if any man is clean, and was not on a journey, and did not make the Paschal sacrifice, that soul shall be cut off from among his people, because he offered not sacrifice to the Lord in due season." From these we have it that the Paschal Lamb was truly and properly a sacrifice and victim, and described absolutely as a sacrifice in Scripture; besides, to be offered to God through immolation, which is of a true and proper sacrifice.

Add, that in the same way we read in the Gospel, "And on the first day of unleavened bread, when the Pasch was immolated." (Mark 14:12).

Next, what could be clearer than the words of Paul in 1 Cor. 5:7, "Christ our Pasch has been immolated?" They will not deny that the passion of Christ was a true sacrifice. But why does Paul call the sacrifice of Christ the immolation of the Pasch if the immolation of the Pasch was not a true sacrifice? Nor is it opposed that it was not offered by the priests alone, but also many who were not priests. This sacrifice was established before the family of Aaron was selected for the priesthood, and therefore, insofar as the purposes of this sacrifice are concerned, it remained an ancient privilege that every head of house exercised the priesthood. See *Philo* (*de Vita Moysis*, lib. 1).

But now, let us see what Chemnitz will raise in objection to our argument in his *Examination of the Council of Trent*, pp. 758-759. His first objection is taken from the testimony of St. Augustine (*de Unitate Ecclesiae, contra litteras Petiliani*, cap. 16): "Let them not gather and relate matters which are couched in obscure, doubtful, or figurative language, which everyone can interpret as he likes, according to his own view. For such passages cannot be rightly understood and explained, unless, first, those things that are most plainly derived are held with a firm faith. Bring forth something which does not need an interpreter, nor from which you might show something that was said on another matter and that you dared to twist to your own opinion." And in Chapter 19, "These are mysterious, secret, and symbolic; we beg of you something obvious that does not require an interpreter. ... For if something that has been posited ambiguously can be interpreted for us and for you, certainly, it would not help your cause at all, seeing that if we wished to use such things, we could use countless pieces of evidence which likewise would not help our cause at all. But truly, such evidence sustains a bad cause by making delays."

I respond: The testimonies of scripture that exist under a figure, because they can be explained in different ways, do not establish matters of faith unless they would be certain from another passage of Scripture; just the same they must be taken up. For Scripture usually explains some figure in three ways. *Firstly*, when it explains what was said under a figure immediately and in particular with its own words. Hence, from the parables of the Lord on the good and wicked fish in the same net, and on the sheep and goats in the same sheepfold, and similar things, Catholics refuted the Donatists who denied that both good and evil men are in the Church, since the Lord himself explained the parables, applying these to the Church (Matt. 13:41; 25:32. On that matter see Augustine in the third day of the brief conference). *Secondly*, when Scripture does not immediately explain a figure, nevertheless it approves the explanation of the Church, when it displays the testimony to it that it is a pillar and foundation of truth (1 Timothy 3:15), and Augustine, who hands down this form of argumentation in *contra Cresconium*, 1, 33 and frequently in other places). *Thirdly*, when Scripture teaches in certain words a figure in Christ contained in a figure that is going to be fulfilled by Christ, and from there we gather from manifest reasoning in what time, and place it was fulfilled, although Scripture did not explain it. For, when it is certain that something is a figure, at the same time it is certain that it should be fulfilled; hence if we can conclude from reason either in such a time and place it was fulfilled, or absolutely was not fulfilled, we firmly prove what we propose.

Thus, our argument from the figure of the Paschal Lamb and the explanation of the same figure has the testimony of Scripture in the second and third manner. For, in the first place we advanced the consensus of the ancient Greek and Latin fathers, which is the consensus of that Church which both we and our adversaries do not doubt is the true Church, and hence according to the Apostle is the pillar and foundation of truth. Next, Scripture witnesses that figure was fulfilled by Christ, as we showed from the same Apostle in 1 Cor. 5:7. And we concluded from the manifest circumstances with evident reason, that the figure was either never fulfilled, or it was fulfilled in the institution of the Sacrament at the Last Supper.

Moreover, in the places which Chemnitz cites, Augustine speaks on those figures whose explanation has not testimony from Scripture, and therefore adds that they are always obscure, hidden and requiring interpretation, to the extent that they can be twisted into various senses at will. He does not simply reject the argument from figures, but from figures that are "obscure and not yet explained," either in another passage of Scripture or by the Church. Otherwise, in that same book *On the Unity of the Church*, in ch. 13, Augustine proves the Church consists in the good and the wicked, both from the parables of the cockle and the good and evil fish, and similar figures. He only rejects the argument from those figures for which the interpretation is uncertain, such as that from the Canticles, "where do you lie at noon?", which the Donatists always threw about to prove the Church is only in Africa, to which Augustine rightly objected Psalm 47:3, "The sides of the north, the city of the great king," and similar equally obscure passages.

Additionally, in the same book Augustine asks for clear testimonies of Scripture from the Donatists, and he did not freely admit obscure ones, because he had clear testimonies for his own side. For, it was a question on the place of the Church, whether it was in Africa alone, or the whole world. And because there are a great many testimonies which teach without any obscurity that the Church was going to be throughout the whole world, Augustine duly required from his adversary similar testimonies; for what is clear and proper should not yield to what is obscure and under a figure. But in other more obscure questions, such as the question of Baptism was in that time, Augustine did not challenge them to clear testimonies of Scripture, but the authority of the Church, which could not err in its explanation of Scripture, as is clear from *Contra Cresconium* (*loc. cit.*). This is why if Chemnitz thinks his cause is the same as that of Augustine, let him advance clear testimonies of Scripture which do not need interpretation, where we shall read that the celebration of the Eucharist was not a sacrifice, and then he can rightly reject arguments from figures with Augustine.

Chemnitz objects *secondly*, that many absurd things would follow if the figure of the Paschal Lamb were applied to the Eucharist. In the first place, the figure will not correspond to the prefigurement, since the immolation of the Paschal Lamb was bloody, but the Eucharist is unbloody. Then, the Paschal Lamb was not immolated by the priests, as the Eucharist is, but by the multitude. And lastly, the sacrifice of the Paschal Lamb was not propitiatory for sin, as we say the Eucharist is, but done in memory of the liberation from Egypt.

I respond: The Eucharist was not only prefigured by the Paschal Lamb, but also by the sacrifice of Melchisedech, and by the Manna, and other things in the Old Testament. Thus, not everything which took place in the Paschal Lamb pertains to the figure of the Eucharist, but only those things which are not opposed to the fulfillment of the other figures. Therefore, from the figure of the Paschal Lamb we have in the Eucharist the true flesh and blood of Christ, the Immaculate Lamb is immolated, but only in an unbloody fashion and under the species of bread and wine, that the other figure of the sacrifice of Melchisedech offered in bread and wine would have place. And also, in this way the oblation and eating of the lamb pertains to the figure of the Eucharist, the mode of bloody consumption does not pertain to that figure, because it would be opposed to the figure of the sacrifice of Melchisedech, just as on the other hand, the form or outward species of bread and wine in the sacrifice of Melchisedech pertains to the figure of the Eucharist; the inward substance of bread and wine do not pertain to this figure,

Book I, Ch. VII: The Paschal Lamb

because they would be opposed to the figure of the Paschal Lamb, which requires the true substance of flesh in what was prefigured, lest what was prefigured would be more vile than its figure. Moreover, that the mode of bloody sacrifice would not impede, the Paschal Lamb was no less a figure of the Eucharist, as is clear from Augustine (*City of God* 17, 20; and *contra advers. Leg. et Prophet.* 1, 18), and from Leo I (*Serm. 8 de passione Domini*), who taught that all the sacrifices of the Old Law, although they were bloody, were figures of the Sacrifice of the Eucharist.

Now, what pertains to the other absurd argument presents no difficulty. For, the fact that it is said in Scripture that the Paschal Lamb ought to be immolated by the multitude of the children of Israel is not so understood as if each and every one of the people should immolate the Lamb, but that it should be immolated in each house and in every household, by the head of household, and while he makes the immolation, the rest do so through him, as willing participants in the sacrifice. The fact is also observed in the Church in regard to the Eucharist; for the priests who are fathers of the household of Christ properly and personally immolate it, but the people immolate it through them, and share in the sacrifice together with them in will and participation.

Lastly, the third absurd objection which Chemnitz advances is of no weight at all. For the sacrifice of the Eucharist, as we have said, was not only foreshadowed by the Paschal Lamb, but by many other types. The Paschal Lamb was indeed a type of the Eucharist, not as a propitiatory sacrifice, but as a commemoration of liberation and as properly Eucharistic; moreover, the sacrifices, a great many of which were done in the old law for sin, as propitiatory sacrifices were figures of the same Eucharist.

Thirdly, Chemnitz makes the objection that the Paschal Lamb bore the figure of the Lord's passion. With great labor, he strives to prove from the Scriptures and even from Ecclesiastical Testimony taken from the Preface of the Mass.

But the argument has already been answered. The Paschal Lamb was a type of both things, the passion and the Eucharist; nay more, it could not be a type of the Eucharist, without also being of the passion, since the Eucharist is a representation and commemoration of the passion. And it is not proper to the Paschal Lamb, but in common with all the sacrifices of the old Law, that it was at the same time a figure of the Lord's Passion and the Eucharist.

CHAPTER VIII

The Sacrifice of the Mass is Proven from the Figures of Different Sacrifices of the Old Testament

THE *THIRD* ARGUMENT is taken from Exodus 24:8, where the dedication and celebration of the Old Covenant is described. For, after the law was given on Mount Sinai, God composed the Covenant with the Hebrews and promised them many benefits, and in turn they promised God obedience to the commandments. Moreover, this covenant was ratified with a solemn sacrifice, and the sprinkling of blood in these words, "This is the blood of the Testament,[6] which God has entrusted to you," as the Apostle recites it in Hebrews 9:20, suborning the words of Moses from Exodus 24:8. This figure was fulfilled in the Last Supper, in the institution of the Sacrament of the Eucharist, as we proved above (*de Eucharistia* lib. 1), nor does it appear that anyone could deny it. For in the first place, Luke 22:20 and Paul in 1 Cor. 11:25 say, "This chalice is the new Testament in my blood." Matthew 26:28, and Mark 14:24 say, "This is my blood of the New Testament."

Next, the Fathers clearly teach that Christ established the New Testament in the Last Supper. Tertullian (*in Marcionem*, 4), says: "In the commemoration of the Chalice, he constituted the Covenant signed with his blood." Chrysostom and Theophylactus clearly teach the same thing in those passages gathered from Matthew and Paul, and likewise Ambrose on the Pauline passages, as well as Bede on the passages from Mark and Luke (*loc. cit.*).

Besides, the Lutherans cannot deny it, seeing that their particular argument against the Mass is this: "The Mass is the Testament of Christ; therefore, it is not a sacrifice." Luther places more importance upon this argument before all others, in his book *De Babylonica Captivitate* (cap. 1) and *De Abroganda Missa*, and in other places. Chemnitz also puts forward the same argument (*Examination*, 2. Part., pp. 753 & 802). Others commonly put forward this argument. Later, we will see the reason why this argument should be of such great importance. In the meantime, we will take what they give, that the Mass is the Testament of Christ; from

---

6 Translator's note: In this place we have used the word "testament" to translate the Latin *testamentum*, which means covenant. The reason for this more literal rendering is to not lose the sense of the argument which follows in this chapter, where Christ's *testamentum* is compared to a legal testament, which in Latin is the same word.

there it manifestly follows that in the Last Supper Christ established his Testament, and hence fulfilled the figure of the Old Testament.

Lastly, it happens that if the Testament of Christ was not made in the Last Supper, certainly it took place on the Cross, as some seem to suspect. But all the conditions of the Testament square with the Last Supper, whereas none of them with the Cross. *First*, the one who gives witness, should live until the Testament has been signed and completed. Christ lived throughout the course of the Last Supper, but died on the cross. This is why St. Paul rightly does not say in Hebrews 9:17 that the New Testament was made by the death of Christ, rather *it was confirmed*; for the Testament does not come into effect while the one who made it lives. *Next*, the one who made it should be in his own power. Christ, in the Last Supper was in his own power, whereas on the Cross not only was he taken and bound, but also condemned and placed on a gibbet. *Thirdly*, the one who made the Testament always entrusts something to heirs. Christ said in the Last Supper, "This is my command, that you love one another." And again, "Do this." On the cross it is read that he entrusted nothing. *Fourthly*, the one who makes the testament promises or relinquishes something, namely, he normally expresses something, as well as the persons to whom he relinquishes something. In the Supper, the Lord expressed the remission of sins, which is the promise proper to the New Testament (Jeremiah 31:34), and he also expressed the heirs, when he said, "For you and for many." On the Cross he did nothing of the sort, with the exception alone of the promise made to the good thief. *Fifthly*, the one who makes the Testament, applies witnesses, and just as Moses did not employ just any witness, but called together the people themselves when he ratified the Old Testament in the name of God. So also, Christ should have called witnesses, and he did not call anyone but the very Church; he did that in the Last Supper, for all the Apostles were present for the Pasch, and they were the true Fathers of the whole Christian people. But they were not present at the cross, nor could they easily have been called there. *Sixthly*, the ones who makes the Testament usually explain the Testament themselves in clear words. On the Cross, Christ did not name the Testament, but in the Last Supper he clearly expressed the word "Testament", and even with nearly all the words that Moses had once used, as when he had said, "This is the blood of the Testament, which God has entrusted to you," so he said, "This is the New Testament in my blood." *Seventhly*, the one who makes the Testament, composes a public deed which should perpetually have the force to be applied to his inheritance. Christ composed such a deed in the Last Supper while he instituted the Sacrament; on the cross he did nothing of that sort. Therefore, it remains fixed and, certain that in the Last Supper he established the New Testament and hence fulfilled the figure of the Old Testament.

Now, with this foundation posited, we make the argument in this way: The blood of the Old Testament in Moses was the blood of the victim that had already been immolated, and was truly and properly sacrificed, as is clear from Exodus 24:6; consequently, the blood of the New Testament with Christ is the blood of the victim that was immolated and was truly and properly sacrificed. Moreover, that is the blood of Christ, as he says, "this is my blood," so he was the victim immolated and sacrificed in the Last Supper.

One could not answer that the blood of Christ in the Last Supper was going to be the blood of the victim on the cross. For in Exodus, before the victim was immolated, the blood was sprinkled on the people with these words: This is the blood, etc. So also, Christ, before he ought to have make himself the victim and immolate himself, said about the blood, "This is the blood, etc." Besides, no reason is produced that before the blood of the victim should be drawn, then the victim be immolated, seeing that on the contrary from the immolation the blood follows. Next, since in the figure of the Old Testament (Exodus 24) we find three things: firstly the promulgation of the law in the presence of the people; secondly the immolation of the victim of the covenant, or of the peacemaking; thirdly, the aspersion of the blood and the eating of the victim, and Christ fulfilled the first when he says, "This is my command, etc.", and the third when he says, "Eat, this is my body; drink this is my blood." Now, who would believe that the second was omitted, namely the immolation of the victim? We find no response to this argument either from Chemnitz, or others.

So far, all those passages of the Divine Scripture can be referred where various sacrifices, properly speaking, are described in the Old Law. For they were all types and figures of the Sacrifice of the Eucharist; from which it follows that even the Eucharist should be a true sacrifice.

Chemnitz responds to this argument (*Loc. cit.*, pg. 771), that the sacrifices of the Old Testament were indeed figures that would be fulfilled in the New Testament, but the fulfillment is in the one sacrifice of the Cross, and now it is also fulfilled in the spiritual sacrifices of good works.

On the other hand, we prove the figures were sacrifices not only

Book I, Ch. VIII: The OT Sacrifices

of the cross and of good works, but even of the Eucharist, and in two ways. 1) From the Fathers. In his book *Against the Jews*, Tertullian clearly says the sacrifice of Abel was a figure of the Sacrifice of the Eucharist. Likewise, St. Justin Martyr in the *Dialogue with Trypho*, says, "The oblation was a figure of the Eucharist." Chrysostom (*on Psalm 95*), says, "A new supervenient grace with the one sacrifice embraces all the sacrifices of the ancients." St. Augustine (*City of God* 17, 20), says: "The table which the priest of the New Testament furnishes, concerning his body and blood, *i.e.* the sacrifice which succeeded all sacrifices, which was immolated in the shadow of things to come. For this reason, we also see that word in Psalm 39 of the same Mediator: 'You have desired a body for me', because his body is offered for all those sacrifices and oblations, and ministered to the participants." Pope St. Leo I (Serm. 8 *de passione Domini*), says: "Now that the many carnal sacrifices have ceased, all the differences of hosts, one oblation of your body and blood fulfills, and just as the sacrifice for every victim is one, so now one from every nation becomes a kingdom." See also Isichius (in *Leviticus*, lib. 5); Isidore (*de officiis*, 1, 17); and St. John Damascene (*de fide*, 4, 14). From such testimonies of the Fathers we see that the lie which Chemnitz puts forth (*loc. cit.*, pg. 778), is clearly refuted, namely: "That disputation was unknown to the ancients, which by the abrogation of the Levitical sacrifices, apart from the Sacrifice of Christ on the cross, some ceremonial sacrifice would succeed in the New Testament."

Secondly, it is proven that the sacrifice of the cross was not a fulfillment of those figures except inasmuch as its sacrifice and a few other ceremonies. Moreover, many other ceremonies of sacrifices, which without a doubt were under a figure, such as those which were offered in the tabernacle in the sight of the multitude of the faithful people, that a hand was placed upon the victim, that the victim was eaten immediately after it was immolated, and other similar things, could not be fulfilled on the cross. This is why they were either fulfilled in the Eucharist, or they were simply not fulfilled.

CHAPTER IX
The Sacrifice of the Mass is Proven from Predictions of the Prophets

THE FOURTH PRINCIPAL argument can be taken from the Predictions of the Prophets. As St. Augustine rightly says (*Epist. 49*, qu. 3), "Our sacrifice has not only been shown by the Evangelists, but even from the Prophetic books." Six testimonies are usually brought forward, but the last is the most important. So, we will only touch upon the others briefly, so that we may be permitted to tarry much longer upon the last.

1) The *first* testimony is contained in 1 Kings [1 Samuel] 2:35, near the end, where a certain unnamed prophet foretells to Heli the priest that a time will come when not only his priesthood, but that of his fathers will cease, and a new priesthood will rise which walks in the presence of the Christ of God for all days. Many Fathers explain the passage to mean the priesthood and sacrifice of Christians, which succeeded the Aaronic will remain even to the end of the world (Cyprian, *Contra Judaeos*, 1, 17; Augustine, *City of God*, 17, 5; Eusebius, *demonst. Evang.* 4, 26; Gregory, Bede and Eucherius in their commentary on this passage).

On the other hand, one could object that the prophecy seems fulfilled in Samuel, or in Sadock. For Samuel succeeded Heli, and then Solomon threw out Abiathar, who descended from the lineage of Heli, and constituted Sadock in his place, and Scripture adds (3 Kings 2:27) that it came to pass that the word of the Lord was fulfilled against Heli in Silo.

Augustine responds to this objection (*loc. cit.*), that the prophecy was fulfilled in Samuel, or Sadock, insofar as they bore the figure of the Christian priesthood. Therefore, the ejection of Heli was a figure of the ejection of the Aaronic priesthood, and the assumption of Samuel and Sadock was a figure of the assumption of the Christian priesthood. Augustine proves this from the fact that when Scripture says that Heli was going to be cast out with his fathers, clearly speaks about Aaron, accordingly it names him, who was first constituted a priest by God in the exodus from Egypt.

2) The *second* prophecy is taken from Proverbs 9:1-2, "Wisdom built herself a house, she has hewn her out seven pillars, slain her victims, mingled her wine and set forth her table." On this passage, Cyprian says: "By Solomon the Holy Spirit foretold a type of the Lord's Sacrifice, of the host that was immolated, and of bread and wine, even calling to mind

Book I, Ch. IX: The Predictions of the Prophets 75

the altar and the Apostles." See also St. Augustine who explains this whole passage on the Eucharist in *City of God* (17, 20).

3) The *third* testimony is taken from Isaiah 19:21. "And the Lord shall be known by Egypt, and the Egyptians shall know the Lord in that day, and shall worship him with sacrifices and offerings." Eusebius (*loc. cit.* 1, 6), as well as Jerome in his commentary on this passage, prove the law was translated, and in the same way the priesthood was translated, since among the Egyptians, that is, among the gentiles, sacrifices would be offered to the true God. Calvin has a response to this (*Instit.* 4, 18 §4), that Isaiah speaks on spiritual sacrifices which all Christians offer, but it does not avail. For in the same passage (verse 19), mention is made of an altar set up in a visible place for the Lord, "In that day there shall be an altar of the Lord in the midst of the land of Egypt." No visible altar is needed for spiritual sacrifices.

4) The *fourth* testimony is found in Isaiah 66:21, "And I will take from them priests and Levites, says the Lord." This is similar to what we find in Jeremiah 33:17-18, "There shall not be cut off from David a man to sit upon the throne of the house of Israel. Nor shall there be cut off from the priests and Levites a man before my face to offer holocausts, and to burn sacrifices, and to kill victims continually." Jerome explains these passages from Isaiah, and Theodoret those of Jeremiah, in regard to the priests of Christ, who will perpetually remain even to the end of the world. It cannot be explained otherwise, since clearly both Prophets speak about the conversion of the gentiles and the building of the Church.

Chemnitz (*Exam.* 2 parte. Pag. 753), acknowledges that these passages should be explained in regard to the priests of the New Testament, nor does he give any other response except that these prophecies were partly fulfilled in Christ, who was the true priest, and succeeded the priests of the Old Testament, and partly fulfilled in all Christians, who are spiritual priests. But neither exposition touches the matter. Not in regard to Christ alone can these prophecies be understood, since they clearly place priests and Levites, nor can they be understood in regard to all Christians, since both Prophets distinguish those who are going to be priests from the rest.

Someone will say: "These prophecies speak about the ministers of the New Testament who succeeded the ministry of the Old Testament in the ministry of doctrine, and of the sacraments, although they did not succeed in the ministry of sacrifice." But if that were so, why are they called *priests* (*sacerdotes*)? Why would Jeremiah say that *holocausts* are going to be offered? Therefore, *true* priests should succeed the old, who truly and properly offer sacrifices.

5) The *fifth* testimony is of Daniel 8:11 and 12:11, where it is said that Antichrist is going to remove continual sacrifice. The martyr Hippolytus explains this passage in regard to the sacrifice of the Mass in his book on Antichrist. Nor is it opposed that Daniel seems to speak about Antiochus Epiphanies; for he speaks about Antiochus as he bore the figure of Antichrist, which is clear from the comparison of this passage with that of Apocalypse 13.

Chemnitz answers (*loc. cit.* pg. 733), that the passage is literally understood on Antiochus and merely allegorically on Antichrist; but no solid arguments may be deduced from allegories. For John (Apocalypse 13) and Paul (in 2 Thess. 2) explain it, and even Daniel himself explains it when he says that king, who will abolish continual sacrifice is going to battle all gods, and act against the God of their fathers. But this cannot be understood on Antiochus, seeing that it is certain that he openly worshiped the gods of his fathers, as Jerome shows in his commentary; rather, everything that Paul writes is suited to Antichrist, namely that he will raise himself above everything which is called God.

Secondly, Chemnitz responds that this passage of Daniel can be understood on spiritual sacrifice, *i.e.* on the preaching of the word, and the administration of the Sacraments, nay more, he tries to show that continual sacrifice was removed by Antichrist because the Roman Pope, as he says, abolished the purity of the word and the Sacraments. But all these are utterly vain. For, in the first place, it is one thing to abolish, and another to corrupt. Antichrist will not corrupt, but simply abolish continual sacrifice, at least from public Churches. For that reason, it is added in the same place that the place of sacrifice will remain desolate. Next, in Scripture, nothing is called a sacrifice absolutely and especially in the singular except that which is truly and properly a sacrifice. Then, the continual sacrifice among the Hebrews was not spiritual sacrifices, but a sacrifice *properly* so called, *i.e.* two lambs who were offered daily as a holocaust, one in the morning and the other in the evening, as is clear from Exodus 29:38 and Numbers 28:3. This is why Daniel, when he speaks of a continual sacrifices, is talking about the *true* and *proper* sacrifice, whose type was that sacrifice of the Hebrews.

CHAPTER X
That the Mass is a Sacrifice is Proven from Malachi

THE CHIEF TESTIMONY for the sacrifice of the Mass is contained in the prophet Malachi, 1:10 and in these words: "I have no pleasure in you, says the Lord of hosts, and I will not receive a gift of your hand. For, from the rising of the sun even to the setting, my name is great among the gentiles, and in every place there is offered to my name a clean oblation; for my name is great among the gentiles, says the Lord of hosts."

This testimony cannot be understood on the sacrifice of the Cross, because that was not offered in every place, but only once in *one* place; nor on some Jewish sacrifice, because the Prophet says it was going to be offered by the *gentiles*, and clearly that is opposed to the sacrifices of the Hebrews. It is also not speaking about the sacrifices of the pious gentiles who were in the world before the arrival of Christ, such as Melchisedech, Job, and others like them. For these holy men were very few among the nations, and especially in the times of the Prophets when idolatry clearly filled the whole world, so that David said, "God is known in Judea, in Israel his name is great" (Psalm 75:1). But Malachi gives a prophecy in a contrary manner in verse 11, "My name is great among the gentiles, and from the rising of the sun to its setting, etc." Again, this passage of Malachi cannot be understood as some suppose, on the sacrifices of the idolaters among the gentiles; for that oblation was not *clean* in any way, nor offered to the true God, but to foreign gods, "The things which the gentiles sacrifice, they sacrifice to devils and not to God."

This is why the exposition of Benito Arias Montano[7] can in no way be admitted. For it is not only opposed to all the Fathers (whom we shall cite shortly), but also to the Apostle himself, and most clearly to the truth. Otherwise, why did so many thousands of martyrs prefer to shed their blood than communicate in the sacrifices of the gentiles, if these were sacrifices that were clean and pleasing to God?

"Yet", he says, "The gentiles knew there was a certain great God from the motions of the heavens, and they sacrificed to him." I respond: They certainly knew God, but they did not glorify him as God; they served him more as a creature than as a creator, as the Apostle says in Romans

---

7 Translator's note: Benito Arias Montano (1527-1598) was a Spanish Orientalist. The work where he authors the opinion that Bellarmine inveighs against is *Antiquitatum Judaicarum*.

1:21. So, they either did not sacrifice to that God, or very few of them did, and they did this very rarely. But Malachi speaks about sacrifices which are offered *in every place*, of the sort that the gentiles of that time did not offer except to idols and demons. Therefore, it remains that even our adversaries affirm with us that Malachi gave a prophecy about the sacrifice of the Christian Church, which also succeeded the Jewish sacrifices and is pleasing to God, as well as clean, and that the gentiles, once converted, offer it to the true God continually. Nor is it opposed that Malachi speaks in the present and not in the future. The Prophets do that because they are so certain about future events that they gaze upon them, prodded by God's revelation, as if they were present.

The whole controversy in regard to this passage is whether Malachi spoke on a sacrifice *properly speaking*, namely of the sort that in the Church is the Eucharist, or altogether nothing; or, on the other hand, whether he spoke of a sacrifice improperly speaking, such as prayers, praises, good works, patience in persecution, and similar things. Philipp Melanchthon (*Apologia Confess.*), Calvin (*Instit.* 4, 18 §4), Chemnitz (*Exam.* Pg. 760) and others contend that Malachi spoke about spiritual sacrifices, and sacrifices improperly speaking.

Moreover, Chemnitz introduces three arguments for his opinion, which can easily be answered. The *first* argument: "Malachi does not say there should be a sacrificing priest with miming gestures, rites and actions over bread and wine to represent the passion of Christ and that action is a sacrifice pleasing to God for the living and the dead, etc."

I respond: This is not an argument but an imposture. It is not a question of gestures and rites, but of *the substance of the thing*, i.e. our question is concerning the oblation of the sacrifice properly speaking, since we have shown from the testimony of the Prophet that a sacrifice properly so called will be in the Church.

The *second*: "Malachi foretells that there is going to be a clean sacrifice in the Church in general, but he does not explain what kind of sacrifice. Moreover, we find in the New Testament the sacrifices of the faithful are spiritual sacrifices (1 Peter 2; Romans 11; Hebrews 12; Philipp. 2), consequently, the Prophet speaks about a spiritual sacrifice."

I respond: If in the New Testament, we would only read of spiritual sacrifices of the faithful, then the argument of Chemnitz would rightly conclude the matter. But we read nothing of the sort. Moreover, we may not conclude from the fact that there are certain spiritual sacrifices in the Church that there are no sacrifices *properly speaking*; or that the Prophet speaks of *spiritual sacrifices*. Otherwise, because in the Old Testament there were also spiritual sacrifices, we would be able to conclude, in the same manner, that there were no sacrifices, properly speaking, in the Old Testament. Moreover, when Malachi says, "I will not receive a gift from your hand," we would understand him to speak about a spiritual sacrifice, not a proper sacrifice, which is clearly false.

He takes the *third* argument from the Fathers, which we will bring to naught later.

Against these arguments, Catholics prove the words of this Prophet should be understood on sacrifices properly speaking.

1) The *first* argument is taken from the term which the Prophet uses. For he says מנחה *minchah* without regard to any circumstance, where there are two considerations. *Firstly*, Scripture does not usually absolutely place a term when it speaks about what is improperly called a sacrifice, but when it is joined to something, such as *sacrifice of praise, sacrifice of justice, sacrifice of jubilation*, etc., whereas in this passage *clean oblation* is placed absolutely. Next, this Hebrew term מנחה *minchah* properly means a certain species of outward sacrifice, which from similar things, was confected with oil and frankincense, as is clear from Leviticus 2:2.

Calvin and Chemnitz respond to this first argument. Calvin says that the Prophet uses the term for sacrifice because it is the custom of the Prophets, when they prophecy on the conversion of the gentiles, they describe the outward spiritual cult by the rite of the Law; for in this way they place for the conversion to the Lord the ascent to Jerusalem, for the adoration of God, every kind of oblation of gifts; dreams and visions for a fuller knowledge of him, whereby in the kingdom of Christ the faithful were going to be given, etc.

I respond: It cannot be denied that often in the Scriptures of the Old Testament, future affairs are described by types and external rites of the law, such as when the Church is understood allegorically through Jerusalem, and clergy through Levites, the sacrifice of the Eucharist by sacrifices of sheep and oxen. Nevertheless, it usually happens that when new and future things are described which were not then in use, they are described through figures or terms then known because they could not be understood otherwise. But with those things which are common to all times and places, which were no less in use than they are now, there is no reason why they should be signified through figures. Moreover, spiritual sacrifices, prayers, hymns, almsgiving and similar things are common to every place and time, and occur everywhere in Scripture, both in the Old and the New Testament. This is why by the term מנחה *minchah*, one should not understand a spiritual sacrifice, which was not new or future, nor in any way unused, or unknown, but some true sacrifice that is going to be celebrated in the Church, and then was unknown; the Eucharist is really of such a sort. For, we do not understand the Prophet so crassly that he would show that now it is fitting to offer *minchah* properly so called, *i.e.* a similar sprinkling with oil and a wafting of incense, rather, we understand the prophet through a known term to have described a new and true sacrifice, through something foreshadowed in the ancient.

It is also false when Calvin says that oblations of every kind of gift are placed in Scripture for the future adoration of God in the Church. Truly something future *and new* should correspond to those oblations; but adoration was always in use.

At any rate, Chemnitz approaches the question in another way. He writes that this term מנחה *minchah* is received in the Scriptures for spiritual sacrifices; for we read in Psalm 140 (141):2, "The lifting up my hands as an evening sacrifice," and the name of this oblation is found in Romans 15:31, and Philipp. 2:17, for the conversion of the gentiles.

I respond: David very properly took up evening sacrifices for a true and outward sacrifice, which was daily offered according to the law at evening, in Leviticus 6:9. He also did not mean to say that the elevation of his hands in prayer is the evening sacrifice, for the elevation of hands can be done at any time, rather, he prays to God that "he shall find his prayer pleasing," just as he is usually pleased with the evening sacrifice. For he says in this way: "Let my prayer be directed like incense in your sight, the elevation of my hands the evening sacrifice," namely, let the prayer be directed just as incense, and the elevation of hands be like a certain evening sacrifice. Daniel could also say this more clearly, when he says in 3:39, "In a contrite heart and humble spirit let us be received, as in holocausts of rams and bullocks, and as in thousands of fat lambs." Moreover, those passages of Romans 15:31 and Philipp. 2:17 do not bear on the matter. For in each passage the word sacrifice is placed, and oblation with a circumstance, but not absolutely, for he calls the oblation "for the gentiles," or "of faith". Therefore, our first argument remains, taken from the term oblation.

2) The *second* argument is taken from the term *clean*. For the Prophet opposes the clean oblation of the Church to the unclean oblations of the priests of the Jews. This argument can be concluded in two ways. *Firstly*,

from the opinion of our adversaries, that good works which proceed from us are all unclean, since they are sins, and by their nature mortal sins. Therefore, through the oblation which the Holy Spirit calls clean, we should not understand our works, that is, sacrifices improperly so called, but *a sacrifice instituted by God*, which has its force from God himself and not from us.

Chemnitz responds: Our works are indeed as unclean as a polluted cloth, nevertheless, in the Scriptures sometimes they are called clean and acceptable to God, such as in 1 Peter 2:5, "Offering spiritual sacrifices, acceptable to God through Jesus Christ," and the faithful are said to lift up pure hands (1 Tim. 2:8), and all things are called clean by the clean (Titus 1:15).

But I would gladly ask of Chemnitz in what way these works are said to be clean and acceptable. For, they are either truly and properly clean and then the Lutheran opinion on the goodness of our works goes to ruin, or they are not truly and properly clean but are called such either on account of the imputation of God, or any other cause you like. Then, if Malachi is speaking on a spiritual sacrifice, these words would be fitting: "A clean oblation offered to my name", is so explained: an oblation truly unclean is offered to my name, but which I will repute as clean. Such an exposition is absolutely absurd; for the teaching of Malachi shows that oblation pleases God, *because it is clean*; moreover, it would not be clean because God reputed it as such.

Secondly, according to the Prophet, the sacrifice is clean of itself, and generally, to the extent that the malice of ministers could not make it unclean, and he opposes this to that sacrifice which can easily be polluted and which is not always clean. It is clear, for he says on the Jewish sacrifice in verse 7, "You offer polluted bread upon my altar," and in the next verse, "If you offer the blind for sacrifice, is it not evil? And if you offer the lame and the sick, is it not evil?" There he shows those sacrifices could be polluted. Nor is it credible that their sacrifices were generally rejected only by reason of the pollution on the side of those offering it, because our sacrifice could be rejected for the same reason. Besides, many Jews offered sacrifice well; why if these were the cause of rejection, would God have rejected these in particular, or those, rather than all in general? Therefore, all things were rejected in general because the cause was general, seeing that all things were guilty of pollution.

Still, the reason why he opposes a clean sacrifice to them generally, and not only those guilty of pollution, is clear because he says in verse

11, "In every place a clean oblation is offered." For, if it were clean by reason of those making the offering, he would not say a clean offering is made in every place, since there are bad ministers in many places that would pollute what is, in itself, a sacrifice. Rather, it is said in every place a clean offering is made because it is such a thing *in itself*, nor can it really be polluted from the malice of the ministers. Besides, if the reason for the repudiation of the former sacrifices was that they were guilty of pollution, certainly Malachi would have opposed the sacrifice of those not guilty of pollution to them. But spiritual sacrifices, since they depend upon our work, are guilty of pollution, and really, they are often polluted no less now by Christians than formerly by the Jews. As a result, the Prophet speaks about the sacrifice of the Eucharist, both because only one is truly clean, and because it cannot be polluted by the malice of any minister, seeing that Christ is the particular priest, and he is the same sacrifice.

3) The *third* argument is taken from those words of verse 10, "I shall not receive the offering from your hands, etc." From here it is gathered that the oblation of the Church is not only clean, but also *new*, and did not exist before. That clean oblation succeeds the oblations of the Jews which are rejected under the pretext of pollution. Moreover, it would not succeed the old if it was in use together with them; so, it should be a new oblation. And besides, the Prophet distinguishes the sacrifice of the gentiles from the sacrifice of the Jews, and hence speaks about a new sacrifice, and one which was not in use among the Jews. Moreover, it is certain that spiritual sacrifices of prayers, psalms and similar things were all used by the Jews. Consequently, Malachi does not speak about a spiritual sacrifice, but about a sacrifice properly speaking. A sacrifice like this would not exist in the Church if the Eucharist is not a sacrifice properly speaking.

4) The *fourth* argument is taken from the antithesis between contempt and the glory of God, which the Prophet describes in this passage. St. Malachi says that through the Hebrew priests the name of God was scorned and despised; but by the oblation of the gentiles it is glorified. For the Hebrew priests offended God in the public and visible sacrifice, thus the glory of God should come into being among the gentiles even from the public and visible sacrifice. Otherwise there was greater contempt inflicted upon the name of God in the sacrifices of the Jews than glory in the sacrifice of the gentiles, for in the former the contempt would have been inward and outward, private and public; moreover, in the latter

glory would only be private and, for the most part, inward.

5) The *fifth* argument is taken from the antithesis of the priests. Malachi does not oppose all of the people to all Christians, but merely the priests of the Old Law to *certain men* who properly succeed those priests. Therefore, he does not speak about a spiritual sacrifice; all Christians customarily offer them, rather, about a sacrifice properly speaking, which can be offered only by true priests. Now, the fact that he is speaking only about the priests, and not about all the people, is clear from the words in verse 6, "To you, O priests, who despise my name, etc." Moreover, the fact that he only opposes the priests to them, but not all the people, is clear from the same Prophet. After he says in 1:11, "a clean oblation offered to my name, etc." he explains in 3:3 *who* will offer this clean oblation: "He will cleanse the sons of Levi and shall refine them as gold and silver, and they shall offer sacrifices to the Lord in justice." There, for the sons of Levi, the Levites of the Old Testament cannot be understood, because the Prophet is clearly speaking about the sacrifice of the Christian Church, and the Levitical priests had already been cast out. Next, from the beginning of the chapter, verse 1, we read: "Behold, I send my angel." The Lord himself explains these words on John the Baptist in Matt. 11:10, and from there we are compelled to understand this whole passage on the arrival of the Lord and the time of the New testament. Nor can all Christians be understood by the sons of Levi, because the sons of Levi were only one part of the people of God, not the whole people; this is why a certain part of the Christian people corresponds to them, not the whole people. And it is confirmed from Isaiah 66:21, where we previously showed the priests are distinguished from the Christian people, when he says, "I shall take priests from them." So not all the Christian people are properly priests, but certain men taken from them, and hence, there should be a sacrifice, properly speaking, which they alone offer, and not the whole people.

Then, we add the consensus of the ancient Fathers who always understood this passage of Malachi on the sacrifice of the Eucharist, not good works, which everyone can do. St. Justin Martyr, in his *Dialogue with Trypho* (ch. 41), explains this passage with precise words on the sacrifice of the Eucharist which is offered to God throughout the world in the species of bread and wine (as even Chemnitz witnesses): "He then speaks of those gentiles, namely us, who in every place offer sacrifices to Him, *i.e.* the bread of the Eucharist, and also the cup of the Eucharist, affirming both that we glorify His name, and that you profane it."

Chemnitz attempts to twist this citation from that which Justin adds in the same place, that the Eucharist is done in memory of the passion of Christ, and in thanksgiving to God, who made the world for us, and freed us from sin. Hence, he also gathers that the sacrifice, on which Malachi speaks and according to Justin is a spiritual sacrifice, *i.e.* the memory of the Lord's passion, and thanksgiving made to God for the benefit of creation and redemption.

Yet he labors in vain. For by these words, Justin explains the *final cause* of the sacrifice foretold by Malachi, not the sacrifice itself. For he says the sacrifice is the oblation of the Eucharist confected from bread and wine, moreover, he says the cause of the sacrifice is the memory of the Lord's passion, and thanksgiving. And rightly, if one were allowed to use sophistry in this manner, we could prove that there were never any sacrifices, properly speaking not even among the Jews, for all were done in representation of the passion of the Lord, and thanksgiving, or for some similar reason.

Irenaeus (*Adversus Haereses* 4,17), says, "He took that created thing, bread, and gave thanks, and said, 'This is my body.' And the cup likewise, which is part of that creation to which we belong, he confessed to be his blood, and taught the new oblation of the new covenant; which the Church, receiving from the apostles, offers to God throughout all the world, to Him who gives us as the means of subsistence the first fruits of his own gifts in the New Testament, concerning which Malachi, among the twelve prophets, foretold: 'I have no pleasure in you, says the Lord of hosts, etc.'"

Chemnitz even tries to twist this passage to his own opinion, but his argumentation is so weak that it hardly needs any response. He says that Irenaeus speaks on the oblation of almsgiving, which used to take place during the act of the Lord's Supper; and he calls these almsgivings a sacrifice which can be said to be offered for God, while that which is offered for the poor is for God's sake, according to the Scripture verse, "A man that is merciful to the poor lends unto God" (Proverbs 19:17), and that, "I hungered and you gave me to eat" (Matthew 25:34), for Irenaeus selects these passages in chapter 17.

But Chemnitz does not even notice that Irenaeus makes an argument from similarity. When he meant to show that sacrifice is shown to God not because he needs it, but because it is useful for us and an act of thanksgiving to show it to him, then he introduces the example of almsgiving which is said to be done for God, when still, it is not useful for God, but for us. Moreover, because Irenaeus understands Malachi in regard to a sacrifice, properly speaking, he is not talking about almsgiving, which is clear from these words which we find in chapter 17: "Manifestly showing, by these words, that the former people [the Jews] shall indeed cease to make offerings to God, but that in every place sacrifice shall be offered to him, and a pure one, and his name is glorified among the gentiles." And from these which can be found in chapter 18, "The class of oblations in general has not been set aside; for there were oblations both there [among the Jews], and here [among Christians]. Sacrifices there were among the people, and there are also sacrifices in the Church." There, Irenaeus says that our sacrifice succeeds the former, which ceased among the Jews; and God did not absolutely set aside sacrifices, but a certain kind of sacrifice, namely of *the Jews*. Moreover, among the Jews almsgiving, prayers, as well as other sacrifices improperly speaking, have never truly ceased, whereas immolations, properly speaking, which could not be done except in Jerusalem, truly ceased. Consequently, Irenaeus speaks about sacrifice properly speaking, and he meant that the sacrifice of the Eucharist is such a thing. Lastly, these words of chapter 17: "He taught that new oblation of the New Testament." Do these not clearly show what we mean? For the new oblation is not almsgiving, nor was it proper to the New Testament since it is done even among the Jews, and it was then in use.

Now, Tertullian, (*Contra Marcionem*, 3,22), declaring the sacrifice foretold by Malachi, says: "*In every place sacrifice shall be offered unto my name, and a pure offering.* Such as the ascription of glory, and the blessing, and praise and hymns. Now, inasmuch as these things are also found among you, and the sign upon the forehead, and the sacraments of the Church, and the offerings of the pure sacrifice, etc."

Chemnitz pounces on this citation on account of the terms, *ascription of glory, praise*, and *hymns*. But Tertullian is describing briefly, and in his fashion a little more obscurely, the whole rite of the sacrifice of Mass. Accordingly, in that sacrifice, both before and after the consecration, and the oblation of the sacrifice, God is praised, prayed to, and hymns are sung, as is known. Moreover, what Tertullian calls a blessing is the consecration of the Eucharist itself, which is why he adds right away, "the sacraments of the Church, and the offerings of the pure sacrifice." Next, Tertullian alludes to the first oblation of this sacrifice. The Lord, in the Last Supper, first gave thanks, then blessed and at length sang a hymn; for when the hymn was sung, he went out onto the Mount of Olives, as we read in the Gospel. Tertullian expressed nearly all these things in words, when he says, "The ascription of glory, praise and hymns."

Chemnitz advances two other passages from Tertullian. One is from his book against the Jews, where he says that Malachi spoke about spiritual sacrifices, not earthly ones. The other is from *Contra Marcionem*, book 4, where we read a simple prayer from a pure conscience is the sacrifice that Malachi speaks of.

But the response is rather easy. Tertullian does not call the Eucharist a spiritual sacrifice because it truly isn't, rather it is a sacrifice properly speaking; both because it is from the *Holy Spirit*, not devised by man and carnal senses, and also because it does not consist of an earthly victim, but *a heavenly one*, nor is it sacrificed in a carnal mode, through a sword, fire, and effusion of blood, but rather *in a spiritual mode*, through the blessing of words and a consecration. It will not seem hard for anyone that is able to think, that the sacrifice of Abel is called a spiritual sacrifice in respect to the sacrifice of Cain by the same author (*ibid.*), because without a doubt, Abel offered sacrifice with the guidance of the Holy Spirit, whereas Cain had for his guide the sense of his flesh when he offered sacrifice. But if the sacrifice of Abel, although it could be called a spiritual sacrifice, did not cease to be a true, more correctly, even a bloody sacrifice, how much more could the Eucharist be called a spiritual sacrifice, and still retain the name and notion of a true sacrifice? Add, that Tertullian says (*ibid.*) the sacrifice of Abel was a figure of the Eucharist, from which it follows, the Eucharist was called a spiritual sacrifice in this way from it, just as the sacrifice of Abel.

In the other citation Tertullian does not expound on the testimony of Malachi through prayer, where he names sacrifice, but where he names *incense*. For in the Hebrew as well as the Septuagint, we read: "Incense is offered to my name, and a clean sacrifice." There Tertullian interprets *incense* as prayer, because Irenaeus did it before him (*loc. cit.*), and after him Jerome in his commentary on Malachi; but they commonly explain the latter term, sacrifice, on the Eucharist.

Cyprian (*Contra Judaeos*, 1, 16), places in the title of the chapter, Let the old sacrifice be purged, and the new celebrated. And then he cites this passage of Malachi. Moreover, there is no new sacrifice except for the sacrifice of the Eucharist; for those spiritual sacrifices, which the heretics call to mind, were always present.

Eusebius of Caesarea (*Demonst. Evang.*, 1, last chapter), commenting on Malachi 1:11, says: "We sacrifice to God on high the sacrifice of

Book I, Ch. X: The Prophecy of Malachi 87

praise; we sacrifice the full and most holy sacrifice to God, bearing the odor of sweetness; we sacrifice in a new fashion, according to the New Testament, a clean host." In these words, he very clearly describes the sacrifice of the Eucharist; for this alone is proper for the New Testament, and it is offered in a new fashion, it is satisfactory and most holy to God. Prayer and almsgiving are sacrifices, but they are not proper to the New Testament, nor are they offered in a new fashion, nor are they satisfactory and most holy to God, etc.

Chemnitz cites from the same author (*ibid.*, 1, 6) another testimony. Eusebius writes that the sacrifice of Malachi means that the gentiles in the whole world were going to offer the incense of prayer, and a clean sacrifice not through blood, but through pious actions.

But he doesn't seem to have understood Eusebius, for this is the Greek of Eusebius: Τὸ δὶ εὐχῶν θυμίαμα, which does not mean "incense of prayer", as if prayer were incense, or sacrifice, which Malachi is speaking about. Rather incense, or the sacrifice which is carried out through prayer, *i.e. through the words of consecration*. The Fathers customarily name the words of consecration prayers or mystical prayers. Next, even if through incense we should understand prayer; just the same, the following words pertain to the Eucharist; for it is the clean sacrifice, which is not offered through blood, but through pious and religious actions, i.e. through mystical consecrations. Therefore, in each passage, Eusebius understands the sacrifice foretold by Malachi as the Eucharist.

St. John Chrysostom (*in Psalm 95*), after he cited the words of Malachi, adds: "Look at how profitably and clearly he has interpreted the mystical table, which is the unbloody host. Moreover, he calls the pure Thymiama (incense) sacred prayers, which are offered after the host." From that passage another of the same Chrysostom can be explained, namely his second homily *against the Jews*, which Chemnitz cites. There, he understands the words of Malachi in regard to the spiritual cult, which succeeded the carnal cult of the Jews. For he calls the spiritual cult the sacrifice of the Eucharist, because, as we have already said, it is not effected in a carnal manner through the sword and the effusion of blood, but through the Holy Spirit and through the words of consecration. This is why Chrysostom (*ibid.*), writes that ours is called a clean sacrifice, because it is so excellently clean, that in comparison to it all others seem unclean. Such an encomium certainly does not square with our works, which are sacrifices improperly speaking, but best fits the Eucharist.

Jerome, in his commentary on Malachi, although he understands incense as prayer (a citation which Chemnitz doubles down on but in vain), nevertheless, he understands the oblation of the Eucharist through sacrifice, for he says a clean host is offered to God in the ceremonies of Christians.

Augustine (*Contra advers. Legis et Prophet.*, 1, 20), treating on this passage of Malachi, says, "The Church through the successions of the Apostles immolate the sacrifice of praise in the Body of Christ." There, that he speaks on a true sacrifice, which can only be offered by priests, properly speaking, it is clear from these words: *through the successions of the Apostles*. For they alone rightly immolate the sacrifice of the Body of Christ, who legitimately succeed the Apostles, who were the first instituted as priests by Christ. This is why what Chemnitz answers to this passage is frivolous, for the reason that it is not against him, or for us, because Augustine does not call to mind miming representation. For, as we have often said, the controversy is not on that representation, but on the oblation of the Eucharist made to God. What Chemnitz also adds, that Augustine understands prayers for the word *incense*, has already been shown for what it is.

Augustine also speaks on the sacrifice of the Body of the Lord in *City of God* (18, 36): "This sacrifice is offered to God in every place, from the rising of the sun to its setting, through Christ's priesthood after the order of Melchisedech, while the Jews, to whom it was said, 'I have no pleasure in you, neither will I accept a gift at your hand,' cannot deny that their sacrifice has ceased. Why do they still look for another Christ, when they read this in the prophecy, and see it fulfilled, which could not be fulfilled except through Him?" (You can see the same in *ibid.*, 19, 23; *oration contra Judaeos*, 9, and *in Psalm.* 106, on the words, *He turns a wilderness into pools of water*).

Theodoret, in his commentary on Malachi, says with clear words that according to the prophecy of Malachi, no the immaculate lamb is immolated in place of irrational victims, which took place in the law of the Jews.

John Damascene (*de fide* 4,14) says, "This is that pure and unbloody sacrifice which the Lord foretold through the Prophet was going to be offered from the rising of the sun even to its setting." Lastly, Rupert in his commentary clearly explains the prophecy on the sacrifice of the Eucharist.

CHAPTER XI
The Sacrifice of the Mass is proven from John 4

THE *FIFTH* ARGUMENT can be taken from chapter 4 of the Gospel according to John, where the Lord himself seems to explain the prophecy of Malachi (which we have already discussed), when he says in verse 21: "The hour comes when you shall adore the Father neither on this mountain, nor in Jerusalem." And again, in verse 23, "The hour comes and now is, when the true adorers shall adore the Father in spirit and in truth." For in this passage, not any prayer you like is understood by adoration, but *solemn* and *public* prayer through sacrifice, properly speaking. We shall prove it with three arguments, if first we may briefly show that it is not unusual in Scripture to understand sacrifice by adoration.

In Genesis 22:5, when Abraham was prepared with sword and fire for the sacrifice, he said to his household: "Stay here with the ass, I and the boy will go with speed as far as over there, and after we have adored, will return to you." In this passage, *to adore* (*adorare*) means to sacrifice; for otherwise he could have given adoration anywhere, if it only meant a certain bow of the head. But the Lord commanded him to offer sacrifice on the mountain, and he set out for it, as we have said, to offer sacrifice prepared with sword and fire. Again, in John 12:20, we read, "There were certain gentiles among them, who went up to adore on the day of the feast." In Acts 8:27, "The Ethiopian Eunuch came to adore in Jerusalem." In these and similar passages, adoration means sacrifice; therefore, men came from far off regions to Jerusalem because they could not duly offer sacrifices to God in any other manner, whereas simple adoration, such as prayers, they could have done anywhere.

Since these have been addressed, we move to the arguments. 1) The *first* argument: we prove that the words of the Lord, "the true adorers shall adore the Father in spirit and truth," must be understood on sacrifice; this is deduced from the principal scope of the whole passage. The Samaritan woman proposed the question for the Lord in regard to the schism of the Jews and the Samaritans: "Master, I see that you are a prophet. Our fathers adored on this mountain, and you say that Jerusalem is the place where it is right to give adoration." This question must necessarily be understood on adoration through sacrifice. For (as we can understand from Josephus, *Antiquit.* 11, 8), the schism of the Jews and the Samaritans arose from the fact that the Samaritans built a temple on mount Garizim, and pressed for sacrifice to be made there. But the Jews taught the contrary, that sacrifice could be made only in the temple of Jerusalem. Consequently, this question, which then disturbed many, the Samaritan woman proposed to Christ as to a Prophet.

Besides, these words of the Samaritan woman compel us to understand sacrifice in the word *adoration*; for she speaks about adoration bound *to a certain place*, and which otherwise could not be done with due observance. But if the matter so stands, it is necessary that even the Lord's response on adoration be understood by sacrifice, otherwise the Lord would not satisfy the question that was proposed. So when the Lord says, "Woman, believe me, that the hour comes when you shall not adore the Father either on this mountain nor in Jerusalem," the sense will be: The time will come when adoration through sacrifice will not be bound to this mountain, or Jerusalem, but in every place sacrifice shall be offered to the Lord. And this is what Malachi foretold, "In every place a clean oblation is offered to my name."

Moreover, the following words of verse 23, "The true adorers will adore the Father in spirit and truth," have this sense: True adorers, i.e. those who truly worship God, namely Christians, will adore the Father, i.e. they will sacrifice to God; in spirit and truth, i.e. in a spiritual, and true sacrifice, not a carnal sacrifice or a type as the Jews did. For the spirit is opposed to the flesh and the truth is to the figure; the Jewish sacrifices were carnal, because they consisted in the slaughter of flesh and the effusion of blood, and at the same time were types and shadows of future things. Yet, the Eucharist is a spiritual sacrifice because (as we already said), it is effected by the Holy Spirit and the words of consecration, and at the same time, it is true and the fulfillment of the old figures. Even if it is a type in respect to the sacrifice of the Cross, nevertheless, in respect to the sacrifices of the Jews, it is not a type, but must be said to be true. In this way, Chrysostom, Cyril, and Euthymius explain the phrase, "In spirit and truth" in their commentaries on this passage. Nevertheless, they can also be so distinguished, as Theophylactus and St. Thomas distinguish them, as a spiritual cult, opposed to the carnal cult of the Jews; moreover, the true cult is opposed to the false cult of the Samaritans, who really did not legitimately, and through this not truly worship God in their sacrifices.

2) The *second* argument is introduced from the words of verse 21, "The hour comes, and now is." These words manifestly mean the Lord speaks about a new adoration, which did not exist previously, and which

will have its beginning in Christ. But simple adoration, and all sacrifices improperly speaking, such as hymns, prayers and almsgiving, were always in use both in the law and even before the law; consequently, the Lord does not speak about simple adoration, but on adoration through *sacrifice*, and through sacrifice not improperly speaking and common in every age, but through a sacrifice *properly* speaking, and proper to the New Testament, as well as the Christian Church.

3) The *third* argument is taken from the fact that, without a doubt, the Lord is speaking about *outward, public and solemn* adoration, not internal and private. Not only does the question of the Samaritan woman demand it, but besides, the Lord very clearly speaks about adoration among Christians who will succeed that which among the Jews could only be done legitimately in the temple of Jerusalem—but that was outward, public and solemn. Otherwise, simple adoration, and sacrifices improperly speaking, can always be done and often only in the mind. Thus, the Lord is not speaking about that type of adoration, or about those sorts of sacrifices, but on the *true, outward, and public* sacrifice of the Church, which is either nothing, or it is the Eucharist.

Add that Theodoret and Rupert would have it in their commentary on Malachi, that this passage of John is altogether the same as the prophecy of Malachi explained in the last chapter. Even Eusebius asserted this before them (*Demonst. Evang.* 1, 6). This is why, if the passage of Malachi is understood on a sacrifice, properly speaking, as we have already sufficiently shown above, certainly even this passage of John will have to be understood on a sacrifice properly speaking.

CHAPTER XII
The Sacrifice of the Mass is proven from the Words of Institution

THE SIXTH PRINCIPAL argument is taken from the institution, and first celebration of this mystery which is found in Matt. 26:26, Mark 14:22, Luke 22:19, and 1 Cor. 11:24. Furthermore, the argument is of this sort: During the Last Supper, Christ offered himself to God the Father under the species of bread and wine, and commanded the Apostles and their successors to do the very same thing until the end of the world. But this is a sacrifice, truly and properly speaking, offered and instituted to be offered; therefore, the celebration of the Eucharist is a sacrifice properly speaking. The assumption of the argument is beyond controversy, but our adversaries pertinaciously deny the proposition. Moreover, before we progress to prove it, it will be worthwhile to briefly refute the imposture of our adversaries.

John Calvin, in his *Antidote to the Articles of the Parisians*, imagines that Catholics prove the proposition of our argument in this way: "Christ said, do this. But to do this is to sacrifice according to Virgil. So, when I do it with a calf, therefore the Lord commanded sacrifice." Then, he answers the argument that he has fabricated in this way: "When the Lord said 'Do this', he did not speak in Latin so that a Virgilian passage would have place, but in Aramaic, or Hebrew, where grammatical subtleties do not have place; hence the argument concludes nothing." Martin Chemnitz (*Exam. Conc. Trid.*, 2 part., pg. 740) mocks Catholics because they use that argument from the vocabulary to make something found in Virgil to be received for that which is to sacrifice.

But our adversaries err in two ways. First, they do not relate the arguments of Catholics in good faith, for no Catholic argues so ineptly. Then, it is false, what they assume, that in Aramaic or Hebrew the verb (*do*) cannot be received for *sacrifice*. Nothing appears more often in Scripture than that verb in this meaning. In Leviticus 15:15, Moses, speaking on the two turtle doves to be offered in sacrifice, says, "He will offer one for sin, and the other for a holocaust." There, the word עשה *asah*, properly means to do: ועשה אתם הכחן *vehhasch ahottham hacchohen*. In 3 Kings 18:23, Elijah says to the prophets of Baal, "Let two bulls be given us, and let them choose one bull for themselves, and cut it into pieces and lay it upon the wood, but put no fire under; and I will do up a bull, and lay it on the wood: ואני אעשה את חפר האחד *vehani ehhesche eth hepar haechad*. In Hosea 2:8, "I gave her grain, wine and oil, and multiplied her silver, and gold, which they have done in the service of Baal: עשו לבעל *hhaschu lebahhal*. See similar things in Leviticus 9, 14, 23, 24; Numbers 6, 8, 14, 28; 3 Kings 8; Ezekiel 46, and other places.

But after passing over these, we will prove the proposition of the argument, that in the Last Supper, the Lord took and commanded his body to be offered under the species of bread and wine. Truly, if he offered something, he also commanded it to be offered, which is certain from those words of Luke 22:19, "Do this in memory of me," for the word *hoc* proves, as we showed above, that it is the very thing the Lord did in the Supper.

Moreover, the fact that the Lord offered his body to the Father in the Eucharist at the Last Supper, and that he did not merely extend them something to eat, is where the entire difficulty consists, as even Chemnitz and others affirm. We prove the former, first from the foregoing in the 1st-3rd principal arguments. For he was not truly a priest according to Melchisedech, nor did he fulfill the figure of the Paschal Lamb, nor was there truly blood at the Supper, or blood of the New Covenant, unless he offered himself in sacrifice in the Last Supper, as we have sufficiently and profusely demonstrated.

Apart from these arguments, we have three others. *First*, Christ said, "This is my body, which is given for you" (Luke 22:19), or, as Paul has it, "which is broken for you" (1 Cor. 11:24). Likewise, "This chalice is the New Testament in my blood, which is being shed for you", and Matthew and Luke add, "for the remission of sins" (26:28). These words are in the present tense, *given, is broken, is being shed*, they do not mean to be given, or shed for the Apostles to eat and drink, but it is given and shed *for God in sacrifice*. The Lord did not say, "it is given, broken, shed to you," but "for you". And besides, mere food and drink was not given, or shed, except for the Apostles who were present, and nevertheless, the Lord also says, "It is shed for many" (Matthew 26:28). Therefore, the sense is, it is given for you and for many, and poured for God in a propitiatory sacrifice, clearly for the remission of sins.

No response can be made to this argument except that which Chemnitz offers (*Exam.* 2 part. Pg. 716). He says the words, "it is given, it is broken, is shed," refer to the cross, so that the sense would be: This is my body, which a little later will be given up to death: and this is the blood which a little later will be shed on the cross; for the fact that it was going to happen later is not said to be strange. And Chemnitz offers proof that it in this place the present should be received for the future with these arguments. *Firstly*, because in the Canon of the Mass,[8] we read: *Effundetur* (will be shed). *Secondly*, because if in the very action of the Mass blood were shed, the Mass would not be an unbloody sacrifice. *Thirdly*, Scripture hands down that the blood of Christ was shed on the cross. *Fourthly*, in Scripture the present is often received, or even the past for the future, as in these words: "I place my soul; a child was born for us; the Lamb was slain from the beginning of the world." He adds *fifthly*, that if these words, "which is given for you," were the substantial words of the sacrifice of the Mass, a great crime would be thrust upon the Canon of the Mass, because it overlooked those words.

But these arguments of Chemnitz have little strength. To the *first*, not only the Canon of the Mass, but even the Vulgate edition of Luke 22:20 and St. Cyprian (*Epistles*, 2, 3) read it in the future: *effundetur* (will be shed). But these readings are not contradictory, nay more one leads to the other; for from it, what the Lord said in the present, *funditur*, i.e. it is offered, and poured in sacrifice to God in representation of the shedding that was going to take place on the cross, and at the same time it also follows that then, even to the end of the world the blood of Christ is going to be shed, i.e. *offered and poured out to God in the sacrifice of the Mass*, which succeeded all the old sacrifices. Therefore, they are all true readings, or we might say, it is shed now in the Supper, or it will be shed, i.e. on the cross, or it will be shed, i.e. thereupon in the sacrifice repeated through the Church.

To the *second*, his blood was not shed in the Supper in its proper species, but in the species of wine, for the blood is said to be shed in the Supper while held in a liquid species in the chalice, offered to God, and thence in the same species poured out into the mouths of those receiving it. But this effusion does not make a bloody sacrifice, since blood did not really come forth from his body.

To the *third*, the Scripture most truly hands down that the blood of Christ was shed on the cross, but it does not deny that it was shed in the Supper, actually it teaches that very thing; nor are those opposed to each other, as we said above.

To the *fourth*, I do not dispute that often in Scripture the present or past tenses are received for the future; but more often the present is received for the present, than it is for the future, and nobody, I believe,

---
8 Translator's note: In the Ordinary Form (1970) this is Eucharistic Prayer I.

Book I, Ch. XII: The Words of Institution

would deny that. Chemnitz must prove that in this passage, *datur* (it is given) and *effunditur* (it is shed) are received for the future, not the present, that way I might omit how inadequate the example he adduces is, "The lamb was slain from the beginning of the world." If, as he bids, you explain the past for the future, this will be the sense: The lamb will be slain from the beginning of the world. No man could see how the sense could include such an opposition.

To the *fifth*, the words, "Which is given for you," are not the substantial words of the sacrifice, as if it were necessarily required to pronounce them that the sacrifice be carried out; still they are of this sort, that they manifestly show the sacrifice was offered by Christ in the Last Supper.

As a result, Chemnitz has not proven what he wished, but we, on the other hand, prove the words, "given" and "being shed" should be related to the action of the Supper, and must be received in the present. *Firstly*, because the proper and simple sentence of this passage requires it.

Secondly, because Paul in 1 Cor. 11:24, said, "Which is broken for you." *Frangitur* (it is broken) does not suit the body of Christ except in the species of bread. This is why St. John Chrysostom (*Hom. 24 in 1 Cor.*) writes that Christ allowed the breaking in the Sacrament which he refused to allow on the cross. And although, no matter how the breaking could be accommodated even to the passion of Christ in its proper species, on account of the breaking of the skin and nerves, and veins, etc., still there can hardly be any doubt that the Apostle considered the species of bread, when he says, *frangitur*. For Scripture properly is accustomed to use this voice when it speaks about bread, such as, "Break your bread for the hungry," (Isaiah 58:7); "The bread which we break," (1 Corinthians 10:16); "They broke bread in their houses," (Acts 2:46). Still, we cannot understand the words "This is my body which is broken for you," in regard to bread alone; for the bread is not broken for us, but *by us*. It is fitting therefore, to understand these words on the true Body, but *under the species of bread*, so that the sense would be: This is my body, which now is broken for you in the species of bread, i.e. given and immolated to God.

Thirdly, because Luke 22:20, when he says, "This chalice is the New testament in my blood, which is shed for you," the subject of shed (*funditur*), is not the word *blood*, but the word chalice (*calix*), as it appears in the Greek text, where we find τοῦτο τὸ ποτήριον ἐκχυνόμενιον. But certainly, if Luke meant to say the blood was merely going to be shed on the cross, he would have said: This chalice is the New Testament in my blood, namely the blood which is shed, but now he says, "this is the chalice ... which is shed. Therefore, he showed the blood which was in the chalice is shed, and hence was shed in *the Last Supper*.⁹

The *second* principal argument to prove the aforesaid proposition, that Christ offered himself in sacrifice at the Last Supper, is taken from the true presence of the Body and blood of Christ in the Supper, which the Lutherans concede and the Calvinists would concede, were it not, as they contend, opposed to the clear words of Scripture. For the Body and Blood of Christ are taken in the Supper, as flesh and blood of the victim offered for us; so necessarily in that Supper it was first immolated and offered to God, then taken by us.

The Lutherans do not deny that the body and blood of Christ are taken as a participation of the victim, and if they would deny it, it shall easily be proven. In the first place, the body and blood are consecrated apart from each other, that we would understand the presence of the body and the blood in the Supper were slain *ad modum*, and are of a dead body. Next, the body and blood are in the Supper as food and drink. But flesh and blood are not suitable food unless first the animal should die; Christ does not die, however, except through immolation. This is the argument of Gregory of Nyssa in his *First Oration on the Resurrection*, where he gathers that Christ was immolated in the Last Supper because we could not otherwise eat his flesh. Augustine also (*Confessions*, 9, 13) says his mother served the altar every day, from where she knew the holy victim is dispensed.

Chemnitz (*loc. cit.* 2 part. Pg. 772-773) thinks he has an outstanding response to this argument. For he says that the true and real presence of the Body of Christ does not suffice for sacrifice; for even in the womb of his mother, and afterward the true and real body of Christ was in the manger, but there was still no sacrifice. Therefore, he would have it that four conditions are required for a true sacrifice. *Firstly*, the substance of the thing, which is immolated; *secondly*, a certain action prescribed by God to offer it; *thirdly*, a certain person assigned by God to offer; *fourthly*, that it is done from that intention and toward that end which has been prescribed in the word of God. From these conditions he says that only the first is present in the celebration of the Last Supper, the rest

---

9 Translator's note: There is a distinction in the Latin that is impossible to render into English on account of the propriety of the Latin words. *Effunditur* would mean in the context of blood, that it is shed from the act of killing, whereas the same word in the context of a chalice would mean pouring out or to drain, as in drinking it.

are altogether lacking.

I answer the *first:* That the body of Christ was truly and really present in the womb of his mother, or in the manger has no bearing on the matter. For he was not in the womb or in the manger as a victim, but as *a living infant*, whereas he was at the Last Supper as a *victim*, as they affirm. For, Chemnitz himself (that I might omit others) so writes on pg. 717 of his work, "There (in the Supper) the victim was arranged and taken, which was offered for us once on the Cross." Thus he. Consequently, we draw up our argument: The body of Christ, as it really was present in the Last Supper, is a certain victim; thus, it took place when some immolation of the victim preceded. I ask what was that immolation? You will say: The immolation of the cross. But when the Apostles first partook of that victim, Christ had not yet been immolated on the cross. Besides, now the victim which is on the altar cannot be said to have been made through the immolation of the cross; for that immolation took place only once, and the victim made through it, would shortly thereafter cease to be a victim. For the Body of Christ, when it appeared to the disciples after the resurrection, and while it ascended into heaven, could not be called a victim; much less, now that he lives and reigns in heaven, can he be called a victim. Since he became a victim through the immolation of the Christ, he ceased to be a victim; if the body of Christ begins again to be a victim, it should be done through another immolation. But the immolation of the cross cannot be repeated, therefore a new immolation is required. This is why either the immolation, which places the victim on the altar, or in the Last Supper is itself an action, and the celebration of the mystery of the Eucharist, or there is no victim in the Sacred Supper.

Now, what pertains to these three conditions of sacrifice, which Chemnitz thinks are required in the Eucharist, we can easily demonstrate them. For in the first place, certain persons were appointed to the sacrifice, these are the Apostles and those who succeeded them, for the Lord said to them alone, "Do this." The intention and end are prescribed in the word of God, you can find them in the same passage: "In memory of me." For, as Christ was the end of the preceding sacrifices, he represents the sacrifice of the cross as a future event; so, the end of the sacrifice of the Eucharist is to commemorate and represent the sacrifice of the cross, as a past event. And just as those old sacrifices did not lose their true and proper notion of a sacrifice from the fact that they were representative, so also the sacrifice of the Eucharist does not lose its true and proper notion of sacrifice because it is at the same time commemorative of another sacrifice.

One condition remains to be shown, namely *the action of offering*, which we know for certain to be present even if we cannot easily distinguish it and separate it from the other actions which took place at the same time. From the first condition, which Chemnitz admits, the second is necessarily inferred, which he denies. Where there is a victim, necessarily an immolation ought to precede and hence an oblation; since a victim does not come into being except through immolation. But the action of immolation and oblation is sufficiently manifest in the Eucharist, namely in the very *consecration*. Our adversaries should not ask that we show where the Lord said: I offer, or I sacrifice, or where he commanded: offer, or sacrifice; rather, it is sufficient enough if the very *action* of offering and immolating is shown. For in the Old Testament we never read that the priests said, "I offer, or sacrifice," rather in this very thing, which for the honor of God and to show the death of Christ, they placed slain animals upon the altar to offer them to God, and they were reckoned to have sacrificed. Just the same, the Lord also is not read to have said on the cross: "I offer myself, and I sacrifice," and just the same is there anyone who doubts that voluntary ascent of the cross was a true oblation? As a result, that action, oblation and immolation must be said to be in the same manner, whereby the body of Christ is placed on the table to the honor of God, that it should be consumed, and is done to represent the passion of the same Christ. Moreover, that action is a consecration, for through the consecration it happens that the body of Christ is truly and visibly present upon the table and suitably present to represent the passion and death of the same.

The *third* principal argument to prove the same proposition is taken from the Fathers who clearly say that Christ offered himself to God the Father under the species of bread and wine.

Irenaeus (4, 17), "He taught the new oblation of the New Testament." Cyprian (*loc. cit.*), "Who is a greater high priest of God than the Lord Jesus Christ, who offered sacrifice to God the Father and offered the same thing which Melchisedech offered, namely bread and wine, i.e., his body and blood." Ambrose in Psalm 38, says in these words: "The man passed in appearance. We see the prince of priests coming to us; we see and hear him offering his blood for us. Let us follow him, as best we can, priests that offer sacrifice for the people. For even if we are weak in merit, nevertheless, we are honorable in sacrifice because even if now Christ does not seem to offer, nevertheless he is offered on earth when

Book I, Ch. XII: The Words of Institution

the body of Christ is offered; nay more, he is made known to offer in us, whose word sanctifies the sacrifice which is offered." Gregory of Nyssa (*loc. cit.*) says, "For the ineffable and secret, and who cannot be discerned by men, in the mode of sacrifice, by his disposition anticipates the violent attack and offers himself as an oblation and victim for us as the priest and lamb of God. When did he do this? When he offered his body to be eaten and his blood to be drank by his household." John Chrysostom (*homily 24 in 1 Cor.*) says: "He commanded himself to be offered in place of brute animals." And in *homil. 2 on 2 Timothy*, he says, "The very sacred oblation, whether Peter, or Paul, or any priest of whatever merit offers it, it is the same as what Christ himself gave to his disciples, and what priests now also confect; the one has nothing less than the other. Why is that? Because men do not sanctify this, but Christ who already sanctified it." Augustine, in Psalm 33, conc. 2, says: "He established sacrifice, according to the order of Melchisedech, with regard to his body and blood." (See also *de Baptismo* 3, 19; *Contra Faustum*, 20, 21; *Epistle 5 to Marcellinus, City of God*, 17, 20 and lib. 83 q. 61). Leo (*Serm. 7 de Passione Domini*), says: "As shadows yield to the body, etc." Isichius, *on Leviticus*, 2, 8, says: 'First the Lord dined on the prefigured sheep with the Apostles, then he offered his sacrifice." Rupert (*in Exodus*, 2, 6), says: "Suffering agony in the meanness of the passion, earlier he immolated himself to God the Father with his own hands, receiving bread, etc."

CHAPTER XIII
The Sacrifice of the Mass is Proven from Acts 13

THE SEVENTH ARGUMENT is taken from the words which St. Luke places in Acts 13:2, where he relates the ordination of Paul and Barnabas: "While they were ministering to the Lord and fasting, the Holy Spirit said to them: Separate me Saul and Barnabas, for the work whereunto I have taken them." That ministry shown to the Lord does not appear to have been anything else but sacrifice, and the sacrifice of the Mass, for either this sacrifice is in the Church, or none at all.

Moreover, it is proven that sacrifice is meant from the phrase, "while they were ministering." Firstly, from the Greek of this verse, λειτουργέω; even our adversaries confess, above all in the *Apology for the Augsburg Confession*, in the article on the Mass, that the term λειτουργέω does not mean any ministry, but a *public ministry*. Therefore, in this passage not some mere private and internal ministry is shown, but a *public*, and hence, *external one*. Nor can it mean the ministry of the word, or of the Sacraments because although these are public, they are not shown to God. We do not preach for God, nor dispense the Sacraments to the Lord, but to the people. Yet, here it is said, "While they were ministering to the Lord."

Someone will say, "Those who preach or offer the Sacraments to the people can be said to minister to the Lord, because they do it for his honor." But if that were the reason why Luke wrote, "While they were ministering to the Lord," he would not have added, "And fasting," for to fast would also be to minister to the Lord in that manner. For he that fasts well fasts in honor of God, according to that of Romans 14:6, "He that eats, eats for the Lord, ... he that does not eat, does not eat for the Lord."

Besides, the word λειτουργέω, although it could be accommodated to sacred and profane ministries, nevertheless, when it is accommodated to sacred things, as it always is in Scripture, is everywhere received for the ministry of Sacrifice, as is clear from Luke 1, Hebrews 2, 8, 9 and 10. This is why in this passage Erasmus, who is usually in the service of our adversaries, ventured to translate it: "while they were sacrificing," and hence it also came to pass, that the Greeks call the celebration of Mass λειτουργείαν.

CHAPTER XIV
The Sacrifice of the Mass is Proven from 1 Corinthians 10

THE LAST ARGUMENT from these which are sought from the Scriptures is found in what the Apostle says in 1 Corinthians 10:14 et seqq. "Flee the service of idols. I speak as to wise men: judge for yourselves what I say. The chalice of benediction, which we bless, is it not the communion of the blood of Christ? And the bread, which we break, is it not the partaking of the body of the Lord? For we, being many, are one bread and one body, all that partake of the one bread. Behold Israel according to the flesh; are not they, that eat of the sacrifices, partakers of the altar? What then? Do I say, that what is offered in sacrifice to idols, is anything? Or that the idol is anything? But the things which the heathens sacrifice, they sacrifice to devils, and not to God. And I would not that you should be made partakers with devils."

From these words we gather three arguments. *One*, from the comparison of the Lord's table with the table of the gentiles and the Jews. Clearly, the Apostle compares the Lord's table, from where we take the Eucharist, with the altar of the gentiles, where immolation is made to idols, and with the altar of the Jews, where carnal sacrifices are immolated to the true God. From there, it follows that the Lord's table is also a certain altar, and hence the sacrifice of the Eucharist. An altar was never properly raised except for sacrifices properly speaking. Some even think, such as Abbot Haymo, and several serious authorities, and not without probability, that he expressly calls the Lord's table an altar in Hebrews 13:10, in these words: "We have an altar, whereof they have not power to eat who serve the tabernacle." Nevertheless, because there are not lacking among Catholics those who understand the cross or Christ himself for an altar in this place, I do not insist upon this passage.

The next argument is taken from the comparison of the Eucharist with the sacrifices of the gentiles and of the Jews. For the Apostle clearly says that we are faithful to take the Lord's body and blood from the table as the Jews take their holocausts and the gentiles what has been sacrificed to idols from their altars or tables. Such a comparison, introduced by the Apostle, would necessarily be inadequate and wrong if the Eucharist is not a sacrifice immolated to God, just as those foods of the Jews and gentiles are sacrifices to God, or immolations to idols respectively.

The *third* argument is taken from the comparison of the society which we have with God through the eating of the Eucharist, and what the gentiles have with the idols through the eating of what has been sacrificed to them. Paul teaches that they who eat the food of idols are so joined with the idols that they are reckoned true idolaters, therefore from the beginning he says, "Flee the service of idols." He uses this argument: He that eats what is offered to idols becomes a partaker of the altar of idols, therefore he consents in the sacrifice of idols, nay more he becomes the companion of those immolating to idols. Therefore, it is idolatry; for sacrifice is the proper act of *latria*. This is why if the comparison of Paul is apt, it will also be fitting to argue in this way in regard to the Eucharist: he that eats the Eucharist becomes a partaker of the altar of the Lord, therefore he consents in the oblation made to God of the Eucharist, nay more, he becomes a companion of those offering it; therefore, he honors God with this oblation by the cult of *latria*.

Chemnitz responds to these arguments (*loc. cit.* 2 part. Pag. 767). And *first*, in his fashion, he acts completely impudent and with buffoonery; "From the sacrifices of the heathen, which are offered to demons, they do not fear to fetch a stipend for their miserable Mass, not for any different reason than we find in Virgil, when he says:

Vos mihi Manes
Este boni, quoniam Superis aversa voluntas."[10]

Thus he. Little does the impious heretic notice that in this way he mocks the Apostle himself, and insults him. If we are thought to seek a stipend from the gods of the underworld, by the comparison of the Eucharist to the sacrifices of the gentiles, how much more will Paul be thought to have asked the help from the gods of the underworld, who proved that food offered to idols must not be eaten by making the same comparison of the Eucharist to the sacrifices of idols? But let these impious trifles, or rather blasphemies, be done with; we solicit our stipend not from the gods of the underworld, but from the words of Divine Scripture, and from the comparison placed in the same Scripture.

Next, Chemnitz gets a little more serious, and says two things. *Firstly*, the table of the gentiles, with which the Apostle compares the table of the Lord, is not an altar to idols, but a common table in which they usually ate. He shows that there was no custom of the gentiles to recline at altars, rather they drew up the remains of what was immolated for their

---

[10] "Oh, infernal gods befriend me, since the powers above prove so hostile." Aeneid, XII, 646-7.

Book I, Ch. XIV: 1 Corinthians 10

dinner at home, and invited their friends to it. However, Blessed Paul speaks about the table, in which they ate what was sacrificed to idols, so, he does not speak about the altar, but on the common table. Besides, for Paul there was no question whether it was lawful for Christians to be present at their sacrifices and to sacrifice to demons, for that was well known to Christians; but whether it was lawful to go to the dinners of the gentiles, where food immolated to idols was placed to be eaten.

This first answer of Chemnitz avails little. In the first place, it is false that the gentiles had no custom of reclining at altars. For, I ask, what is it that Paul says in 1 Cor. 8:10, "If anyone will see him that has knowledge reclining in an idol's temple, etc."? For what is an idol's temple except a place where there is an idol? Nor is it opposed what Paul says in 1 Cor. 10:27, "If any of the infidels invite you and you are willing to go, eat of anything that is set before you. ... If any man says, this has been sacrificed to idols, do not eat of it, etc." Both are true; for indeed the gentiles both reclined at the altars of idols, and also drew up the remnants of what had been immolated for dinner at their home. This is why Chemnitz badly proposes the question of the Apostle. For even if there was no question: whether it was lawful to sacrifice to idols; nevertheless the question was not whether it would be lawful to be present at the dinners of gentiles, but whether it would be lawful to eat what was immolated to idols, and especially in a temple to idols; and Paul denies it is lawful, because this is to be made a friend of demons, and interpretatively to sacrifice to demons.

Next, even if the gentiles did not have a custom of reclining at the altars of the idols, as Chemnitz falsely says, nevertheless the table of demons, to which the table of the Lord is compared, still would signify the altar itself, not the common table. For where the Apostle names the table of demons, he is not speaking about the table where food is eaten, but of the table where it was immolated, and from where the immolated foods are brought to the common table, as is manifestly clear from the comparison with the altar of the Jews: "Behold Israel, according to the flesh. Are not they who eat of the sacrifices, partakers of an altar?"

Next, the same is gathered from the fact that the Apostle calls the table of the gentiles the table of demons; for he calls it the table of demons because it was consecrated to demons. For he would not call the common table of the gentiles, to which he also permitted the faithful to approach, the table of demons. Besides, he would not have compared it to the table of the Lord if he were speaking about a common and profane table, unless Chemnitz would have it that the table of the Lord is a common and profane table.

For this reason, the Apostle, when he deters the faithful from the table of demons, he says the reason is that they should flee the worship of idols; consequently, he speaks about a table in which immolation is made to idols, from which one who takes food is reckoned an idolater.

Next, the same Paul, in the same chapter, says it is licit to go to the tables of the gentiles, and there to eat what has been offered to idols, if one did not know the food was immolated to them, and he says at the same time: "You cannot be a partaker of the table of the Lord and the table of demons," therefore, unless the Apostle were to oppose himself, then by "table of demons" he cannot have meant a table of the gentiles where food offered to idols was only eaten materially.

Moreover, what Chemnitz says, that the Apostle writes one is free, still it is not fitting that the faithful become partakers at the same time of the table of the Lord and the table of demons; it is most absurd and false. For the Apostle does not say one is free, but he says absolutely, "You cannot be a partaker of the table of the Lord and the table of demons." And what more absurd thing can be said than that the faithful are free to participate at the table of demons and to become partakers with them?

Lastly, add that even if we cannot settle the matter, that through the table of demons an altar of idols is understood, nevertheless, our argument is solid regarding the comparison of the table of the Lord with the altar of the Jews, which the Apostle expressly names.

But Chemnitz was not so stupid that he didn't see that his answer could be refuted in this way; so he adds a second answer, and says they who take the Eucharist participate in the sacrifice carried out on the cross, just as those who ate the food immolated to idols participated in the sacrifice carried out on the altar of idols.

But he cannot evade it in this way. For the Apostle does not compare the table of demons with the cross, but with *the table of the Eucharist*; hence, he means the table of the Eucharist is the true altar raised for sacrifice, and in this he placed the comparison; because just as the gentiles ate what was immolated on the altar, so we eat that which is immolated on the table of the Eucharist. Next, as we said above, the sacrifice made from the immolation on the cross existed at a certain time, and later ceased to be, and cannot be done again except through a new immolation. And that is all from the testimonies of the Scriptures.

CHAPTER XV
The Sacrifice of the Mass is proved from the tradition of the Fathers, and first from the terms Sacrifice, Oblation and Immolation

HITHERTO, we have taken testimonies for the Sacrifice of the Mass from Holy Scripture; now we approach the second place, namely the testimony of the ancient Fathers. Chemnitz rightly says (*Exam. Conc. Trid.*, 2 part. Pg. 775), that most good minds are moved by the consensus and testimony of antiquity, especially that which was in the purer, best and most prosperous times of the Church. But because it would be too long to examine each individual testimony separately, as we did in the disputation on the truth of the Lord's body in the Eucharist, we will reduce all of them to a few headings, and at the same time we will refute the responses to our adversaries.

1) The *first* heading, or argument, is taken from the words *sacrifice, host*, and *victim*, as well as from the verbs *to offer, to immolate*, and *to sacrifice*, which the Fathers use when they speak about the celebration of the Lord's Supper. For everywhere both the Greeks and the Latins not only say the Eucharist is a sacrifice, or an oblation, but they say *it is offered, immolated, and sacrificed to God*. It is not necessary to mark down citations where terms of this sort are found, for our adversaries themselves confess that they are very frequently found among the Fathers. Chemnitz (*loc. cit.* pg. 782), says: "It cannot be denied that the ancients, when they speak about the celebration of the Lord's Supper, take up the vocabulary of sacrifice, immolation, oblation, host and victim. Likewise, they use the verbs *to offer, to sacrifice, to immolate*." Thus he.

Consequently, he sufficiently shows the manner of speaking which the Fathers intended; for if they thought the Eucharist was merely a sacrament and not also a sacrifice, as our adversaries suppose, there is no reason why they would speak about the Eucharist any differently than Baptism. None of the fathers call Baptism a sacrifice, a host, or a victim, nor do they say to baptize is to sacrifice or immolate. Besides, what reason would there be for the Fathers to speak differently of the Eucharist than our adversaries do? How believable would it be that the ancient Fathers, who use our manner of speech, would agree with our adversaries?

But let us say what our opponents answer. Luther (*de Capt. Babyl.*

cap. 1), cautiously says that perhaps the Fathers call the prayers which are said in the Mass sacrifice, and not the Eucharist itself. But then he saw that this answer was not sufficient since the Fathers always call the Eucharist a sacrifice, and what is more, say it is offered to God by the priests, as we will show shortly. So, he boldly bid farewell to the Fathers: "If they have nothing which should be said, it is safer to deny everything which concedes that the Mass is a sacrifice." And in the beginning of his book *On the Abrogation of the Mass*, he so writes in the beginning, "I confess, in the first place, facing those who will shout that I have taught against the rite of the Church, against the statutes of the Fathers, I say I will hear none of it." And later he says that he does not care what the Fathers say on the Mass, but only for what they ought to have said. He has similar things in his book against the king of England, "Lastly, the king introduces the sayings of the Fathers for the Sacrifice of the Mass, and mocks my foolishness because I above all should know. This is what I said, Thomistic asses have nothing which they produce except a multitude of men and ancient use." And he says (*ibid.*), that he does not care if a thousand Augustines or a thousand Cypians stood against him. Then, in his book *On the Abrogation of Private Mass*, he says, "We will not pay attention if Papists shall shout out, 'the Church, the Church! The Fathers, the Fathers!' because as I said, they are sayings of men or deeds; we care nothing in such great reasons. For we know the prophets fell, and even the Apostles. By the word of Christ, we judge the Church, the Apostles, and even the angels themselves!"

John Calvin (*Instit.* 4, 18 §10), answers that in the beginning the Fathers called the Sacrament of the Eucharist a sacrifice because it is a memorial of the sacrifice of the cross. Chemnitz profusely follows up this answer, and so a little later we will refute it with the answers of Chemnitz, especially seeing that Calvin does not seem to place much faith in it. For a little later (*ibid.* §11), he not only affirms the ancients used terms that mean sacrifice, but even acknowledges that in their mode of action they approach the notion of sacrifice, and so rebukes them, although he inadequately attempts to excuse their sense: "I also see the ancients twist this memorial into another purpose than the institution of the Lord (the Supper somehow seemed to them to present the appearance of a repeated, or at least renewed immolation), nothing can be safer for the pious than to be satisfied with the pure and simple ordinance of God, whose Supper it is said to be, simply because his authority alone ought to appear in it. ... (§12) And certainly, if we consider that it is the Lord's

Book I, Ch. XV: The Tradition of the Fathers

Supper, and not man's, why do we allow ourselves to be turned aside one nail's breadth from Scripture by any human authority, or a length of prescription?"

Therefore, Luther and Calvin are not men of sound mind, by Chemnitz's judgment, since they are not moved by consensus and the testimony of the ancients, and of the true and most prosperous Church of Christ. Moreover, Chemnitz himself, to persuade his readers that he is of sound mind, says four specific things about the testimonies of the Fathers. *First* (pg. 776), he talks nonsense about the state of the question; for he writes that the historic representation which the Popes call the Mass cannot be proven to be a sacrifice from the fathers. But we have already responded that the state of the question is not on the ceremonies and rites of the Mass (for we will treat these in their proper place), but on the *substance of the sacrifice*. This is why we are not held in this place to prove the rite of Mass from the Fathers, but only that the Eucharist *is offered to God*, and not only distributed to the people, for that is what we are now disputing.

Secondly (pg. 780), he treats on the words *Mass*, and *sacrifice*, and he hands down six rules for explaining the passages of the Fathers which seem to assert that the Mass is a sacrifice. *a)* That they speak about almsgiving which is done in Mass, for the people offered bread and wine, from which a certain part was consecrated in the Eucharist, part given for the use of the poor; moreover, almsgiving is a certain kind of sacrifice. *b)* They speak about the prayers which were done in celebration of the Lord's Supper, for prayers are a kind of sacrifice. *c)* They speak about the action of thanksgiving, to which men are roused in the celebration of the Lord's Supper, from the consideration of the benefits of God; for to give the thanks pertains to the sacrifice of praise. *d)* That they speak on preaching and the annunciation of the death of the Lord, which was usually joined with the celebration of the Supper; for Paul, in Romans 15:31 calls the ministry of the Gospel a sacrifice. *e)* That they speak on various exercises of piety which occur in the Lord's Supper, such as faith, penance, hope, love; for St. Peter calls these spiritual holocausts. *f)* That they speak on the oblation of the faithful which they dedicate and consecrate, *i.e.* his body and blood. For Paul, in Romans 12:1, calls it a pleasing sacrifice to show obsequiousness to his body.

But all these arguments have no bearing on the matter. For the Fathers speak on the oblation of the Eucharist; they clearly say it is licit *for priests alone* to offer that sacrifice to God. Almsgiving, however, prayers, praises and the rest of the things that Chemnitz laboriously amasses are offered by the whole people. For Tertullian (*de velandis virginibus*), "A woman is not permitted to speak in Church, nor teach, nor to intinct, or offer." He has the same in *de exhortation castitatis*, that the office of the priest is to teach, to intinct, and to offer. Epiphanius likewise (*Panarion*, haeresi 79), contends with many words that women are not permitted to offer the sacrifice, and therefore Christ did not even permit his Mother to sacrifice, but only his Apostles whom he had ordained. The Council of Nicaea (can. 14), and Jerome (*Epistola ad Evagrium*), as well as other Councils and Fathers everywhere hold that deacons do not have the power to offer the sacrifice, rather, it is the office of the priests. But who ever denied that deacons, or even the laity, and women may offer alms, prayers and other spiritual sacrifices, improperly speaking?

Besides, the Fathers say with clear words that the sacrifice, which the priests offer in the Church is the very *body and blood of the Lord*, and hence these answers of Chemnitz are vain; unless perhaps one meant by some unheard-of figure of speech, to understand alms and prayers by the Body of Christ.

St. Andrew the Apostle, as the priests and deacons of Achaia write on his passion, said to Aegea the Proconsul, "I offer the immaculate lamb on the altar, whose flesh all the believers then eat, the lamb that was immolated is preserved whole and living." The martyr Hippolytus, in his oration on Antichrist, introduces Christ speaking to the priests in this way: "Come, O bishops and priests, who daily immolate my precious body and blood." Ambrose (on Psalm 38), says, "Even if now Christ does not seem to offer, nevertheless he is offered on earth, since his body is offered." And in his commentary on Luke 1, the same author says, "Christ is present, Christ is immolated." Gregory of Nyssa, in his *Oration on the Resurrection*, says, "The Lord, anticipating the attack of the Jews, offers himself as a victim, at once as the same priest and lamb. But you will say to me, when does he do this? When he gave his body to be eaten and his blood to be drank by his household." John Chrysostom (*Homily 24 in 1 Cor.*) says, "He commanded that he be offered in place of victims and cattle." And in *Homily 17 on Hebrews*, he says, "He is offered in many places, not many Christs, but the one Christ everywhere, here and there fully present, one body, not many bodies." The author of the commentary, which is attributed to Ambrose on Hebrews 10, and after him Primasius on that passage, says the same thing. Augustine (*Quaest. Evang.*, lib. 2 q. 3), giving the account as to why the Lord commanded the leper to offer

Book I, Ch. XV: The Tradition of the Fathers

sacrifice for his cleansing according to the rite of Moses, says, "Because this sacrifice had not yet been instituted, the holy of holies, which is his body." He says the same thing in *de Trinitate* 4, 14, "What can more thankfully be offered or received than the flesh of our sacrifice, the body effected by our priests?" Cyril has similar things (*de adoratione in Spiritu et Veritate*), and Leo (in *Sermon 8 de passione*). Fulgentius (*ad Monimum*, 2, 2) and other Fathers everywhere. And the Council of Nicaea itself, in that canon which Calvin and others receive, clearly says that the lamb of God is immolated on the table in an unbloody manner.

Now, since Chemnitz is not unaware of these things, he adds a third proclamation (pg. 778), "But they receive not only those exercises of piety, but the very action of the Lord's Supper, and the very body and blood in the Supper, called a sacrifice, oblation, host and victim by the ancients; but I do not deny this, etc." Then he places three methods for the explanation of the citations of the fathers, which they call the very action of the Supper, or the Body of Christ; we will refute these kinds of methods separately, while omitting the third, because it only pertains to those passages of the fathers which say the sacrifice of the altar is propitiatory, which is a different controversy to be explained later in its proper place.

Therefore, the *first* method is that they call the action of the Supper a sacrifice, because the consecration and dispensation of the Eucharist is a certain sacred action; which is called by Dionysius in Greek ἱερουγία, while the Latins say "to sacrifice", which in Greek is: ἱερουγεῖν. He tries to prove it, for Paul (Romans 15:31) describes by the terms of sacrifice and oblation, the ministry of the Gospel, because it is a certain sacred action. And Augustine (*Epist. 59 ad Paulinum*) calls the oblation of the holy altar that which is offered to God, when that which is in the Lord's table is blessed and sanctified, and broken as well as prepared to be distributed. And Cyprian (*Epistles*, 2, 3) where in the beginning of the Epistle he places the argument on the Lord's sanctifying chalice, and the ministration to the people; then he emphasizes the words of sacrifice and oblation, and that Christ took up the chalice not only with water, but wine and mixed with water, and blessed it and distributed it to his disciples. And Cyprian brings this out in this way: "Christ offered not only water to God the Father, but wine mixed with water in the chalice." For that oblation seems able to be this which Catholics teach, for the body and blood, not wine and water, Catholics say is offered to God. So Cyprian calls the oblation made to God the very consecration of bread and wine, in the same way as in Acts 13:2 Luke said the Apostles ministered to the Lord, although, in Chrysostom's interpretation, he speaks on the preaching of the Gospel. This is why Augustine, in his twenty-third epistle, says Christ is immolated for us, and in Psalm 77 [78] he says he is immolated for the faithful, where he calls this immolation a consecration made for the use of the faithful. Then, Cyril, in his epistle to Nestorius, calls it an unbloody sacrifice, or latria, when that which has been confected, we name the body and blood of Christ; when we approach to the mystical benedictions, we are sanctified, made partakers of the body and blood, Christ the redeemer of all. Thus Chemnitz.

I respond to this first method: By saying many things Chemnitz says nothing, but only pours cloudiness upon the matter by misdirecting the minds of the simple. If only the action of the Supper were called a sacrifice, because it is a certain sacred action, why would not the action of Baptism be said to be a sacrifice in the same manner, and of the same kind as the action of the Supper, seeing that both are mere sacraments according to adversaries.

Next, let it be the case that any sacred action you like can be called a sacrifice, on account of the similitude of vocabulary, because sacrifice expresses making something sacred; still, not any sacred action you like can be called an oblation, as is known. Not anyone that does a sacred action immediately offers it on an altar. But the Fathers clearly say that the sacrifice of the Body of the Lord was offered in the Last Supper. Therefore, the words of the Fathers cannot be explained on the consecration of the bread alone, ordered for the communication of the faithful, since that cannot be called an oblation.

Besides, even if the word for sacrifice was ambiguous, and could be received for any sacred action you like, nevertheless, when that term is attributed to a permanent thing, i.e. when the action of sacrificing itself is not called a sacrifice, but *the thing which is sacrificed by that action*, then certainly the word sacrifice cannot be explained for a sacred action. But the Fathers call the sacrifice the very body of Christ which is offered; for they say very circumspectly that in the Sacred Supper the sacrifice of the body of Christ is offered to the Lord. Consequently, the teaching of the Fathers cannot be explained in regard to the sacred action of consecrating and dispensing the Eucharist, seeing that the *action itself* is not, nor cannot be called in any way the body of Christ.

Lastly, add that Chemnitz does not prove what he assumes very well, and he constituted the whole strength of his answer in that *sacrificium*

Book I, Ch. XV: The Tradition of the Fathers 111

(sacrifice) and *sacrificare* (to sacrifice) in Latin are the same as ἱερουγία, and ἱερουγεῖν in Greek. Although the etymology of sacrifice is taken from a sacred action, seeing that to sacrifice is to make something sacred, nevertheless, not any sacred action you like is a sacrifice, rather, only that whereby something is offered to God with some certain solemn rite, and there is a real consumption of that thing, as we showed above. This is why learned Latin interpreters of Greek books do not translate anything as sacrifice apart from the word θυσίαν, which properly means sacrifice, while on the other hand, the term ἱερουγίαν, or any other general word that is likewise ambiguous, they will only render it as sacrifice when it is clear from the context that it is a true sacrifice. This fact can easily be picked out from the testimonies brought forward by Chemnitz. The word ἱερουγίαν, as it is found in Dionysius, translators render as a sacred ministry, but not as a sacrifice; and the fact that Dionysius believed a true sacrifice is offered to God in the Mass is clear from what he says in *the Ecclesiastical Hierarchy* (3, 3), "The priest justifies himself because he offers the salutary host, which is greater than him." Also, in Paul (Rom. 15:16), the word ἱερουργοῦντα, the translators do not render the one sacrificing, as they should according to Chemnitz, but the one sanctifying, moreover the word προσφορὰν most rightly translates to oblation, but that word of sacrifice is not read in the whole chapter.

Moreover, Augustine clearly calls the oblation of the altar the Lord's body, which is offered to God on the altar as a true and proper sacrifice. Thus, the words that Chemnitz cites do not oppose this. For Augustine does not say that oblation is made to God when it is broken on the table to be distributed (for Chemnitz cites him in bad faith), but after he said that which has been blessed and broken on the table, etc., after interposing many words he says everything is dedicated to God which is offered to him, especially the oblation of the holy altar. Thus, Chemnitz adds these with what came above, as if they made one sentence, when they pertain to different sentences.

Now Cyprian, when he arranges the plan of his epistle in regard to the sanctification of the chalice and the ministration to the people, he does not understand a simple consecration through the word "sanctification" (namely a consecration merely ordered to communion), rather, he understands a consecration ordered to *sacrifice*. He frequently says the sacrifice is offered to God. This is why Cyprian insists on the terms *sacrifice* and *victim*. Chemnitz, however, supposes Cyprian said bread and wine were offered in oblation by Christ, not the body and blood; he does nothing against our teaching. For Cyprian speaks on the oblation of bread and wine which preceded the sacrifice, and which necessarily require a subsequent sacrifice, for bread and wine are offered as we see even now takes place at Mass, just as the matter of a future sacrifice that is going to be blessed by God.

In regards to the passage of Acts, we have already discussed it above, and there we showed that the opinion of those that by the words, "While they ministered to the Lord," the Mass is understood is more probable. But even if we were to admit another opinion as probable, say that Luke speaks of preaching, still Chemnitz would profit nothing from it. The words of Luke are general, and they do not contain some certain ministry; for Luke does not say, while they were offering the sacrifice of the Body of Christ to the Lord, rather, "while they were ministering to the Lord." Now, although it would be adequate to say that to minister to the Lord means that they preached, and in the same manner, it could mean they dispensed the sacrament of Baptism or the Eucharist, nevertheless, it could only be said ineptly and by a rather unusual figure of speech that they offered water to the Lord, or he that dispenses the Eucharist offers the body of Christ to God. Consequently, seeing that the fathers everywhere say that in the Last Supper the body and blood of Christ was offered to God in sacrifice, these words cannot be distorted in this way, as Chemnitz would have it.

In regard to the citations of Augustine, where Christ is said to be immolated for us, or the people, we can easily make a response. "For us," or "for the people" means the sacrifice is offered to God *for our benefit*. Even the sacrifice of the cross, which is the truest sacrifice offered to God, can be said to have been done for us, because it was offered on our behalf. Nay more, Augustine, in a later passage, speaks on the sacrifice of the cross, and there says Christ is immolated for us when we begin to participate in the fruit of his death; equally it is for us, as if Christ were the first offered on the cross [for that purpose].

Next, Cyril holds nothing against our teaching. For he calls the unbloody consecration *latria*, and the communion of the Eucharist, insofar as through those actions we offer to God a sacrifice, and then we consume it, or partake in it. But he does not appeal to *latria* except as the primary end of that action is immediately to worship God with that cult due to him alone, which is only through a sacrifice, properly speaking. Hence it is a fact that neither Cyril nor the other Fathers who call the Mass unbloody *latria*, ever call the celebration of Baptism an

Book I, Ch. XV: The Tradition of the Fathers

unbloody latria, because Baptism, without a doubt, refers immediately to our sanctification not to render the worship due to God alone. That is enough for the *first method*.

The *second* method of Chemnitz for explaining the sayings of the Fathers is that we would understand the Lord's Supper to be called a sacrifice, oblation, and immolation by the Fathers because it is a certain representation and commemoration of the true sacrifice, namely the death of Christ [on the cross]. According to this method, Christ is said to be immolated in the Last Supper, not because he is really and properly immolated in himself, but because he is immolated in the Sacrament, i.e. in the image and similitude. Such a solution, as we showed above, Chemnitz receives from Calvin, and proves it from the Fathers who often say Christ was only truly immolated once, and the Eucharist is a representation of that immolation. For Augustine holds this in the teachings of Prosper of Aquitaine, *de fide ad Petrum,* ch. 18, *contra Faustum,* 20, 18, and *in Epist.* 23 and 120, *in Psal.* 79, as well as Ambrose, Chrysostom and Theophylactus on Hebrews 10.

Then, Peter Lombard asks in the *Sentences* (4 dist. 12), if the priest is said to properly carry out a sacrifice, or immolation, and he responds that what is offered and consecrated by the priest is called a sacrifice and oblation because it is a memorial and representation of the true sacrifice and holy immolation made on the altar of the cross. There Chemnitz claims that the Council of Trent, in its 22nd session, canon 1, declared anathema to this opinion of Lombard which was confirmed from the Fathers. For Lombard teaches from the Fathers that the sacrifice of the Mass is so-called because it is a memorial of the sacrifice of the cross, not because it is properly a sacrifice in itself. The Council, however, says, "If anyone shall say that in the Mass a true and proper sacrifice is not offered to God, let him be anathema."

I respond to this second method: it is very true what the Fathers say, that Christ was only immolated once and the memorial and similitude of that immolation is the action of the Sacred Supper; for they speak on the immolation in its proper species, or concerning the *bloody* immolation, which truly and properly, only happened once; now it is not done properly, except through *representation*. But this is not opposed to the fact that the Fathers believed that in the Mass a true and proper sacrifice is offered to God.

Moreover, when Lombard asks whether what the priest carries out is said to be a sacrifice and immolation, he receives the words "sacrifice" and "immolation" for *killing*, but if he had asked more clearly what the priest does, whether it must be called the killing of Christ, then he answers most rightly that Christ was truly only immolated once, i.e. he was killed, but now he is not immolated properly, i.e. killed, rather only in the sacrament and in representation. However, whether what the priest does is a sacrifice properly speaking, but unbloody, Lombard does not ask, rather he presupposed, as was known to all, from the daily celebration of the sacrifice itself. Even St. Thomas, and the other scholastics were not anxious about such a manner of speech, because it was not called into controversy then, but only by what notion the sacrifice of Mass can be called the immolation of Christ, i.e. the killing, and therefore they normally answer it is said to be an immolation because it is a representation of immolation, or because it has the same effect with the very true and real killing of Christ. This is why the Council of Trent taught nothing contrary to the doctrine of Lombard, or the scholastics.

However, the fact that the Fathers conveyed that the sacrifice was not only commemorative, but also true and proper, is proven *firstly* because Augustine (*loc. cit.*), just as he says the action of the Supper is a commemoration of the sacrifice of the cross that has already been carried out, so also he says the sacrifice of the Old Testament was a commemoration of the future sacrifice of the Cross, and still it cannot be denied that those were true sacrifices in themselves, and sacrifices properly speaking.

Secondly, if the Fathers thought the sacrifice of the Eucharist was not a sacrifice except by representation, they never would have spoken of a multitudinous number of victims offered to God, and sacrifices on the altar, as Cyprian says everywhere (*epistles*, 1, 2; 2, 3; 3, 2; 3, 6; 3, 25; *sermon on almsgiving*, and in another *on the Lord's prayer*), rather it would only be in the singular, *sacrifice*. It is one thing that it is a representation, and therefore, the word cannot be spoken except in the singular. For this reason the Calvinists never say that many consecrated loaves are the bodies of Christ, because they represent one body, and we say in regard to images that we have or have seen that there are many images of Julius Caesar, but we do not say, except inadequately, there are many Julius Caesars.

Thirdly, Baptism is a sacrament that is representative of the death of Christ, as the Apostle teaches (Romans 6:3). For, while we are immersed in water, we are put to death with Christ, and when we emerge from the water, we rise again with Christ; and still none of the Fathers ever called

Book I, Ch. XV: The Tradition of the Fathers

Baptism a sacrifice offered to God. Consequently, that representation is not the only reason there could be as to why the action of the Last Supper is called a sacrifice.

Fourthly, if the celebration of the Eucharist was not a new, real and true oblation made unto God, but only some image and representation of the oblation carried out on the cross, we could not truly say to God, "I offer this to you", or, "Receive, O Lord, this sacrifice." Who says to someone: "I offer to you;" or: "Receive," then really offers him something which only represents an offering, except perhaps because he wanted to mock the man whom he pretended to honor? This is why our adversaries, although they understand this well enough, altogether refrain from terms of this sort in their celebration of the Supper, and especially rebuke us for them. But the Fathers very frequently spoke this way, and especially Augustine (*City of God*, 8, 27): "Who ever heard a priest of the faithful, standing at an altar built for the honor and worship of God over the holy body of some martyr, say in the prayers, I offer to you a sacrifice, O Peter, or O Cyprian?" Add that the fathers not only say that they offer, but even say through this oblation that the oblation of the cross is commemorated, where they distinguish two oblations: the one representing, and the one represented; one unbloody, the other bloody. Augustine (*Contra Faustum*, 20, 18) says: "Christians, after commemorating the sacrifice, celebrate with the most holy oblation and participation of the body of Christ." There, it is also observed in passing, that just as the participation of the Lord's body does not cease to be a true and real participation, although it is commemorative, so also, the oblation, which took place once with that participation does not cease to be a true and real oblation, although it is commemorative of the other oblation.

Fifthly, the Fathers often add an epithet to the word sacrifice, which is only appropriate for a true sacrifice, and which would be inadequate to say of a mere representation. Cyprian (*Epistles*, 2, 3) calls it a full and true sacrifice. Chrysostom (*hom. 60 ad populum*) and all the Greeks call it a fearsome sacrifice, and full of awe. Augustine (*City of God*, 10, 20), calls it the supreme and truest sacrifice. Again (*de spiritu et litera*, 11) he calls it a most true, and singular sacrifice. Eusebius (*demonst. Evang.*, last chapter) calls it a full sacrifice unto God.

Next and lastly, it happens that the Fathers clearly say through this sacrifice, that now it is offered to God throughout the world, and the cult of *latria* due to him alone is shown to the same, as is clear from Augustine (*loc. cit.*) where he proves we do not have saints for gods, because no one says at the altar, "I offer to you O Peter, or Cyprian;" and from Cyril and the other Greeks, who, as even Chemnitz witnesses, call this sacrifice unbloody *latria*. But if it were no sacrifice at all except a representation, and a memory of the sacrifice of the cross, it would not be the cult of *latria*; for to not commemorate the sacrifice of another, but truly and properly to sacrifice is the cult of *latria*. Thus, the second method devised by Chemnitz is refuted.

The *last* pronouncement of Chemnitz on the testimonies of the fathers is found in his work (*Exam. Conc. Trident.*, pg. 798-799). After he had given all the solutions, when he adverted to the fact that he could not really satisfy his readers, he also, along with his teachers Luther and Calvin, bade farewell to the fathers, and forgot about that which he had written previously, that good minds always paid head to the consensus of most of antiquity: "No matter how excellent the teaching of the ancient authors, it is the canonical Scripture which is the rule, and norm of faith, and judgment in this controversy." And a little later, he calls the testimonies of the Fathers blemishes; at length, he gives three reasons why he would rather, with his own, call the Eucharist a sacrament and not a sacrifice, although all the Fathers called it a sacrifice. The *first* is, that Scripture never calls the Lord's Supper a sacrifice; *second*, because the term sacrifice in no small way obscures the true doctrine and use of the Lord's Supper; *thirdly*, because the theatrical sacrifice of the Popish Mass has been skillfully constructed from that catechesis of the term sacrifice, poorly interpreted.

In the first place, these reasons contain the greatest rebuke of the Fathers; they show the Fathers did not speak according to the fashion of Scripture, and obscured true doctrine and the use of the Lord's Supper, and by their license, and impropriety of speech, produced the greatest harm to the Church. But who would believe that about such learned men who flourished in the purer, best and most prosperous times of the Church, as Chemnitz said earlier?

Next, the first reason is utterly inept, let us say nothing of the second and third which contain mere calumnies. For if the word sacrifice displeases him because Scripture does not use it, why, by the same reasoning, would the word *sacrament* not displease him? I do not believe they will show the place in Scripture where the Lord's Supper is called a sacrament. What is it that Chemnitz is talking about, when he says, "This consideration from the blemishes of some of the ancients shows why we prefer to call the Lord's Supper a sacrament rather than a sacrifice.

Book I, Ch. XV: The Tradition of the Fathers

Firstly, Scripture, which is the most right of all, and can give the most suitable names in these very matters, in no place calls the Lord's Supper a sacrifice"?

Additionally, Scripture calls the Lord's Supper a sacrifice in clear words found in Isaiah and Malachi, as we showed above; moreover, Paul so clearly compares the Lord's Supper with the sacrifices of the Jews and gentiles, that one would have to be blind to not see that Paul thought it is a sacrifice.

CHAPTER XVI
The Sacrifice of the Mass, Properly Speaking, is Proven from the Rite of Altars

THE SECOND HEADING, from which we can discern the teaching of the ancient Fathers is taken from the rite *of altars* erected for the celebration of this sacrifice. One is not accustomed to raise altars except for sacrifices properly speaking. Our adversaries do not deny this, so Calvin (*Institutes* 4, 18 §12) speaks in this way, on the difference of the Sacrament of the Eucharist, and a sacrifice properly speaking: "He gave us a table upon which we dine, not an altar upon which to offer a victim." And Peter Martyr, in his book against Stephen Gardiner (*parte 3, in responsione ad objectum 16*, pag. 710), writes that no altar should be in a Church. And then, there is no other reason why in this time, our adversaries everywhere tear down altars and substitute meal tables for them, except that they understand altars are clear signs of sacrifice properly speaking. Add, that what we said above (chapter 2) where from Scripture and the Fathers, and from the Hebrew, Greek and Latin word we offer that very thing. This is why if the ancient fathers always had altars to celebrate the Eucharist, we will be able to show, and at the same time will have proven that the Eucharist in their teaching was truly and properly speaking, a sacrifice.

The first testimony is in the Canons of the Apostles (3 & 4) where there is a clear mention of an altar erected to offer the Eucharist. Dionysius also, in *The Ecclesiastical Hierarchy* (ch. 3) mentions an altar. Tertullian (*On Penance*), numbers among other signs of the humility of penitents, is to fall on their knees before the priest, to kneel before the altars of God, etc., and in his book *on Prayer*, in the last words, he says: "Your station will be more solemn if you stand near the altar of God." Cyprian (*Epistles* 1, 9) bids that sacrifice not be offered for a certain Christian that had died, who had abandoned a priest as a procurator of temporal affairs; and he gave the reason that he was not worthy for sacrifice to be offered for him, since he had removed a priest from the altar of God. Eusebius (*Demonstrat. Evangelic.* 1, 6), says many things about the altar of the Church. Optatus of Milevis (*Contra Parmenianum*, 6), says, "Why is it a sacrilege to break the altars of God upon which even you once offered [sacrifice]?" And he calls the same altar the seat of the body of Christ

Book I, Ch. XVI: The Rite of Altars

(*ibid*). Ambrose (*epistles*, 5, 33) says, "Soldiers compete to greet and rush upon the altar to show peace with a kiss." St. Anthony, as Athanasius writes in his life, when he foresaw that the Arian heresy would come about, it seemed to him that he saw wild mules overturning the altars of Christ with their feet. Gregory Nazianzen (*oration in Gorgoniam*) writes that he laid prostrate at the altar and invoked him, who usually worshiped upon that altar. Gregory of Nyssa (*de Baptismo*) says that an altar is by its nature a stone, but by consecration it becomes holy. St. John Chrysostom (*hom. 53 ad populum*) says, "If anyone wills to undermine this altar, wouldn't you bury him with stones? And in *homily 20 on 2. Cor.*, he says, "You honor the altar which receives the body of Christ." Jerome (*contra Vigilantium*), Augustine (*City of God* 8, 27; 22, 8), and other fathers, even ancient Councils, frequently mention an altar.

But perhaps someone will object that Minutius Felix, in his dialogue titled *Octavius*, introduces the pagan Caecilius speaking in this way with Octavius the Christian: "Why do you (Christians) have no altars, no temples, no idols?"

But the answer to this is easy; for Christians in those times were afraid lest any pagan would be present at their sacred rites for two reasons. *First*, because they were not fit to gaze upon such mysteries. *Second*, due to fear of the persecutors on whose account they also were frequently compelled to carry out divine rites in crypts, caverns, or certainly in private houses. This is why it was commonly thought that Christians were atheists, because they were not seen to sacrifice to any god openly. Moreover, not only in the time of Minutius Felix, but even much earlier Christians had altars, as is clear from the citations of Tertullian, Dionysius and Clement, who are all older than Minutius, and from Cyprian, who lived at the same time.

CHAPTER XVII
The Sacrifice of the Mass is proven from the word "Priest".

THE THIRD HEADING is taken from the term *priest* (*sacerdos*). Both Calvin and Peter Martyr (*loc. cit.*) affirm that priests are properly ordained for sacrifice; so, they contend that Christ did not give priests to the Church, but only ministers of the word and the Sacraments.

Moreover, the ancient Fathers use this word so frequently, that Chemnitz was compelled to confess in the second part of his *Examination* (pag. 1140) where he disputes on the Sacrament of Order, that the use of calling ministers of the Church priests, and their ministry a priesthood was strengthened among the Fathers, although in the New Testament a word of this sort in this meaning is not found; which of course is true. Not only Augustine (*City of God* 20, 10) and Chrysostom (*de Sacerdotio*), whom Chemnitz cites, and all later writers everywhere use this word; but it is also found in those more ancient. Gaudentius, in his *second treatise on Exodus*, says, "The Lord entrusted to his faithful disciples, whom he constituted the first priests of his Church, to exercise these mysteries of eternal life without ceasing, which is necessary to be celebrated in the Churches of the whole world by all priests." Likewise, Jerome (*Dialogus contra Luciferianos*) says the same thing, as well as Ambrose (*in Psalm 38*), Eusebius (*Demonstrationum Evangelicarum* 5, 3), and all others use this word. And what is more, St. John the Apostle himself exercised the priesthood and bore the pontifical veneer as Polycrates writes (cited by Eusebius *Hist.* 5, 23).

We are also not hindered by the fact that in the New Testament Ecclesiastical ministers are not called priests, for the reason is obvious. The Jewish priesthood still flourished in the time of the Apostles, and they offered bloody sacrifices in the temple of Jerusalem, so the Apostles (under the Lord's inspiration) did not use the words priesthood, sacrifice, temple, altars and similar things, so that Christian sacrifices might be more easily distinguished from the Jews, and lest they might be thought to renew or confirm those same rites if they used the same terms. But a little after the temple in Jerusalem was destroyed, and the sacrifices of the Jews ceased altogether, the ancient Fathers freely began to use the words temple, altar, priesthood, and sacrifice, as the matter itself demanded.

This is why Calvin is manifestly deceived, or rather more lies (*Institutes* 4, 18 §10) when he says the Fathers so claimed the honor of the priesthood for Christ alone, that perhaps Augustine (*contra Parmenianum* 2, 8) would affirm it as a term of Antichrist if any bishop would make himself an intercessor between God and men. For Augustine is not speaking to Parmenianus about a priest, but about *a mediator*, and not any mediator, but on a mediator *through the mode of redemption*, which is proper to Christ alone. For by the mode of payer there are many intercessors and mediators, as the Fathers everywhere affirm. For Basil speaks of the holy martyrs this way (*in orat. In 40 Martyres*), and Jerome (*epist. Ad Fabiolam on the priestly garment*) calls bishops trustees, i.e. mediators, between God and the people through the oblation of the sacrifice of the altar, which is also found in Chrysostom (*de Sacerdotio*, lib. 6). Augustine not only calls bishops and presbyters intercessors, but priests by name (*de Civitate Dei*, 20, 10). "Bishops and presbyters are properly called priests."

The response of Chemnitz (*loc. cit.*) does not avail, where he affirms the word priest is found among the Fathers, but would not have it received for the ministry of sacrifice, but for the ministry of the word and the sacraments; for he contends that is the only ministry given in the New Testament to show men whom the Fathers customarily call priests. This, I say, is not a sufficient answer. For in the first place, it would follow that all the Greek and Latin Fathers either ignored the force of this word, or that they labored to abuse it. As the Apostle says in Hebrews 5:1, "Every priest ... is constituted in those things which pertain to God, that he would offer gifts and sacrifices." And in 8:3, "Every high priest is constituted to offer gifts and sacrifices." And from there the same Apostle proves that Christ is not a priest if he has nothing to offer. So who would believe the most learned Fathers attributed the word priest to those who only teach the people and administer the sacraments, but offer no sacrifice to God? Besides, to teach and administer the sacraments is not only suited to bishops and priests, but even to deacons, and nevertheless, the Fathers do not call deacons priests, as is clear from St. Augustine (*loc. cit.*), where he says that bishops and presbyters are properly called priests; and from the Fourth Council of Carthage (chapter 4) where it is clearly said that deacons are not ordained to the priesthood, but *to ministry*.

Someone will say: Deacons could not administer all the sacraments, and therefore perhaps were not called priests. But priests cannot administer all the sacraments, as is clear from the Sacraments of Order and Confirmation, and nevertheless, they were called priests. Therefore, for that reason alone, the Council of Nicaea relates, in canon 14, that clearly deacons do not have the power to offer sacrifices, but only to assist the priests in sacrifice.

CHAPTER XVIII
The Sacrifice of the Mass is Proven from the Liturgies

THE FOURTH HEADING is taken from the rite of celebration. In all the ancient liturgies which are extant, those of James, Clement, Basil, and Chrysostom, as well as the writings Ambrose (*de Sacramentis*, books 5 and 6), and Cyril of Jerusalem (*Catechesis Mystagogica*, books 4 and 5), who explain a great part of the liturgy, it is abundantly clear that the Fathers celebrated the mystery of the Eucharist in a rite that they had no doubt was a true sacrifice. They are full of the words oblation, sacrifice, victim, signs, blessings, elevations, and other rites of this sort. This is why Luther (as we noted above) in his book on the formula of the Mass, removed the whole Canon, because he did not think his position that the Mass is not a sacrifice could be defended if it remained intact. Moreover, nearly all of the Canon, whose words have not been changed very much, is found in the Liturgies and in the books of Ambrose and Cyril (*loc. cit.*), and certainly all those things are found which offended Luther, namely the words *oblation* and *sacrifice*.

Calvin (*Institutes* 4, 18 §11) says that the Fathers cannot be excused because they sinned in the manner of action: "For they imitated a Jewish custom more proper to sacrifice than either Christ ordained or the reasoning of the Gospel allowed." Clearly, Calvin, who was born yesterday knows better what Christ ordained than James, the brother of the Lord, who was present with Christ himself at the Lord's Supper, or Clement who learned from Peter the Apostle, or Basil, Cyril, Ambrose, and Chrysostom who preceded Calvin by 1200 years.

CHAPTER XIX
The same Is Proven from those for whom the Sacrifice of the Mass is Offered

THE LAST HEADING whereby we especially know the teaching of the Fathers is so clear that our adversaries have no way out but to reject the Fathers altogether, is taken from those for whom the Fathers offered the sacrifice. If the Eucharist were nothing else but a Sacrament, then it would be of no benefit except to those receiving and eating it, just as Baptism does not benefit anyone but those who are baptized. Our adversaries do not even deny it. Melanchthon, Calvin, Chemnitz and others say the whole controversy between us and them is whether the Eucharist should not only be distributed to those who will eat of it, but even offered for the salvation of others, both the living and the dead. For the latter do not doubt that it pertains to the truest sacrifice. By and by, they do not doubt it pertains to the truest sacrifice.

Now the Fathers, in the liturgies we cited, not only offer the Eucharist for the sins of the living and the dead, for peace, for safety, and then for every necessity both spiritual and temporal, but they even teach everywhere in their other books that it should be done. We will add such testimonies in the proper place below, when we come to the question: Whether this sacrifice is propitiatory. In the meantime, one or another of the Fathers will suffice.

John Chrysostom (*hom. 79 ad populum Antiochenum*) says, "The priest assisting at the altar, is bidden to offer to God for the bishops, for the Church and those governing the Church." And in Homily 72 on Matthew, he adds it is also offered for the sick, for the healthy, and for the fruits of the earth. In Homily 21 on Acts, as well as *de Sacerdotio*, book 6, and other places he adds for the dead. Augustine (*City of God*, 22, 8) writes that the sacrifice of the Eucharist is offered by his priests for the home to be freed from the disturbance of demons, and in *Confessions* (9, 12) he writes that the sacrifice was offered for his dead mother. And lest we might think it is mere ceremony to offer for the dead, he writes the same thing in *Enchiridion*, ch. 110, that this host is a propitiation for those that are not very wicked. But that is enough from these. If anyone wishes for a collection of testimonies, let him read John Garetius.

CHAPTER XX
The Sacrifice of the Mass Is Proven from the Union of Law and Sacrifice

I COME now to the arguments which can be sought from the argumentation of the Scriptures and a profitable reading of the Fathers.

The *first* argument is taken from the union which exists between religion, or law, and sacrifice; and we can come to a conclusion with this syllogism. There is such a union between law, or religion, and outward sacrifice, properly speaking, that it is altogether necessary that either law and religion are truly and properly not found in the Church of Christ, or a sacrifice properly speaking that is also external is found in the Church of Christ. If you take away the Mass, then no external and proper sacrifice is found in the Church; therefore, the Mass is an external sacrifice, properly speaking.

The first proposition is proven: *firstly,* from the fact that nearly every religion, whether true or false, applies sacrifice to God always, and in every place and time. From here it is gathered that it comes about from the light and instinct of nature, and is a certain first principle begotten in us by God. What Chemnitz says in the *Examination of the Council of Trent* (2 part. Pag. 743) is very false, where he tries to evade this argument by calling it an instinct of corrupted nature, which is the font and root of all superstitions. For, even if corrupt nature is really the font, as it was of idolatry and all other superstitions, nevertheless, when all the gentiles came together as one on some principle, then without a doubt it is not from the corruption of nature, but from the good of nature, i.e. it came about from the light which God had sowed into them; the things that come about from corruption are not the same among all. Consequently, that God exists, must be worshiped, invoked, that he must be honored by sacrifices, and similar things which are generally found among all and were always the same, come from nature. But that there are many gods, idols must be worshiped, men offered in sacrifice, and other things, which are different in many ways, they are from corruption. Besides, that which comes about from corrupted nature is not common to the good and bad, nor is it approved by God. But that sacrifice must be offered to him, many of the best and most holy men felt, such as Noah, Abraham, Job, Melchisedech, etc.; God himself approved the sacrifices and also commanded them to be done. As a result, the instinct to offer sacrifice does not arise from the corruption of nature.

Secondly, the same proposition is proved: sacrifice began with religion itself, and is extinguished with it; therefore, a certain union between these is plainly necessary. The antecedent is clear. For the first men, whom we read worshiped God, were the sons of Adam, Cain and Abel; moreover, we read in Genesis 4:3 that they offered sacrifices to God. Then, after the flood was dispelled, seeing that religion was again renewed, all sacrifices were renewed through Noah (Genesis 8:20). Then, when on account of various persecutions, true religion was brought into danger, the prophets lamented nothing more than the cessation of sacrifices. In 3 Kings [1 Kings] 19:10, Elijah says, "For the children of Israel have forsaken your covenant; they have thrown down your altars, and they have slain your prophets." In 2 Chronicles 15:3, Azariah says, "And many days will pass in Israel without the true God, and without a priest, a teacher, and without the law." Daniel 3:38, the three holy children say, "At this time there is no prince, leader, prophet, holocaust, sacrifice, oblation, incense, nor place of firstfruits before you that we may find mercy." In Daniel 12:11, it is said that Antichrist is going to take away continual sacrifice, namely, he will thoroughly abolish religion. Then, in Hebrews 7:11 the Apostle says that the people, under the Levitical priesthood received the law, and then he adds after that priesthood had been translated [to the New] it is necessary that the translation of the law would take place.

It is proved *thirdly:* A sacrifice properly speaking is the proper worship of God, i.e. what is due to him alone by the consent of all. For all kinds of honor are in some manner common with creatures, as we proved in our treatise *On Canonizations*. As a result, there can be no religion without a sacrifice properly speaking. For religion was established to worship God; however, a religion does not worship God, but rather more afflicts him with ignominy, which does not show a cult due to him alone. Certainly, among men, if anyone did not give a title of honor to a king, of the sort suited to kings alone, namely "your majesty," even if he preserved all lower titles, would not only be judged to have failed to give the king honor, but even to afflict him with contumely.

Now the assumption of the first syllogism is proven, namely, that after one removes the sacrifice of the Mass, no sacrifice properly speaking remains in the Church. For, if any could be assigned, it would be the sacrifice of the cross. Our adversaries assign that one, and also would have it that it is the sole and true sacrifice of the Christian religion.

Book I, Ch. XX: The Union of Law and Sarifice

But we will show that the sacrifice of the cross, although it was the truest sacrifice, is not of the kind that is required to constitute and preserve law, or religion; Christ willed there to be such a thing even to the consummation of the world. Therefore, if we have no other, it plainly follows that we have no religion.

It is proved *firstly* because the sacrifice of the cross is not proper to the Christian religion, rather it is common to all true religions which were from the beginning of the world. For even in the law of nature, in written laws, all sacrifices look to this one, and they declare this one, and however many just men there were from the beginning of the world, they were just on account of the participation of this sacrifice; consequently, the Christian religion is not distinguished from the ancients by the sacrifice of the cross.

Secondly, the sacrifice of the cross was carried out once, then ceased, and does not remain except through its effect and power, as is known; nay more, it never existed during the time of the Christian religion, for that only properly began after the death of Christ. But the proper sacrifice of religion should accompany it perpetually, as we have shown above.

Thirdly, any religion you like requires an external and visible sacrifice, to which men of that religion come together to carry out, and which they can repeat. But nothing of this sort is found in the sacrifice of the cross. For, in respect to Christians it is invisible, since it is discerned by faith and not the eyes; for this reason, the people cannot assemble at it, nor, even if it were discerned, can it be repeated by the people, or Christian priests, for it is not lawful for Christians daily to kill Christ.

Fourthly, the sacrifice of the Christian religion should be a certain rite received by Christians from God, pertaining to that cult which is called *latria*, as Augustine rightly affirms (*Contra Faustum*, 20, 21). But the slaying of Christ, which is called the sacrifice of the cross, cannot be called a rite seeing that it was the very truth which all rites represent; and much less can it be called a rite given to Christians unless someone would have it that God commanded of us the supreme crime, namely the killing and death of Christ. Lastly, it can scarcely be called the cult of latria when to kill Christ should rather be called a supreme sacrilege.

The testimonies of the Fathers are added, which we cited above, in explaining the definition of sacrifice which they say is the unique sacrifice of the Eucharist and the singular sacrifice of Christians.

Therefore, let the testimony of Cyprian be added on the Lord's

Supper, where he says if the Eucharist were exhausted by eating, the sacrifice would not remain with us and through this the whole religion would cease.

Someone will say, why is it that Paul, in Hebrews 7;12, when he says that after the priesthood was translated, the law should also be translated, does not also say the priesthood of Aaron had been translated to St. Peter and his successors, but only to Christ?

I respond: The Apostle does not say the Levitical priesthood was translated from Aaron to Christ, but that the Levitical priesthood was translated *to the priesthood according to the order of Melchisedech*, which is eternal, and should be perpetually active in the Church. This is why when later, he says the priesthood of Christ is according to the order of Melchisedech, he does not consider it as he precisely offered the sacrifice of the cross, but as *he sacrifices himself perpetually in the Eucharist through his ministers*; in this manner, as we showed above, he has a perpetual priesthood.

CHAPTER XXI

The Sacrifice of the Mass is proven from the comparison of the Christian law to the Mosaic

THE SECOND PRINCIPAL reason is introduced from the comparison of the Church and the Synagogue, or the law of the new and the old, the Christian people and the Jewish. This is the argument: Among the Jewish people there were sacrifices properly speaking; therefore, among the Christian people there should also be sacrifices properly speaking.

The consequent is proven: for the antecedent is beyond controversy. *Firstly,* Christ did not altogether abolish what God had established in the Old Law, which was not contrary to his Father or himself. Rather, he either perfected or changed it into a better thing, as is clear in the Commandments and the Sacraments. For he did not abolish the commandments, but explained them (Matthew 5:27), and added counsels which are conducive to perfect observance of the Commandments. For equal reason, he did not abolish the sacraments of Circumcision, the Paschal Lamb, and similar things, rather he changed them into other things which are truly and properly called Sacraments, or rather, as Augustine says (Epistle 118), fewer, easier, and more excellent. Consequently, in the same manner he ought not to have altogether abolished sacrifices, but to change them.

Secondly, sacrifice is the supreme worship which can be shown to God. Without any controversy, things are better than words, and among words, sacred are better than profane; among sacred things, the public are better than the private; among public things, those of which the very substance is consumed in the honor of God, than those which are of only one use. Moreover, such is a sacrifice properly speaking, as everyone knows. This is why if this kind of worship was in the Old Law, but not in the New, then God was by far endowed with greater honor in the Old Law, than in the New. Hence, Christ could not have procured the glory of his Father, as he said, but ignominy.

Thirdly, the reasons why the people of the Jews had external sacrifices, properly speaking, are all found in the Christian people. They had external and visible sacrifices because that people was also external and visible, namely not consisting in the spirit alone, but in spirit and flesh. Whereas the Christian people are also external, visible and consist of the flesh and the spirit. The former had sacrifices that they might often represent and commemorate the death of Christ, which is of singular price and our singular salvation, since they could not look upon it in the present. But we also cannot look upon the death of Christ in the present; as a result, we need a sacrifice whereby we might daily commemorate the sacrifice of the cross. The former had sacrifices to please God, or to obtain benefits from him, or to make thanksgiving for what they had obtained. Now, for the same reasons, we also need sacrifices, nay more, the more benefits we receive from God, so much the more are we obliged to offer sacrifice. This is why Peter of Cluny correctly writes that heretics, who desire to abolish sacrifice from the Church, attempt it at the suggestion of the devil that the nation which apart from so many others had been ordained by God would become, among other things, ingrate.

Fourthly, Christians really retain all the other kinds of honor and cult with which the Jews worshiped God, namely adoration, invocation, the solemn pronouncement of vows, hymns, psalms, canticles, feast days, fastings, almsgiving, and similar things. So, who could persuade himself, that the only kind of honor which is proper to God is forbidden us by Christ, when he permitted all the others, especially seeing that Christ procured nothing more ardently than the glory and honor of God?

Now, those who say an internal cult is more noble than an external one do not satisfy the matter. Christians furnish an internal worship to God. For, even if an internal cult were more noble than an external one, nevertheless, both furnish *an internal joined with an external*, or an internal cult with an external protestation of it. However, sacrifice itself is a sign, and protestation of the supreme internal cult, as Augustine often teaches (*City of God*, book 10). This is why the three children in Daniel 3:39 say, "That we may find your mercy; nevertheless, in a contrite heart and humble spirit let us be accepted. As in holocausts of rams, and bulls, and as in thousands of fat lambs; so, let our sacrifice be made in your sight today." The holy children desired to be placed in captivity so that their affected internal sacrifice might so please God, in just the same way he would be pleased if they could show and profess him by the outward sign of sacrifices.

Fifthly, sacrifices were not instituted first in the law of Moses, rather, they have their origin from the law of nature, as is clear from the sacrifices of Abel, Noah, Melchisedech, Job, and others. Therefore, even if Christ meant to abrogate everything that was instituted in the Mosaic law, still, he should not altogether abrogate sacrifices.

CHAPTER XXII
The same is proven from the difference between the Sacrament and the Sacrifice

THE THIRD REASON can be taken from the difference that exists between a sacrament and sacrifice. For it is common to all the sacraments, that they are given by one and received by another; but no one administers a sacrament to himself. We see that it happens this way in Baptism, and the other Sacraments; for no one is permitted to baptize himself, even if extreme necessity is present. For equal reason, no one confirms himself, no one absolves himself, no one initiates himself into Holy Orders, no man anoints himself. Thus, in the same manner, if the Eucharist were merely a sacrament, no man could minister it to himself; nevertheless, the contrary has always been in use for what pertains to those who consecrate the Eucharist.

Next, all of the Sacraments consist in action, not in some permanent thing, as is clear from Baptism and the rest of the Sacraments. For the water is not consecration, rather *the washing* is the Sacrament of Baptism. The Eucharist alone does not consist in action, but *in a permanent thing*, as we proved above. Hardly any other reason can be given for this difference except that the Eucharist is not only a Sacrament, but ought also to be a *sacrifice*.

Then, no other sacrament really contains the Body of Christ, rather they are only visible signs, containing virtually the grace of sanctification; no other thing is required for the notion of the sacrament, since the Sacraments are nothing other than instruments of sanctification. This is also why the Eucharist can truly and properly be a Sacrament, even if it did not really contain the Body of Christ. What reason is there that the Eucharist should necessarily contain the real body of Christ, except that it could truly and properly be offered to God the Father, and hence truly and properly be called a sacrifice? And it is a marvel why the Lutherans concede the Body of Christ is truly and really present in the Sacrament of the Eucharist, and at the same time they admit the victim is the most excellent of all which have been offered, and nevertheless they pertinaciously deny it can even be offered to God; as if it were not altogether explored and certain that the best of all which we have should be offered to God.

CHAPTER XXIII
The Same is Proven from the Consensus of the Church

THE LAST REASON: In my judgment, the most efficacious argument of all those that do not please them, and whom the smoke of pride has not altogether blinded, is taken from the consensus and testimony of the whole Christian Church, Greek, Latin, and Barbarian; which flourished for a thousand years. For our adversaries affirm that the Pontifical Mass, as it is now, is a sacrifice. Luther expressly holds it in his book against the King of England. Calvin (*Institutes*, 4, 18 §1), and Chemnitz (*Exam.* 2 parte, pg. 774), and others. Moreover, the Mass, as it is now, was fully developed in the time of Pope St. Gregory I, as Chemnitz affirms on page 826 and 827, where he disputes on the canon of the Mass. It is also certain that since the time of St. Gregory nothing has been added to the Canon of the Mass. Moreover, Gregory lived nearly a thousand years ago, therefore, by the testimony of our adversaries, the Mass began to be considered a sacrifice in the Church nearly a thousand years ago.

However, this teaching was not received in Rome alone, but throughout the whole world, and even our adversaries affirm this. For Luther (*De Capt. Babyl.*, cap. 1) says, "The Mass is everywhere believed to be a sacrifice which is offered to God. Then they add the sayings of the Holy Fathers, so many examples, and the vast usage which has constantly been observed throughout the world. ... Let us not be moved because the whole world has the contrary sense and use." And in the beginning of his book *On the Abrogation of Mass*, or rather in the dedicatory epistle of that book, he says, "Certainly it is a great thing to oppose the custom of so many centuries, the sense of such a multitude, and the authority of such great men." Later (*loc. cit.*) he clearly says that he opposes the whole world by himself. For there he creates the objection to himself: "You alone know? Have so many in the whole world erred? Have so many centuries erred? ... Join me in battle. Let my readers understand that I do battle with that teaching, whereby the Roman Antichrist and his prophets have soaked the whole world." And further on, in §18 he says every king of the earth, and the people even to the present have drunk the teaching that the Mass is a sacrifice.

And although our adversaries would not say it, nevertheless, the matter is most certain. For it is a fact that the same Mass has always been

Book I, Ch. XXIII: The Consensus of the Church

present among the Latins, from those who explained it in different times, such as Isidore, Amalarius, Walfrid Strabo, Rupert, Hugh of St. Victor, Innocent III, Bonaventure and others; and similarly among the Greeks it is crystal clear from the monk Maximus, Germanus of Constantinople, Simon of Thessalonica, Nicholas Cabasilas, and now at length from the *Censure of the Orientals against the Augsburg Confession*, ch. 13.

So from this most certain principle, and from the concession of our adversaries, namely that the Mass has been held as a sacrifice for no less than a thousand years through the whole world, if what we teach is not true then it necessarily follows: *Firstly*, the whole Church perished and lost Christ her spouse, as well as her inheritance; for the Church of Christ could not exist which was openly a slave to idolatry for so many ages. *Secondly*, it follows that what was foretold by the prophets is false, namely in Hosea 2:17, and others, who foretold that after the coming of the Messiah idolatry would cease. *Thirdly*, the promise of Christ in Matthew 16:18 would be false, namely, "The gates of hell will not prevail against her." *Fourthly*, the teaching of the Apostle in 1 Tim. 3:15, that the Church is the pillar and foundation of truth, would be false. *Fifthly*, all the saints, a great many of whom lived in these last centuries, whose lives were full of miracles, would actually be impious idolaters. *Sixthly*, God, although he revealed many things that were not necessary, still this most supreme mystery he revealed to absolutely nobody, no matter how holy, before Luther. But if these are completely absurd, and in no way believable, certainly it follows that what we teach with the Catholic Church is true, which even our adversaries correctly understand, if they do not altogether give it in a reprobate sense. For, that consequent cannot be denied by any reason; the whole world believed Mass is a sacrifice for a thousand years, therefore either the Mass is a sacrifice, or for a thousand years the faith of Christ ceased to exist on earth, perished in the Church, idolatry returned, and the prophecies of the Prophets and Christ himself were in vain.

CHAPTER XXIV
The Objections of Luther are Answered

AT LENGTH, we are now going to answer the objections of our adversaries, Luther, Calvin, and Chemnitz, seeing that the rest hardly assert anything new. *First* Luther. In his books *On the Babylonian Captivity*, and *The Abrogation of the Mass*, he proposes two arguments, and he confidently opposes these to all the testimonies of the saints, and the consensus of the whole world through all centuries. 1) His first argument is taken from words; 2) the second from the example of Christ.

The first is of this sort: The Lord's Supper is a sacrament, and the Testament of Christ; for he says, "This chalice is the new Testament in my blood," therefore it cannot be a sacrifice. For the notion of sacrifice is altogether opposed with the notion of the Sacrament and the Testament. For a sacrifice is something which we offer to God; but a Sacrament is given to us by God, and similarly the Testament contains the promise of inheritance made to us. Besides, the promise of the Sacrament and the Testament is received in faith; on the other hand, a sacrifice proceeds from faith. A sacrament and a Testament descend to us from God, the sacrifice ascends from us to God. Likewise, just as a prayer and what is received in prayer cannot be the same thing, so a testament and a sacrifice cannot be the same thing. Lastly, just as it is ridiculous to say through the Testament something is given to the testator by the heir, when it should be the other way around, namely something is given to the heir by the testator, so also it should seem ridiculous if anyone would say through the Sacrament of the Eucharist we offer something to God when he rather more promises and gives something to us. Luther uses this argument again and again through many pages, and he calls it the foundation of his whole doctrine on this matter; and on account of this ignorance of the business, he pronounces all priests and bishops idolaters, together with their fathers.

I respond: The argumentation of Luther fails in three ways: *Firstly*, because it assumes the sacrifice is a work which we show to God, and he opposes it as our action to the action of Christ. But we do not say this, rather, we assert both the Sacrament, or the Testament, and the sacrifice are a work and action of *Christ*. The same Christ who offers himself as food through the Eucharist, offers himself to the Father in the Eucharist and daily offers himself in sacrifice through the ministers of the Church. Nay more, among other goods which Christ left for us in his testament while he was dying, one was his body and blood, which we use both that we might offer them to God, and that from there our souls may take refreshment. Nor is there a difference in what pious men do when they compose their testament; for first they give something to God in the use of the Church or the poor, then they leave behind the inheritance to their sons.

But even if this sacrifice were altogether our work, still the argument of Luther would not conclude the matter; for he errs *secondly,* because he confuses the promise with the seal of the promise. Accordingly, in the Sacrament, and Testament of Christ, Luther's doctrine must distinguish the promise, which consists in the words, "Take, eat, etc." and the seal, which is the very body and blood of the Lord under the species of bread and wine. From these two the promise is not the sacrifice. And this argument of Luther proves it, if it proves anything at all. It is one thing, that something is promised to us by God, and that we offer something to God. But the seal of the promise is no reason why there cannot be sacrifice, for why cannot God take a victim offered to him, at his institution and command, in the seal of the promise? Nay more, God really acted in this way in the Old Law. He sealed the Old Testament in Exodus 24:8 with the blood of a victim, then it was immolated to him while Moses said, "This is the blood of the covenant which the Lord has made with you." So, all the sacrifices of the old law were also true sacrifices, and still the seal of the promise was that the Messiah was going to come and die. Why would it be a marvel if the blood of the Lord appearing upon the altar through the consecration were at the same time the blood of a victim offered to God, and the seal of the divine promise.

Thirdly, Luther's argument fails because he does not distinguish the formal notion of the Sacrament, the Testament and the sacrifice. For so the argument proceeds, as if we were to say a sacrifice, *qua* sacrifice, is a sacrifice or Testament, and conversely, to give is the same as to receive something; to ask is the same as to promise something. But we are not so dimwitted or unlearned to say something like this. Rather, what we say is this: the Eucharist is a sacrament insofar as it is an outward and visible sign of inward grace and refreshment, which is conferred unto us while we receive the Eucharist in due ceremony; it is the same thing as the Testament insofar as it is the public and authentic instrument of the Divine will, and promise; it is the same thing as the victim and sacrifice insofar as it is offered to God. Nor is it incompatible for one and the same thing to be received and given, nor does the consequent avail, that we receive the Eucharist from God, therefore we cannot offer the same to him. For we have nothing altogether which we offer to God, except that which we have received from him, according to that of David (1 Chronicles 29:14), "All things are yours, and we have given you what we received from your hand."

Now, the *second* argument of Luther is taken from the example of Christ, who is read to have sat in the Last Supper and distributed the sacrament to the disciples, but not that he offered something to the Father.

I respond: The example of Christ particularly favors us. For even if the Evangelists do not expressly say that Christ offered himself to the Father in the Last Supper, they also do not expressly say that he did not. Besides, we know from the circumstances, figures and prophecies of that passage, as well as from what the Prophets foretold, and finally from the express testimony of the most ancient Fathers, that Christ offered himself to the Father in sacrifice at the Last Supper, and also commanded this to be done, when he says, "Do this." It is also not a new mystery of faith. For no Evangelist writes that in the Last Supper Christ immolated the Paschal Lamb, and that he ate the kidneys while holding a staff in his hand. Nor do the Evangelists expressly write that he ate the Paschal Lamb, and still no one doubts these very things were done, since the Lord was most observant of the law and commanded the Pasch to be prepared. Furthermore, the Evangelists do not expressly say that Christ placed wine in the chalice which he called the chalice of his blood, for these words, "I will not drink from this fruit of the vine," we showed above were said about the chalice which he was going to drink after the eating of the paschal lamb, not on the chalice of the Eucharist (*De Eucharistia*, book 4, cap. 10);[11] and still who at this time would deny that there was wine in the chalice? For all writers hand that down. This is why if Luther desires to prove from the example of Christ that the Mass is not a sacrifice, let him advance some certain testimony where we

---

11 Translator's note: In that citation, Bellarmine refers the reader again to *On the Eucharist*, book 1, chapter 10, in the tenth argument. There, the essence of Bellarmine's exegesis is that the words, "I will not drink of the fruit of the vine, etc." do not refer to the consecrated chalice, but to the wine drank during the rite of the Paschal Lamb. His Protestant interlocutors had argued that since Christ says I will not drink of the fruit of the vine after the consecration, it is still wine. Bellarmine shows that this is not so, but that there were two chalices.

shall read that Christ did not offer himself at the Last Supper; for these negative arguments, "It is not held expressly in the Scriptures, therefore it didn't happen" are already ridiculous, even for children.

Besides these arguments, Luther has a characteristic imposture in the beginning of his book on the *Abrogation of Private Mass*, where he says that the Pope will advance the decretal epistles to cite for the foundation the words of Paul: "after the priesthood was translated it is necessary that the translation of the law should take place," and from there deduce that after the ascension of Christ the priesthood was translated to Peter from Christ, and thence from Peter to the Pope, and from the Pope to his successors. Illyricus again repeats this imposture of Luther in his *Apology for the Antwerp Confession*, cap. *de Missa*, where he also adds the Pope speaks of the priesthood according to the order of Melchisedech.

But there are three lies here: *First*, that the Pope would say he will advance such things in the decretal epistles and lay them for a foundation. For that canon, *Translato Sacerdotio* is not found in the first title, but in the second, nor is it in the beginning since two other canons precede it.

The *second* lie is that the Pope said these things. For in that whole canon, we do not even find the name of Christ, nor Peter, nor the Pope, rather the very words of Paul are placed with some annotations of St. Augustine, which only contain the fact that the law and priesthood are altogether connected.

The *third* lie is that in that canon there is a question on the priesthood of Christ, or Melchisedech. For it is expressly a question on the Levitical priesthood, as the *Gloss* notes twice. Therefore, these are mere dreams of Luther, that the priesthood was translated from Christ to Peter, and from Peter to the Pope.

CHAPTER XXV
The arguments of John Calvin are Answered

JOHN CALVIN (*Instit.* 4, 18 §1) proposes five arguments, where he says that he will clearly prove from the word of God that the sacrifice of the Mass afflicts Christ with a manifest insult, buries and oppresses his cross, obliterates his death, takes away the fruit which he brought into being for us, and weakens and dissipates the sacrament, in which the memory of his death was left; all such arguments he carries out in the following sections.

1) The *first* argument is of this sort. Christ is a priest forever; so, there should be no substitutes or vicars for Christ. Consequently, there are now no priests on earth; hence no sacrifices, for in the old law priests were multiplied because death forbade them to remain, as the Apostle says (Hebrews 7:23). Nor can one answer that those who are now ordained priests do not succeed Christ, but are his assistants. For the Apostle (*loc. cit.*) does not concede the multiplication of any priests, except on account of the death of the preceding. Christ, however, lives forever, and remains a priest, therefore, he alone exercises the priesthood, or if there are many priests on earth, their priesthood is abrogated in Christ.

I respond: No Catholic affirms that the priests who are in the Church *succeed* Christ, this is why it was not necessary for Calvin to refute it. Moreover, we already refuted this in the lies of Luther and Illyricus about what is contained in the decretal letters. Further, what attains to vicars and assistants, or rather more ministers of Christ in the priesthood according to the order of Melchisedech, it is false that the multiplication of these is incompatible with the unity and eternity of the priesthood of Christ. For, Christ is not only a priest, but he is also our sole and eternal teacher, as he says in Matthew 23:8. Nay more, it also pertains to the priesthood to teach, as Calvin himself affirms (*ibid.*, 4, 1, §5) and yet, because Christ does not now teach us himself in human fashion, and visibly as the nature of men requires, it is not opposed to the unity and eternity of his magisterium that many men who are called doctors and teachers, and in this matter vicars, assistants and ministers of Christ, as it is clear from Paul who calls himself a doctor and teacher in 1 Timothy 2:7, as well as 2 Tim. 1:11. In 1 Cor. 3:5 and 9, he calls himself and a few others helpers *ministers of God*, and in 2 Cor. 5:20, he says, "For

Book I, Ch. XXV: Calvin is Answered 139

Christ, therefore, we are ambassadors, God as it were exhorting by us. For Christ, we beseech you, be reconciled to God." By such words he makes himself both a legate and vicar of Christ. The same can be said about the office of shepherding, and administering the sacraments. For Christ is the pastor of all the sheep, and he is the one who baptizes and confers the rest of the Sacraments in the consensus of all, and still who ever denied that there should be many pastors and ministers of the Sacraments in the Church, who do these things visibly in place of Christ as his ministers? Why do our adversaries also wish to be called pastors, doctors and ministers, and why do they teach and baptize daily and yet not think that they detract from the sole magisterium and pastorship of Christ? As a result, in the same manner, because Christ does not now offer sacrifice visibly and in human fashion on earth, it is not opposed to his unique and eternal priesthood that he should have on earth priests, ministers and vicars through whom he does it. Nay more, as we showed above, Christ cannot truly be called an eternal priest for any other reason than that he sacrifices through ministers, in the same way it is certain that he does not sacrifice properly in his own person.

Now, the answer to the passage of the Apostle which seems to absolutely exclude the multiplication of priests in the New Testament is rather simple: The Apostle absolutely excludes the multiplication of priests *in that same dignity and power*, but not of inferior priests who are said to be ministers in respect to Christ. For in the old law on account of the death of Aaron, Eleazar succeeded him in dignity and power; Phineas succeeded Eleazar, and so the rest; and if Aaron never died, no one would have succeeded him. Nevertheless, while Aaron lived there were many other lower priesthoods. So therefore, no man succeeds Christ in the same dignity and power, because he never dies; nevertheless, while he lives many other inferiors are ordained who are his vicars and assistants. We also see in the temporal kingdom, where a king lives for some time, he is never succeeded, although he usually has many viceroys or ministers through whom he pronounces the law in different provinces.

2) The *second* argument of Calvin is like this: An altar cannot be raised since it would overturn the cross of Christ, nor can the sacrifice of the Mass be offered without injury to the sacrifice of the cross. The sacrifice of the cross has infinite and eternal force; therefore, we do not need another sacrifice; thus, to multiply so many sacrifices of the Mass is nothing other than to deny the virtue and sufficiency of the sacrifice of the cross. Nor does the escape of some avail, who say the repetition of this

sacrifice is necessary so that the force of the first oblation of the sacrifice of the cross would be applied to individuals. Really, the means instituted by Christ are sufficient for this application, namely the preaching of the word and the administration of the Lord's Supper. The Apostle confirms all of these things from Hebrews 9:25 and 10:10, where we read that Christ appeared once through immolation; likewise we are sanctified once by the will of God through the oblation of the cross; likewise Christ, with one oblation consummated the sanctified forever, then once the remission of sins was acquired, no further oblation remains. Lastly, we add the voice of Christ, John 19:30, "It has been consummated," with which words the Lord witnesses that with his one sacrifice whatever was needed for our salvation was carried out and completed.

I respond: What the Apostle says in Romans 3:31 about the law and faith, "Do we then destroy the law through faith? God forbid, rather we establish the law." We can say the same thing about the cross and the Mass. We never overturn the cross by the Mass; God forbid, rather, we establish the cross. For how would the Mass overturn the cross when it is nothing other than the continual commemoration of the cross? But to the argument: We affirm the sacrifice of the cross has infinite and eternal force to sacrifice, and we also concede that it follows from there, that there is no need for another sacrifice of the cross, or a repetition of the same sacrifice of the cross; i.e. we have no need for another Christ to die for us, or that the same Christ to die again and again. On the other hand, we do deny that it follows that sacrifices representing the sacrifice of the cross and applying its fruit to us cannot be multiplied without injury to the cross of Christ. If it were so, not only would Masses be abolished, but we would also prove that the sacrifices of the Old Testament were carried out in injury to the cross of Christ. For the sacrifice of the cross cannot only have force to sanctify men in the future, but also *in the past*, which is why it is said that the lamb slain from the beginning of the world (Apocalypse 13:8). So those consequents of Calvin: The sacrifice of the cross is the most perfect, therefore an altar cannot be raised because the cross of Christ is overturned; for, if something would avail against the altar of the Church it will also avail against the altar of the Synagogue; we do not say with the Manicheans that the Old Testament raised so many altars in insult to the cross of Christ so that we might yield to Calvin.

Moreover, that which Calvin adds, that the fruit of the cross is sufficiently applied through the preaching of the Word and the

Book I, Ch. XXV: Calvin is Answered 141

administration of the Lord's Supper, hence there is no need for the sacrifice of the Mass, concludes nothing. In the first place, by the same argument I might prove the Lord's Supper is unnecessary, because the fruit of the cross is sufficiently applied in Baptism. I might even be able to show that Baptism is redundant, because faith could be aroused by the preaching of the Word alone, whereby the fruit of the cross is applied. As a result, it pleased God to institute different means whereby we might obtain the fruit of the cross more easily, sweetly and fully, and we contend that one of these is the sacrifice of the Mass. And still our adversaries have not been able to show the contrary. Next, even if the sacrifice of the Mass were not necessary, or useful to apply the fruit of the Cross, still it would not follow that it is in injury of the cross, which Calvin meant to show, nay more, it would not follow that it is not necessary. It would still be necessary to constitute religion, which cannot exist without an outward sacrifice, to honor God with the supreme worship due to him alone, to commemorate the sacrifice of the cross, and other purposes which we have spoken of above.

The passages drawn from Paul are easily answered. Those words in Hebrews 9:25, "Nor that he should offer himself often," etc., by the consensus of all the commentators on this passage must be received in regard to a *bloody* oblation. Right after that Paul adds in verse 26, "Otherwise he should have suffered often from the beginning of the world." Thus, the sense is: Christ did not enter into heaven through the first offering of himself, i.e. through his death, and then go out, and by offering himself, and dying, enter in again, and repeating this often, just as the Levitical priest was entering the sanctuary through a victim, and was going out and, again and again entering through another victim, and then going out; otherwise it would be necessary that Christ offer himself from the beginning of the world for each generation and to suffer death; rather by one oblation, i.e. by one death, he cleansed the sins of the whole world and opened the entrance to heaven for all men. So, we see the Apostle does not exclude any repetition of the oblation of Christ, but only that which *requires his death*.

So also, those words of Hebrews 10:10, "We are sanctified through the oblation of the body of Christ once," and those of verse 14, "By one oblation he perfected forever those who are sanctified," must similarly be understood in regard to a *bloody* oblation. The sense is: We are sanctified through the one death of Christ, nay more we are also perfected, obtain not only the remission of sins, but even the trappings of justice, and beatitude itself, and this forever, i.e. for every age and generation, so that now we do not need another Christ who shall redeem us by his death, or that the same Christ should die often for us or for others.

Moreover, what we find in verse 18, "Where there is a remission of sins, there is no more an oblation for sin," which our adversaries continually raise in argument, if it proves anything, it only proves that after the sacrifice of the cross there is no place for any *propitiatory* sacrifice, but not any sacrifice absolutely; for there are many sacrifices truly and properly speaking which are not propitiatory. This is why Calvin does not cite Paul very faithfully to argue there is no further oblation, when Paul said very clearly there is no oblation *for sin*.

Now, we do not admit that it can be gathered from this passage that the Mass is not a propitiatory sacrifice or an oblation for sin. For two things are required for the remission of sins. *a)* One, that the price of liberation is found, or the just satisfaction that is also due to divine justice; *b)* Second, that the price be applied to men in particular. What attains to the *first*, the sacrifice of the cross remitted all sins, past, present and future, accordingly it acquired the most sufficient price for the sins of the whole world, and so, after that sacrifice was carried out, and sins were remitted, no similar oblation remains for sin, i.e. for acquiring the price for the remission of sins. And it is this alone that the Apostle writes in that passage. Insofar as the *second*, the remission of all sins had not yet taken place; for there still are and will be even to the end of the world, men for whom the price of liberation and the remission of sins must be applied, and therefore, the victim remains for sin, namely the sacrifice of the Mass.

Someone will say: It seems that when the Apostle says, "Now there is no oblation for sin," he considers the Jewish sacrifices which were said to be for sin, and he teaches those sacrifices are all abrogated, since the remission of sins has already been carried out; therefore, Paul not only excludes a new oblation whereby the price is acquired, but all other oblations for sin, even if they are only representative of and applicable to the sacrifice of the cross.

I respond: We are not compelled to say the Apostle considered the Jewish sacrifices; for his teaching only demands this, that once the price for the remission of sins was acquired, an oblation to acquire that price is not required. Nevertheless, it can be conceded that Paul looked to those sacrifices of the old law not as they were representative, and in some manner applicable to the sacrifice of the cross, but as they were *figures and promises of the future sacrifice*; for after the sacrifice of the cross was completed and the price acquired, the figures promising it were in vain, because now we have it. However, the fact that Paul does not exclude sacrifices that were representative of and applicable to the sacrifice of the cross is manifestly clear from the fact that otherwise one would be able to exclude Baptism and the Lord's Supper, which are also Sacraments representing and applying the fruit of the cross; nay more, the word, and faith, and prayer and all means or instruments whereby the fruit of the cross is applied. For we can argue this way: Through the cross all sins have been remitted, therefore all instruments of justification are in vain.

Next, Calvin incorrectly uses "It has been consummated." It does not mean, as he dreams up, that by the singular oblation of the cross everything which was necessary for our salvation is consummated and completed, as if everything else, doctrine, sacraments, examples and all labors are redundant and meet their end at the cross. Rather, it means, as Chrysostom, Augustine, Cyril, Theophylactus and others explain, the punishments and afflictions which were going to be suffered in the flesh were completed, because they fell on the same man, the oracles of the prophets were completed, which foretold his passion.

3) The *third* argument of Calvin is taken from the fact that the sacrifice of the Mass would cast the one death of Christ into oblivion, and cast it out from the memory of men. For the confirmation of the Testament depends upon the death of the testator; therefore, the confirmation of the Testament of Christ depends upon the death of Christ. But the Mass is a new Testament, nay more, there are as many Testaments as there are Masses, consequently, that they be ratified, it is necessary for Christ to die as often as Mass is said; therefore, that one death of Christ is either not believed, or comes to nothing. Besides, it is necessary for the victim which is offered to be killed and broken; so, if Christ is sacrificed in each Mass, it is necessary for him to be cruelly killed every moment in a thousand places. Nor does it avail, if they would answer that the sacrifice of the Mass is ἀναίμακτον (bloodless); for it does not depend on the will of men to change the nature of sacrifice, and the Apostle says, "Without the effusion of blood there is no remission."

I respond: If Catholics were to say Christ truly dies in the sacrifice of the Mass, Calvin's argument would seem to have some force; but they all say that Christ does not die except in *the sacrament*, or in the *sign* representing that one death, in which he died. Only, far be it that the Mass would cause men to forget the death of Christ, it would rather more bring it about that it should never be forgotten. But Calvin says, "If the Papists would say that they do not want to kill Christ, nor could, nevertheless it follows that they prove our arguments from their own dogma." Let us see whether this is so.

The *first* argument from the word Testament proves nothing. The Mass is not a new institution of the Testament of Christ, rather it is *a repetition* of the same thing which Christ once did, and confirmed by his death. In the same way among men, when a testament has been confirmed by death, more often than not it is shown in court, and recited, or even described to apply to this or that heir, it is not necessary that the testator should die again. It is enough if it is certain that the testator is dead, and he did not revoke or alter his testament before death.

But on the other hand, Calvin struggles to prove that individual Masses are new testaments, i.e. different from that testament which Christ made in the beginning and confirmed by his death. He says, "Individual Masses promise a new remission of sins and a new acquisition of justice; therefore, there are as many new and diverse testaments as there are Masses."

I respond: The remission of sins and the acquisition of justice which the Mass promises, in respect to what is promised, which it did not have beforehand; but in respect to the sacrifice of the cross, on which Calvin should speak, it is not new, but rather is the very thing which has been produced by the sacrifice of the cross. As we have often said, the sacrifice of the Mass applies the fruit of the sacrifice of the cross. Moreover, the whole error of our adversaries is in this, that they have falsely persuaded themselves that we attribute to the Mass the force to remit sins without any order to the sacrifice of the cross.

Now I answer that argument from the slaying of the victim: The sacrifice of the Mass is the truest sacrifice, and still it does not drive out the true slaying of the victim. For killing is only required in the oblation of a living thing and which is offered in the form of a living thing; just as when lambs, bulls, birds and similar things are offered, the destruction of which consists in death. But when the form of the sacrifice is lifeless, like bread, wine, incense and similar things, killing cannot be required, but only *the consumption* of that thing is appropriate. Consequently, in the Mass, Christ is indeed offered, who is a living thing, and is offered in the form of a living thing so much as representation, where only a representative death is required, but not a real death; but as it is a real sacrifice, properly speaking, it is offered in the form of bread and wine according to the order of Melchisedech, and hence in the form of a lifeless thing. Wherefore, in the Canon, where the words of the principal oblation are found after the consecration, we say: "We offer the bread of eternal life and the chalice of eternal salvation." This is why the consumption of this sacrifice should not be killing, but *eating*.

Now, to that, "without the effusion of blood no remission takes place," I respond: The Apostle speaks on the sacrifice of the Old Law, in which there was no sacrifice for sin without the effusion of blood. For he also says in Hebrews 9:22, "Almost all things, *according to the law*, are cleansed with blood; and without the shedding of blood there is no remission."

Besides, the teaching of Paul can also be received absolutely and generally, not that as often as remission is made, then it is necessary for blood to be shed, but that remission never takes place except *in virtue of the effusion of blood*, whether it takes place now, or already has, or is going to take place.

Then, in the sacrifice of the Mass, it can rightly be said that the blood of Christ is shed, as the Lord himself says, "This is my blood which is shed for you," or we may consider it a mystical effusion of blood, or a real effusion, that is, an offering or oblation of the Lord's blood. In the use according to the Scriptures, the bread is said to be broken when it is distributed, even if the loaves are given whole; so also the wine can be said to be poured, when it is distributed, although full cups are given, and in the same way the body under the species of bread is broken, and the blood shed under the species of wine while it is offered and given to God in sacrifice.

4) The *fourth* argument of Calvin is taken from the fruit of the death of Christ: The Mass snatches away from us the fruit of the death of Christ, while we do not recognize and consider what it does. For who will believe he has been redeemed by the death of Christ where he sees a new redemption in the Mass? Who trusts that his sins have been remitted where he sees a new remission?

I respond: This argument is not very different from the previous ones; for it rests upon a false foundation, that in the opinion of Catholics, the Mass has the force of expiating sins without the sacrifice of the cross. For if we were to say this, Calvin would quite correctly gather that the Mass snatches away from us the fruit of the death of Christ. But because no Catholics teach that, Calvin merely punches the air.

Otherwise, he still insists: "It will not do to say that the only reason for which we obtain the forgiveness of sins in the Mass is that it has already been purchased by the death of Christ. For this is the same thing as to boast that we are redeemed by Christ on the condition that we redeemed ourselves."

I respond: It is a marvelous boldness, or perhaps malice, of this man that he has not yet been able, or certainly refuses to understand the teaching of Catholics. For in the first place, the Mass is not our work, rather it is *Christ's*; he is the true priest who offers sacrifice through ministers, and through it purges and remits sins. This is why even if the Mass had the force *per se* without the sacrifice of the cross, still we would not redeem ourselves, rather, Christ would redeem us. Next, we do not make the comparison in this way, as Calvin does incorrectly, of the passion of Christ with the sacrifice of the Mass, that we would say from the passion of Christ we only take the example of redemption. For we say from the passion of Christ the whole price of redemption has been acquired, and on that account we are all redeemed by that death, which pertains *to the sufficiency of the price paid for all*; however, through the sacrifice of the Mass that price is applied, as it is also applied through the sacraments, although in one way or another, as we will say in the proper place later on. Therefore, just as the one who baptizes is not said to merely take up an example of redemption from the passion of Christ, nor to properly redeem, but merely apply the price acquired by the passion, so also it should be considered in regard to the sacrifice of the Mass.

5) The *fifth* argument has already been answered, as it advances nothing apart from that which Luther was saying, that the same thing cannot be received and given. That is all the arguments from the *Institutes*. He adds two others in the *Antidoto Parisiensis*, art. 6, which can be briefly answered.

The *first* is this: "The institution of Christ so has: 'Take, and eat,' but not 'offer', consequently, there is no sacrifice from the institution of Christ, rather it is plainly opposed with it."

I respond: There is nowhere that we read Christ had said: Do not offer," but if we did the sacrifice of the Mass truly would be opposed to the institution of Christ. But if Calvin would insist on the fact that Christ did not say "offer", that has already been answered above, both because nothing can be gathered from a pure negation, and Christ clearly commanded it to be offered, when he said, "Do this."

The *second* argument from this tract is the following: "No man should take up the honor of the priesthood unless he has been called by God, as the Apostle witnesses. But no one apart from Christ is read to have been called."

I respond: Since Christ called the apostles to the honor of the priesthood with these words: "Do this", no man can say they were not called by God, except one that would deny Christ is God. Moreover, those who succeed the Apostles by legitimate ordination are no less reckoned to be called by God than formerly they were judged to be called by God who were substituted for Aaron by carnal generation.

CHAPTER XXVI
The Objections of Chemnitz Are Answered

MARTIN CHEMNITZ, in *The Examination of the Council of Trent* (2 part. Pag. 800 et seq.) proposes his arguments under the heading: "Arguments showing the abomination of the Popish Mass." There are six arguments.

1) The first is of this sort: "To institute worship outside of the word of God and without the word of God is vain, nay more idolatry, since it is written: 'They worship me in vain with mandates and doctrines of men.' But the theatrical representation through words, rites, gestures, just as it is done in a Popish Mass, has no authority from the word of God, nor an example of Christ or the Apostles. Popish writers affirm that the Apostles only used the Lord's prayer in the celebration of the Supper, and they note which Roman Pontiffs conjured up individual acts and stages of mystical drama and in what time, etc."

I respond: We have often discussed the proposition of this argument in other disputations. Moreover, in this citation, even if the proposition were true, still nothing concludes the argument, for there is a defect in the assumption. As we have often said, our question is not on the ceremonies of the Mass, but on *the substance of the sacrifice*; moreover, we proved above from the testimonies of Scripture, the Fathers and the whole Church that it was instituted by Christ.

2) The *second* argument of Chemnitz: "To transfer the Sacraments from what was instituted by Christ into another action different from the whole kind, is a monstrous sin. Christ prescribed an action of a sacrament, and not of a sacrifice in the words of institution; therefore, the Popish Mass is an insult."

I respond: The assumption of the argument needs to be proved; for it is false, as we showed above and with clear argumentation.

3) The *third* argument: "Since Christ was about to die, he instituted the administration of the Supper in the form of a Testament. Moreover, it is a great crime, even for the testament of men, when someone rearranges it when it has already been ratified and confirmed; therefore, it is manifest that the Popish Mass, which reorders something in the Testament of the Son of God, is a great crime."

I respond: The last bit needs to be proven. That the Mass reorders something in the Testament of the Son of God is false, seeing that the

Mass is nothing else but the repetition of a thing which Christ, when he was about to die, commanded to be repeated. But it is easy for our adversaries to pour out words, even when they have nothing whereby they can prove what they say.

4-6) The *fourth* argument: "The Pontifical Mass is opposed with the Sacrifice of the cross, etc." The *fifth:* "The Mass is opposed to the sole priesthood of Christ, etc." The *sixth:* "The Mass obscures the Lord's Supper, and the other means instituted by Christ to apply the fruit of the passion of Christ." *I respond:* All of these are taken from the *Institutes* of Calvin, and we answered them in the last chapter.

CHAPTER XXVII
The Last Objection Is Answered, and it Is Explained in What Part Of the Mass the Essence of Sacrifice Properly Consists

IN THE LAST place a certain objection must be answered, some of which the heretics make to attack the Mass, and some of which Catholics make to explain the matter better.

If the Mass is a sacrifice, properly speaking, certainly in some part the notion of a sacrifice, properly speaking, will be found and explained by the definition above; but there is no part of it where it is shown in this way. After the Mass of the Catechumens, which certainly does not consist of the notion of the sacrifice, five parts are found. *Firstly*, the oblation of bread and wine; *secondly*, the consecration and changing of the bread into the body, and the wine into the blood of the Lord. *Thirdly*, the oblation of the body and blood by express words. *Fourthly*, the breaking and mingling of the Sacrament. *Fifthly*, the distribution and consumption of the same. That the sacrifice of the Mass does not consist in the oblation of the bread and wine is beyond controversy; for earthly things cannot be that one sacrifice which the Fathers affirm flourishes in the Church in place of all the ancient sacrifices.

In the consecration, which is the *second* part, no oblation appears which has the intrinsic notion of a sacrifice. Besides, there is no sensible change of the thing which is offered during the consecration. Such a change seems altogether to pertain to the outward notion of the sacrifice.

The oblation of the body and blood, namely the *third* part, which follows the consecration, cannot pertain to the essence of the Mass; hence the notion of a sacrifice should not be constituted in it. For Christ the Lord, whom we hold to be the author of this sacrifice, distributed the sacrament immediately after the consecration and commanded it to be eaten. For he says, "Take and eat, this is my body." Therefore, there was no time in which the Lord could offer the consecrated bread to God. Then, if it is true what St. Gregory writes (*Epistles*, 7, 63), the Apostles merely added the Lord's prayer to the words of consecration, certainly not even they made that oblation which we make after the consecration; as a result, that oblation does not pertain to the essence of the sacrifice.

Moreover, the breaking (*fractio*), which is the *fourth* part, without a doubt does not have the Lord as an author. For the Lord indeed broke the

Book I, Ch. XXVII: The Essence of the Sacrifice

bread, but he broke it either before the consecration, as many hold, or immediately after to distribute it to the disciples. But our breaking takes place after the consecration with many actions interposed, and it is not done for distribution, but to show a certain mystery.

Next, the eating, or consumption, does not properly seem to be a sacrifice, since it is done by the priest alone. And although it may pertain to the essence of a sacrifice, still the whole essence of the sacrifice cannot be constituted in that alone. For without oblation and dedication preceding, it cannot be a sacrifice. Moreover, this is the reason why among Catholics, during the Good Friday liturgy it is not thought that the sacrifice of the Mass is properly celebrated, although a true host is present and it is broken and consumed, because there is no consecration and oblation.

I respond: For us to explain the whole matter easily and briefly, two things must be made clear. *First*, what the sacrifice of the Mass properly is, by receiving the sacrifice for that which is sacrificed. Then, what the sacrifice of the Mass properly is, by receiving the sacrifice for the action of sacrificing. Both will be made clear from the following opinions, or propositions.

1) The first proposition: *It should not be denied that the bread and wine are offered in some manner during Mass, and hence pertain to the thing which is sacrificed.* This is clear *firstly* from the liturgy itself. For when we say before the consecration, "Receive, O Holy Father, this immaculate host," certainly the pronoun *this* shows the sense of the "it" which we then hold in our hands; the *it* is bread. And in the liturgy there are several similar sentences which clearly show the bread is offered.

Then, the Fathers everywhere hand down the same thing. Irenaeus (4, 17) says the Church offers the sacrifice from created things, i.e. from bread and wine. Cyprian (*Epistles* 2, 3) says Christ offered the chalice to the Father with wine mixed with water, and in his sermon on Almsgiving, while rebuking rich women who did not offer bread to be consecrated, he says, "You come to the Lord's day rich and opulent without sacrifice, and take the bread from the sacrifice which the poor man offers." There, he understands bread for sacrifice, which was going to be sacrificed to God by the priests. St. Gregory (*Dialogues*, 2, 23), speaking on St. Benedict, says: "Go, and see to it that this oblation is offered to the Lord for them, and they will no longer be excommunicated. Such an oblation was immolated for them, etc." And in 4, 55, he says: "Offer this bread to the all-powerful God for me." Similar sentences are found everywhere.

2) The second proposition: *The body and blood of Christ are that sacrifice which is properly offered and sacrificed in the Mass.* This is most certain and proven by a great many testimonies.

3) The third proposition: *The bread and body of the Lord, the wine and blood of the Lord, are not two sacrifices, but one.* We do not offer bread to God simply, but bread *that has been consecrated and changed* into the Lord's body: nor do we offer the body of the Lord absolutely, for then, it should either be a bloody sacrifice, or really no sacrifice; rather we offer the Lord's body *in the species of bread*, confected from bread. Therefore, just as the Jews offered living sheep, and even dead ones, and although the living and the dead differ by species, if they seemed physically to be the same by nature, still it was one sacrifice, not two; for the living sheep was being offered to be consecrated to God by death, and then to be consumed by fire. So also, although the bread and body of the Lord are different things, if they are considered by nature, nevertheless they make one sacrifice because the bread is going to be changed into the Lord's body, or the Lord's body offered to God in the species of bread. Besides, it is from here that in the Mass bread is not offered as a perfect sacrifice, but as an *inchoate* sacrifice and *to be perfected*, as is clear from those words: "Bless this sacrifice prepared unto your holy name." And in the Secrets, we read as often: "The gift we offer to be consecrated by you." This is why Irenaeus most rightly says, "He declared the chalice to be his blood and he taught it was the new oblation of the new Testament." (4, 17). There, the oblation of the New Testament is properly called wine changed into the blood of the Lord.

From here, note all those passages of the Fathers who teach the sacrifice of the Church is one, which succeeds the whole multitude of ancient sacrifices: Leo (*serm. 8 de passione Domini*), John Chrysostom (*in Psalm 95*), and Augustine (*de Spiritu et litera*, 11, 3; *Contra Donatistas*; *de Baptismo*, last chapter; *contra advers. Leg. et prophet.* 1, 20; *Crontra Cresconium* 1, 25; *De Civitate Dei* 8, 27).

Hence it is clear how improbable the opinion of Gaspar Cassali (*de sacrificio*, 1, 20) is, which affirms there are two sacrifices of the Eucharist, one of the bread and one of the wine, one the Lord's body the other his blood.

4) The fourth proposition: *The oblation of bread and wine preceding the consecration pertains to the integrity and fullness of the sacrifice, but still not to its essence.* The fact that it does not pertain to its essence seems to be beyond controversy. For the vocal oblation, as we showed above, is

not necessary for a sacrifice; it is enough if he demonstrates to God that he offers something which he *really* offers. And although some oblation necessarily requires the essence of the sacrifice, still it is not necessary that it precedes the immolation; for the oblation can be the oblation itself. Moreover, from the fact that it pertains to a certain integrity, it is clear that in all liturgies, no matter how ancient, Greek or Latin, part of the action is the oblation of things that are going to be consecrated. And although the Lord did not offer bread to be consecrated in those words, in the manner whereby we offer it, nevertheless he offered *in some manner*, as Cyprian clearly writes (*Epistles*, 2, 3) and it is gathered from the ceremonies of lifting the eyes to heaven and giving thanks, which the Lord did before the consecration, which is witnessed partly by the Evangelists, and partly by the most ancient liturgies.

5) The fifth proposition: *The oblation which follows the consecration likewise pertains to the integrity of the Sacrifice, but not the essence.* The fact that it does not pertain to the essence is proved both from the fact that the Lord did not employ that oblation, and neither did the Apostles in the beginning (as is proven by Gregory), and from the fact that the words of this oblation are not said in the person of Christ, but in the person of the minister himself and the Church, as is clear from: *Unde et memores nos servi tui*, etc.[12] Moreover, the sacrifice is principally offered in the person of Christ. Therefore, this oblation being subsequent to the consecration, is a certain witness that the whole Church consents in the oblation made by Christ, and offers it together with him. Moreover, the fact that it pertains to the integrity is clear from the most ancient liturgies which, without a doubt, take their origin from the Apostles. For even if in the beginning the Apostles are said to have only added the Lord's prayer, nevertheless, afterward they had composed the rite of celebration for the same and added many other things, as can be understood from the Liturgies of James and Clement.

6) The sixth proposition: *The breaking of the sacrament does not pertain to the essence, but only to the integrity.*

That it does not pertain to the essence should be clear from the very use of the Church. For if perhaps, when in the sacrament itself, the sign of the cross is expressed over the chalice, the consecrated bread would fall into the chalice, it is not usually broken, but left whole even to the consummation, but still the sacrifice is not believed to have been invalid,

---

12 Translator's note: This prayer immediately follows the consecration in the Roman Canon, or Eucharistic Prayer.

or essentially changed. Add the fact that it does not seem that the Lord used this ceremony, as we said from the beginning. That it pertains to the integrity, is clear from all the Greek and Latin liturgies.

7) The seventh proposition: *The consumption of the Sacrament that is made by the people is not part of the sacrament, but that which is done by the sacrificing priest is the essential part but not the whole essence.* What attains to the people's consumption, is very certain; for those who eat the victims, are partakers of the altar, as the Apostle says in 1 Cor. 10:18 and Hebrews 13:10. But it is not the same to offer sacrifice and participate at the altar. The consumption, however, which the sacrificing priest makes, is not as much a consuming of the victim as it is a consummation of the sacrifice, and is properly considered to correspond to the burning of the holocaust. Therefore, it has always been judged as so necessary by the Church, that if perhaps the priest would die before the consumption, or the consumption were impeded in another way, it will be necessary for another priest to succeed him and consume the sacrifice, as is clear from the Council of Toledo, (12, can. 5) and from the rubrics of the Mass.

The fact that it is an essential part, is because in the whole action of the Mass (as we will demonstrate soon), there is no other real destruction of the victim apart from this; a real destruction is required, as we proved above, when we constituted the definition. This is why Abraham the Patriarch, although he had taken his son and set him upon the altar, and took up his hand to sacrifice him, because still a real slaughter was absent, it is not said that he sacrificed, except in will. Nor is it opposed that the very consumption does not seem to take place in the person of Christ, who is still the primary priest. For Christ indeed does not eat himself, nor did he immediately consume the Sacrament; nevertheless, he can be said to consume because *he gives it to be consumed.* In just the same way in the sacrifice of the cross Christ himself truly sacrifices himself, because he offered himself to be killed, although he did not kill himself. For even in the Old Testament, from the notion of a holocaust there was combustion, which still was not done immediately by the priest, but by fire; but the priest is said truly to burn the victim when he adds fire to it.

8) The eighth proposition: *The Consecration of the Eucharist pertains to the essence of the sacrifice.* This opinion has been proposed so generally because it has many authors. For among the Greeks Nicholas Cabasilas clearly teaches it in his explanation of the Sacred Liturgy (cap. 32) and from the Latins, Rudyard Tapper (*in defensione articul. 16 Lovaniensuium*);

Book I, Ch. XXVII: The Essence of the Sacrifice

Jodocus Tiletanus (*responsione ad Apologiam Illyrici*, 15); Gaspar Casalius (*de sacrificio*, 1, 20); Alanus (*de sacrificio* lib. 2 cap. 15) and others, but not everyone explains it in the same manner.

Some think, therefore, the essence of a sacrifice consists in the consecration, because through the consecration there is a true and real change of bread into the body of Christ; moreover, a true sacrifice requires a true and real change of this sort in which the thing would cease to exist, for the honor of God.

But this opinion has no light arguments against it. For, in the first place, if it were true, it would follow that bread alone is properly sacrificed. For a sacrifice is properly called what is really changed, so that it would cease to exist; but the bread is only changed. Moreover, nobody can deny that it is quite absurd, because if it were so, then the Church would have a lifeless sacrifice, and one of much less value than what the Jews had. Next, the change which is placed as if it were the form of the sensible and outward sacrifice should be outward and sensible. But the change of bread into the Body of Christ is altogether internal and not perceptible to any of the senses, except only by faith. Thirdly, the sacrifice of the Church would not be the same as the sacrifice of the cross in regard to the thing offered; nor would it be true, what the Fathers say, that in the sacrifice of the Mass, the sacrifice and the priest are the same; nor that which Chrysostom, Ambrose, Primasius and others note in their commentaries on Hebrews 10, that the sacrifices of the Jews were many, because they offered one lamb today, and another tomorrow, but ours is one because we always offer the same Christ, for even we, if we were to use bread, would not offer the same thing.

Others would have it, therefore, that the essence of sacrifice consists in the consecration, but through it truly, although mystically, Christ is immolated in an unbloody manner. For, when by the force of the words, "This is my body," only the body of Christ without soul and blood will begin to be on the altar; and by the force of the other words, "This is the blood" the blood alone begins and is apart from the body on the altar. Where the true body and blood are separated, there is a certain true immolation; certainly, it follows by the force of the whole consecration that Christ is truly immolated, and still the immolation is unbloody because the natural concomitance[13] prevents the blood or the soul would be truly separated from the body.

This opinion does not seem to satisfy the matter in a way to put

---

13 Translator's note: For more on natural concomitance, see St. Thomas, III, q. 76.

the mind at rest. For in the first place, the true and real sacrifice, and the real death or destruction of the thing immolated would be wanting; moreover, the consecration is not a true and real death, but only mystical in its effects. Nor does it seem enough to answer those who say the consecration of itself conveys a true death, rather, it happens through the natural concomitance, that a real death would not follow. For if the natural concomitance impeded death, by this very fact it impedes the sacrifice. Certainly if in the time of the Old Testament, a priest who was going to immolate the lamb were ready to kill it so that he could sacrifice of himself, but then some impediment would appear and the lamb would not be slaughtered, then it would not be said that sacrifice was really carried out, except in the will.

Besides, if through the consecration a true and real immolation took place, still, it would not thereby happen on the altar, but in heaven. The immolation is said to be done in that place where the living animal is killed, but the place where this division of the body of Christ from the soul, and blood (if such a thing takes place by the sacramental words), would not be on the altar, but in heaven. There, the division should be done, where the matter was before the division. Christ, however was in heaven before that division, not on the altar. Consequently, according to this teaching the immolation did not take place on the altar, but only parts of what was immolated are placed on the altar after the immolation. But who would concede that the immolation, which is the sacrifice of the Christian religion, is not celebrated on earth but only in heaven?

Next, in the Mass there is either the true and real sacrifice and slaying of Christ, or there is not. If there is not, the Mass is not a true and real sacrifice; for a true and real sacrifice demands a true and real slaying, seeing that the essence of a sacrifice is placed in that killing. Moreover, if that happened, it would be true to say Christ is really and truly killed by Christian priests; but this is clearly a sacrilege, not a sacrifice.

So, after omitting these, I think the matter must be explained this way. In the consecration of the Eucharist there are three things in which the notion of a true and real sacrifice consists. *First*: The profane matter is consecrated; for bread is an otherwise earthly and common thing, but through the consecration it is turned into the body of Christ, the most sacred thing of all.

Someone will say: From this it seems to follow that only bread is properly sacrificed, because what we said above is absurd. The fact that something becomes sacred from the profane, it is properly sacrificed;

Book I, Ch. XXVII: The Essence of the Sacrifice

therefore, if bread becomes sacred from profane, bread will properly be sacrificed.

I respond: The fact is, it becomes so sacred from the profane that what remains, is without a doubt properly sacrificed. Moreover, among the Jews, when a sheep was being consecrated and the same sheep was being sacrificed, because it remained the same even after death, at least in regard to the material part, and a sheep is described both living and dead. But the bread does not remain while it is consecrated, rather it is turned into something else, and consequently, it is not bread, but that which it becomes from bread that is properly sacrificed.

Secondly, in the consecration that thing which has been consecrated from the profane is offered to God, while it is placed on the altar of God. For, as we said above, to place the victim on the altar is really to offer it to God, and because by the force of consecration it happens that the body and blood of Christ begins to really be upon the altar by the medium of the hand of the priest, so by the words of consecration a true and solemn oblation is celebrated. Now, the fact that at some time the sacrifice was celebrated without an altar is not opposed to what we just said. For here we do not make a disputation on the altar stone, rather, we call everything an altar where *the victim that was effected by the words of consecration* is received. Nor is it opposed that it would seem to be an oblation of an invisible thing, although still, an external and sensible victim is required in an external sacrifice, properly speaking. For, the body of Christ is not a victim in the sacrifice of the Mass absolutely, but as it is *in the species of bread*, moreover it is visible in the species of bread.

Thirdly, through the consecration, the thing which is offered is prepared for a true, real and external change and destruction which was necessary for the notion of the sacrifice. For, through the consecration, the body of Christ receives the form of food, moreover, the food through consumption and through this it is ordered to this change and destruction. It is also not opposed that the body of Christ suffers no wound in itself, and the Eucharist does not lose its nature when it is eaten, for it ceases to be *sacramental*, and hence it ceases really to be on the altar, when it ceases to be sensible food.

St. Thomas seems to be of the same opinion as I, since in II IIæ q. 85, art. 3, when he teaches that it pertains to the notion of the sacrifice that something should become in regard to the matter offered as the animals that were killed and burned to the honor of God; he did not add that which takes place in the sacrifice of the Mass consists in the conversion of the bread and the body of the Lord, but in the fraction, benediction and consumption of the bread.

After prefacing this explanation, our eighth and last proposition is proved. *Firstly*, because the sacrifice of Mass is offered *in persona Christi*; moreover, the priest does nothing as clearly *in persona Christi* as the consecration, in which he says, "This is my body."

Secondly, because Christ himself offered sacrifice either by consecrating and consuming, or he did not offer sacrifice in any manner. As we showed above, it is nothing other than the action of Christ which can be called the sacrifice, either before or after the consecration.

Thirdly, because in the beginning the Apostles, if they added nothing to the words of consecration apart from the Lord's prayer, it is necessary that by consecrating they offered sacrifice; and the Lord's prayer cannot be called a sacrifice.

Fourthly, because the representation of the sacrifice of the cross consists in the consecration, as St. Thomas teaches (III q. 80, art. 12 ad 3). But at the same time there should be real and representative sacrifices; accordingly, the real itself is representative of the other.

Fifthly, because this is the teaching of the ancient Fathers. For Irenaeus (4, 17) says Christ then taught the oblation of the New Testament, which the Church repeats throughout the world, when he says "This is my body." Cyprian, in his sermon *de Coena Domini*, says that when the bread is blessed in the words of Consecration, then the Eucharist becomes at the same time our nourishment and a holocaust. Chrysostom in his homily on the treason of Judas, says the words of the Lord: "This is my body" furnish the foundation for sacrifice until the end of the world. Gregory (*Dialogues*, 4, 58) when he says in the very hour of immolation that the choirs of angels are present at the words of the priest, heaven is opened, nay more joined with the highest, one thing is made from the visible and the invisible, he clearly teaches the immolation takes place in the consecration. For that is the hour in which Christ truly begins to be on the altar under the species of bread at the words of the priest; for the lowest is joined to the highest, earth is aligned with heaven, and one thing is made from visible and invisible; nor is there any doubt that on account of the presence of Christ, the Angels come down to earth from heaven. Thus, enough has been said on the first controversy.

ON THE MOST HOLY SACRIFICE OF THE MASS
BOOK II

ON THE MOST HOLY SACRIFICE OF THE MASS

BOOK II

CHAPTER I
We Lay Down the First Controversy: Whether the Mass is a Propitiatory Sacrifice

SINCE the primary controversy has been put to rest, others follow that are certainly briefer, and easier, but still, in which we agree even less with our adversaries than in the first. This is the second controversy: *What kind of sacrifice the Mass may be: Only Eucharistic and honorary, or is it also propitiatory and impetratory?* For, as in the beginning of the first book of the last treatise, it was explained that there are three kinds of sacrifices, or rather more four, seeing that the last of the three is divided into two kinds. *One* is that in Scripture it is called a holocaust, which is also λουτρευτικόν, and can be called honorary, of the end which is the sole worship and honor of God. The second is called in Scripture a sacrifice for sin, which is also called propitiatory; whose end is apart from the worship of God, a propitiation of the wrath of God and a remission of sins. The *third*, in Scripture it is called a peace-offering, and this is twofold: one is the Eucharist, that is what has been offered for thanks giving for benefits received; the other can be called in the common terminology impetratory, whose purpose is impetration of a benefit.

Our adversaries easily concede the Mass is a sacrifice εὐχαριστικὸν (of thanksgiving) and λατρευτικόν (of worship), but they would not allow that it is a sacrifice properly speaking, but rather improperly, and broadly speaking, as we showed above. They argue that the very distribution and consumption of the Eucharist is done in honor of God, and in the action of thanksgiving for the benefit of the passion of Christ that has been received. These things are fitting for the Eucharist even if it is nothing other than a Sacrament. Moreover, they do not, by any reasoning, admit that it is a propitiatory and impetratory especially for anyone other than the very ones who receive it, nor could they unless they would affirm the Eucharist is not merely a sacrament, but also a sacrifice properly speaking; for the Sacraments do not benefit anyone other than those who receive it. See Luther *de cap. Babyl.*, 1, *Apologia Confess. August.*, in art. *De Missa*; *Wittenberg Confession*, cap. 16, (which is on the Eucharist). Likewise, John Calvin (*Instit.* 4, 18 §13-16), as well as

Chemnitz (*Exam. Conc. Trid.* 2 part, sess. 22 cap. *de Missa*).

The Catholic Church of Christ teaches, and has always taught the contrary. The Council of Trent, to thoroughly declare the whole matter (sess. 22 ch. 2), specifically taught that the sacrifice of the Mass is not only propitiatory for punishment, but even for sins, not only for light faults, but also for grave ones, even mortal sins, for it shows this when it says: "Crimes and sins, even heinous ones." Besides, an impetratory sacrifice is not only for spiritual benefits, but even temporal ones, and so, it can be offered for sins, punishments, and for any and all necessities. To defend and explain such an opinion in order, we will prove: 1) The sacrifice of the Mass is propitiatory; 2) it is impetratory; 3) we will show that both are suited to it *ex opere operato*, and we will briefly explain what is the proper essence of the sacrifice; 4) we will answer the objections of the heretics.

CHAPTER II
That the Mass Is a Propitiatory Sacrifice Is Proven

THUS, that the sacrifice of the Mass is *propitiatory* is proven:

1) *First*, from the testimonies of the Old Testament. For the Scripture of the Old Testament clearly teaches the sacrifices in the natural and Mosaic law were propitiatory. We read in Job 1:5 that St. Job, who lived according to the natural law, offered sacrifice to God daily for the sins of his children; and in 42:8, God himself commanded Job to offer sacrifices for the sin of his friends. In Leviticus 4:5-6, different sacrifices for sin are described. These and similar testimonies prove that the sacrifice of Mass is propitiatory in three ways: *a) Firstly*, because those sacrifices were types and figures of this our sacrifice, as we proved in the last book.

b) Secondly, because if the sacrifice of the cross, which is uniquely propitiatory, does not prevent the Old Testament sacrifices from being propitiatory in their mode, nor should it prevent the sacrifice of the Church from being propitiatory. For the sacrifice of the cross had force from the beginning of the world, and will have it until the end of the world; moreover, on that account, if it would prevent our sacrifice from being propitiatory, it would also prevent the Old Testament sacrifices, and vice versa, if it does not prevent them, nor should it prevent ours.

c) Thirdly, because our sacrifice is truly and properly speaking a sacrifice, no less than the Old Testament sacrifices (as we showed in the last book), it is also a commemorative sacrifice of the Lord's passion, just as they were, even more expressly than they were. Lastly, does it not contain a victim more pleasing to God than they? What reason can there by why the former could be said to be propitiatory, and the latter cannot?

Calvin answers (*loc. cit.* 4, 18 §13) that the Old Testament sacrifices are called propitiatory not because they truly made expiation for sins, or pleased God, but because they foreshadowed the coming sacrifice of the cross, whereby sins would truly be cleansed.

But even if the sacrifices of the Old Testament were nothing other than types and shadows, still the answer of Calvin does not satisfy. They were not only types and shadows of the sacrifice of the cross, but even of the sacrifice of the Eucharist. This is why Augustine (*quaest. 56 in Leviticum*) says, "This one sacrifice was shown in those sacrifices, in which a true remission of sins takes place, by taking the blood of that sacrifice as food; not only should no one be forbidden to drink, they should rather more be encouraged." Next, if those sacrifices only showed the coming cleansing, but also did not cleanse in some manner, then the words of scripture (Leviticus 4:26) will be false, which are often repeated: "Let a sacrifice be offered, ... and the priest will pray for his sin and it will be forgiven him." And likewise, what we read in Job 42:8 would be false, where the Lord wanted his wrath placated by sacrifices. Then, those sacrifices did not expiate sins, in regard to fault in the presence of God, as though they would justify and men would be effected friends of God *ex opere operato*: for the Apostle rightly says in Hebrews 10:4 that it is impossible for the blood of goats and calves to take away sins; just the same they made expiation for the legal faults, and also propitiated God in regard to temporal punishments, and even in regard to the faults from the faith of those making the offering, whose protestations of faith were those sacrifices.

2) The second argument is taken from the words of institution. For those words, "This is the blood which is shed for you in remission of sins," clearly teach that Christ offered himself in the Last Supper as a sacrifice for the sins of the Apostles. Moreover, our sacrifice is the same as that which was offered in the Last Supper; for the Lord commanded the Apostles to repeat the same thing afterward.

Besides, the sacrifice of the Mass is a sacrifice applying the promises of the New Testament. Consequently, even in Luke 22:20, it is called the New Testament, as we explained above. But among the promises of the New Testament there is one on the remission of sins, as is clear from Jeremiah 32:40 and Hebrews 8:12.

Lastly, the Lutherans affirm, or rather more contend, that the Eucharist was instituted for the remission of sin; this is why it is necessary to remit sins either as a sacrifice or as a sacrament. And indeed, as a sacrament, it was not properly instituted for the remission of sin, but for *the preservation of spiritual life*. As a sacrament, it does not benefit anyone but *the one receiving it*; moreover, the one receiving it is commanded to prove himself beforehand, nor can he approach with sin on his conscience unless he would eat and drink judgment on himself (1 Cor. 11:29). So, it follows, that the Eucharist was instituted for the remission of sin as *a sacrifice*. And our adversaries do not rightly understand what they say when they argue the Eucharist was instituted for the remission of sin, and still contend it is only a sacrament and not

Book II, Ch. II: Mass is a Propitiatory Sacrifice

also a sacrifice.

3) The third argument is taken from the Apostle, who says in Hebrews 5:1, "For every high priest taken from men is ordained for men in the things that pertain to God, that he may offer gifts and sacrifices for sin." There, we see the particular office of any priest you like is to make an offering for sin. So, if (as we proved in the last book), we have a priesthood and a sacrifice in the Church, it is necessary that we have it to cleanse sins. Besides, just as the Apostle says in Hebrews 10:18 "Where there is a remission of these, there is no longer an oblation for sin," so we can say on the other hand: Where the remission of sins has not yet taken place, still a victim remains for sin. But the remission of sins has not yet taken place, rather it happens daily, and will happen even to the end of the world; consequently, a victim for sin still remains and will remain even to the end of the world.

Secondly, it is proven from the testimonies of the ancient Fathers. James, in his liturgy, says, "We offer the unbloody sacrifice for our sins and the ignorance of the people." Justin, in the *Dialogue with Trypho*, says the sacrifice of a cow that had been offered for lepers, was a figure of the Eucharist, which is offered for the expiation of sins. Origen (*homil. 13 in Leviticum*), when he brought forward the words of the Lord, whereby we are commanded to consecrate the mystery of the Eucharist in his memory, notes: "It is this commemoration alone, which makes God well disposed toward men." Athanasius, in his sermon on the dead, which Damascene cites in his sermon on the same argument, says: "The oblation of the unbloody host is a propitiation." Basil, near the beginning of his liturgy, says, "Make us worthy to stand with a pure heart before you, and to minister to you, and that we may offer this most revered sacrifice to wipe out our faults, and for the sin of your people, etc." Cyril (*Catech. Mystagogica*, 5), calls the Eucharist a victim of propitiation, and later he says, "We offer Christ, slain for our sins, that we may also render him well disposed to us and others, for he is most kind." Chrysostom (*on the priesthood*, 6) says, "The priest has been deputed for all the world that he may intercede and, as an intercessor with God, see to it that he is made propitious not only for all men that are living, but even for the dead." Likewise, in his liturgy, "Strengthen us, O Lord, so that we offer unto you this spiritual and bloodless sacrifice on account of the sins and iniquities of your flock, that you would forgive our sinfulness." He says the same thing in *Homily 3 on Ephesians*, where in every place that he speaks of the sacrifice of the Eucharist, he calls it a salutary victim.

Lastly Damascene (*de Fide*, 4, 14) says that by this sacrifice, the filthy are cleansed of their sins.

From the Latins Cyprian, in his *Sermon on the Lord's Supper*, says that the Eucharist is a holocaust to cleanse our iniquities. Ambrose (*de Officiis*, 1, 48) speaking on the Eucharist, says, "Christ offers himself as a priest to forgive our sins." And in his *Exhortation to Virgins*, in the very last words he calls the sacrifice which is offered on the altar a salutary victim, whereby the sin of this world is destroyed. Jerome (*Comment. In Titus 1*), says: "If laymen are commanded to abstain from sex with their wives on account of prayer, what should be thought about a bishop who daily offers unblemished victims in sacrifice to God for his own sins and those of the people?" See the same in his epistle to Damasus on the prodigal son, and in his *Epistle to Fabiola* on the garb of a priest. Augustine (*quaest. 57 in* Leviticum), says, "In many sacrifices which were offered for sin, this our sacrifice is shown, in which there is a true remission of sins." And in *City of God*, (20, 25) he writes that the sacrifice for sin is offered in the Church even to the day of Judgment, but no later, because after that day there will be no sins which can be remitted. In his work *Contra Cresconium* (1, 25) he calls the sacrifice of the Eucharist the sole sacrifice of our salvation. In *Sermon 11 On the Saints*, which is *4 de Innocentibus*, when speaking on the altar, he says, "There the blood of Christ is shed for sins." Gregory (*Dialog.* 4, 58) says, "This victim singularly saves the soul from eternal ruin." See also homily 37. Bede (*Hist. Ecc. Ang.* 4, 22) says: "This salutary sacrifice avails for the eternal redemption of soul and body."

Let us add the third Council of Braga, which was celebrated before the time of Bede. There, in canon 1, we read: "Although every crime and sin is blotted out by the sacrifices offered to God, something will be given from the rest for the expiation of delicts when there is an error in the very offering of the sacrifice."

Lastly, the there be added all the testimonies that are going to be brought forward in the following controversy, whereby we will prove the sacrifice of the Eucharist is propitiatory for the dead. Those who assert this sacrifice is propitiatory for the dead, necessarily assert it is propitiatory; for the moment, however, we merely take up the proof. Thus, from the testimonies of the Fathers.

CHAPTER III
The Sacrifice of the Mass Is also Impetratory

Now, the fact that the Lord's body is not only a propitiatory sacrifice, and can be offered for the remission of sin, but even that it is *impetratory* for every kind of good thing, and is also rightly offered for these, can easily be proven from the testimonies of Scripture and the Fathers.

Firstly, in the Old Testament there were victims not only for sin, but also as peace-offerings, both for thanksgiving and also a votary for obtaining some benefit, as is clear in Leviticus 7:11 and elsewhere; and David (2 Kings, 24:25) offered a peace offering for averting a plague, and he obtained it. Onias offered a salutary victim to save the temporal life of Heliodorus, which he also obtained in 2 Macc. 3:32. In 1 Ezra 6:17, the Jews immolated victims for the life of King Darius and his sons. This is why, if it is true what several fathers write, that all the differences of the victims of the Old Testament are contained in the one of the Eucharist (Chrysostom in *Psalm 95*; Augustine *contra advers. Legis et prophet.*, 1, 20; Leo *serm. 8 de passione Domini*), then it is necessary that the Eucharist be offered even for obtaining benefits of this sort.

Secondly, what the Apostle writes in 1 Tim. 2:1-2, making supplications, prayers, entreaties, and acts of thanksgiving for kings and all who are on high, that we might live a peaceful and tranquil life, the holy Fathers explain it on the *public* prayers which are in the Mass, meaning the Apostle commanded this so that sacrifice would also be offered for temporal peace and the peace of the Church. See Augustine (*Epist. 59 ad Paulinum*), and the commentaries of Chrysostom, Theophylactus and Oecumenius on this passage, as well as Ambrose (*de Sacramentis*, 6, last chapter).

Thirdly, all the liturgies of James, Clement, Basil, and Chrysostom more than once command that kind to be offered and prayed for an abundance of crops and other temporal benefits.

Fourthly, the ancient writers everywhere witness it. Tertullian (*ad Scapulam*): "We sacrifice for the salvation of the Emperor." And in his work *de Corona*, he writes that the oblation is customarily made for his birthday. Cyril of Jerusalem (*Catechesi Mystagogica* 5), says: "After that spiritual sacrifice has been confected, and that unbloody worship through the very victim of propitiation, we ask God for the common peace of the Churches, for the peace of the world, for kings, for soldiers, for our countrymen, for the sick, and the afflicted, and at length, for all who need help." St. John Chrysostom (*In Acta Apostolorum*, hom. 18 & 21 and other places) often teaches the sacrifice is offered for the fruits of the earth, and for other necessities. St. Augustine (*City of God*, 22, 8) calls to mind the sacrifice of the Eucharist is offered to cleanse the house from the disturbance of demons. Prosper of Aquitaine (*De Praedictionibus Dei*, 6) writes that in his time the sacrifice of the Mass was offered for those possessed by demons, and again for their cure, and again offered in thanksgiving. Gregory the Great (*Hom. 37 in Evangelia*) and Bede (*Hist. Angliae*, 4, 22) write that in different times a miracle took place when the sacrifice of the Mass was offered for a man held captive in another region and, unknowing that it was done for him, his bonds were untied in the very hour of the sacrifice.

Fifthly and lastly, reason itself teaches this, for if the oblation of the Eucharist avails for the forgiveness of sins, certainly it ought to avail also for other necessities which arise from sin. And if God, being pleased by this sacrifice gave favor to his enemies, how much more easily will it be added, on account of the same sacrifice, that he gives good temporal things to his friends and those reconciled if it will be useful for them.

CHAPTER IV
The Proper Efficacy of the Sacrifice of the Mass is Explained

Now it follows that we explain whether the Sacrifice of the Mass has force *ex opere operato*, and at the same time, as we promised, what the proper efficacy of the sacrifice is. Moreover, we must preface three things: *The first* is that the sacrifice of the Mass is offered by three: Christ, the Church, and the minister; but not in the same mode. Christ offers as *the primary* priest, and he offers through a human priest, as through his proper minister. The Church does not offer as a priest through a minister, but as *the people through the priest*. Therefore, Christ offers through the lower, the Church through the higher; for the priest, insofar as he is so much greater than the rest of the people, and indeed who, as a certain mediator, intercedes with God for the people, and is not a minister of the Church in that matter, rather, of *Christ* the principal mediator. It follows from this that the Church does not properly sacrifice by exercising the sacerdotal act, rather, it only offers the thing that is going to be sacrificed to the priest, or sees to it that the sacrifice takes place, or certainly consents to the sacrifice, and offers in will and desire with the priest.

Here, we must also observe that the whole Church offers all the sacrifices which are offered by all the priests, but not in the same mode. Some only offer habitually, those who are away and do not think about sacrifice, but still habitually desire it to be offered; some offer in act, who namely are present at the sacred rites and offer with an actual desire; some besides also offer causally, because they are the causes why the sacrifice is made, whether by exhorting, or asking, or commanding. Lastly, the minister himself offers, as a true priest, but ministerial.

Secondly, we must remember that we often said during the disputation *On the Sacraments in General* that what is done *ex opere operantis* has force because it has force from the goodness, or devotion of the one who carries out the work, so that a work has much, little or no value according to how great, little or no goodness and devotion the one who works it has; such is the value of our prayers and merits. However, something has force *ex opere operato* because it has value of itself, provided it is done just as the law prescribes, irrespective of the goodness or malice of the minister working it, so that a work will always have the same value, nor be done any better from the goodness of the minister, or worse from his iniquity. Not even our adversaries dispute that this is the value of Baptism, although they abhor the term *ex opere operato*; nevertheless, Baptism is the same thing, and effects the same thing, whether it is conferred by a good or evil minister. This is why the controversy is: whether a sacrifice has force from its own work, of the kind the sacraments have, or from the goodness of the minister, such as our prayers have.

Thirdly, we must consider the value *ex opere operato* can be found in some work in two ways: *a)* In one way, if that work is a certain instrument efficiently and immediately producing the effect, just as by the mode of nature, and in this mode, the sacraments have force *ex opere operato*. This is because the sacramental action is an instrument of God, because he efficiently and immediately justifies, unless an obstacle were placed in the way, nor does the virtue of this instrument depend on the goodness of the minister, but only on the institution of God. *b)* In the other mode, if the work, which is done, is not an instrument efficiently and immediately producing the effect, but still infallibly and independently would move God to produce the effect from the goodness of the minister. In human affairs, an example could be if someone were unknown to, or even unseen by a ruler, but asked something of him in the name of another man, to whom the prince could deny nothing; the supplication of this man would infallibly obtain and still not have force *ex opere operantis*, i.e. from the good quality of the supplicant, since he himself were unknown or unseen by the prince.

Now that we have noted these things, I will posit a few propositions, whereby the whole matter shall become clear. The first proposition: *The Sacrifice of the Mass does not only have force chiefly ex opere operantis, but also ex opere operato*. We say *only*, because it cannot be denied that the sacrifice also has force from the goodness and devotion of the sacrificing minister. If other works of virtue please God, insofar as they proceed from the charity and devotion of some friend of his, why, by the same reasoning, would that most excellent work of religion not please him? Rather, we deny that from here, the sacrifice of the Mass only has force, or chiefly has force; on the contrary, we assert that it has force especially *ex opere operato*.

Such a teaching is common among the theologians, although only one or another may be found who disagrees; and it is also of the Council of Trent, sess. 22, cap. 2. There, when the Council teaches that sins are remitted by this sacrifice, it explains that it is the same reason as the host, and the same one offering who was in the sacrifice of the cross; however the host is the same and the one offering it, who was on the cross, whether the minister is good or bad. Without a doubt, this is also the reasoning of all the Fathers, nay more of the Scriptures, from which it was proven above that Christ is the one who (as the primary and eternal priest) now offers himself through the hands of all the ministers: this is why the principal effect of this sacrifice does not depend on the goodness of the immediate minister.

The second proposition: *The Sacrifice of the Mass does not have force ex opere operato to the mode of the sacraments.* I shall explain this proposition. A sacrifice is not worked efficiently and immediately, nor is it properly an instrument of God for justification, which the Council of Trent teaches (sess. 22, cap. 2) when it says through this sacrifice great sins are also forgiven, because God has been pleased by this sacrifice and concedes grace and the gift of penitence. So, the sacrifice does not justify immediately, in the way Baptism and absolution do, rather, *it obtains the gift of penitence*, whereby a sinful man wills to approach the sacrament and be justified through it. St. Thomas had already taught the same thing (4 dist. 12, q. 2 art. 2 q. 2 ad 4), where he says the sacrifice justifies those for whom it is offered, not as a proximate cause, rather by obtaining a gift of contrition.

This teaching of St. Thomas and the Council are proved *firstly*, because if the sacrifice would justify immediately, a disposition in the one for whom the sacrifice is offered would necessarily be required ahead of time. But if it were true that it is not lawful to offer sacrifice for those whom we know gladly remain in sin, nor for the obdurate and impenitent, still the contrary of this would be most certain; they would also sin who would ask sacrifice to be offered for themselves unless at the same time they were prepared to receive grace, which nobody doubts is false.

Secondly, it is proved from the sacrifice of the cross. For, the sacrifice of the Mass can have no greater force than the sacrifice of the cross, seeing that the sacrifice of the Mass has its force from the sacrifice of the cross, however the sacrifice of the cross does not efficiently and immediately justify, but only imperatorially and meritoriously, otherwise all men would immediately become justified, and the Lord would have offered himself in sacrifice to God for all men. Besides, what is not *in re* cannot be worked efficiently. The sacrifice of the cross is not presently *in re*, but only in the mind of God, hence it is not worked efficiently. So, as the sacrifice of the cross does not immediately justify sinners, but pleases God and obtains that through due means sinners are guided to salvation, so also the sacrifice of the Mass does not justify men immediately, but obtains that grace and the gift of penitence are given to men from the merit of the sacrifice of the cross.

Thirdly, it is proved because the sacraments of Baptism and Penance were established to immediately abolish sin, the former for unbelievers, the latter for the faithful; or, the former for washing away original sin, the latter for actual sin. Therefore, it is not believable that God established another means which has precisely the same effect, or cause, which accounts everything in number, weight and measure.

The third proposition: *The sacrifice of the Mass has force through the mode of impetration, and its proper efficacy is to obtain something.* It is proved *firstly*, because this is the efficacy of a sacrifice in general, and hence, is of this sacrifice; for a sacrifice is properly of the one praying and entreating, and it is applied to assist prayer. St. Gregory of Nyssa (in his *second oration on the Lord's Prayer*) beautifully explains that προσευχή, i.e. prayer, comes from εὐχή, i.e. a vow, because vows, i.e. promises and oblations usually precede the prayer, so that the prayer will more easily obtain its purpose. Thus, we see in Virgil, *Aenea cessas in vota, precesque?*[14]

This is why, like prayer, just as it can be meritorious insofar as it is done by a just man and from charity, and at the same time is also satisfactory insofar as it is a laborious work, so also a sacrifice, which is a type of prayer, or if I may say, real, not merely verbal, is properly *impetratory*.

Secondly, it is proved because the sacrifice of the Mass has a special force, because Christ the high priest offers it. Christ, however, now does not merit, nor can satisfy, but only obtain, consequently force and efficacy are the proper *impetration* of this sacrifice.

Moreover, from here three things follow which illustrate this matter in no small way. *a*) The *first* is the difference between the sacrifice of the Mass and the sacrifice of the cross, insofar as they are both offered by Christ. The sacrifice of the cross was truly and properly meritorious, satisfactory, and impetratory because Christ was mortal then, and could obtain merit and make satisfaction; the sacrifice of the Mass, as I have said, is properly only impetratory because no Christ is immortal,

14 Aeneid VI, 51: "Why have you stopped your vows and prayers?"

Book II, Ch. IV: The Efficacy of the Sacrifice

and can neither obtain merit nor satisfy. However, when it is called propitiatory, or satisfactory, it must be understood by the notion *of the thing which is obtained*. For, it is called propitiatory because it obtains the remission of sin; it is satisfactory because it obtains the remission of punishment; it is called meritorious because it obtains the grace of doing good and acquiring merits. Still, I would not deny it is also called satisfactory because from the institution of Christ by this sacrifice of the same passion of Christ it is applied to abolish the punishments, either of the living or the dead, which sometimes remain after the sin has been forgiven, which must be washed away in this life or in Purgatory.

b) The *second* is for the sacrifice of the Mass, although the goodness of the minister offering it is not necessary, still the goodness of *someone* offering it is necessarily required. Since a sacrifice is intended for impetration and is similar to a prayer, certainly it cannot be pleasing or obtain anything unless the one offering would be pleasing; This is why it is said in Genesis 4:4, "God regarded Abel and his offerings." Nor is it opposed that in the Sacrifice of the Mass, the very thing which is offered is of itself most pleasing to God. For it is not the matter itself, but the *oblation* of that thing which is properly a sacrifice. Sacrifice is an action, not a permanent thing. Hence, although the thing itself might please of itself, nevertheless the *oblation* of the thing is not pleasing unless the one *offering* it is pleasing, and especially with God, who possesses all things, and who needs nothing. Thus, in the Gospel when the holy widow made the oblation of two petty farthings, it pleased God more than the hypocrites who offered many golden coins from pride. All things being equal, the oblation of a more excellent thing, and hence the most pleasing oblation of the body of the Lord, is clearly the most excellent of all things.

c) The *third*, is the sacrifice of the Mass, as it is offered by Christ, has force *ex opere operantis*, but infallibly; because it is pleasing from the goodness of Christ offering it, which is always the same and cannot be diminished or increased. However, as it is offered by a man, it has force *ex opere operato* because it is pleasing to God, even if the man who offers it is not pleasing to God. So, what is needed of the worker in respect to Christ, is the work to be worked in respect to the minister. Still, when it is said absolutely that the Mass has some force *ex opere operantis*, it is always understood on the value which it has from the goodness of the minister, because he is the one who properly works it; for Christ does not work it except through the minister.

The fourth proposition. *The value of the sacrifice of the Mass is finite.* This is the common opinion of the theologians, and it is proven clearly from the use of the Church. If the value of the Mass were infinite, it would be worthless to offer many Masses to obtain the same thing. If one is of infinite value, certainly it would be sufficient to obtain all things; why would it be otherwise? It is confirmed from the sacrifice of the cross, which was offered for only one purpose, not for any other, nor is it ever repeated if only because that one sacrifice was of infinite value and price, and it acquired the remission of all sins, past and future.

Now, although the matter is certain, still the reason is not as certain; it seems a marvel why the value of this sacrifice is finite when it is the same sacrifice as the sacrifice of the cross, and it is the same Christ who offers this very host, pleasing to God in an infinite manner. It seems to me, save for better judgment, that there are three reasons for this. The *first* is taken on the side of the victim which is offered. For in the sacrifice of the cross it was destroyed for the honor of God, it was the physical Christ in human form; in the sacrifice of the Mass it is only the sacramental that is destroyed. The physical Christ, however, is more noble and precious than the sacramental. Moreover, this argument only proves the sacrifice of the cross was greater than the sacrifice of the Mass, but it does not give the reason why the latter is finite and the former was infinite. For there is not an infinite distance between the physical and sacramental Christ, nor was the sacrifice of the cross of infinite value because in it the physical humanity of Christ was destroyed; rather, because the son of God suffered that destruction of his own will, and offered himself in sacrifice which is truly and infinitely pleasing to God, since he was also true God.

The *second* reason is more efficacious, which is taken on the side of the one offering. For, in the sacrifice of the cross, the one offering is the very person of the Son of God *per se*, but in the sacrifice of the Mass the one offering is the Son of God *through a minister*. However, there is a great difference between the action of the Son of God *per se* and through a minister; for the former is an action immediately supposing the divine; the latter a *human*. This is why, although the action of the minister is much more pleasing insofar as it is *in persona Christi* than if it were done in his own person, nevertheless, without a comparison it is more pleasing which is done immediately by Christ himself. In the same way among men, a request of an envoy in the name of his ruler avails much more with some prince than in his own name; nevertheless, a request of the prince himself would avail all the more if he asked something himself.

The *third* reason is taken from the very will of Christ. Even if Christ could obtain anything from God by himself, or offered through a minister and for whomever you like, still he refuses to ask or obtain it unless a certain measure of the fruit of his passion be applied for individual oblations either for the remission of sins or for other benefits which we need in this life. This is why he willed that we not ask from curiosity. Still, it seems that he willed both this holy sacrifice to be repeated in this manner, without which religion cannot consist, and also, because the order of divine providence requires it. This is also the reason why Christ assiduously intervenes for us in heaven when still, it seems by a unique intervention he could immediately obtain everything, and similarly why he did not want the infinite price which he acquired on the cross, whereby the whole world could immediately be saved, to be applied for this purpose except that it be applied to some and in a certain measure. All of these constitute the reason, why Christ willed everything to be done according to the order of divine providence.

CHAPTER V
We Answer the Objections of our Adversaries

Now we must refute the objections which our adversaries usually make against the efficacy of a propitiatory and impetratory sacrifice. However, the chief arguments of the heretics were already answered in the previous book since they confuse everything.

One argument remains from Luther, which is in his book *On the Babylonian Captivity*: "The baptism of one does not benefit another, nor can one be baptized for another; consequently, the reception of the Eucharist cannot be done by one man for another. Therefore, the Mass is not a propitiatory sacrifice because if it were, then Mass and communion of one man would benefit another."

I respond: There is quite a difference between the reception of a sacrament and the oblation of a sacrifice. The reception of a sacrament is ordered to the sanctification of the one that receives it, and so, it does not sanctify anyone but the one who receives it. But the oblation of a sacrifice is ordered to obtain benefits for all those on whose behalf it is offered. This is why the sacrifice, as we said above, is similar to prayer which attains to the efficacy; for prayer does not only benefit the one praying, but also those for whom the prayer is made. From these we gather that the consumption of the Eucharist, which is done by the priest, as the reception of the sacrament, is beneficial for him alone; but as it is the *consummation* of the sacrifice, it benefits all those for whom the sacrifice has been offered.

Secondly, others make the objection, and among them Chemnitz (*Exam.* 2 part, pg. 405, and 861): "If the Mass were a propitiatory sacrifice and remitted sins, it would not be profitable to come so as to partake of the sacraments for the remission of sins. The remission of sins would be secured through one Mass said by another without any labor, and trial; through the sacraments it can be secured with labor and danger."

I respond: If the Mass would immediately remit sins, the argument would conclude something; but we do not teach this, rather only that through the sacrifice of the Mass *the gift of repentance is obtained* whereby sinful men are moved to desire and seek the sacraments, in which they will be justified, as we said above.

Thirdly, someone could introduce an argument against the answer we have given from experience. For, often Masses are said for sinners, who still do not receive the gift of repentance; consequently Mass does not, *ex opere operato*, confer the gift of repentance. And the same argument can be made against the force of this sacrament to obtain other benefits. Those for whom the sacrifice of the Mass is offered do not always obtain them.

I respond: The sacrifice of Mass, when it is offered for sinners, infallibly obtains a new and certain divine *assistance*, whereby sinners are led to repentance; but that help works in different ways, for different dispositions of men. If a man for whom Mass is offered was disposed to contrition, it will be effected in him, and that contrition is properly the gift of repentance, by the force of the new assistance. This is what the Council of Trent and St. Thomas say (*loc. cit.*). But if a man were not disposed, a certain new disposition will be effected in that man, but it will be in vain if he rejects the calling of God by his own will. So, it is no wonder if sinners are not always converted, when the sacrifice of the Mass is offered for them, although, without a doubt *they are always assisted*. Add the fact that it is not necessary for the effect of the sacrifice to come into being immediately, rather only that God gives aid and grace *when it seems opportune to him*. For even the sacrifice of the cross did not immediately have its effect, and the prayer of St. Stephen obtained the conversion of Paul, but it was going to take place in a time determined by God.

What attains to temporal benefits, however, there can be many reasons why they are not immediately obtained, although the efficacy of the sacrifice is infallible. Either God does not bestow these things because he does not think they are useful for eternal salvation, or he delays them so as to concede them at a more opportune time; or lastly, those for whom the sacrifice is offered are unworthy to receive those temporal benefits, and conversely they are worthy of being severely castigated. For even if the sacrifice is offered to please God in regard to unworthy men, still, sometimes the defects of men are too great for God to be placated by one or another sacrifice. Accordingly, as we said, the value of the Mass is finite and limited.

CHAPTER VI
The Sacrifice of the Mass Benefits all the Living

THE THIRD QUESTION follows: For what persons may and must the sacrifice of Mass be offered? There are six kinds of men in regard to whom there seems to be no doubt. Some are still living, or are living members of the body of the Church; or they are dead members, or in no manner, i.e. neither the just nor sinners, but the faithful; or lastly the impious and the infidels, those who are dead, others now abide in Purgatory, others in heaven, others are sentenced to eternal punishment in hell.

And from those who live within the Church, and those who are in hell, i.e. on the first and the last there is no controversy. All Catholics teach the sacrifice can be offered for all those who are within the Church, whether they are just or sinners, nay more it is also really offered daily. We say in the Canon: "We offer for all right worshipers of the Orthodox Catholic and Apostolic faith." The heretics, however, have nothing special to say on this matter.

For those who are in hell, it is certain the sacrifice cannot be offered, nor do any heretics or Catholics deny it; for the sins and crimes of those damned to hell are unpardonable. This is why St. Augustine clearly teaches (*de origine animae* 1, 9 &11) the sacrifice cannot be offered for children that died without Baptism; and in the *Enchiridion*, (ch. 109-110), he says the sacrifice would be of no benefit to the damned if it were offered for them. But we said enough on the matter in *On Purgatory*, book 2, in the final chapter.

On those who are alive and outside the Church, the matter can easily be explained. In the first place it is certain that the sacrifice at least indirectly benefits them and can be offered for them indirectly. While we offer the sacrifice for the increase of the Catholic Church by uniting it and cleansing it, it is certain that it is lawful to indirectly offer it for the conversion of infidels and heretics. Besides, in our Missals there is a proper Mass to end schisms, although in that place the sacrifice is offered for the peace of the Church, nevertheless, it is implicitly offered for schismatics, namely that they be converted. Lastly, in the offering of the chalice, while we are bidden to pray for the salvation of the whole world, certainly we also pray in some manner for unbelievers.

Book II, Ch. VI: Mass Benefits the Living

Next, it is certain from the nature of the thing, if there is no prohibition of the Church, it is lawful to offer it for men of this sort. For the sacrifice of the cross was offered for all; therefore, why could Mass also not be offered for all? Next, in the ancient Church it was offered for rulers and kings who were all still infidels; thus, the saying of the Apostle (1 Tim. 2:1-2), "I will prayers to be said, etc." is commonly explained by the Fathers on the prayers which were made in the sacrifice. Chrysostom (*homil.* 6 on this epistle), says it was offered for a pagan king. And Tertullian (*ad Scapulam*), says, "We sacrifice for the salvation of the Emperor." And in the Old Law, as we showed above, sacrifice was offered for the life of king Darius, and his sons, in 1 Esdra 6:10, while in 2 Macc. 3:32 it was offered for the health of the pagan Heliodorus. Besides, Clement (*Const.* 8, 18) teaches that the Apostles offered the sacrifice of the Eucharist for the kings of their time, and also for Catechumens and for the return of those who lived in error. And in the Liturgy of James a prayer is pronounced to uproot heresies. Chrysostom and Basil, in their liturgies, pray in a similar fashion for the whole world, and namely for those who are in error to be recalled from error. Besides, Chrysostom says (*de Sacerdotio*, 6) that the sacrificing priest prays for the sins of all men, for God to become well-disposed toward them, and in his *homily on Adam and Eve*, he says that priests publicly pray for unbelievers, heretics, Jews, catechumens, etc. In the Roman Ordinal, where it describes the third scrutiny which takes place on the Wednesday after the fourth week of Lent, a proper Mass is instituted for Catechumens, and within the action in these words: *Hanc igitur oblationem servitutis nostrae*, etc., is expressly added to be offered for the Catechumens. As a result, there can be no doubt that it is absolutely lawful to offer sacrifice for those who are outside the Church.

What St. Augustine says is not opposed (*de orig. animae* 1, 9), namely: "Who can offer the sacrifice of the body of Christ [for anyone], except for those who are the members of Christ?" As St. Thomas rightly answers this objection (4 dist. 12 qu. 2 ad 4), it should be understood on those who are members of Christ *in act*, or *in potency*; for then it is also offered for the members of Christ when it is offered for some men in order that they become members of Christ. Add that Augustine does not speak in that citation about any but *the dead*, and because the dead are either members of Christ in act, or in no manner at all, therefore he could say absolutely that it cannot be offered for the dead unless they were members of Christ.

But although the matter so stands, nevertheless the Church (*c. A nobis*, on the sentence of excommunication), has forbidden public prayer to be made for those who have been excommunicated, and consequently for heretics who are always excommunicated; hence it also forbade the sacrifice of the Mass to be directly and expressly offered for them; for the sacrifice is always public.

But someone will ask whether in places where infidels reign, such as in Greece where the Turk rules, and in India, in Japan, or among the Chinese where pagans reign, the sacrifice may be especially offered for the king. *I respond:* I think it is lawful provided that king were not an excommunicate, just as heretical kings, but rather a pagan or a heathen. For this is the tradition and Apostolic custom is (as we showed earlier). Nor is there any manifest prohibition of the Church that I know of.

Again, someone will ask whether it is lawful in this time to offer the sacrifice of the Mass for the conversion of heretics or other infidels. There is reason to doubt it, because the whole liturgy of the Latin Church, which is now in use, is referred to the faithful, as is clear from the prayers of oblation, both inside and outside the Canon.

I respond: I think it is lawful provided nothing is added to the Mass, rather, the sacrifice is only applied through the intention of the priest for the conversion of infidels or heretics. Many pious and learned men make this argument, and we cannot rebuke them, nor is there an express prohibition of the Church. Nevertheless, the safest course is what others do, who so moderate their intention that they intend directly to offer Mass for the increase, unity and peace of the Church, which abides among heretics, or pagans. Those who offer it in this way have the same effect as the former, seeing that the Church cannot be increased, united and made peaceful in those places unless the infidels or heretics are converted, and at the same time their intention is more in conformity with the Ecclesiastical rite than those of the other opinion.

CHAPTER VII
The Sacrifice of the Mass Is duly Offered for the Dead Abiding in Purgatory

WE HAVE two controversies with the heretics of this time on the dead. One is on those who are in Purgatory; the second on the Blessed.

In regard to the first, all the heretics named in the previous controversy (*loc. cit.*) especially detest sacrifices for the dead, although they have only the most trifling argument against it. They argue that when Christ said, "Take and eat," he spoke about the use of the Eucharist; but the dead do not receive nor would it avail them to eat. Moreover, Calvin uses this argument (*Antidoto articulorum Parisiensium*), as well as Chemnitz (*Exam. Conc. Trid.* 2 part, last argument), and others; but still, it concludes nothing. The fact that the dead do not eat proves they cannot participate in the meat of the sacrifice, but it does not prove they cannot participate in the fruit of the sacrifice; accordingly Job offered sacrifice for his absent sons, and the Jews for the king of Babylon who was similarly absent, and not uselessly. When the Lord said, "Take and eat," he was speaking to those whom he offered the sacrament, but not to all of those for whom he offered the sacrifice; for we read (*ibid.*) that he offered his blood to the Lord, for them and for many.

Therefore, we now move to confirm the most certain truth of the matter. *Firstly*, from the custom of the Old Testament, and from the very authority of Scripture. In 2 Macc. 12:43, Judas Maccabaeus commanded sacrifice to be offered for the sins of the dead, and Scripture, while praising this deed says (v. 46): "It is a holy and wholesome thought to pray for the dead that they may be loosed from sins."

I know that our adversaries usually answer that this book is not Canonical; but this is an old refrain, and we have refuted in several places (*On the Word of God*, book 1, and *On Purgatory*, book 1). But let's grant for the sake of argument that it wasn't canonical, still who would deny it is an ancient historical book, and trustworthy any less than Josephus or Sallust? It relates the dead of Judas and the custom of the Jews offering sacrifices for the dead; there is no reason why it should not be thought to be true. For if Josephus relates the same thing, or any other trustworthy author, nobody would doubt it. Therefore, we at least have that it was a custom of the ancient Church which was good and praiseworthy, or it is proved from that the fact that it was rebuked not by Christ, nor the Apostles, nor by any Council, or any doctors, not even by the enemies of the Church. Add, that Augustine, whom we follow more securely than Calvin, proves from this passage that sacrifices offered for the dead benefit them (*Care for the dead*, 1, 1; *On the origin of the soul*, cap. 11).

We take the *second* argument from the custom of the universal Catholic Church. As Epiphanius writes (*in compendiaria doctrina*), and Augustine (*On the care for the dead*), ch. 1; *Sermon 34 on the words of the Apostle*), the universal Church prays for the dead in the Sacrifice of the Mass. That is also clear from all the liturgies, that of James, Clement, Basil, Chrysostom, Ambrose, and others. And lastly, it is clear from the Councils of every province, in which sacrifice for the dead is called to mind as something received and common (See for Africa, the third Council of Carthage, ch. 29 and the fourth Council of Carthage, ch. 79; for Spain, the first Council of Braga, cap. 34 and 39; for France, the Council of Cabilonensi (Chalon-sur-Saône), as it is found in the canon *Visum est, de consecrate*. Dist. 1; for Germany, the Council of Worms, ch. 10; for Italy, the 6 Council under Symmachus; for Greece, ch. 69 of the headings collected from the Greek synods by Martin of Braga). From this the lie of Chemnitz is refuted, for in his *Examination of the Council of Trent*, part 3, in his treatise on Purgatory, he writes that although the custom of offering sacrifice for the dead existed in a few places, it did not exist in the whole Church.

The *third* argument is taken from the Apostolic tradition. It is certain that this rite of offering sacrifice for the sins of the dead was entrusted to us by the Apostles; for Rabanus clearly teaches it (*de Inst. Clericorum* 2, 44) and before him Isidore (*de Officiis Divinis*, 1, 18), and before Isidore Chrysostom (*hom. 69 ad populum Antiochenum*), who says: "The Apostles did not rashly decree that, among other things in these awesome mysteries, the commemoration of the dead should be made, for indeed they know well that thereby great profit and advantage comes to them." He holds the same in *Hom. 3 on Philippians*. Gregory of Nyssa teaches the same thing, as well as others whom St. John Damascene cites in his *Oration for the dead*. The same is clearly gathered from the Liturgy of James, who was an Apostle, and Clement who wrote the things that he received from the mouth of the Apostles.

Next, it is proven from the rule of St. Augustine (*De baptismo*, 4, 24) which is that it is certainly believed to come down to us in Apostolic tradition, "which is preserved in every Church, nor was instituted in

Book II, Ch. VII: Mass Is Offered for Souls in Purgatory

some Council, but has always been preserved and retained." Moreover, that such a rite existed cannot be denied. For it is preserved in every Church, as we showed above, and the fact that it was instituted by no Council, rather always preserved is clear from the testimonies of the most ancient Fathers who preceded Councils, where mention was made on the sacrifices for the dead. The first Council in which mention of this matter occurs was the third Council of Carthage, which was celebrated around 417 A.D. But Eusebius of Caesarea mentions sacrifices for the dead (*Vita Constantini*, lib. 4) who lived a hundred years earlier than the Council of Carthage; Tertullian also calls it to mind (*de Corona militum*) and he lived two hundred years earlier than that Council; lastly Clement calls it to mind (*Const.* 8, 19) who lived three hundred years before the same Council.

Chemnitz (*loc. cit.*) works very hard to respond to this argument. *First*, he admits that Chrysostom says this rite was instituted by the Apostles, but then tries to show the teaching of Chrysostom is false for three reasons: *a)* This Apostolic constitution is not found in any place in the divine Scripture; *b)* because Jerome and Gregory say the Apostles only added the Lord's prayer to the consecration; *c)* because Tertullian (*loc. cit.*) writes that this rite flowed from custom.

Now, even if we would only have Chrysostom on our side, we would rather believe him than Chemnitz, since the authority of the former avails much more than all the arguments of the latter. Then, when he says that it is not found in the Scriptures, who would deny it? We do not relate this constitution of theirs to Scripture, but to the unwritten *tradition* of the Apostles. Certainly, the rule of St. Augustine avails to investigate traditions of this sort.

In regard to what is alleged from Jerome and Gregory, it is partly true and partly false, and altogether impertinent. It is true that Gregory said it, false that Jerome says the same thing. In *Contra Pelagianos*, book 3, Jerome says that Christ taught the Apostles to recite the Lord's prayer in the sacrifice of the Eucharist, but he does not say *alone*. The whole thing is impertinent, both because the Apostles could have added only the Lord's prayer at first, then later added other prayers, and also because they could offer the sacrifice for the dead without any certain prayer, for a mere inward intention of the mind would abundantly suffice for this purpose.

Lastly, what Chemnitz adds from Tertullian is refuted by the same author. Tertullian does not say that this rite of offering sacrifice for the dead flowed first from custom, but what had come down from Apostolic tradition was *retained and confirmed* by custom. "Tradition is the authoress, custom the strengthener, and faith [their] observer" (*loc. cit.*, 4). Add, that Tertullian does not speak on the sacrifice for the dead absolutely, but on the *annual* sacrifice. This is why it could happen that the annual sacrifice could flow from the custom of some, but this very thing is an argument that sacrifice for the dead was already then received in use. Although Tertullian does not clearly say that this tradition is Apostolic, nevertheless he does not deny it, and it can be gathered from the rule of Augustine that it is necessarily Apostolic.

The *fourth* argument is taken from the heresy of Aërius, which was publicly condemned in the Church. Aërius taught that sacrifice must not be offered for the dead; seeing that the ancient Church condemned this heresy, and even by the testimony of our adversaries it was the true Church, then it also likewise condemned all the Lutherans and Calvinists.

This argument greatly pricks Melanchthon, and therefore in his *Apology for the Augsburg Confession*, in his disputation on the word *Mass*, near the end, tends the wound by applying the medicine of a lie. "Our adversaries falsely citing against us the condemnation of Aërius, whom they say was condemned because he denied that in Mass an oblation is made for the living and the dead. ... Epiphanius witnesses that Aërius thought prayers were useless for the dead; he rebuked it, and we do not hold Aërius for our patron." Thus he. Now we find two characteristic lies.

One, that the Lutherans do not have Aërius as a patron when they deny that prayers are useful for the dead. For I ask: who among the Lutherans does not oppose Purgatory? Which of them do not mock prayer for the dead?

Secondly, the idea that Aërius denied prayers but not oblations for the dead is a lie, and will be clearly refuted by the words of Epiphanius, Augustine and Damascene, three of the holiest witnesses. Epiphanius (*Panarion, haeres.* 75) shows somewhat obscurely that Aërius denied the commemoration of the dead within the sacred mysteries; but in another book, which is called *Anacephalaeosis*, that is, *A summary of all heresies*, he says: "Aërius taught many things against the Church, in faith he was the most perfect Arian; to be sure he amply taught that one must not offer for those who had died." Augustine (*de haeresibus*, c. 53) says that Aërius added his own doctrines, and among these he numbers in the first place that one must not pray, or offer the sacrifice for the dead. Damascene (*de centum haeresibus*) says, "Aërius denies anything should

Book II, Ch. IV: The Efficacy of the Sacrifice

be offered for the dead."

The *fifth* argument is taken from the testimonies of the most revered Greek and Latin Fathers. Tertullian (*de Corona*), says, "We offer sacrifices for the dead on the anniversary of their birth [into heaven]." He has similar things in *de Monogamia*, and in his *Exhortation to Chastity ad uxorem*, (book 2).

Cyprian (*Epistles* 1, 9), says: "His ancestors, Bishops, religiously considering the dangerous consequences of clergymen's undertaking secular administrations, did wholesomely provide and decree that no Christian departing this life should nominate any clergyman to be either tutor or curator to minors. If anyone should do this, let no one make an offering for him, nor celebrate the sacrifice for his rest."

Eusebius of Caesarea (*Vita Constantini*, 4, 17), from the version of Christophorson, writes that Constantine obtained what he had desired, that he would be buried in the Basilica of the Apostles, and already enjoyed the communion of prayers which were poured forth there, as well as the mystical sacrifices.

Cyril of Jerusalem (*Catech. Mystagogica*, 5) says, "We believe that it is a particular help to souls for whom the act of prayer of that holy and tremendous thing is offered, which has been placed on the altar of sacrifice."

Ambrose (*Epist.* 2, 8 *ad Faustinus* on the death of his sister) says: "Therefore, I judge that one must not weep for her as much as to pursue her with prayers, nor should you be sad with tears, rather, you should commend her soul to the Lord with oblations." See his prayers for the death of Theodosius, Valentinian and Satyrus, in which he promised to offer sacrifices for all of their souls.

Ephraim, in his testament (which is extent in Surius, tomus 1), asked for the sacrifice of the altar to be offered for his soul. Epiphanius, in his *Compendium of Doctrine*, places among the dogmas of the Church to pray for the dead, as well as to carry out the divine cult and dispensation of the mysteries for the same. Chrysostom has already been cited above, and his testimonies in Homily 69 *ad populum*, as well as *Homily 3 in Philippians* are very clear.

Augustine mentions this rite in nearly all the volumes of his works (*Confessions*, 9, 12-14; *Epist. 64*; *Enchiridion* 110; *Care for the dead*, 18; *City of God* 20, 9; *de sancta Virginitate*, 45; *On the Origin of the Soul*, 9 & 11; *Tract. In Joan.* Tr. 84; *Serm.* 17 and 34 *on the words of the Apostle*).

Possidius in his *Life of St. Augustine*, writes that sacrifice was offered to God for his death. See Gregory (*Dialog.* 4, 55) and Theophylactus (*In Luke* 12), as well as Damascene (*loc. cit.*), Bede (*Hist. Ecc. Ang.* 4, 22 and 5, 13).

From these testimonies it can be known how trifling and inept the answers which our adversaries customarily give to them really are. Some contend we do not have any testimonies but Gregory and more recent authors, to prove sacrifice for the dead, such as Melanchthon (*loc. cit.*).

Others concede that we also have the testimonies of Augustine and Epiphanius, but none older, such as Chemnitz (*loc. cit.*). But we have cited a great many Fathers, not only Gregory, but even those more ancient than Augustine and Epiphanius, such as Ambrose, Ephraim, Nyssa, Cyril, Eusebius, Cyprian and Tertullian.

Others contend that those Fathers speak on the sacrifice of prayers and almsgiving, not on the sacrifice of the Lord's body, when they say sacrifice is offered for the dead. In this way, Chemnitz explains the citations of Tertullian and Cyprian, and George Mayer in the citations of Augustine in his *Refutation of the Profanation of the Supper*. But they are clearly deceived. Cyprian says the sacrifice is celebrated for the dead on the altar. Augustine, however, distinguishes three things which are offered for the dead, and he says they all benefit them, alms, prayers and sacrifices, as in the *Enchiridion*, can. 110, and *Sermon 34* on the words of the Apostle, as well as *On the care for the dead*, c. 18. Likewise, he says for sacrifice to be offered for the dead is our price (*Confess.* 9, 13); the sacrifice of the Lord's body and blood (*de Orig. Animae*, 1, 9 & 11); and the sacrifice of the Mediator (*Quaest. 1 ad Dulcitium*) and the sacrifice of the altar (*On the Care for the dead*, 18).

But Chemnitz opposes this and says in the celebration of the Eucharist it was customary to call the dead to mind, but not for the purpose that the oblation of the Eucharist would be a propitiation for the sins of the dead. Rather, at that point the confession and witness of that article, *the Communion of the Saints* was added, namely that we would profess that both the living and the dead pertain to the Body of Christ and the Church.

But this is a mere fiction. For Cyril, Chrysostom, Ambrose, Augustine and others we have cited clearly say that the sacrifice of the Eucharist brings great benefit to the souls of the dead in respect to rest; and Augustine, in *Enchiridion* c. 110, uses the term *propitiation* when he says, "It is not a propitiation for the very wicked." And lastly, the same Augustine, wherever it is a question on this matter, always distinguishes the saints, especially the martyrs, from other dead faithful, and he says that both are commemorated in the sacrifice of the altar, but the saints so they will pray for us, and others that we might pray for them. But if it were merely a commemoration, and a witness of communion and fellowship, they would all be commemorated in the same way. See the citations of Augustine in *Tract. In Joan.*, tract. 84, and *de Sancta Virginitate*, cap. 45, and *Serm. 17* on the words of the Apostle.

CHAPTER VIII
The Sacrifice of the Mass is Rightly Celebrated in Honor of the Saints

FROM those for whom the sacrifice can be offered, only the saints remain, who now reign with Christ in heaven. Now, because our adversaries, and especially Chemnitz, wrap the whole state of the question with deceit and wrongly attach to us what we would never dream up, we must lay out the argument this way: Firstly, we must diligently explain the teaching of the Church, and then clear up the state of the question. Then, the truth is going to be proved. Lastly, we will respond to objections.

1) What pertains to the *first*, the teaching of the Church is contained in these three headings. *Firstly*, the sacrifices do not benefit the saints in regard to the remission of sin or punishment, nor in regard to the increase of grace or essential glory. This is certain among Catholics, nor is there any contention with the heretics. This is why St. Augustine (*Tract. In Joan.* 84; *Serm.* 17 on the words of the Apostle, and in other places), stipulates that in the sacrifice of the Mass the saints are remembered, but no prayer is made for them. And on that account we ask in our liturgy that the oblation would benefit the saints in regard to glory not because we pray for the saints as much as they will pray *for us*; for we ask from God the grace to offer the sacrifice in a holy manner, piously, devoutly and rightly so that the saints can thereby rightly rejoice and glory be given to them in the presence of men. In a similar way, when Cyprian, Cyril, Epiphanius, Augustine and Chrysostom (whom we will cite below for proof of the first proposition), say the sacrifice is offered for the Apostles and Martyrs, we do not understand it is offered for their salvation, but for their honor.

2) *Secondly*, sacrifice is not offered to the saints, and hence neither are Churches, and altars are not raised to the saints, though all of this can be done in their *memory*, as we will address soon. This is held expressly in the Council of Trent (Sess. 22, cap. 3) and in Augustine (*City of God* 8, 27), where we read: "We do not constitute churches, priesthoods, rites and sacrifices to the martyrs." Chemnitz cites these words (*loc. cit.*, pg. 818), and adds an impudent lie. "Still, this has been done in the Papacy, and is still defended." But in the same way he could lie against Augustine and say: Still, this was done in the time of Augustine and he defended it. For in that sense Augustine denies altars, churches and sacrifices

Book II, Ch. VIII: Mass Is Offered in Honor of the Saints

are made to the saints, and we equally deny it, and just the same, in another sense with the same Augustine, we assign Churches, altars and sacrifices to the saints. Augustine denies, and we with him, that sacrifices are offered to the saints, and hence churches and altars raised, so that in these *sacrifice be made to the saints*; rather he conceded, and we equally concede with him, that sacrifices were offered in memory of the saints, and hence churches and altars are erected *in memory* of the saints, whereby Churches and altars, in which sacrifice is offered to God alone, are everywhere described by Augustine as being in the memory of the saints.

We shall prove all these things from the words of Augustine himself. In that passage which Chemnitz cites (*City of God*, 8, 27) Augustine explains what he said in this way. Churches and sacrifices are not constituted to the saints: "Who ever heard a priest of the faithful, standing at an altar built for the honor and worship of God over the holy body of some martyr, say in the prayers, I offer to you a sacrifice, O Peter, or O Cyprian?" And in *Contra Faustum* (20, 21), he says: "But we do not build altars to any martyr, rather to the God of martyrs, although it is to the memory of the martyrs. No bishop officiating at the altar in the saints' burial place ever says, 'we bring an offering to you, O Peter! Or O Paul! Or, O Cyprian! The offering is made to God, who gave the crown of martyrdom, while it is in memory of those thus crowned." Moreover, the fact that churches are dedicated in the sense which we have said is clear from the same Augustine in *City of God* (1, 1): "The places of the martyrs and the basilicas of the Apostles witness this." And in his work *On the Care of the Dead*, ch. 1, he calls to mind the basilica of St. Felix. See the many testimonies of the different Fathers on the Churches of the saints in our work on the Saints, book 3 chapter 4.

3) *Thirdly*, the sacrifice of the Mass was not instituted per se to honor or invoke the saints as its proper end. We assert this against the calumnies of Chemnitz (*loc. cit.*, pg. 810) where he says that Catholics teach the Lord's Supper was instituted so that they might implore the saints in its celebration, etc. We affirm that the sacrifice of the Mass was instituted *per se to worship God and make him well-pleased*; it will be a true sacrifice even if no commemoration of the saints is made in it. This is why we judge, in regard to the sacrifice, that it only pertains *secondarily and consequently* to the cult and invocation of the saints. By the very fact, thanks are given to God in the sacrifice for the victories of the saints, the honor of the saints follows; and because we honor them

in this way, it follows in turn that they remember us in heaven and pray for us. Moreover, we can understand this from our liturgy itself. There is no place in it where the saints are directly invoked except for two or three times in some versicle, and in the confession which is made before the *Introit* of the Mass. Otherwise, the oblation itself is expressly directed to God alone. Likewise, the Collects, both those said aloud and in a low voice, as well as all the prayers of the Canon are directed to God, none to the saints. But if the Mass were instituted *per se* to the cult and invocation of the saints, certainly the saints would be invoked directly in the Canon itself, as they are invoked in the Litanies.

Accordingly, the state of the question is not what Chemnitz proposes, namely whether the Lord's Supper was instituted for the cult and invocation of the saints; rather, whether *it is opposed* to the institution of the Lord's Supper that in its celebration the saints are commemorated, and consequently that the saints are honored and invoked either directly or indirectly. Now, all Catholics affirm both, i.e. that it is not only in conformity with the institution that the saints be named with honor in the sacrifice, but even invoked. Both of these are manifest from the Council of Trent (*loc. cit.*), and from the Liturgy itself. On the other hand, Chemnitz admits that the first was a custom in the early Church, and can be tolerated to a certain extent, whereas he would have it that the second pertains to a manifest profanation of the Lord's Supper, and on another front it attacks the institution of the Lord, but not as clearly and palpably. This is why we will briefly confirm both teachings.

So, in regard to the second, I state these propositions:

The First Proposition: *It is not opposed to the institution of the Lord's Supper that the saints be named and honored in it.* It is proved firstly from the Apostle in 1 Tim. 2:1, where he commands prayers and thanksgiving to be made in the sacrifice of the Mass (for the Fathers explain this passage in regard to this sacrifice, as we showed above), for all, and especially for kings. Thus, the Apostle means that in the Mass we should not only pray to God to receive benefits, but even to give thanks for what has been received. It is a singular benefit, however, that God has conferred grace upon our brethren to conquer the world and saint, and that he crowned them with glory and honor after that victory; this is why it will be licit, or rather more worthy and just, to offer sacrifice to thank God for the victory and triumphs of the saints, and for this we will also name the saints themselves in the sacrifice with honor and exultation.

Secondly, it is proven from the testimony of all the liturgies, of James,

Clement, Basil, Chrysostom, and others, for in all of them the saints are named, and not only once.

Thirdly, it is proven from the fathers. For Cyprian (*Epist.* 3, 6) asks that the day of the death of each martyr be annotated and written for him so that he could offer sacrifice for them, namely on the anniversary of their passion. Epiphanius (*Panarion, haeres.* 75), and Cyril (*loc. cit.*) clearly write that in the sacrifice the Apostles and Martyrs are named. Chrysostom (*in Acta*, homil. 21), not only says they are named, but he affirms the saints have a remarkable honor because they are named in the presence of the Lord, while that terrible sacrifice is carried out. Augustine (*de Sancta Virginitate*, c. 45, and elsewhere), frequently says the saints are named in the sacrifice, and especially in *City of God* (22, 10), "And in this sacrifice they are named in their own place and rank."

Fourthly, it is proven from the advantage of this institution: it is beneficial *a)* to profess the communion of saints. For the sacrifice of the true body of Christ is offered in the name of the whole mystical body, and should be offered; hence, just as the living bishops, kings, and many others are named, and also the dead, either those in purgatory, or in heaven; for all pertain to the same body. Add that, as Augustine writes (*City of God* 10, 6; 22, 10) in the sacrifice of the altar the general sacrifice is signified, whereby the universal mystical body of Christ, i.e. the whole city of the redeemed, is offered to God through Christ the high priest, and because to the bond of this body the saints also pertain, who are in heaven, therefore they are also named in their rank in the sacrifice of the altar.

b) Another advantage is the arousing of holy imitation. St. Augustine touches upon this (*City of God*, 8, 27), when giving an account of why there are commemorations of the saints made during the sacred rights, he says: "by doing so, we may both give thanks to the true God for their victories, and, by recalling them afresh to remembrance, may stir ourselves up to imitate them by seeking to obtain like crowns and palms, calling to our help that same God on whom they called."

The Second Proposition: *It is not opposed to the institution of the Lord's Supper that the saints are invoked in it by that mode which they are usually invoked by the Catholic Church.* I explain. The saints can be invoked in three modes in the sacrifice of the Mass. *a)* In one mode, through the oblation itself, so that the oblation would be offered to them; for the oblation itself is a certain tacit, but also most efficacious invocation; and in this mode the Church does not invoke the saints in the Mass, nor could she invoke them without the sin of idolatry, as we said above.

b) In the mode of prayer directed to them, as when we say, "St. Peter, pray for me"; and in this mode the saints are not invoked in the Mass, as we said above, except in passing in some versicle after the reading, and that only in one or another Mass. Still, there is nothing absurd about that mode. For if it is licit to ask from the living that they help us with their prayers while we exercise so sublime a ministry, from where we also say in the liturgy, *Orate fratres*,[15] why would it not be lawful to ask the same of the saints? But it is not necessary to dispute on this fact now, because our adversaries do not oppose those versicles which are sung in the Mass of the Catechumens, since that is not properly the sacrifice. In the Mass of the faithful, however, which begins from the oblation, the saints are never directly invoked.

c) In the mode through prayers directed to God, as when we ask of God that he help us by the intercession of the saints, and in this mode, the saints are invoked in the Mass both in the canon and outside of it; and this is what our adversaries rebuke. As a result, we need prove only this.

It is proved *firstly* from the Fathers. St. Cyril of Jerusalem (*Cateches. Mystag.* 5), explaining the rite of the sacrifice of the Mass, says: "When we offer this sacrifice, we commemorate those who died before us; first the patriarchs, prophets, Apostles, and martyrs so that God would receive our prayers with theirs." Basil, in his liturgy, after the consecration, calling to mind the Patriarchs, Prophets, Apostles and martyrs, the Holy Mother of God and all the saints, says: "That you would make constant use of the prayers which they offer to you on our behalf, and by that fact we celebrate their memory so that when we, being equally protected, have confidence in their memory and legation for us, we dare to approach you through them, and exercise this tremendous and sacred office.". Chrysostom in his liturgy, says: "O God look upon us with the supplications of the incorporeal heavenly beings, St. John the Baptist the forerunner, the holy and glorious Apostles, and of the saint whose memory we commemorate and all your saints." And again, "Make firm our steps with the prayers and supplications of the Theotokos and ever Virgin Mary, and all the saints." Augustine (*Tract. In Joan.* 84), says: "We do not commemorate them [the martyrs] at the table in the same way as we do others who now rest in peace, as that we should also pray for them, but rather that they should pray for us." He says the same in

---
15 Pray brethren.

Book II, Ch. VIII: Mass Is Offered in Honor of the Saints 195

Sermon 17 on the words of the Apostle.

Secondly, it is proven from reason. The saints, without a doubt, may and must pray for us in heaven, therefore it is good to ask from God both that he would cause the saints to pray for us and that he would graciously hear them praying for us; these two things are asked in the Mass. The consequent is clear and certain. If the prayer of the saints is one of means of our salvation, why would we not be allowed to ask from God that he would help us through this medium? And if we are allowed to ask that he might direct us through good teachers on earth, that he might teach us and guard us, why are we not also allowed to ask that he do the same through the suffrage of the angels and the saints? And if we are allowed to ask God to rouse those who live here to pray for us, and graciously hear them, why is it not also lawful to pray for the saints?

The antecedent of this argument, however, we profusely proved in *On Canonizations*; nor do our adversaries fight much on this matter. For even if they pertinaciously deny that we must invoke the saints because they do not believe they can hear our prayers, nevertheless, they affirm that *in general* the saints are solicitous for the Church and pray for it, and also that they really pray (Melanchthon *Apologia for the Augsburg Confession*; Brenz in the *Würtemberg Confession*, c. on the invocation of the saints; Chemnitz in *Exam. Conc. Trid.* 3 part; even Calvin in *Instit.* 3, 20 §21 &24). They are not opposed to this opinion, although they bitterly suffer to admit it. And rightly it cannot be denied unless first one would deny Scripture, which witnesses it in 2 Macc. 15:14, Jeremiah and Onias being dead, prayed for the people; and in Apocalypse 5:8 twenty-four elders are described in heaven to offer incense, whereby John himself explains it means the prayers of the saints. Moreover, one would have to deny the unity of the body of the Church, or the communion of saints, which we confess in the Apostle's Creed. For if we are one body, and the others members of the other, certainly we should be anxious for one another; for this is the nature of members, as the Apostle teaches in 1 Cor. 12:26. Lastly, Augustine (*Quaest. 108 in Exod.*) says God is well pleased by the prayers of the martyrs for the sins of the people, and in *Quaest. 149*, he says we can be relieved by the merits of the saints with God, when our evil merits weigh us down.

It remains, that we answer the objections of Chemnitz. His first argument (*loc. cit.* p. 810), "Christ says 'Do this not in commemoration of the saints, but of me.' And besides, he gave us his body and blood in the Supper that, once he had entered the throne of grace, we might obtain mercy through the merits of the singular oblation of Christ; therefore, the Lord's Supper is profaned when it is asked from God that we may be fortified by the aid of divine protection through the merits and prayers of the saints."

I respond: Christ never said *do not do this in memory of the saints*, nor did he say: Do this in commemoration of me alone; this is why it cannot be rightly assumed that the commemoration of the saints is contrary to the institution of the Supper. Besides, even if the Lord had said: Do this in commemoration of me alone, our adversaries would still gain nothing. The Lord is speaking not on any commemoration you like, but on that whereby his *passion and death* are represented through the mystery of the Supper. In that kind of commemoration it is not customary, nor can the Church commemorate the saints in the Mass; for the Eucharist is not a symbol of the passion of the saints, but of Christ alone. Therefore, there is another commemoration of the saints which we celebrate in the sacrifice, clearly, we name the saints that we might offer sacrifice to God in thanksgiving for their victory, as we said above.

Now let us respond to the other part of the argument: On the one hand, we anticipate and beg mercy from God by the intercession, and merits of Christ, and on the other, through the merits and prayers of the saints. For, we ask mercy from God through the merits of Christ *immediately*; for he alone is our immediate intercessor with God. But we ask mercy from God through the merits and prayers of the saints, *through the medium of the same Christ*; for even when they pray for us, they pray through Christ. Therefore, just as our prayer to God on our own behalf is not vain, nor causes injury to Christ, although he is our advocate with God because we pray to God for ourselves through him, so the prayers of the saints for us are not vain or an injury to Christ, although Christ is our advocate, because they ask through Christ. And just as the saints can pray to God for us, not withstanding the intercession of Christ, so even we can ask from them to pray for us and ask from God that he would move them to pray for us as well as graciously hear our prayers, notwithstanding the intercession of Christ.

His *second* objection is from Augustine (*City of God* 22, 10), who says that in the administration of the Lord's Supper the saints are named by the priest, but in no way are they invoked by the priest.

I respond: If Chemnitz were to cite the words of Augustine, his deceit would be utterly clear to everyone without so much as a word from us. These are Augustine's words: "We immolate the sacrifice to the one God

Book II, Ch. VIII: Mass Is Offered in Honor of the Saints

of the martyrs and ourselves; and in this sacrifice they are named in their own place and rank as men of God who conquered the world by confessing him, but they are not invoked by the sacrificing priest. For it is to God, not to them, that he sacrifices, though he sacrifices to their memory, for he is God's priest, not theirs."

Here you see firstly, that Augustine does not say, "In the administration of the Lord's Supper," but "We immolate the sacrifice;" and he repeats two or three times that the priest offers the sacrifice to God, not that he administers the Supper. Secondly you see that Augustine clearly says the sacrifice is made in memory of the saints and the saints are named in it; this is not only against the novelties of these sects who make no mention of the saints in their Supper, but is expressly against Chemnitz who a little while ago argued that Christ said do this not in commemoration of the saints. Thirdly, you see that Augustine, when he denies the saints are invoked, speaks about invocation through *the sacrifice*, i.e. on the oblation which, as we said above, is a most efficacious invocation; he speaks formally when he says: "they are not invoked by the sacrificing priest," as is clear from the following words: "For it is to God that he sacrifices, ... because he is God's priest, not theirs."

What Augustine does not deny, however, is that the saints may and must be invoked in the Mass in the same way in which the Catholic Church does, and this is clear from *Tract. In Joan.* 84, which we cited above, where he says the saints are commemorated at the Lord's table not that we might pray for them, but that they may pray for us. From these it is clear how inane is Chemnitz' victory dance on account of this passage of Augustine, and how unduly and impudently he calls the Council of Trent the Whore of Babylon.

The *third* objection is from the history of antiquity; Chemnitz lays out the progress of history in this way. First, he says, in the primitive Church there was a custom that the anniversary of the martyrs was solemnly celebrated in those places where the bodies of the martyrs were buried; and he bases this on the epistle of the Church of Smyrna cited by Eusebius (*hist.* 4, 15). Secondly, he says in the progress of time it happened that the bodies of the saints were placed under the tables, and he shows this from Ambrose (*Epist.* 10, 85). Thirdly, he says in the prayers of the Church the martyrs were commemorated because the Church prayed that at some point it would become a sharer in the eternal life of those martyrs; that which he shows from the epistle of the people of Smyrna. Moreover, he says these three things are consistent according to the use of the purer Church, and Scripture. Fourthly, he says that in the time of Augustine foreign and vicious opinions began to arise on individual intercessions of martyrs for those who kept their cult, on the merits and works of the martyrs. Fifthly, he says that Augustine was ambiguous on these opinions, as though they were neither ancient nor certain, which he shows from *City of God* (22, 10), and *On the Care for the dead*, (c. 16). Sixthly, he says that Augustine, little by little began to make something of these opinions; but Jerome, Basil, Nazianzen, were more rash on this question. Seventhly, he says in the last times, an article of faith was fabricated on the patronage and merits of the saints, and what is more horrible, the very action of the Lord's Supper began to be twisted.

From this long narration, Chemnitz tries to persuade the simpler minded that the matter of the invocation of the saints in Mass is new, and confected by papists. But if anyone were to judge the matter more attentively, Chemnitz and his associates are clearly refuted from this very disputation. For the first three points, which our adversary affirms were in the purer Church and are consistent with Scripture, do nothing against us, since they do not contain anything contrary to our doctrine; rather they do much against our adversaries, since they are altogether contrary to their writings and deeds. For they do not celebrate the memory of the saints with the relics of the saints, nor place the bodies of martyrs under the sacred table, but they rather cast them out; nor, at length, do they make any mention of the saints in prayers and the mystery of the Eucharist; this is why we conclude from the testimony of Chemnitz, that Chemnitz and his associates have withdrawn from the use of the purer primitive Church, consistent with the Scriptures.

The Fourth point is false and can be refuted from his sixth. For if Basil, Nazianzen and Jerome follow these opinions on the intercessions and merits of the saints, as he holds in the sixth heading, therefore those opinions did not begin in the age of Augustine, as he holds in the fourth heading, for the age of Augustine is later than that of Basil and Nazianzen. Add, that the teaching of the Church on the invocation of the saints did not begin even in the age of Basil, but is by far more ancient. For Eusebius is more ancient than Basil, and he says: "We profess that we offer prayers to the saints, whose intercession is no small assistance with God" (*Praeparat. Evangeli.* 13, 7). And Irenaeus is older than Eusebius, who says: "That the Virgin Mary would become the advocate of the virgin Eve" (*Adversus Haereses*, 5, 19).

Book II, Ch. VIII: Mass Is Offered in Honor of the Saints

The fifth heading contains a manifest lie and imposture. For Augustine (as he is cited by Chemnitz), does not hold it as ambiguous and an uncertain thing whether the saints help us and are our intercessors and advocates, and as such to be invoked by us; rather, only *how* they help us, when miracles take place at their tombs. For Augustine was uncertain as to whether it was done by a work of the angels, or whether through the very souls of the martyrs, or in another manner; and after he left this as ambiguous, he asserted the matter as beyond doubt that those who invoke the saints are assisted by them. In *City of God* 22, 8, he proves this very thing with nearly innumerable examples, and affirms it as most certain.

The sixth heading does not need any refutation, since I do not know who would not see how great a prejudice Chemnitz makes for his cause when he so openly dared to rebuke the pillars of the Greek and Latin Church, Basil, Nazianzen, Jerome and Augustine.

The seventh heading is absolutely false, and it is clear from the testimonies we cited above, those of Cyril, Basil, Chrysostom and Augustine, who plainly write that in the sacrifice of the altar we ask the intercession of the saints from God. What a lie, that he conceives it was made up more recently, when it was in the use of the Catholic Church 1200 years ago!

CHAPTER IX
On Private Masses

Now, the controversy on private Mass follows. After Luther, other authors wrote on this subject such as Brenz (*Confess. Wirt.* Cap. de Eucharistia) and Chemnitz (*Exam. Conc. Trid.* 2 part., pg. 858 et *seqq.*), and Melanchthon (*Augsburg Confession*, and in his *Apology* for the same in the article on the Mass). We will treat this controversy in this way: *first*, we shall teach that private Mass can be said in six ways, and is licit in all of them. Then we will refute the objections of our adversaries.

1) *Firstly*, A Mass can be called private by reason of the place, for those Masses which are celebrated in some private oratory or chapel can be called private, if they are compared to those which are celebrated in a public Church. There is no great controversy on these; even if our adversaries display how much they hate these Masses, and call them "corner Masses" through a contumely, still we have manifest examples of these in antiquity. In the first place, the Lord established the Mass in a private house, and in the beginning, the Apostles broke bread around their homes (Acts 2:46). Lastly, the holy bishops during the period of persecution did not only carry out the sacred rites in private homes, but even in crypts and caves. In fact, St. Lucianus offered sacrifice in prison, and when he was on the ground straddled with chains and could not get up, he used his own chest as an altar, as Nicephorus relates (*hist.* 8, 31).

Sometimes the Fathers offered sacrifices in private places not only due to persecutions, but even for other reasons. Gregory Nazianzen offered the sacred rites in an oratory built in his tiny cell, as Sozomen witnesses (*hist.* 7, 5), and even Chemnitz cites that passage. St. Ambrose, as Paulinus witnesses in his life, while in the house of a certain noblewoman, after she asked him, he offered sacrifice there. St. Augustine witnesses that a certain one of his priests offered the sacrifice of the Lord's body and blood in a country house (*City of God* 22, 8). Theodoret (*Historia religiosa*, c. 20) writes that he celebrated the sacred mysteries in the little cell of Maris the anchorite. Gregory I (*hom. 37 in Evangelia*) writes that Cassius, the bishop of Narniensis (Narni), a very holy man, sometimes celebrated Mass in the bishop's oratory, because being impeded by illness he was not well enough to come down to the Church; and in an epistle (book 5 epistle 43), to John the bishop of Syracuse he commands that he not forbid Masses to be celebrated in the house of Venantius. St. John the Almsgiver, as Leontius writes in his life, saw that when the people went out from the Church, in which time he celebrated the sacred rites, turning to them he said: "Sons, I come down to the Church for your sake, for I am able to say Mass for myself in the chancery." Lastly (so as to pass over other examples), John Damascene, in his *History of Barlaam and Josaphat*, writes that Blessed Barlaam was a priest and in his cell, with only Josaphat present, customarily offered the sacrifice of the Mass.

2) *Secondly*, a Mass can be called private by the time; what is celebrated on feast days is public, and what is celebrated on an ordinary day private. And although our adversaries do not keep the sacred Supper but rarely, and nearly only on Sundays or greater feasts, still they do not openly rebuke the use of daily Mass, and certainly it cannot be rebuked in any way. For in the first place, it is called a continual sacrifice in Daniel 12:11 because it should be celebrated continually and daily.

Then, it cannot be denied that formerly Masses were celebrated each day in many places. For Cassius celebrated Mass each day, as St. Gregory witnesses (*loc. cit.*, hom. 37). Augustine (*Epistle 23*) says Christ was immolated once on the cross, and immolated every day in the Sacrament for the people. Chrysostom (*hom. 3 in Ephesians*) writes that the customary oblation is made daily at the proper time. Jerome (*On Titus 1*) says priests daily sacrifice for the sins of the people and their own. Hippolytus the martyr, (*Oration on Antichrist*), writes that Christ is going to say on the day of judgment: "Come O bishops who daily immolated my body." Lastly, St. Andrew, as we read in his history, sacrificed the immaculate lamb each day. But our adversaries do not labor very much on this matter.

3) *Thirdly*, a Mass can be called private from its end; namely that it is celebrated for some particular man, or business, as for this or that dead man, for this or that necessity. Indeed, if some Mass were applied to one man alone, while excluding all other men, then it could truly be called private, but there has never been such a thing, nor was there ever in the Church. For every Mass is offered by a public minister, and in a public name for the *whole Church*, which is on earth, or in heaven, or in Purgatory; for each of these are mentioned in any Mass you like. If, however, a Mass should be specifically applied to one, still not that it would exclude the rest, then it will be able to be called a private Mass, and it will be, if compared to others, which are applied to no one in particular.

There is also no doubt that private Masses of this sort were in the use of the ancient Church and are licit. In the Old Testament a great many sacrifices were carried out for particular things. In Leviticus 4 and 5, sacrifices are prescribed for the priest, for the ruler, for any private man you like, for the synagogue, etc. In Job 1:5 we have sacrifice for the sons of Job, and in Job 42:8 sacrifice for his friends. In 2 Macc. 3:32 for Heliodorus.

In the New Testament, concerning the births of the saints (which we defended above), all were private in this third mode, and we have a characteristic example, apart from those which we already conveyed, cited by Bede (*Historiae* 4, 14) where the holy Apostles Peter and Paul appeared to a certain man and commanded Masses to be celebrated on the day of King St. Oswald, and it was clear that this vision was true from the miraculous events which the same Apostles foretold were going to happen. For equal reasoning Mass for the dead, as many as there were, were particular and private; for so Augustine writes on the death of his mother in *Confessions* 9, 12: "When the sacrifice of our redemption was offered up unto you for her, the dead body being now placed by the side of the grave, etc." Lastly, that sacrifice was offered by a priest of the same Augustine for the liberation of a house from demonic disturbance (*City of God* 22, 8), and others of that kind, without a doubt were private nor can they be rebuked unless all antiquity were to be rebuked.

4) *Fourthly* a Mass can be called private from the fewness of those who are present: for it to be called public, it is done in the presence of the people. Such a Mass is usually called parochial, or conventual, which is not celebrated unless the people are present; private, however, to that which the people are not expected, rather is held at the will of the priest whether many are present or just a few. Our adversaries do not rarely rebuke Masses that are private in this way. Certainly, Melanchthon in the *Apologia for the Augsburg Confession*, draws forth arguments to prove there should not be any Mass but one, namely that to which the people are present; still others from our adversaries do not wish to dispute the matter. Brenz (*Confess. Wirtemburgensi*, cap. de Eucharistia), is content that Mass is celebrated if at least two are present, one who consecrates and administers the sacrament, and the other to whom it is offered. And the testimonies brought on behalf of private Masses by reason of the place prove this very thing. St. Gregory also speaks on private Masses (*Epistles, 4, 43 ad Castorium*) where he forbids public Masses to be offered in the monastery lest popular gatherings would take place in

the solitude of the people of God. From such a citation it is gathered that Masses are called public in which a multitude of the people are present, while private Masses are those which are celebrated without a gathering of the people within a monastery or in another place.

This is why Melanchthon is clearly deceived in his *Apologia* when he says before the times of Gregory there was no mention made of private Masses. For in Gregory private Masses were thought to be those which are celebrated without a gathering of the people, as is clear from this place; St. Augustine witnesses that a priest said a private Mass in a country home (*loc. cit.*), and Ambrose in the house of a certain Roman matron as Paulinus witnesses, and likewise by Theodoret in the cell of St. Mare; as well as by Lucianus in prison. Nay more, by the Apostles when they broke bread around homes, as we cited above; and by Christ himself who did not call the people together, but only the primary twelve disciples.

5) *Fifthly*, Masses can be called private which are said in the same Church, on the same day apart from the one [parochial Mass]. For only one is usually a public and solemn Mass which is said at the high altar; the rest which are said on lesser altars on the same day can be called private, although many might be present to hear it. And indeed, all of our adversaries especially hate and rebuke this multiplication of Masses. But we will prove they are licit. First, from the Old Testament in which a great many sacrifices were offered on the same day and place.

Secondly, there were many priests in the same Church. In the time of Pope St. Cornelius in Rome there were forty priests, as he writes to Fabius (and Eusebius witnesses *hist.* 6, 33), and thereafter the multitude of priests always increased more and more. However, they celebrated daily, therefore, either all others ceased from offering the sacrifice or many offered it on the same day and in the same place. Moreover, that there were those who offered sacrifice daily there can be no doubt; for it is clear from the testimonies we cited above, where we argued on Private Mass with respect to the time.

Thirdly, the testimony conferred above from Bede (*loc. cit.*) proves the same thing. There, the Apostles commanded Masses to be celebrated on the day of St. Oswald through all the oratories of the Monastery. What Eusebius writes is similar (*Life of Constantine*, 4, 45) that the bishops were invited to the dedication of the Church to celebrate the feast day with unbloody sacrifices offered to God.

Fourthly, the most ancient custom of the Church proves the same thing, that on Christmas day each priest offers the sacrifice of the Mass three times; Gregory calls this rite to mind (*homil. De Natali domini*) and before him Telesphorus in his decretal epistle. But if one priest can offer the sacrifice three times on the same day, why could many not offer sacrifices each day?

Fifthly, the multitude of altars in the same Church proves the same thing. Ambrose, in *Epistle 33*, says "They attacked the altars, etc." speaking about one basilica. Gregory (*Epistles*, 5, 50 to Palladius) writes that in one Church there were thirteen altars; William Abbot, in his life of St. Bernard (1, 12) writes that in the Church of the monastery of St. Bernard there were three altars, one in memory of the Blessed Virgin, one for St. Laurence, the third for St. Benedict. See also Peter Damian in the beginning of the life of St. Romauld. Why so many altars if the sacrifice can be offered only once a day in one Church?

Next, Prosper (*de praedictionibus dimidii temporis*, c. 6) writes that twice within a few hours sacrifice was offered in one place. Leo I (*Epistle 81 ad Dioscorum*) teaches that the Roman Rite be preserved in Alexandria in regard to repeating the sacrifice on the same day.

6) Lastly, a Mass can be called private in which the priest alone communicates; and this is a private Mass, on which our adversaries chiefly make trouble, and which they approve in no way. But that it is licit is proved *firstly* by the argumentation of the Council of Trent (sess. 22 cap. 6) which is like this: Masses in which the priest alone communicates, even if they can be called private, by reason of communicating sacramentally, still are not absolutely private, but *public and common*, therefore they should not be rejected and condemned as private. The antecedent is proved by the Council in two ways. *Firstly*, because in Masses of this sort many often communicate spiritually, hence the fruit is public and common; and through this also the Mass is on this side public and common. *Secondly*, because the priest is a *public* minister, and offers the sacrifice for *the whole Church*.

Chemnitz tries to refute this whole argument (pag. 868) but he does not so much refute the reasoning of the Council as he shows himself to be a liar and inept. *Firstly*, he marvels why the Council would dare to call these Masses common and deny they are private when through many centuries they have been called private by Catholics, and seeing that Gregory frequently mentions private Masses in his epistles, as well as the Gloss on the canon, *et hoc attendum, de consecr.* Dist. 1, which calls them private.

Moreover, this whole thing is a lie; for the phrase "private Masses" is not extent in any writing of Gregory. We do indeed once find the term "public Masses" (*Epistles* 4, 43), but as we said above, Gregory does not call a Mass public because people communicate in them, but *a multitude of the people is present*, and he contrasts Masses to these, in which the people are not present or some would communicate in them, or none. In the same manner the phrase public Mass is received, as well as specific, or private cited in the canon and the Gloss.

Secondly, Chemnitz opposes the argument which the Council introduces from spiritual communion, and because he cannot deny spiritual communion, he falsely imputes to this Council a new lie that it affirmed through spiritual communion the institution and precept of Christ on receiving the Eucharist is satisfied.

But nothing of this sort is found in the Council; nay more, in sess. 13, can. 9, the Council teaches that adult faithful are held, at least once a year to receive sacramental communion, namely, that in that manner they would satisfy the institution and precept of Christ.

Thirdly, he opposes the second argument of the Council taken from the fact that the priest is a public minister, and says the argument is not valid, because the minister of the word is also a public minister, and nevertheless, he cannot preach unless the people are present; the one who baptizes is a public minister and still he cannot baptize unless some one is present to be baptized.

But these are mere ineptitudes. On the one hand, the priest is a public minister when offering the sacrifice, on the other, in preaching and administering the sacraments. In offering sacrifice, he directs his action to God for the people's sake, while in preaching and administering the sacraments, he directs his action to the people for God's sake.

And from here another argument arises from the nature of sacrifice: If our adversaries would concede the Mass is not only a sacrament, but also a sacrifice, perhaps they would easily agree in this matter; accordingly, in regard to the sacrifice, as it is a sacrifice, it is of no importance if many or a few, or no one is present or communicates, since the sacrifice is offered to God for the people; for the priest can offer for the people even if the people are neither present nor communicate. This is confirmed from the Old Law, when the sacrifices were offered for sin, the one for whom it was offered ate nothing from it, as is clear in Leviticus 6:30, and 7:7, and still these were beneficial. And it is again confirmed from similar things. For the sacrifice is similar to prayer, as we said above, nay more it is a type of real and very efficacious prayer. Hence prayer is beneficial for the one for whom it is made, even if he is not present and does not know it is done, and this has been investigated and is most certain.

Next, it is proven from the custom of the ancients. For, even if we did not expressly read that sacrifice was offered by the ancients without the communion of anyone apart from the priest himself, still, we could easily gather it from conjectures. The *First* conjecture is from the Council of Nantes, cap. 30, which is cited by Ivo (*Decret.* Part. 3 cap. 70) where the priests are commanded not to celebrate Mass alone unless they would have at least someone who might make the responses. From that we understand plainly that certain priests were accustomed to celebrate Mass alone, and hence without any communicants. Likewise, from the Council of Toledo, 12, can. 5, where certain priests are gravely rebuked who offering the sacrifice did not communicate. The Council says, "What kind of sacrifice is it, in which the sacrificing priest himself is not discerned to have participated?" Such words show clearly enough that in a sacrifice of this sort there was altogether nobody that communicated, and still the Council does not require anything else than that the priest himself would communicate; hence it admits the thing as ratified and, as it appears, customary that there were sacrifices in which the priest alone communicates. Moreover, this Council was celebrated around nine hundred years ago.

The *second* conjecture: Certain men initiated the sacred rites without any certain care of souls, who, moreover, could not administer the sacrament to anyone, and still, without a doubt celebrated Mass. We have an example in St. Paulinus of Nola, who was ordained a priest, as he himself writes in epist. 6 *ad Severum* in the priesthood of the Lord, but he was not bound to a certain Church.

The *third* conjecture: A great many priests celebrated daily, as we showed above, and still the people rarely communicated in many places, as can be seen in the complaint of Chrysostom (*hom. 3 in Ephesians*), where he says: "The daily oblation is held in vain when there is nobody who participates in it." And in *Homily 17 on Hebrews*, he writes that a great many only approach for communion of the sacrament once a year. Ambrose (*De Sacramentis* 5, 4) also says the Greeks usually communicate after a year.

The *fourth* conjecture: Many sacred rites are done for a cause so particular that it does not in any way have the appearance of truth that communion was administered in those rites: e.g. when Augustine writes

Book II, Ch. IX: Private Masses

in *Confessions* 9, 12, that sacrifice was offered for his mother, when the body was placed in the ground, and when he writes in *City of God* 22, 8, one of his priests offered sacrifice in a country house, to free it from the disturbance of evil spirits. Now we will answer the arguments of our adversaries.

CHAPTER X
The Arguments against private Masses Are Answered

1) THE FIRST OBJECTION is of Chemnitz (*Exam.* 2 part. Pg. 862, and I will omit the story he creates on the origin of private Mass because he proves it with no argument). He takes it from the words of Luke 22:19, "Do this in my memory." For Christ commands that we do what he did; but he did not only consecrate, but also gave the sacrament to those who were present to eat, this is why to consecrate and not distribute is to profane the Lord's Supper itself.

I respond: The Lord commanded what he did to be done, but for *place, time and person,* for that is the force of affirmative precepts. And without a doubt, he did not command the sacrament to be dispensed to the unwilling or the unworthy. This is why if there is no one who wishes or who can communicate, we are not held to administer the sacrament; still, nor are we required to cease from the celebration.

Someone will say: If it is lawful to divine the actions which the Lord joined by his example, at some time to consecrate the sacrament and administer it to no one, it will also be lawful to consecrate or minister and not receive.

I respond: The notion of all these actions is not the same. For the consecration and consummation are in regard to the essence of the sacrifice, therefore in no way can they be omitted; but the dispensation of the sacrament is not in regard to the essence, nor the integrity, but only the affirmative and necessary precept of the Lord, and therefore it is indeed to be done, but for *place, and time,* as we said.

2) The *second* objection: The synaxis of the Apostles is described in Acts 2:42 by the breaking of bread; therefore, distribution and dispensation of the sacrament was in the use of the primitive Church in the celebration of the Lord's Supper.

I respond: Nothing can be said more truly, but it does not thereby follow that the sacrifice cannot ever be offered without dispensation. For in every one of our Churches the synaxis is celebrated with the dispensation of the sacrament, and still the sacred rites which are celebrated in private oratories and chapels without such a dispensation are not condemned by that fact.

3) The *third* objection: St. Paul, in 1 Cor. 10:16, while describing the rite

Book II, Ch. X: Private Masses Are Defended 209

of the Lord's Supper, clearly writes that the Lord's body is communicated and distributed to the faithful, and the faithful are partakers of the Lord's table, not as spectators of one man eating, but by eating themselves.

I respond: In that passage the Apostle does not describe the rite of the Lord's Supper to declare that it is the very celebration of this mystery, or it especially consists in something, but only to show that those who take the Eucharist are partakers of the Lord's table, and become companions of Christ. In the same way, they are companions of demons when they partake of the altar of idols, who knowingly eat the food offered to idols. Thereby it does not follow that Mass without the communion of the people is illicit, or those who are present at Mass and do not communicate receiving nothing useful. For, while affirming this very true proposition, it can also be gathered from Paul, whoever really eats the Eucharist is joined with Christ; while denying this is false; we do not find in Paul: He that does not really take the Eucharist except by desire alone is in no way joined with Christ or is present at the sacrifice in vain.

4) The *fourth* objection: In 1 Cor. 11:20-21, the Apostle makes an opposition between the Lord's Supper and a private supper, and so much that he confirms where a private supper is carried out, there the Lord's Supper cannot be celebrated. Moreover, he defines a private supper where someone who is at the Lord's Supper eats and busies himself privately, not together with the others participating; he says it is no different than if some supper would be prepared where one is fed but the other is compelled to go hungry. Chemnitz says, "This passage strikes the private Masses of the papists like lightning, in which only the celebrating priest communicates sacramentally; and the teaching of Chrysostom on this place of Paul is most clear: 'What is the Lords they do in private; for the Lord's Supper should be common, etc.'"

I respond: First, when Paul makes the opposition of the Lord's Supper to a private supper, he does not speak about the Eucharist, but about a dinner party which formerly was customarily done in the Church for the refreshment of the poor, which they called the dinner party of the Lord [agape], as Chrysostom interpreted it, because it was done to represent the Last Supper of the Lord with the disciples, since it was also done in a sacred place, and then because it was joined with the communication of the Eucharist. That this dinner party is understood by the Lord's Supper is clear from those words of 11:21, "One eats, another is drunk." For you cannot be hungry in the communication of the Eucharist, or found drunk, since the Eucharist is the food of the mind, not the stomach. Next, the same is clear from what Paul proposed. He wants (as Chrysostom and all other expositors of this passage say) to rebuke the Corinthians because they did not make those dinners greater, as they should, but the rich dined elegantly while the poor were apart and hardly found sufficient refreshment; so he rebukes this abuse with these words in verse 20-21: "It is not now to eat the Lord's Supper. For every one takes before his own supper, etc." This is: These dinners of yours, as they are now celebrated, do not fully represent the Lord's Supper. For the Lord reclined together with his disciples in the same table, even if, he being the Lord, they served him; moreover, you exclude your brothers from your table because they are poor, etc. All of these pertain to those *dinner parties*, not to the Eucharist, for what pertains to the Eucharist, all partake equally sober and just as elegantly when the Lord's body is given to them in the restrained species of bread. Therefore, the whole argument of Chemnitz turns on an equivocation.

Secondly, even if Paul spoke about the Eucharist when he opposed the common supper to the private, as Theodoret and some other ancient writers teach with probability, nothing could be gathered from that in favor of our adversaries. Paul rebukes the private supper in which others were *excluded*, not to which they are not compelled. Moreover, our Mass does not exclude communicants; nay more, as the Council of Trent affirms (sess. 22 cap. 6), the Church desires that in each Mass, those who are present would communicate; but if there are not any who wish, it is no fault of the priest, nor can he be rebuked as if he alone wished to participate in the Lord's Supper.

5) The *fifth* objection: In the ancient Church the distribution of the Sacrament always took place in the action of the Lord's Supper, as is clear from the description of all the Liturgies which are extent in the Fathers.

I respond: The contrary is gathered even from the many examples which we advanced above. Moreover, in the Liturgies mention is made of the distribution, because, as we said, the distribution of the Sacrament may and must always be done in a Mass of those priests who have the office to care for souls, if some are prepared to communicate. Yet, he must not cease from offering sacrifice as a consequence of no one being present who wishes to communicate.

6) The *sixth* objection: The commentary, that the celebration of the Lord's Supper benefits those who do not communicate but are merely present and hear, and watch with devotion what the priest does, was not

Book II, Ch. X: Private Masses Are Defended

only unknown to antiquity but is often and gravely rebuked by ancient authors. Chrysostom (*Homily 3 on Ephesians*) says, "The daily oblation takes place in vain when there is no one who will partake of it at the same time. ... Whoever is not a consort of the mysteries is impudent and assists as a wicked man. ... If anyone has been called to a dinner, has washed his hands and reclines, and still tastes none of the food, does he not insult the host who called him? How much more will it be for a man who is the sort that altogether will not come?" Chemnitz adds: "You hear not words, but thunderbolts against the papist persuasion on the spectacle of private Masses."

I respond: The use of assisting at the sacrifice of the Mass but not communicating sacramentally was known to the ancients. That is clear from the Council of Agde, celebrated a thousand years ago, where in canon 18 all the laity are commanded to communicate at least three times a year, on Christmas, Easter and Pentecost, and still in canon 47 the same laity are commanded to be present at Mass on Sundays, even to the blessing of the priest which is given a the end of Mass. Besides, the Fathers did not doubt that the Mass benefited those assisting it, although they did not communicate, and it is most certain from what we said above about Masses for the dead and for any necessity. If the Mass is beneficial for the dead, as all the fathers unanimously affirm, and also the living who are absent, the sick, those making a journey, nay more even infidels and heretics, how much more will it benefit the faithful who are present and offer it together with desire?

I say two things to the citation of Chrysostom: The words, "The daily oblation is made in vain," do not mean absolutely the oblation is carried out in vain, rather, it is in vain insofar as *it is ordered to communion*. Since the celebration of the Mass is partly ordered to offer sacrifice to God, and partly to refresh the people with that sacred bread, when there is nobody to communicate, it is done in vain insofar as it is ordered to the second end, but not insofar as it is ordered to the first end. So even if Chrysostom were to say it is done in vain, still he did not omit the daily sacrifice on that account, which he certainly would have if he thought it was absolutely done in vain.

Now, to what Chrysostom says, that it would be better not to be present at the sacrifice than to be present and not communicate, I say that Chrysostom spoke certain things through hyperbole, since he merely desired to exhort men to communicate frequently and worthily. Since he says men excuse themselves from communion because they said they were unworthy and unprepared, when he took notice that the reason of the whole forfeiture was negligence and idleness, he vehemently complained of them, and says they are also unworthy to pray together with the rest, nay more they are worthy to be sent out of the Church during the time of sacrifice, in the same way as the penitents and Catechumens were sent out, and it would be better for them if they did not come; and other things were said for the sake of hyperbole, which is most certain. It is similar to what the Apostle says in 1 Cor. 6:4, "Set those who are the most despised in the Church to judge." Paul does not really command the most despised to be set up as judges, rather, he so speaks because he desired there to be no quarrels in the Church, or all Christians to be so wise and good that the least would suffice to judge temporal controversies.

Moreover, there can be no doubt that Chrysostom was not of the opinion that he thought the sacrifice conferred no benefit to those who are present and do not communicate. We see this both from the places cited above where he writes that the sacrifice benefits the dead and the living who are absent, and also from *Homily 3 on the incomprehensible nature of God*, where he gravely rebukes his listeners because they left after the sermon ended and were not present for the sacrifice. There he says nothing about communion, although he knew a great many either do not communicate, or do so rarely. Rather, he only exhorts them to remain and pray together, and look to Christ who shows himself in the mysteries.

7) The *seventh* objection: In the ancient Church private Masses, in which the priest alone communicates, were forbidden as Chrysostom witnesses (*hom. 18 on 2 Cor.*), where he writes that in the celebration of the Eucharist it does not happen, as it did in the Old testament, that the priest alone eats the offerings.

I respond: (*loc. cit.*) Chrysostom only makes the distinction between the Sacrifices of the Old Testament and of the New, because in the former, either the priest alone ate the victim, or he ate the greater part and the people obtained the lesser from what was immolated. In the latter, however, the priest and the people eat the whole victim, namely the same and whole body and blood of Christ. But this does nothing against private Masses, since if it is often the case now that the priest alone eats the victim, it is not the fault of the priests or the nature of the sacrifice, but *the negligence of the people*.

8) The *eighth* objection: The tenth canon of the Apostles commands

Book II, Ch. X: Private Masses Are Defended 213

those to be excommunicated who do not remain in the Church even while Mass is carried out, and do not receive holy communion. Furthermore, this canon is renewed in the Council of Antioch (cap. 2) and is also extant in the decree of Anacletus (epist. 1) and is cited by Gratian, can. *Peracta, de consecr.* Dist. 2: "After the consecration has been carried out let everyone communicate that does not wish to lose the ecclesiastical house; for the Apostles so decreed, and the Holy Roman Church holds." Therefore, private Masses were forbidden at that time.

I respond: First, these canons command that the faithful should communicate in Mass, but they do not forbid the priest to offer sacrifice if the people are not present or refuse to communicate. Next, the canon of the Apostles is explained in the Council of Antioch, that we understand it does not condemn those who absolutely do not communicate, but those who do not for a certain reason, namely those who turn away from holy communion on account of some *superstition* or *perverse opinion*. Moreover, the decree of Anacletus, if his epistle were to be consulted, and not only the fragment which is cited by Gratian, obliges only *clergy* solemnly ministering with the Bishop on solemn days; this is why, if on some day it were not solemn, or someone would offer sacrifice without the solemn ministry of other clergy, he is not compelled by this decree to give communion. Lastly, it is certain that this decree, which was without a doubt from human law, not divine, if it did pertain to the people it was abrogated through the progress of time; for it is certain in the time of Ambrose and Chrysostom as we cited above, that the Greeks did not usually communicate except after a year.

9) The *ninth* objection: Humbert writes against Nicetas, that Mass is incomplete in which the consecration, fraction or distribution and communication are not done together, and Strabo (*de rebus Ecclesiasticis,* c. 22) teaches likewise, that a legitimate Mass is one in which the following are present: A priest to make responses, those who are to offer and communicate. Two decrees are cited for the same purpose, of Pope Soter (cited by Gratian cap. *Hoc quoque,* de consecr. Dist. 1), the other of the Council of Nantes, cited by Ivo (*Decreti* part. 3 cap. 70).

I respond: If the Mass is received precisely for the sacrifice, it is certain that it is complete and legitimate even without communicants, provided the sacrifice is consumed by the priest. Nevertheless, since, as we said, the celebration of Mass is not only ordered to offer the sacrifice to God, but also to nourish the people with spiritual food, on that account, on the side of the former, it cannot be denied that a Mass is more complete and legitimate where those who are present communicate, than where they are lacking; and the cited authors mean this alone. Hence, those decrees of Pope Soter and the Council of Nantes do not pertain to the matter, for they do not command that those who are present communicate, but only that those who are present *respond to the priest*. There we must note in passing the lie of Chemnitz, for he writes that the Council declares a ridiculous thing, that the priest whisper to the walls in place of the people. But the Council makes no mention of the people, rather, it commands that at least one man will be present to make the responses in Mass lest it would look like the priest says to the walls: *Dominus Vobiscum*, and *Orate fratres*.

10) The *tenth* objection: [A private Mass] is a laughing stock, because in a Mass, in which no one communicates, the priest says, "Whatsoever we have received from this participation of the altar, and the sacraments which we have received." Likewise, that the hosts should be broken; for the *fractio* is ordered to distribution, as Augustine teaches in *Epistle 59 ad Paulinum*.

I respond: Those words are said in the number of the multitude, both on account of the communicates that are present, if any are there, and also on account of those who communicate elsewhere; for since we are one body, not only when we are present but even when absent we pray for all. It is similar to the Lord's prayer, which anyone can recite alone in his bedroom, and still it is composed in such a way as though it should only be said by a multitude gathered together.

What pertains to the *fractio*, is that it is not only ordered to distribution, but also to *signification*; for in the Mass of Chrysostom the *fractio* is done in four parts in the manner of the cross, and one of these pieces is placed in the chalice with a certain recitation of words, as the Latins also do. This is why when Chemnitz calls the ceremony of the fraction a laughing stock, he also clearly mocks the ancient and true Church, Greek and Latin. That is all from the objections of Chemnitz.

11) The *eleventh* objection is of Brenz, from the *Würtemberg Confession*, cap. *de Eucharistia*, where apart from those which are common with those of Chemnitz, he makes this argument: "Christ instituted his Supper, not to be a private action of a sacrificing priest, but the communion of the whole Church; therefore those private Masses are not licit in which the priest only reads the words of the Supper and consecrates the Eucharist."

I respond: The Mass of Catholics is never a private action of the priest, but is always *common for the whole Church*, because it is offered by the common ministry for the common advantage of all; hence, in Mass there is the communion of the Church, if by communion you understand the common fruit of the sacrifice. But if by communion, you understand the consumption of the Eucharist, we affirm Christ instituted the Supper that it should be at the same time, both a sacrifice and a communion, but he did not *command* that those two never be separated, as if sacrifice could not be offered to God when no one is present who wishes to communicate.

12) The *twelfth* objection is of Melanchthon in the *Apologia for the Augsburg Confession*, in the article on the Mass, where he produces a certain epistle of St. Francis to all of his brethren, wherein he commands only one Mass to be celebrated in a place, even if many priests are present.

John of Eck responds in his *Enchiridion*, that this epistle is not recognized by the Order of the Friars Minor as a true epistle of St. Francis. Besides, he adds that the author of that epistle only speaks about Maundy Thursday, not on the other days, and rightly, if this epistle were to speak about any day you like, it would contain something clearly false. For the author of the epistle writes according to the use of the Roman Church only one Mass is celebrated in a place. But Pope Honorius III, who sat in Rome during the time of St. Francis, in cap. *Cum creatura, de celebration Missarum*, commands that Mass not be omitted on the anniversary for the dead on account of a feast or feria occurring, but both should be celebrated on the same day.

13) The *last* objection is of others whom Eck relates from St. Basil on Psalm 115, where he says: "I will not sacrifice hiding in a basement, but I will show a public sacrifice to you." Later he says there is one altar of the Church. And it is confirmed from Jerome (*On Amos 3*) where he says there is one altar in the Church.

Eck rightly responds that through secret sacrifice Basil understands the sacrifice *of schismatics*, who separated from the Church and presumed to offer sacrifices in their small assemblies, and therefore, he also acknowledges there is one altar, i.e. one priesthood, one rite, etc. For Basil adds (*ibid.*), "Hear, you who have left the Church and live in public houses, you make wretched fissures in the precious body. ... You erect altars against the altar constituted for you by the Fathers." In the same way Augustine, Optatus, Cyprian and others everywhere describe schismatics when they say certain men erect an altar against the altar. Jerome also distinguishes one altar of the Church against the many altars of heretics because, as he says, there are as many altars as there are schisms. Otherwise, there were many material altars in the Church, as we showed above from Ambrose, Gregory and others, which is why Tertullian (*de poenitentia*) places among other ceremonies of the penitents, that they kneel before the altar of God.

CHAPTER XI
On the Kind of Language

Now the controversy on the type of language follows, whether it is necessary for Mass to be said in the vernacular, as our adversaries contend and among them, especially Chemnitz (*Exam. Conc. Trid.* 2 part. Pag. 883 et seqq.) Yet, we already treated this very question partly in *On the Word of God* (2, 2), *On the Sacraments in Genere*, book 2, in the last chapter. For three things pertain to the Mass. *Firstly*, the reading of the Scriptures and public prayer. *Secondly*, the consecration and distribution of the sacrament of the Eucharist. *Thirdly*, the oblation of the sacrifice. We treated on the reading and the prayer in *On the Word of God* (*loc. cit.*); on the consecration and dispensation of the Sacrament, we treated in the books *On the Sacraments in Genere*, as we have already said. Thus, only the disputation on the very oblation of the sacrifice remains.

But this is rather easy; for in the first place, the oblation of the sacrifice consists more in the thing than in words. For, as we said above, that action whereby the Lord's body is placed on the altar to the honor of God is a true and real oblation, even if it is not said by means of the words, "I offer," or "we offer." Hence, that action necessarily requires some words, namely the words of consecration, but these words are not directed to instruct those who hear them, but *to consecrate the element*, as is known. The element, however, understands no language; this is why it does not pertain to the real oblation, whether the Mass is said in the vernacular, or not in the vernacular.

Secondly, although the oblation itself must necessarily be expressed in words as it really is in the Mass, nevertheless, what language it is done in would not pertain to the oblation; accordingly, the words of the oblation are directed to *God*, not to the people; God however understands all languages.

Thirdly, the words of the oblation are going to be said in a quiet voice, as we will show in the following chapter, therefore it is not necessary that they be recited in a language which the people understand. What use is it to know what the words mean if you can't hear the sound of the word?

Fourthly, the sacrifice is not offered to instruct the people, if it is a question of its primary and proper end, but to worship God, and obtain benefits for the people. As a result, it is not required for the people to understand what is said, rather, it is enough if God understands.

Fifthly, if the sacrifice were going to be offered in the vernacular, two very grave disadvantages would follow. *One*, it would be necessary to frequently change the words of the sacrifice whenever the vocabulary, which is common in one time, would later cease to be the vernacular. The *second*, is that the union of Churches would be disrupted; for an Italian priest could not say Mass in France, nor a French priest in Italy, nor an Italian or French priest in Germany, nor a German priest in Italy or France. The same would be the case in regard to Spain, England, Poland and any other region.

Sixthly, the most ancient custom of the Church agrees. For in the whole East no ancient liturgy is found except in Greek or Aramaic, wile in the whole West there are no ancient liturgies except in Latin. Nevertheless, after the passage of so many centuries all of these languages are now common, while on the other hand, Latin was never common to the Germans, French, English, and Poles; therefore, the Council of Trent, in session 22, last canon, decreed that the Mass should not be celebrated in the vernacular. The arguments which our adversaries object, on the other hand, we have already refuted (*loci citati*). This is why I have not thought to expend the labor to repeat them, especially when they do not concern the action of the sacrifice.

CHAPTER XII
Not everything in Mass must necessarily be said in a loud voice

THE NEXT question is not much different from the previous one, namely on the manner of voice. Our adversaries impugn the Latin Church because it bids many things in Mass to be said in a quiet voice, which was addressed in the Council of Trent, sess. 22 canon 9. There, from the beginning it must be observed that the question is not, "Whether it is licit *per se* to celebrate the whole Mass in a quiet voice", for we are not unaware that the manner of voice does not pertain to the substance of the sacrifice, and these things can be changed according to the judgment of the Church. Thus, the whole question is placed in this: "Whether the custom of the Latin Church of pronouncing certain things in a quiet voice is opposed to the institution of Christ, and hence, is bad and necessarily must be corrected."

Chemnitz (*Exam.* 2 part., pg. 890), contends that it is against the institution of Christ that some things in Mass are read in a quiet voice; but the Council defined otherwise. Moreover, these reasons show that the teaching of the Council is very true. *Firstly*, it is profitable for the reverence of such a mystery that not everything be said in a loud voice. As St. Basil rightly teaches (*de Spiritu Sancto*, cap. 27), it confers much in regard to the dignity and preserves the reverence of the mysteries that men are not accustomed to hear the same thing very often, or rather, that it not be offered to common ears. What kind of mysteries are they that are announced to everyone's ears?

Secondly, we have the example of the ancient liturgies, both Greek and Latin. The liturgies of Basil and Chrysostom, which even Chemnitz notes, prescribe certain things to be said in silence and to be concluded in a loud voice. We also preserve the same thing when we conclude quiet prayers, by raising the voice at the words: *Per omnia saecula saeculorum*. Chemnitz's response is that this is interpreted as if those liturgies prescribed certain things to be pronounced in a moderate voice, so that they may be heard by all, and then are concluded with shouting and song; but this does not have any validity. For in the Liturgy of Chrysostom, where we read: "The priest prays secretly," the Greek word μυσικῶς does not mean in a moderate voice, but in a whisper; nor are the mysteries said which are made public with a moderate voice, but which are altogether hidden. And besides, in that liturgy the priest is advised to recite those prayers in secret while the Deacon sings the Litany in a loud voice, or while the cantors sing other things. Hence, the people cannot attend to those things which the priest says, and so they are truly and properly secret.

In regard to the Latin liturgy we have the testimony of Innocent I (*Epist. 1 ad Episcopum Eugubinum*, cap. 1) where, being asked about the time in which the *pax* should be given in the mystery of the Mass, he clearly shows that particular part of the Mass is secret; nor does he dare to recount the type of things that are recited before the *pax* is given. But if the whole people were accustomed to hear everything, certainly nothing would be secret, nothing hidden and they could easily be committed to writing which was commonly known to all.

Thirdly, we have examples of the sacrifices of the Old Law. For (that I might omit the fact that a great many things in the sacrifice were prayed in mind without any words), in Leviticus 16:17, the sacrifice of incense is solemnly described, and the priest alone is commanded to enter within the veil and offer sacrifice, and pray for himself, the people and all others waiting outside, and not only could they not hear the priest, but they could not even see him. We read that Zachariah, the father of John the Baptist, offered sacrifice in such a rite in Luke 1:10.

Fourthly, Christ himself in the sacrifice of the cross, which was the exemplar of all sacrifices, carried out the oblation in silence, and he did not speak for the space of three hours to those standing about listening, except for seven very brief sentences, as many sentences as there also are which are pronounced in a loud voice in the Canon of our liturgy.

But let us see what Chemnitz asserts in favor of his own opinion.

1) *Firstly*, he objects that the institution of Christ, that he commanded to be done in his memory in his Supper, is not through silence, but, as Paul explains, through announcement. And the argument could be confirmed from the example of Christ himself, who pronounced the words of consecration in a loud voice so that everyone who was present could hear.

I respond: The memory and announcement of Christ should not be done in words as much as *in reality*; for so Augustine writes (*Contra Faustum* 20, 18), when he says: "This sacrifice is also commemorated by Christians, in the sacred offering and participation of the body and blood of Christ." Nor can what Paul commanded be fulfilled in another manner, that everyone should announce the death of the Lord. What

Book II, Ch. XII: Whispered Prayers at Mass Are Licit

kind of disorder would take place if all the people in the Church should announce the Lord's death with words?

What pertains to the example of Christ, it must be known that Christ did not only pronounce the words to consecrate, but also to *teach the Apostles the rite of consecrating*; this is why it was fitting for him to speak in this way, so that he would be heard by the Apostles. The bishops today preserve this when they ordain priests amidst the solemnities of Masses; for they so pronounce the words of consecration so that all these new priests can hear. There is another purpose for those who celebrate Mass for the people.

2) The *second* objection: Christ did not institute the sacraments in such a way that the action would be visible and public, so the word, which is a special part of the sacraments, should be hidden and buried.

I respond: The notion of a sacrament is one thing, and the notion of a sacrifice another; at the present we are arguing properly on the sacrifice. Moreover, the sacrifice does not consist in words, but in the oblation *of a thing*, words, however, are required in the sacrifice of the Mass, not to be themselves the sacrifice, or part of the sacrifice, but only to show the presence of the victim to us. By the words of consecration, as we showed above, it comes about that the Body of Christ is truly present on the altar; this is why the sacrifice will truly be outward and sensible, even if the words, whereby it comes about, cannot be heard. Add, that in the sacraments, to the essence of which the words chiefly pertain, it is not necessary that the words are perceived by those who receive the sacraments, provided they are perceived by those who minister them; otherwise baptism conferred upon infants, the insane, and the deaf would be invalid, which not even Chemnitz would admit. Consequently, we respond to the argument that Christ did not establish the words so they would be hidden and buried, that he also did not establish them in such a way that they must be pronounced to be heard by all who are present. Rather, he only established them to be really applied, and after him it was left to the liberty of the Church to constitute a manner of recitation. Not only do Catholics teach this, but even Chemnitz the teacher and Luther the prophet, in his book *On the Formula of the Mass*, where he permits the freedom to pronounce the words of the Supper in a loud or quiet voice.

3) The *third* objection: The Apostle (1 Cor. 14) clearly distinguishes these two things: To speak in Church on those things which pertain to the public ministry, and to speak privately to himself and to God.

I respond: For St. Paul, to speak in Church is to exhort and instruct the Church; to speak within oneself and to God is to pray, or praise God, as he says in verse 19: "But in the Church I had rather speak five words with my understanding, that I may instruct others also; ... (v. 28) But if there be no interpreter, let him hold his peace in the Church, and speak to himself and to God." Therefore, he distinguishes a sermon from prayer. Moreover, neither pertain properly to the sacrifice; for a sacrifice is not something to say, but *to do*; or if it is to speak in some manner, it is not to speak in the Church, or to the Church, but *to God*. When a man offers sacrifice to God, he acts for God, not for men, although he acts publicly and not privately. This is because he does not act on his own behalf, but on behalf of the universal Church.

4) The *fourth* objection: In the ancient Church, after those who could not be present at the mysteries were dismissed, the prayers were pronounced out loud, the thanksgivings and even the words of consecration themselves. Cardinal Bessarion (*de verbis Coenae*) hands down this very thing on the word of consecration, and the same is clear from the response "Amen" which was made to the words of consecration in the ancient rite. For Dionysius of Alexandria (cited b Eusebius, *Histor.* 7, 9) calls it to mind, as well as Augustine (*ad Orosium*, quaest. 49). It is likewise clear from Chrysostom (*Homily 18 in 2 Cor.*) where we read that the prayers and thanksgivings in the celebration of the Eucharist were common to the people with the priest. Lastly, the same is gathered from the *Novella* of Justinian, constitution 123, where the priests are severely commanded to say what they recite in the celebration of the oblation in a loud voice so that the people could hear it.

I respond: We do not deny that the words of consecration in the Eastern Church are customarily recited out loud, since it is quite certain from the liturgy of Chrysostom. Nor do we condemn this; for we do not contend that these words must necessarily be recited in a quiet voice, rather, that the Church is *free* to establish the rite, and hence neither the rite of the Greeks nor of the Latins can be condemned, nor should they. But although the words of consecration are uttered in a loud voice among the Greeks, nevertheless, certain others are pronounced in a quiet voice and clearly in secret, as we clearly showed from the same liturgy of Chrysostom. As a result, there is no need to respond to the testimony of Bessarion and Dionysius of Alexandria.

To the citation of Augustine, I respond: That book is not of Augustine, as the scholars affirm, nor does it bear on the matter. That author does

Book II, Ch. XII: Whispered Prayers at Mass Are Licit

not speak about the consecration, but the *dispensation of the sacrament*; for he only says that those who receive the blood of the Lord customarily say "Amen", while the priest says, "The blood of our Lord Jesus Christ." Ambrose also calls this rite to mind (*De Sacramentis*, 4, 5).

To the citation of Chrysostom, I respond: Chrysostom chiefly meant that the people should not be idle in Church, but should pray for those things for which the priest also prays. The fact is, that can be done even if both the priest and the people pray in silence. Indeed, Cyprian writes (*On the Lord's Prayer*) that during the time of the sacrifice Anna the mother of Samuel should be imitated, who prayed in such a way that her lips moved, but hardly a word was heard (1 Kings 1:13), and she was a type of the Church, while she prayed in silence. Also, in our liturgy, it is said to the people: *Orate fratres* when the prayer is made in secret. Add, that Chrysostom does not say *all* prayers are common to the people and the priest; this is why even if he spoke on the communion of the same prayers, still our adversaries would gain nothing. For the liturgy of Chrysostom clearly distinguishes what must be said by all, and what must be said by the priest alone, and in secret.

In regard to the *Novella* of Justinian, the response could be made that in the first place, it does not pertain to the emperor to impose laws on the rite of sacrifice, hence he did not greatly report on what he had ratified. But we also answer that this law is not opposed to our teaching. It only commands that what is customarily said out loud in the Eastern Churches should be said in a loud voice. There were some, as is gathered from the *Novella* itself, who pronounced what was customarily said in a loud voice quietly, so in that way they might hide their ignorance; they are rightly rebuked both because they acted against the custom of the Church and because they did it because they were ignorant of reading.

5) The *last* objection: The Popes affirm this is not an ancient usage. Honorius and Belet write that formerly the words of consecration were customarily said in a loud voice, but later it was commanded to be said silently and for this reason: When those words were heard by all, many laity also remembered them. Then it happened that certain shepherds pronounced the words over bread and wine. Immediately the bread and wine were turned into body and blood; and those shepherds, being struck down by God, died. From this history it is gathered that the use of reciting the words of consecration in silence are not ancient, and is born of superstitious opinion, as if those words were magical.

I respond: The miracle which is recalled in this argument truly happened, but different and in a more ancient time than Chemnitz relates. For St. Sophronius writes in his *Prato Spirituali*, cap. 196, that this miracle happened in his time, but he lived before the time of the Seventh Council, as well as John Damascene. For this book is cited by the fathers of the Seventh Council, in the fourth action, and by Damascene (in *Orat. De cultu imaginum*, 3). Hence, this miracle happened more or less nine hundred years ago, and it is also recalled by Alcuin (*de Divinis Officiis*, cap. *de celebratione Missae*), and he lived eight hundred years ago. Moreover, that miracle did not turn bread into flesh, nor kill the shepherds, as Chemnitz gathers from some obscure and more recent authors, rather, when the fire was sent from heaven, the bread, wine and stone upon which these were placed were gone, and the shepherds were astounded to the point that they could hardly speak for a long time. Sophronius does not write that this is the reason why those words should not be said but secretly, although if it were the reason, I do not see what could be objected against it. Certainly, that use is very ancient, even if it did not begin earlier than after that miracle were divinely shown to the world.

CHAPTER XIII
What the Heretics suppose in regard to the Ceremonies of the Mass

WE DISPUTED on ceremonies in our work *On the Sacraments in Genere*, book 2; now we will merely treat on those which properly pertain to the ceremonies of the Mass. Before all, two things must be explained in this place. *Firstly*, it will be made clear what our adversaries suppose on the ceremonies of the Mass, and what is in controversy. *Secondly*, the truth will be proved, and at the same time we will refute the objections.

Many authors write on the ceremonies and parts of the Mass. It seems the first was Gelasius, whose book *De Missarum solemniis* which St. Gregory I abridged, as John the Deacon writes (*Vita Gregorii*, 2, 17), and Gregory himself mentions the very same book (*Epistles* 7, 63). The second was Isidore, after the year 600 A.D., whose two books *De Divinis Officis* are extent. The third was the author of the Roman Ordinal, who seems to have lived after the year 700 A.D. The fourth was Alcuin, who lived in the same century, whose book *De Officiis Ecclesiasticis* is extent. The fifth is Amalarius, in the same century, whose books by the same title are also extent. The sixth was Rabanus Maurus, after the year 800. The seventh, in the same century was Walfrid Strabo. The eighth, after about the year 900, is a solitary book *de Gemma Animae*. The ninth is Micrologus, after the year 1000. The tenth is Rupert Tuitiensis, after the year 1100. The eleventh is Hugh of St. Victor, in the same century. The twelfth is Pope Innocent III, after the year 1200. The thirteenth is Bonaventure, in the same century. The fourteenth is William Durandus, after the year 1300. The fourteenth is Thomas Waldens, after the year 1400. The fifteenth is Conrad Brunus, after the year 1500, and in the same century George Cassander also wrote the Rhapsody, and Rheanus a few things in annotations to Tertullian's book *De Corona Militis*; nevertheless that author must be read cautiously, moreover, even if he was a heretic, still, he seems to have added nothing of his own. It is said that John Garetius and James Pamelius gathered many things in their work *De Liturgia*, but I have not yet been able to see their books.

Now that we have prefaced these, let us proceed to what we proposed.

What pertains to the first, nearly all the Calvinists detest the ceremonies of the Mass and think they must be abrogated. They do not use any in their administration of the Lord's Supper, and Calvin generally rebukes them (*Instit.* 4, 17 §43), where he admits they are very ancient, nay more he writes that they began not far from the age of the Apostles, but he calls them a blight on the Lord's Supper and says they were born from the blindness of human confidence, which cannot contain itself so it plays and runs riot in the mysteries of God.

But Luther and the Lutherans do not altogether reject ceremonies. In their Churches they preserve some, and Melanchthon (*Apologia Confess.* Art. *De Missa*), says customary ceremonies are preserved among them in the Mass, which is true of some but not all.

Moreover, Luther, in his work *On the Babylonian Captivity*, in his chapter on the Eucharist, writes three things about ceremonies. *Firstly*, the Mass is more Christian the simpler and more similar it is to the Mass of Christ, in which there was no vestment, gesture, song, and pomp; in such words he gives a backhanded rebuke to ceremonies.

Secondly, he adds that he must not find fault with the whole Church on that account, which adorned and increased the Mass with many other rites and ceremonies; in his book *On the Formula of the Mass* he permits candles, and incense and some other things of this sort. But this second saying is not particularly consistent with the first. For if the pomp of ceremonies would make the Mass less Christian, as he holds in his first saying, then rightly the Church which brought in that pomp may and must be rebuked, which is contrary to this second saying.

Thirdly, he says that ceremonies without faith are incentives to impiety, more than offices of piety. But if Luther were to speak on Catholic faith, in which we believe the body of Christ is truly present in the Eucharist, and a sacrifice is truly offered to God for the sins of the living and the dead, he would not be wrong to say that ceremonies without faith are incentives to impiety; but because he speaks on a certain special faith whereby he would have it we believe for certain that sins are remitted, consequently, that saying was rightly condemned in the Council of Trent, sess. 22, canon 7. For ceremonies serve to rouse devotion and reverence even in those who do not believe for certain that their sins are forgiven, but we will make a dissertation on this faith in another place.

Furthermore, Chemnitz (*Exam.* 2 part. Pg. 852), posits a fourfold partition of the ceremonies of the Mass. He says that some of them have a divine mandate as well as examples of Scripture, and are substantial, such as to receive bread, to bless, to eat, and to announce the death of the Lord. Certain ceremonies, although they do not have an express

Book II, Ch. XIII: Ceremonies According to the Heretics 227

divine mandate, and are not altogether necessary, they are still pious and good if they are taken for edification, such as Psalms, readings, prayers, and the confession of faith through the recitation of the creed. Some ceremonies are superstitious and impious *per se*, such as an oblation for the living and the dead, the invocation of the saints, satisfaction for the souls in Purgatory, private Mass, the exorcism of salt and the blessing of water. Lastly, others are indifferent, such as vestments, vessels, and the other ornaments which are not repugnant to the word of God. From these he teaches that the first kind were preserved in the first ages of the Church; the third kind must be altogether abrogated; the second and fourth should be retained but at one's pleasure and as something hardly necessary.

We agree with Chemnitz on the first kind; we disagree with him on the third; in the second and fourth we partly agree and partly disagree. But all of these are not for this place: for we do not dispute in this place on any ceremony you like, but only on those which are outside the essence of the sacrifice, on which the Council of Trent speaks; this is why we do not dispute on the first kind. Next, we dispute on ceremonies properly speaking, not on all the parts or causes or effects of the Mass; hence Psalms, readings, prayers, etc. are not proper ceremonies, and through this we do not argue on the second kind. For equal reasoning, oblation for the living and the dead, invocation of saints, satisfaction, private Mass, and similar things are not ceremonies, nor are we disputing on them now. The question at the moment is only on the fourth kind, added with holy water, which Chemnitz posited in the third kind.

Moreover, on this fourth kind, we disagree with Chemnitz and the other Lutherans in three things. *Firstly*, that they apply very few and we a great many ceremonies in the Mass. *Secondly*, that they in no way admit ceremonies to be necessary or able to be commanded by the Church. Even if we were to affirm that they are not necessary of themselves, nevertheless, we judge they can be commanded, and once this command has been made, they cannot be omitted without sin. *Thirdly*, because they attribute no force to any ceremonies, and mock the consecrations of water, salt, incense, and candles, etc.; we, on the other hand, attribute a certain force to the ceremonies from the consecration and prayers of the Church. But in these last questions we have said enough in *On the Sacraments in Genere*, book 2, and in other places. Therefore, we will only need to show in this place that not only those few ceremonies which the Lutherans admit, but all the others which the Catholic Church uses in the Mass are ancient and pious.

But before we come to our ceremonies, we must refute the lies which bubble out of Chemnitz's disputation. Firstly (*loc. cit.* pg. 853), he says the Council of Trent, in sess. 22 cap. 5, approves all ceremonies without distinction, whether they are pious or superstitious. But the Council does not speak about anything but those ceremonies which *the Church instituted*, as is clear from the Conciliar text, and which pertain to the fourth kind posited by Chemnitz, which the same Chemnitz affirms are not superstitious.

Secondly, he says (*ibid.*) that the Council defined all ceremonies which are used in the Mass are from Apostolic tradition, and he shows this is false because in the Last Supper the Lord did not use these, nor did Paul remember them when he described the Synaxis of the Apostles (1 Cor. 11). But the Council does not say all the ceremonies are from Apostolic tradition, but *many*; and the proof of Chemnitz is completely inept. For apostolic tradition began after the Lord's Ascension, and therefore, it is no wonder if in the Last Supper these ceremonies were not used; because clearly the Apostles had not yet instituted them. Hence Paul, in 1 Cor. 11, does not relate the whole Synaxis of the Apostles, but he only relates what he received from the Lord.

Thirdly, he says the ancient Popes amassed ceremonies by mixing up many idle and superstitious rites. That this is absolutely false is clear from the Greek Liturgies as well as the Ambrosian, which the Popes did not establish and still they have more ceremonies than our Roman Liturgy, which Chemnitz calls Pontifical.

Fourthly, he says that among Catholics observance of the ceremonies is thought to be so necessary that they pronounce a man has sinned mortally if he has neglected some of them. But this is also a lie; we do not say that any negligence you like is a mortal sin, rather *contempt* or a *notable negligence in grave matters*.

Fifthly he says the Popes scarcely believe the Lord's Supper is rightly celebrated if the whole apparatus of ceremonies is not used. But if by *rightly* he understands the essential rectitude, as he seems to understand, it is a clear lie; for Catholics constantly teach the whole essence of the sacrifice was instituted by Christ and hence, without these ceremonies which the Church added later, no man doubts that a true sacrifice was celebrated and valid. Moreover, if by *rightly*, Chemnitz understands the accidental rectitude then he says nothing, for who would doubt that a thing was not done correctly if, in doing it, he omitted some things

Book II, Ch. XIII: Ceremonies According to the Heretics

which should not be omitted?

Sixthly, he says Catholics attribute to those rites and ceremonies peculiar merits *per se* and absolutely. But this is a most impudent lie, for Catholics recognize no merits without faith and charity, and only a fool would say that to lift the hands and genuflect and other acts of this kind are *per se* and absolutely meritorious.

CHAPTER XIV
The Ceremonies which Precede Mass Are Ancient and Pious

Now, that we might more easily defend the ceremonies of the Mass, we will recall them all to certain headings. For some are received from the person, others from the place, others from the time, and these consist in things, and are required before the sacrifice. Others consist in action, and are used during the sacrifice, partly toward the Lord, partly toward the people, partly toward the sacrifice itself. On the side of person sacred vestments are required. On the side of the place Churches, altars, sacred vessels such as a chalice, paten, corporal, and likewise candles are required. On the side of time it is required that it is especially done on Sundays before noon and before all food. Let us speak very briefly on each of these.

On Sacred Vestments

We have the first example on sacred vestments from the Old Testament, in which the priest who was going to sacrifice was clothed with certain vestments prescribed by God; moreover, these vestments were types and figures of the sacred vestment with which Christian priests are now clothed as the authors whom I will cite show, one by one, that our vestments correspond to the Jewish.

Next, we have the most ancient use of the Church: for many ancient writers enumerate all the garments which we now use in Mass and explain their meanings, as Innocent III notes (*de Mysteriis Missae*, book 1), along with Rupert (*de Divinis Officiis*), Bonaventure (*de Explicatione Missae*), Strabo (*de rebus Ecclesiasticis*, 24), Hugh of St. Victor (*de sacramentis*, 2, 4) Amalarius (*de officiis Ecclesiasticis*, 2) Rabanus (*de institutione clericorum*, 1) and Alcuin (*de officiis Ecclesiasticis*, cap. *de vestibus sacris*). Some of these authors lived 300 years ago, such as Innocent and Bonaventure; others 400 years ago, such as Rupert and Hugh; others 700, as Strabo and Rabanus, lastly, 800 years ago, such as Amalarius and Alcuin.

Apart from these authors, who enumerate all the vestments in order, they do not say it began in their time, but that they hand down what they received from the ancients; there are no other ancient authors lacking who briefly touch upon something concerning vestments of this sort.

Book II, Ch. XIV: Antiquity of the Ceremonies of Mass

Julian Pomerius, who lived 900 years ago, in the life of St. Ildefonsus, which is extent in Surius (tomus 1), writes that priestly clothing was brought by the Most Holy Virgin from heaven, and given to St. Ildefonsus, which he used in Mass.

Pope Gregory, around a thousand years ago, sent into Britain sacred vessels, relics of the saints, and ornaments of the altar, even priestly and clerical vestments for the new Church, as John the Deacon writes (*Vita Gregorii*, 2, 37) as well as Bede (*hist.* 1, 29).

Jerome (*Contra Pelagianos*, book 1), writes that bishops and priests and every cleric was clothed in white garments in the administration of the sacrifice. Chrysostom says the same thing (*Hom. 83 in Matt.*) who also describes, in the beginning of the liturgy, the prayers which are said while the priests put on sacred vestments. Jerome also writes (*in epist. Ad Heliodorum* on the death of Nepotianus) that when the priest Nepotianus was dying, he gave him his tunic, which he used in the ministry of Christ, but both lived 1100 years ago.

The fourth Council of Carthage, celebrated in the time of Augustine, forbade deacons to use an alb except in the sacred ministry.

The author of questions on the Old and New testament, which is found in the works of Augustine (tom. 4 quaest. 46) writes that the deacons usually used Dalmatics, but this author was scarcely before Augustine's time, as is clear from Question 44.

Sylvester, 1200 years ago, as Damasus relates on his life, constituted that the deacons in the Church use the Dalmatic, and cover their left with a flaxen cloth.

Next, it can be related here what Polycrates writes 1400 years ago, cited by Eusebius (*hist.* 4, 24) that St. John also wore a priestly petalon.

We can also add manifest reason. For just as kings and magistrates do not use common vestments in public actions, but procure another more august, and with certain characteristics whereby their reverence is clearer, and at the same time represent their rule and power, so also, it is altogether fitting that in this public action of the whole Church the priest use a sacred and peculiar garment, suitable both to show the reverence of the mystery and to show the very passion of Christ.

On Churches and the Altar

We already discussed many things about churches and the altar in *On the Church Triumphant* 3, 1, and they are full of writings of ancients both of the Fathers and of Councils, where Churches and altars are mentioned, and in the last book (chapter 14) we advanced several testimonies. Since our adversaries do not so much reject Churches and altars as they do mystical consecrations when they are on a church and an altar, you can see the most ancient testimonies of the same consecration in the Fifth Council of Carthage (can. 6), as well as the Council of Agde (can. 14), and in the writings of the Fathers, Eusebius (*Vita Constantini* book 4), Athanasius (*Apologia ad Constantinum*), Basil (*on Psalm 114*), Gregory of Nyssa (*de Baptismo*) Ambrose (*Epistles*, 1, 5 ad Felicem), Gaudentius, (*in tractatu de dedication*), Augustine (*Serm 251*), and the following in order of time: Gelasius (*in Epist. 1*) and Felix IV in his decretal epistle *De Ecclesiarum et altarium consecration*, and as Pope was a predecessor of Gregory the Great. Felix not only confirms that Churches and altars should be consecrated, but also (which is proper for this place) he witnessed that ancient Canons forbade anyone from presuming to celebrate solemn Masses in any place but those consecrated to God, save for extreme necessity.

On Sacred Vessels

There are many ancient texts extent on sacred vessels. Damasus (*Vita S. Urbani Papae et martyris*) calls to mind silver vessels which were then in the Church for the use of the sacraments. Moreover, Urban sat around the year 230 A.D. Prudentius, in his hymn on St. Laurence, calls to mind golden vessels which were in the time of St. Laurence, i.e. around the year 260 A.D. In the time of Pope Sylvester, around the year 300 A.D., there were many gold and silver chalices, patens, candelabra, and thuribles, as the same Damasus witnesses. Athanasius, in his *Second Apology against the Arians*, writes many things on the mystical cup which the Arians had falsely accused him of breaking. It is certain from this passage that there were sacred chalices of the Eucharist, and they could not be touched by anyone unless they were ordained, nor polluted without sacrilege. Gregory Nazianzen, in his oration himself against the Arians, writes that the Arians plundered sacred vessels which were forbidden for the laity to touch, and therefore he compares them to Nabuzardan and Balthasar, one of whom took the sacred vessels from the temple in Jerusalem, while the other profaned them. Optatus of Miletus (*Contra Parmenianum*, 6), asks of the Donatists why they plundered, melted down and sold the sacred vessels in which the blood of Christ is contained, and likewise the

Book II, Ch. XIV: Antiquity of the Ceremonies of Mass 233

altar cloths and veils. Ambrose (*de Officiis* 2, 28) writes many things on the Sacred vessels, and furthermore, shows that they were golden and consecrated. Augustine on Psalm 113, says: "We also have very many instruments and vessels made of gold and silver for the use of those celebrating the Sacraments, which, being consecrated by the ministry itself are called holy." Lastly, Chrysostom (*Hom. 4 in Matt.*, and more profusely in his book on *St. Babyla* against the gentiles) writes that Julian, the uncle of the Emperor Julian and a certain other man who exercised the office of Quaestor, plundered the sacred vessels of the Church and profaned them; immediately Julian experienced the avenging hand of God, so that he died being gnawed to pieces by worms, and the Quaestor burst asunder from within. Gregory of Tours relates similar examples (*de Gloria Martyrum*, 85) which sufficiently shows that this ceremony of sacred vessels is very ancient and pleasing to God.

But Calvin, in the preface to his work on the *Institutes*, objects with two citations of the Fathers. One is of Ambrose in *de Officiis* 2, 18, where we so read: "The Sacraments do not desire gold, nor are they pleased with gold, since they are not bought with gold." The second is of Acacius, whom Socrates relates (*Hist.* 7, 21), as saying on a certain occasion when he was accused of selling the sacred vessels on account of the poor: "Our God does not need plates or chalices, because he neither eats nor drinks."

I respond: Both citations favor us, for in each one we read the Church abounded in precious and sacred vessels, as well as the fact that they should be diligently preserved unless the great necessity of the poor were to come about. Moreover, in such a necessity the holy fathers meant it is lawful to melt down and sell sacred vessels, and they argue that these precious vessels are not absolutely necessary to administer the sacraments. This is what Ambrose means, when he says, "The Sacraments do not seek gold," not that they must necessarily be driven out; and what he adds, "They are not pleased by gold," does not mean they are displeased by gold, or that they are in no way more pleased by gold than glass, but, they are not *principally* pleased because they are ministered in gold. For if they were displeased in gold, nor any more pleased than in another material, Ambrose would not have saved them for that necessity, but would never have used them to begin with.

The words of Acacius have the same sense; for they mean the golden vessels are of no use to God, but in the Church they are for the honor of God and our benefit; and therefore, when the occasion offered itself whereby they could be more useful to us if they were sold, they should be sold because it will please God more, who desires mercy more than sacrifice. See what we said in book 3 of *On the Church Triumphant*, ch. 6.

On Candles

We are not lacking ancient testimonies on the candles which we use in Mass, and especially while we read the Gospel. Athanasius (*Epist. Ad omnes Orthodoxos*) writes that among the other sacrileges of the Arians, one was that they burned the candles of the Church to idols. Jerome (*contra Vigilantium*) writes that in the Catholic Church candles are lit while the sun glows during the reading of the Gospel, to show the sign of joy. Chrysostom writes in his Liturgy that the priest proceeds to the altar while the minister goes before him with a light. The Roman Ordinal calls to mind the candles which are lit for the Gospel and the oblation of the Lord's body. The fourth Council of Carthage (canon 6) teaches that candles are given to the Acolyte in his ordination by the Archdeacon so that he would know that his ministry pertains to light the candles in the Church. Isidore (*Etymolog.* 7, 12), explains that in that time the Acolyte had to light the candles in the Church not only when the Gospel is read, but even more when the body of Christ is offered. Lastly, Micrologus (*loc. cit.* cap. 11) asserts that Mass is never celebrated without a candle, even if it is celebrated at noon.

On the Day of Celebration

Next, what pertains to the time of celebration of the sacrifice, Catholics understand that it must especially be done on Sunday; the heretics do not oppose this. We have, in the first place, the testimony of Scripture in Acts 20:7, "On the one of the sabbath when we are assembled to break bread."[16] By "one of the sabbath" Sunday is understood, as Chrysostom and Bede explain; and it is clear from other similar places. This is why in 1 Cor. 16:2, it is written: "On the one of the Sabbath let every one of you put away from yourself, etc." All the Greek and Latin interpreters explain it in regard to Sunday, in which Christians usually

---

16 Translator's note: In order to maintain the propriety of Bellarmine's argument, we have been excessively literal here with the phrase *una Sabbati* as it appears in the Vulgate, as Bellarmine is explaining it to his Latin speaking audience. Translations of the Vulgate, as well as those of the Greek where we find the same thing (τῇ μιᾷ τῶν σαββάτων) properly render the Hebrew idiom as "first day of the week."

Book II, Ch. XIV: Antiquity of the Ceremonies of Mass

came together in Church. In Mark 16:9, Christ is said to have risen on the one of the Sabbath, and nobody ever denied that should understand "first day of the sabbath" as Sunday. Moreover, Sunday is called the first of the sabbath, because it is the first day of the week; the Hebrew phrase receives *one* for first, and *Sabbath* for a week.

Next, Justin Martyr, in the *Second Apology*, clearly writes that on the day of the Sun, that is on Sunday (*Dominica*) Christians customarily gathered for the sacrifice of the Eucharist. Augustine writes in *Epistle 188*, that in certain places the sacrifice is customarily offered every day, in others only on Sunday and Saturday, in other places only on Sunday. Whereby we understand that no one ever doubted that Sunday is the most suitable day to celebrate this sacrifice.

On the Hour of Celebration, and on the Fasting Necessary to celebrate the Sacrifice

Among Catholics, the hour of the day most suited to celebrate the sacrifice is before noon, and before all food. Certainly, the ancients offered the sacred rites from 9 in the morning even to 3 in the afternoon, because in that time they continued fasting until 3pm. Sometimes they celebrated just before evening, such as on Maundy Thursday and on Holy Saturday. Sometimes they celebrated in the middle of the night, as on Christmas. See Strabo (*loc. cit.* cap. 23). Now, with the exception of the Mass that is still sung in the middle of the night on Christmas, the sacred rites are celebrated from dawn to noon, and fasting is prolonged from custom.

The Lutherans and the Calvinists openly scorn these things; for Luther writes, in his book against the King of England (published in 1522), that it is an article of the Pope to [celebrate Mass] in the morning and before all food, and he adds: "We, however, merely call these things stupid and brutish, and have a free communion, whether by day or night, or in the morning or the evening. Among us there is no sin if someone modestly eats and drinks before communion." And in his book on the *Formula of the Mass*, he permits fasting, so long as it is free, before communion and only necessarily requires that one approaches soberly, i.e. as he explains, lest someone would belch from drunkenness, or become slow from a full stomach. He says similar things in his book *On the Abrogation of Private Mass*, where still he falsely assigns to Catholics that they teach a man is unworthy of communion who imprudently absorbed a drop of water.

Catholics do not so rigidly explain this fast, nay more, in the case of necessity they permit one to take communion even after food, such as when someone is sick and his life is in danger, and he has not yet received viaticum and there would be a danger in delay; for then communion can be given at any hour. Outside of this case, those who treat on absorbing some drops of water with saliva that reaches the stomach, they did not think it broke fasting, nor were they forbidden from attending the sacred rites or receiving communion. For more on this matter see St. Thomas, III q. 80, art. 8.

Moreover, the fact that our custom is without a doubt most ancient and Apostolic, and necessarily to be preserved with the exception of a case of necessity, can be easily demonstrated. Tertullian (*Ad uxorem*, 2, 5) says, "Will your husband not know what it is which you taste before taking any food?" He speaks on the consensus of all in regard to the Eucharist. Cyprian (*Epist.* 2, 3) objects this argument to himself, which later Luther would make, namely from the example of Christ who offered sacrifice after he had supped, and he answers that Christ offered in the evening for a certain reason, and after Supper, because it was so foretold by the Prophets; still, we should offer in the morning because we celebrate the resurrection of the Lord. He conveys it as though it were a very absurd matter: "Should we, therefore, celebrate after dinner on Sunday?" John Chrysostom (*hom. 27 on 1 Cor.*) says: "You fast before you receive so that in some way you may appear worthy to communicate." Chrysostom also (*Epist. 3 ad Cyriacum Episcopum*) writes that he was accused of offering communion to those who did not fast, and swore that he did not do it: "If I did so, let Christ cast me out of his kingdom."

Augustine (*Epistle 118*, c. 6) proposes the same argument which we said was answered by Cyprian above: "It is evident that when the disciples first received the body and blood of Christ that they did not do so while fasting; still, should we find fault with the universal Church on that account, because it is always received while fasting? Since it pleased the Holy Spirit that in honor of such a sacrament, the Lord's body should first enter into the mouth of a Christian, before other food, consequently through the whole world this custom is preserved. Nor, because the Lord gave it after food, on that account should those brethren that have dined and supped come together to receive that sacrament; or, just as they did whom the Apostle complains of and corrects, when they mixed these things with their own table. For the Savior, that he might more forcefully commend the loftiness of that mystery, willed to fix this last upon the

Book II, Ch. XIV: Antiquity of the Ceremonies of Mass

hearts and memory of the disciples, whom he was about to leave for the passion; and therefore, he did not give a command on what order it was thereafter to be taken, so as to preserve this place for the Apostles, through whom he will manage the Churches." From this testimony we have many things. *Firstly*, the Lord commanded nothing on this matter. *Secondly*, the Apostles, inspired by the Holy Spirit, established that the Eucharist should be received while fasting. *Thirdly*, it is preserved in the whole world by every Church of Christ. *Fourthly*, the reasoning of this matter was on account of the honor of such a sacrament, which is the same reasoning that later authors touch upon, such as Isidore (*de officiis divinis*, 1, 18) and Amalarius (*De Officiis Ecclesiasticis*, 3, 34) and Strabo (*de Rebus Ecclesiast.*, c. 19).

But Luther, as he was the most impudent of all men, mocks the testimony of such a Doctor in his book *De Abroganda Missa*, in the second part, with these words: "They say it is unworthy that anything should enter the mouth of a Christian before the Lord's body. O! festive argument; perhaps it is not lawful for either fog or air to enter the mouth of a Christian before the Lord's body will have entered, so that the priests should be deprived of breath and life, even after Mass and Communion." Thus he.

It is horrendous, bold and positively diabolic to insult the whole Church, not by a strong argument, but by twisting the words of Augustine. Augustine did not say it is unworthy that *anything* would enter the mouth of a Christian before the Body of Christ; rather, that *any food* would enter before the most sacred food of the Lord's flesh. Consequently, we are not forbidden to breath the air, as in Luther's nonsense, but to take *some food*.

Besides these testimonies of the Fathers, we also have the decrees of the most ancient Councils celebrated in different parts of the world. The third Council of Carthage was celebrated in Africa around the year 400, and it so decreed in Canon 29, "The Sacraments of the altar should not be celebrated except by men who are fasting." The same is received in can. 48, and again in the African Council, can. 8. The second Council of Matisconnense (Maconnais) was celebrated in France around the year 500, and in can. 6 it renewed that canon of the Council of Carthage, but added the penalty of deposition from his dignity. The same also established that the remnants of the Lord's body should be given to children to eat, after the appointed fast. The fact that such a use was once in Greece is witnessed by Evagrius (*hist.* 4, 35). The first Council of Braga, celebrated in Portugal around the year 600, stated in Canon 16 that even on Maundy Thursday the Lord's Supper was celebrated while fasting. The seventh Council of Toledo was celebrated in Spain near the same time, and in can. 2, decreed the penalty of excommunication on those who dared to make Mass after receiving food, no matter how scanty. The Council of Constance was celebrated in Germany after the year 1400, a hundred years before the heresy of Luther arose, and in sess. 13 it condemned the error, or the abuse of some who dared to celebrate the Sacrament of the altar after taking food.

At length, let us add the horrible vengeance which God exercised on a certain priest who presumed to celebrate Mass on Christmas but did not fast (Gregory of Tours, *Gloria Martyrum*, c. 86).

Now, let us see the arguments of Luther. Firstly, he objects with the example of Christ, who instituted and ministered the sacrament after dinner. But this has already been answered by Cyprian and Augustine; wo whom we can add that Christ institute and administer the Eucharist after any dinner you like, but after the supper of the *Paschal Lamb*, to show that one supper was a shadow and a figure of another; moreover, it is not lawful for us to set up that Jewish supper since it was abrogated; in the same way that Christ, after Circumcision received Baptism, nevertheless, Christians should not receive Circumcision before they are baptized.

Secondly, he objects with the testimony of the Apostle in 1 Corinthians 11:34, "If any man be hungry, let him eat at home," where it seems the Apostle permits those who intend to communicate but cannot bear fasting, or do not wish to, to approach the Church after they have taken food at home.

I respond: This passage is usually explained in two ways. *Firstly*, that the sense would be: If anyone cannot remain fasting in the Church for a long time, let him first eat food in his home, and so come to Church; Anselm explains it this way, although he adds that a man who has already eaten comes to Church, he should not take the Eucharist. *Secondly*, that the sense is: If anyone being in the Church, cannot bear hunger, he should go out and return home and eat there, not in the Church. Nevertheless, the Apostle did not say this so it would be done, but that men of this sort, slaves to their appetite, should be ashamed, they should be expelled from the Church and sent away to their homes as those who are unworthy of holy communion; this is the way Chrysostom, Theophylactus and others explain it. Such an explanation seems truer, but neither argument favors

Book II, Ch. XIV: Antiquity of the Ceremonies of Mass 239

Luther.

Thirdly he objects that a man is more suitable for communion after taking a moderate amount of food, than fasting, because after food has been taken the head is usually clearer, the mouth cleaner, the breath more unspoiled, etc.

I respond: The Apostolic tradition and the custom of the whole Church should persuade us more than the philosophy of Luther. Besides, what Luther assumes is false; for even if food is beneficial for works of the body, nevertheless it is not for works *of the spirit*. And that fasting confers much upon prayer is especially clear from the divine Scripture, which everywhere joins prayer with fasting. Tobit 12:8, "Prayer is good with fasting," and Judith 4:7, "They humbled their souls in fastings and prayers." Luke 2:37, "Serving God with fastings and prayers." Matt. 17:20, "This kind is not cast out, except in prayer and fasting."

Lastly, he objects: Christ left it free, hence it should be free.

I respond: There are many things that Christ did not command per se, which still he did not wish to be free. Accordingly, he commanded this through the Apostles or their successors, and he said of them in Luke 10:16, "He who hears you, hears me."

CHAPTER XV
On the Ceremonies which Are Done in the Mass, and the Action in which they Consist

Now we must briefly speak on those ceremonies which are used in the very celebration of the Mass, which can be recalled to five headings. Some are assigned to God, such as the elevation of hands, the elevation of the eyes, adoration through bowing, or through genuflection. Others are assigned to the sacrifice, such as the elevation, the *ostensio*, the *fractio*, and the *commixtio*. Others to the celebrating priest, such as striking the breast and the washing of hands. Others to the people, such as the greeting and dismissal. Others are assigned to those which are read at Mass such as the music and the musical instruments. Apart from these, some other ceremonies are common to many things, such as the sign of the cross, the sprinkling with water, incensing, the kiss, etc.

So, the *first* ceremony with respect to God, i.e. the elevation of hands, has an example in Scripture. In Exodus 17:17, Moses obtained his request while praying with his hands elevated. Likewise, in 3 Kings 8:22, Solomon spread his hands to heaven when he was about to pray. In Psalm 140, David says: "The elevation of my hands as an evening sacrifice." St. Paul in 1 Tim. 2:8, "I will that men pray in every place, lifting up pure hands." Lastly, this seems to be a natural ceremony, since it is everywhere read that the pagans lifted up their hands to heaven when they prayed.

The *second*, which is the elevation of the eyes, was familiar to Christ; for in a great many places it is said that he lifted his eyes to heaven (Matt. 14:19; Mark 6:41 and 7:34; Luke 9:16; John 6:5, 11:41 and 17:1). And although in the action of the Supper it is not expressly read that in the Gospel, he lifted up his eyes to heaven, nevertheless it is constantly asserted that he did this by St. James in his Liturgy, as well as Ambrose (*de Sacramentis*, 4, 5). Tertullian (*Apologeticus*, 30) writes that Christians, looking up to heaven with their hands extended, customarily pray with their head uncovered.

The *third*, which is the bowing of the body or genuflection, is a sign of humility and reverence, used everywhere by the saints. In 2 Chron. 6:13, Solomon prays on his knees, in Luke 22:41, the Lord himself prays upon his knees. In Acts 21:5, Paul kneeling down, prayed with everyone who was with him. These ceremonies toward God cannot be

Book II, Ch. XV: On the Ceremonies of Mass

condemned in any way, for, as St. Cyprian teaches (*De Orat. Dominica*), even the expression of the body is pleasing in the sight of God. During the sacrifice, however, the priest does not only bow his head to God, but also to the cross, or a crucifix, and even to the altar itself, and often. That such a ceremony is very ancient can be understood from the Liturgy of Chrysostom, where we find these words: "The priest goes out from a small door, and turning to an image of Christ, after bowing his head, he says this prayer, etc."

The *first* ceremony with respect to the sacrifice, is the elevation of the host that is going to be consecrated in the presence of God, which is done in the Offertory. Such a ceremony cannot be condemned if oblation is conceded, which we defended in the previous book. If it is lawful to offer a visible sacrifice to God, why would it not also be lawful to elevate the very thing in a sign of oblation? We also have an example in Scripture, namely in Leviticus 8:27, 9:21, and 10:15, and other places where the priest elevates that which is offered in the presence of God. Lastly, it is found in the ancient Liturgies.

The *second* which is the *ostension,* or the showing of the sacrament to the people, is very ancient. In the first place, it is found in the Liturgies of Basil and Chrysostom, and among Dionysius (*Eccles. Hierarch.*, cap. 3). And besides, in his work *On the Holy Spirit* (cap. 27) St. Basil calls it to mind as an Apostolic Tradition: "Who among the saints left the words of invocation for us in writing, when the bread of the Eucharist and the cup of benediction are shown?" Chrysostom frequently mentions this rite, which was among the Greeks, that the Eucharist is consecrated at the altar after the veils have been spread, and then after they have been drawn back it is shown to the people. In *Homily 61* to the People of Antioch, he says: "When you see the veils drawn back, then think that the lofty heaven is opened." (See also *Hom. 36 on 1 Cor.*, and *Hom. 3 in Ephes.*)

Third, which is the *fractio* and *commixtio*, is expressly found in the Liturgy of James, and in the Liturgy of Chrysostom: this is why it is also very ancient. Wherefore, Chrysostom (*Hom. 24 in 1 Cor.*) writes that Christ suffered to be broken on the altar, which he refused to suffer on the cross.

There is another ceremony with respect to the sacrifice: The mixing of water and wine. We will say nothing of this now, because we copiously treated on it in *On the Eucharist*, book 4.

The *first* ceremony, which is used in respect to the priest himself, is the striking of the chest; he uses this in the confession, which is made at the beginning of Mass, and at the prayer *Agnus Dei, qui tollis peccata mundi*,[17] etc. And at the words: *Domine non sum dignus*.[18] Moreover, this ceremony shows penance, and is natural; moreover, it has an example in the Gospel. In Luke 18:13, while the Publican was praying, he struck his chest, saying: "God be merciful to me, a sinner." And in Luke 23:48, we read: "They returned striking their chests."

The *second* is the washing of hands, a little before the consecration, which is also found in the Greek Liturgies. Dionysius mentions the same ceremony (*Ecclesiast. Hierarch.*, cap. 3) as well as Clement (*const.* 8, 5) and Cyril (*Catech.* 5), who says: "You have seen the deacon extending water to the priest so he may wash his hands?" And in the same place he gives the reason for this ceremony, and says that washing is not applied to wash the dirt of the body, since nobody would dare come to Church with dirty hands, but on account of the symbol of a pure mind, which those who carry out the sacrifice should possess.

The *first* ceremony with respect to the people is the greeting, made with the words: *Dominus vobiscum*. We will explain this in the next chapter.

The *second* ceremony is the dismissal of the people, by the words *Ite Missa est*, which we will also speak about below; for these ceremonies consist in words, not only in an action.

The *first* ceremony with respect to those which are read in Mass is the music. There is no great controversy on this at present; for even the heretics sing, and besides, we have the example of the Lord himself. In Matt. 26:30, we read that the Lord sang a hymn, in the Last Supper, in which the first institution and celebration of the Mass consists, for the words, "After the hymn was said," which in Greek are: ὑμνήσαντες, properly mean singing. As Augustine teaches on the title of Psalm 72, the very notion of a hymn is music, so that unless it is sung, it cannot be called a hymn. This is why the fourth Council of Toledo, in cap. 12 on hymns sung in the Divine Office, also says we take our example from the Lord. Thus, we gather that what Luther writes in *De Capt. Babyl.* (cap. 1), is false, namely that the Lord's Mass was celebrated without music. We will make a copious dissertation on this matter in out treatise *On the Canonical Hours*, in the next volume.

The *second* ceremony is the musical instruments, which began to be

---

17 Lamb of God, who takes away the sins of the world.
18 Lord, I am not worthy.

Book II, Ch. XV: On the Ceremonies of Mass

used in the Church in the Divine Office in the time of Pope Vitalianus, around the year 660 A.D., as Platina relates from the Pontifical; or, as Aimonius prefers (*de Gestis Francorum*, 4, 114), after 820 A.D., in the time of Louis the Pious. Moreover, instruments of this sort are licit and useful if we use them soberly and seriously, and this certainly cannot be denied since we also have an example in the Old Testament, and we experience devotion roused through them, and weariness diminished, which otherwise arises from the length and gravity of the offices.

Nor does the response of Peter Martyr Vermigli to the example of the Old Testament have any weight. Vermigli writes on 1 Cor. 14, that musical instruments pertain to Jewish ceremonies, and are no more fitting for us than Circumcision, and the New Moon. But he is clearly deceived. Accordingly, Jewish ceremonies were twofold. Some of these were proper, namely those which were instituted to show some future thing, such as Circumcision and the like; these are truly not fitting for us. Others were common even with other nations, and clearly rested upon natural reason, but they were not in signification of future things, such as genuflections, striking the chest, etc., and these are fitting for us, and musical instruments pertain to this kind, since they are used in praise of God on account of the weak, not a few of which are numbered in the Church; for, as I said, they help both to excite piety and to stave off fatigue.

From the common ceremonies, the *first* is the sprinkling with holy water. On Sundays before the beginning of solemn Mass, the priest blesses water and then sprinkles himself, the ministers, the altar and the people; such a sprinkling is a type of expiation, and preparation to the coming sacrifice. We already profusely treated on holy water in *On the Church Triumphant*, 3, 7. Here it will only suffice to mark down that holy water is numbered among the Apostolic Traditions by St. Basil (*On the Holy Spirit*, cap. 27). The sprinkling of holy water customarily used for Mass on Sundays is gathered from Micrologus (*de observationibus Ecclesiasticis*, cap. 46).

The *second* common ceremony is incense; for incense is burned in Mass for the altar, at the Gospel, for the priest, and also for the clergy and people; this ceremony is certainly ancient. In canon 4 of the Apostles it is said that *thymiama*, or incense is offered at the altar when the sacred oblation is celebrated. Dionysius (*Eccles. Hierarch.* 3) describing the rite of celebration of the sacrifice of the Eucharist, also mentions incense. In the liturgies of James and Chrysostom, mention is made of the blessing of incense and incensation of the altar. Besides, Damasus, in the *Pontifical*, for the life of Popes Soter and Sylvester, enumerates a thurible among the other sacred vessels, or a *thymiamateria*; this is why it is false, what Platina (*Life of Sixtus I*), and Polydor Virgil (*de inventoribus rerum*, 1) write, that Leo III, who sat in the year 800, was the first who used incense at Mass. Moreover, what Arnobius writes (*contra Gentes*, 7) that the rite of incense is novel, should be understood on the custom of the gentiles; for among the people of God it is a most ancient custom to use incense in the divine sacrifice, as is clear from Exodus 25:29 and 30:34. Hence, Christians receive the rite of the thurible not from the gentiles, but from the Jews.

The reason why the smell of incense, and the smoke are used in sacrifice, as is gathered from the prayers of both the Greek and Latin liturgies, are: *a)* to show the good odor of the Gospel and of those who should preach the Gospel; *b)* on account of the similitude, which incense has with prayer; this is why it is said in Psalm 140 [141]:2, "May my prayer be directed just as incense in your sight." And in Apocalypse 15:8, John interprets the incense offered to God as the prayers of the saints; *c)* to represent the glory of God. God usually showed himself in a cloud in the Old Testament; *d)* lastly to expel the foul odor if any from the multitude of the people needs to be cleansed.

The *third* common ceremony is the kiss; for the priest frequently kisses the altar itself, then the book of the Gospel, and his minister, and through him he spreads peace upon all the clergy and the people.[19] Such ceremonies are found in all Liturgies, both Greek and Latin, and Justin Martyr mentions them in his *Second Apology*, Tertullian (*on prayer*, c. 29), and Cyril (*Catech.* 5), as well as Chrysostom (*Hom. 77 on John*). There is a twofold reasoning for this kiss, for both the altar and the book are kissed in a sign of reverence, but the brethren in a sign of charity and peace.

The *fourth* ceremony is the sign of the cross, which is the most common and ancient of all. The priest signs himself with the sign of the cross, likewise the book, the altar, the things to be offered, and the oblations, and lastly the people when he blesses them.

Micrologus (*loc. cit.*, c. 14), notes that the sign of the cross is usually

---

[19] Translator's note: In the liturgy of St. Robert's time, and today in the 1962 Missal, a.k.a. the extraordinary form, at a Solemn Mass the priest gives the kiss of peace to the deacon, and the deacon thus to the subdeacon, and the subdeacon to any and all clergy who are present at the liturgy.

Book II, Ch. XV: On the Ceremonies of Mass

expressed once, or three times, or five times over the oblation, but not twice or four times; when it is done once it expresses the unity of the divine essence; thrice the Trinity of persons; five times to represent the five wounds of the Lord.

Moreover, that this is a very ancient ceremony is clear. *Firstly*, from the Liturgies of St. James and others, which are full of signs of this sort. *Secondly* from Chrysostom (*Homil. 55 in Matt.*) and Augustine (*Tract. In Joan.* 118), who say all the Sacraments, and the divine sacrifice itself, are completed with the sign of the cross. *Thirdly*, from Tertullian (*de Corona Militis*), Cyril (*loc. cit.*, 4 & 13), and Jerome (*epist. Ad Eustochium on the care of Virginity*), who teach that the sign of the cross must be used in every affair. But if in every business, why not in the action of the awe-inspiring sacrifice?

CHAPTER XVI
On what is recited in the Mass of the Catechumens

THE LAST CONTROVERSY remains on the truth of the Canon and the other things which are recited in the Mass. Here it must be observed that the Mass is usually divided into four parts. The *first* is from the beginning even to the Offertory, which is usually called the Mass of the Catechumens. The *second*, from the Offertory even to the Consecration which the Greeks call the ἀναφορὰ (anaphora), and some Latins call the *Canon Minor*. *Third*, from the consecration even to the communion, which is called the *Canon Major*. The *fourth* is from Communion even to the end.

On the Psalm Judica me, and Confession

Thus, *first* Psalm 42 [43] which begins *Judica me Deus* is pronounced before the beginning of Mass, and the general confession is made. No man can condemn the Psalm, nor even the confession insofar as it is made to God and those standing about; but insofar as it is made to the saints, our adversaries do not approve of it, because they think the saints cannot hear it, since they are so far away. But the Catholic Church has no doubt that just as the saints know our prayers, so also our confessions. This is both from the rite of invocation of the saints, which was always in use among true Christians (as we profusely taught in *On Canonizations*), and from the miracles which have been worked in every century by the invocation of the saints, many of which Augustine relates (*City of God*, 22, 8). Therefore, we confess to God, the saints and the Church present, because we have offended them all when we sin, just as the Prodigal Son says in Luke 15:21, "I have sinned against heaven and against you."

The use of the confession, however, before the *Introit* of the Mass is ancient, and this is clear from Micrologus (*loc. cit.* cap. 1) where he clearly says the confession is usually done before Mass, as well as from the Liturgy of St. James which begins with the confession.

On the Introit

The introit follows, which consists of an Antiphon, and a Psalm with

Book II, Ch. XVI: On the Mass of the Catechumens

the *Gloria Patri*. It is called the *Introit*, because it is sung by the choir during the entrance of the priest at the altar, as Micrologus would have it (cap. 1), or Conrad Brunus (2, 1), and others, because it is the entrance, i.e. the beginning of the Mass. There is also agreement among the authors, that the use of the Introit was introduced by Pope Celestine I, as Strabo writes (cap. 22) and Micrologus (cap. 1) and others. For in the first place, he did not institute the use of singing one verse, as we now do, but that Psalm 150 be sung antiphonally in order before the sacrifice, as Anastasius the librarian relates. But afterward, to avoid the great length some verses of some psalm were selected which seemed more suitable to excite devotion. Next, Celestine was not absolutely the first to employ the Psalms in the sacrifice, but perhaps he was the first who wished this to be observed in Rome. Otherwise, Dionysius the Areopagate (*Ecc. Hierarch.*, 3) mentions psalms which were sung at the beginning of Mass; and St. Basil, in his Liturgy commands in the beginning that three or four verses of a Psalm be sung. But even if this institution traces its origin to Pope Celestine, it cannot be condemned, since the Introit is nearly always taken from the Divine Scripture, and this use has been retained by the universal Church for over a thousand years.

On the Gloria Patri, etc.

The verse *Glory be to the Father, and the Son, and the Holy Spirit, etc.* which is added to the introit, is supposed by some to have been composed by St. Jerome at the request of Pope Damasus; Alcuin was of that opinion (*loc. cit.*), but what Strabo writes is more true (*loc. cit.* cap. 25), that this versicle was composed by the Council of Nicaea. For this was sung in the Church at the end of Psalms before the time of Jerome and Damasus, as is clear from Theodoret (*Hist.* 2, 42) and Sozomen (3, 19) who write at Antioch in the times of the Emperor Constantine, Catholics and Arians were customarily distinguished because the former would sing *Gloria Patri, et Filio et Spiritui Sancto* at the end of the Psalms, whereas the latter used: *Gloria Patri, per Filium in Spiritu Sancto*.[20] Basil also disputes on this verse *Gloria Patri*, etc., in his book *On the Holy Spirit*, cap. 28. It is also witnessed by the Council of Vaison, which was celebrated 1100 years ago (can. 5) not only in Rome, but also throughout the East, and through Africa, after *Gloria Patri, et Filio, et Spiritui Sancto*, it is customarily added: *Sicut erat in principio, etc.*, Hence, the two epistles,

[20] Glory to the Father, through the Son in the Holy Spirit.

which are usually advanced on this matter, of Damasus to Jerome and of Jerome to Damasus, are spurious and inept, and so relegated to the last page as it were.

On the Kyrie Eleison

The invocation *Kyrie eleison* follows, which the Greeks call the Litany from the word λιτανεύειν, which means to supplicate. This part of the Mass is very ancient, as is clear from the Liturgies of James, Basil and Chrysostom. Basil also explains this supplication in *Epistle 63 to Neocesarien*. Among the Latins it is also a very ancient custom, of singing the same Litany in the Greek language. For St. Gregory (*Epistle*, 7, 63), when he was accused of importing the *Kyrie eleison* and some other Greek ceremonies into the Latin Church, answered that he preserved the ancient ceremonies of the Roman Church, or renewed them, but did not receive them from the Greeks. He proves it from the fact that in the Greek Liturgy, the *Kyrie* is sung by the people, while among the Latins by the priest, and because the Greeks do not interpose *Christe eleison*, as the Latins do, but simply say *Kyrie eleison*. It is, however, most true, what St. Gregory says, that he did not introduce it into the Latin Church, since this form of supplication can be realized from the Council of Vaison, which was celebrated one hundred and fifty years before the time of Gregory. For in that Council (can. 3), the priests in France are bidden to say *Kyrie eleison*, and the reason is given because in the Apostolic See, and through all of Italy, that supplication is said during Mass. Even St. Augustine, in his dispute with Pascentius (*Epistle 178*) says that all Christians, whether Greek, Latin or Barbarian, pray to God for mercy in the Greek language.

On the Gloria in Excelsis

In regard to the *Gloria in excelsis Deo*, which is called the Angelic hymn, nearly all authors hand down that Pope St. Telesphorus began the institution of singing this hymn at Mass. Strabo (*loc. cit.* cap. 22) and all others hand down the same thing. Truly, the first words pertain to the what are found in the Gospel (Luke 2:14) and are recited in the most ancient Liturgy of James, but it is not very certain who added the rest. Innocent III (*de Mysteriis Missae*, 2, 20) writes that the addition is attributed by some to Telesphorus, but most attribute it to Hilary of

Book II, Ch. XVI: On the Mass of the Catechumens

Poitiers. Whoever was the author, it has nothing that gives offense, for even Luther was pleased by it, and that is clear from his work *On the Formula of the Mass*.

On the Dominus Vobiscum[21]

Next, the salutation *Dominus vobiscum* follows. We use such a ceremony whenever we incite the people either to prayer or to attention; this is why it goes before the *Oremus* and before the Gospel, as well as the Preface and other things of this sort. Therefore, it is a certain religious stirring, or invitation, and it serves the place of an adverb of address. It is in the same way as formerly among religious, as Augustine witnesses (*on Psalm 132*), when they called another, they usually said: *Deo gratias*, which many preserve even today. It is also in the same way that St. Paula used *Alleluja* to call the virgins, as St. Jerome writes on her life. Today, in convents *Ave Maria* is usually said. Hence, this salutation: *Dominus vobiscum*, is taken from the custom of the Jews who said when greeting one another: The Lord be with you," as is clear from Judith 6:12, Ruth 2:4, 2. Chronicles 15:2, and Luke 1:27.

St. Peter Damian wrote a whole book on this salutation, which is titled: *De Dominus Vobiscum*, where he proves it should be said, even by those who recite the Canonical Hours. He also advises there, that in Mass Bishops should say: *Pax vobis*, in place of *Dominus vobiscum*, because the Lord (Matthew 10:12) taught the Apostles, for whom the bishops are successors, that they should announce peace when they enter some place. And although the first Council of Braga (can. 21), bid all, both bishops and priests in the Mass to greet the people in the same manner, nevertheless, a custom of this sort of the Churches must be preserved.

That it is a very ancient ceremony in the Mass, however, that the priest greet the people is clear not only from the Council of Braga, which was celebrated 900 years ago, but also from the most ancient Liturgies, of James, Basil, Chrysostom, and others, in which we read everywhere either *Pax vobis*, or, *Dominus vobiscum*, and the response to both is: *Et cum spiritu tuo*.[22]

---

21 The Lord be with you.
22 And with your spirit.

On the Collect

After the salutation the Collect is said, and we must say three things about it. *Firstly*, on the name; *secondly*, on its antiquity; *thirdly*, on the form. On the name, many authors have written things that are not very probable. There are two truer opinions: one, that it is called *collecta* because it is gathered [*colligere*] from few words, whatever is asked of God for the whole people. Strabo (cap. 22) and Micrologus (cap. 3) teach this. The second opinion is perhaps truer, and it holds those prayers are called *collectas* through a figure of speech from the very celebration of the Mass, which ancient writers called *collecta* because the people were gathered [*colligere*] for it. That ancient writers called the celebration of Mass *Collecta* is clear from the words of St. Augustine (*Breviculo Collationis, collatione tertii diei*), who says: "They confessed that they were gathered [*Collectam*], and did what the Lord ordained." The acts of the martyrs are extent in Surius (*Tom. Prim.*), and these seem to be what Augustine cites, wherein we frequently read they made the *Collectam*, or celebrated for them, which is to celebrate the Mass. Tertullian also (*de Fuga in persecutione*) asks: "How shall we gather? How shall we celebrate the solemn rites of the Lord?" So, the prayer, which is said in Mass, seems to have been called the Collect because it is the end, nay more even the beginning and middle of that whole action, which was called *Collecta*.

The prayers are said in the same number and rank at the beginning of Mass, and in the middle, as well as in the end; for which reasoning, sometimes the same Collects are called Masses because they are a certain part of Mass, and by no means the least.

Hence, it can be recognized from antiquity that the use was always in the Church, and that Christians were never gathered except for prayer, as is clear from Justin (*Second Apology*) and Tertullian (*Apologeticus*, c. 39), nay more, by the command of the Apostle (1 Tim. 2:1). The Collects of our Missal, however, which are very beautiful, were composed by ancient Popes, and are said to have been gathered in one place by St. Gregory, as Strabo shows (cap. 22).

What pertains to the form is prescribed in the third Council of Carthage, c. 23, that the prayer which is said in Mass be directed to the Father, still, it does not follow from that that the Son and the Holy Spirit must not be invoked, or are not invoked in Mass; for as Tertullian rightly teaches (*On Prayer*), on account of the unity of essence, the Son and the

Book II, Ch. XVI: On the Mass of the Catechumens 251

Holy Spirit are always understood in the Father. We see the same thing in the oblation of the sacrifice, which is properly directed to the Father, as is clear from the Canon: "We humbly ask you, most merciful Father, through Jesus Christ your son," and still the sacrifice is offered to the whole Trinity as St. Fulgentius proves (*ad Monimum*, 2, 2-5). It is also clearly understood from the conclusion of the Collect, since the Son and the Holy Spirit are invoked at the same time with the Father. While we say the Son and Holy Spirit live with the Father and reign for all ages of ages, at the same time we show that we invoke the Son and the Holy Spirit with the Father.

There are two reasons why the Collects are ordinarily directed to the Father, and not to the Trinity. The first is because the Lord taught us to pray in this way (Matt. 6:9), "Our Father, who art in heaven." And in John 14:13, "Whatever you ask of the Father in my name." The second is because the prayer should always be concluded through Christ, since he is our advocate and the one through whom we ask everything. It would, however, be unsuitable to direct a prayer to the Trinity and conclude: "Through your son, etc.," for we would appear in that way to make Christ the son of the Trinity. But if, while omitting the word "son" we were to say, "Through Christ our Lord," we would seem to divide the persons of Christ; for we include one in the Trinity, whom we invoke, and exclude the other, through whom we invoke. Yet, we remove all these unsuitabilities when we direct it to one person, and because the person of the Father is first, and from that first the rest take their origin, it has seemed best that when prayers must be directed to one person, they be directed to the Father. Still, there are certain Collects which are directed to the Son, and they conclude: "Who lives and reigns, etc." but these are few, and perhaps not as ancient as the others. Perhaps the Church took the time to direct some Collects to the Son lest men would believe none could be invoked with clear words but the Father.

At the end of the prayer the response *Amen* is given, which means truly, or firmly, from the Hebrew אמן *aman*, which in the Hiphil conjugation means to believe, and in the Niphal, to be firm. The Greeks usually translate it as γένοιτο, or may it be, for a man that makes this response desires it truly and firmly to come about, as it was asked in prayer. The use of responding *Amen* is most ancient, as is clear from the Apostle in 1 Cor. 14:16, "How shall those who hold the place of the unlearned say, Amen to your blessing?" The same is clear from Justin (*Second Apology*) and Jerome (*Prologue; on Gal.*, book 2), and Augustine

(*Epistle 107 ad Vitalem*).

On the Epistle

After the Collect the reading follows which is taken from the Prophets or the Apostle; that such a custom is most ancient is clear from Justin (*Second Apology*) where he says that in the Synaxis the readings are customarily read from the Prophets and the Apostles. The same is clear from Tertullian (*Apologeticus*, c. 39), as well as from Dionysius (*Eccl. Hierarch.* 3). Moreover, it seems this custom was received from the Jews, since they have readings from the Prophets on every Sabbath, even today. See Luke 4:16; Acts 13:15, 15:21, 16:14, 17:2, and 18:4.

On the Gradual, Alleluja, Tract, and Sequence

When the reading is finished, some verses are read, which are mostly taken from the Scriptures. Certainly, in the Greek Church the custom is very ancient to place something between the Epistle, and the Gospel, as is clear from the Liturgy of Chrysostom. In the Latin Church, it does not seem to be an ancient and universal custom. For in the fourth Council of Toledo, celebrated 900 years ago, in chapter 11, praises are forbidden after the Epistle; nevertheless, later the Roman custom of interposing the Gradual, and other things of this sort, little by little pleased all, and was received and approved everywhere, as Strabo writes (*loc. cit.*)

Moreover, there are four kinds of these verses: for some are called a Responsory, or Gradual, others the Alleluja, others the Tract, and others the Sequence, or *Prosa*. The responsory is so-called because when one begins, others respond, as Rabanus writes (*de Instit. Clericorum*, 2, 51).

The reason for the name Gradual is not handed down by all in the same manner: the true reason seems to be what Blessed Rhenanus hands down (in his annotations on Tertullian's *de Corona Militis*), namely that it takes its name because it was sung while the Deacon ascends the steps (*gradus*) to sing the Gospel. From which it can also be understood why a versicle of this sort would be sung; namely, lest the time should pass idly, which necessarily had to be placed between the Epistle and the Gospel, while the Deacon prepared himself to sing the latter. Moreover, the fact that there was a custom of the Church, that the Gospel be sung from a higher place which is observed, even now, in many places, is clear from the words of the Roman Ordinal: "When the Deacon goes up to

Book II, Ch. XVI: On the Mass of the Catechumens

read the Gospel, he only ascends to the last step." Cyprian (*Epistles* 2, 5) where he speaks about the Confessor Aurelius, whom he had ordained to read the Gospel in the Church, says he came to the pulpit behind a platform. Lastly, in the ancient Churches stone pulpits were always found instituted for the purpose of reading the Gospel; Micrologus (*loc. cit.* c. 9), as well as others, call these "Ambos" from the Greek word ἀμβαίνω, I ascend, which becomes ἀμβών, which is found in the Council of Laodicea (c. 15), while the Latin translators render it *pulpitum*.

Moreover, *Alleluja*, which means: Praise the Lord, is sung after the Gradual, as Strabo witnesses (cap. 22), and in its place on days of fasting the Tract is usually said, which is composed of other verses taken from Scripture. These verses are called the Tract, however, because they should be sung gravely and in a drawn-out manner (*tractim*) as a sign of mourning, as Durandus would have it. Lastly, on the most solemn feasts, such as Easter and Pentecost, the *Sequences* or *Prosa* are normally added, which are certain rhythmic verses.

Luther condemns none of these, except that we should always say *Alleluja*; for which reason he decreed in his *Formula of the Mass*, that even during Lent and Holy Week *Alleluja* should be sung. But in this matter he rashly moves away from the use of antiquity.[23]

In the first place, in the fourth Council of Toledo (can. 10) it is expressly stipulated that in Lent the Alleluja should not be sung. Augustine (*Epist. 119*, 15) says that is was a well-known usage, that only from Easter to Pentecost and on all Sundays the Alleluja should be sung, as a sign of joy on account of the resurrection of Christ. And St. Gregory was once rebuked because he commanded the Alleluja to be sung at Mass outside of the time of Pentecost, namely on all feast days, except those which fall between Septuagesima and Easter. He answered those who so rebuked him, that he did not begin that practice, rather it was introduced in the time of Pope Damasus, on the authority of St. Jerome (See *Epistles*, 7, 63 to John the Bishop of Syracuse). That the Alleluja is a song of joy, and rightly interrupted on days of penance and lamenting, is clear from the divine Scripture. In Tobit 13, where the glory of the heavenly Jerusalem is described, we read among other things in verse 22: "All its streets shall

---

23 Translator's note: It is worth noting that the Eastern Rites, in Bellarmine's time as well as today, do not receive the custom of omitting the Alleluja during Lent. Although he may or may not have been aware of this, his purpose in arguing the point is that Luther's mind was not to emulate the Eastern practice, but to do the opposite of what the Western Church did.

be paved with white and clean stones; and Alleluja shall be sung in its streets." And in Apocalypse 19:6, the joy of the saints is described, which will be in heaven after the day of Judgment: "And I heard as it were the voice of a great multitude, and as the voice of many waters, and as the voice of great thunders saying Alleluja, let us rejoice and exult."

One thing can be added here from Rupert (*de Divinis Officiis*, 1, 34). The Gradual is a verse pertaining to penance, and therefore is omitted during Paschaltide, and in its place the Alleluja is doubled because the whole period is of remission and joy; just as, on the other hand, from Septuagesima to Easter the Alleluja is omitted and what pertains to penance and lamentation is doubled.

Then the reading of the Gospel follows, which is certain to be most ancient, not only from the Liturgies, but also from the Council of Laodicea (can. 16) and the fourth Council of Carthage (can. 84), as well as of Valencia (can. 2). Likewise, from the Fathers. Chrysostom (*Hom. 6 On Penance*, and *Homily 3 on 2 Thessalonians*); Augustine in his preface to his commentary on the *Epistle of John* where he calls to mind certain readings of the Gospel that are read for a diversity of feast days; Jerome (*Epist. Ad Sabinianum Diaconum*), and at length from the decretal epistle of Pope Anastasius I, where all those present are commanded to hear the Gospel on account of the reverence for the Lord while he is speaking. He did not first institute such a ceremony, as many think. Rather he confirmed it and commanded that it be observed even in those places where it was not. Clement (*Constit.* 2, 57/61) says the Apostles commanded this that everyone, not only clergy, but even laity would rise when the Gospel is read.

Moreover, the ceremonies of seeking the blessing before the Gospel and rousing the people, through those words: "A continuation of the Holy Gospel according to Matthew," and the response, "Glory to you O Lord," are found even in the Mass of St. John Chrysostom, and also among Amalarius (*de Officio Missae*, 18) and Alcuin (*de Officiis Divinis*).

On the Creed

The Creed is rightly pronounced after the Gospel, because faith follows from hearing the word of God. The use of singing the Creed of Constantinople in the Mass is more ancient in the Eastern Church than in the West. In the Mass of Chrysostom, it is expressly found, and the same is gathered in the third Council of Toledo, although it was

Book II, Ch. XVI: On the Mass of the Catechumens

celebrated around a thousand years ago; for in that Council (can. 2) it is decreed that, according to the custom of the East, the Creed should be said at Mass on every Sunday. Strabo also writes (*loc. cit.* c. 22), that among the Germans and French, the use of reciting the creed at Mass became frequent in the time of Charlemagne, on the occasion of Felix, the Bishop of Urgell, who was condemned for heresy in that time.

CHAPTER XVII
On the Offertory, and the Preface

On the Offertory

NEXT in order is the Offertory, which is always taken from the Scriptures, and thereby what is sung while the people offered receives its name, as Strabo hands down (c. 22) as well as Micrologus (c. 10). There are five prayers: The *Suscipe sancta Pater*, *Offerimus tibi Domine*; *Veni sanctificator; in spiritu humilitatis*; and the *Suscipe sancta Trinitas*. These are not very ancient, nor were they read in the Roman Church five hundred years ago; for Micrologus writes (c. 11) that these prayers, *Veni sanctificator*, and *Suscipe Sancta Trinitas* are recited according to the Gallican ordinal, but none of these prayers were established in the Roman Ordinal between the Offertory and the Secret. This is why Strabo, Amalarius, Rupert, Alcuin, and even Innocent III, as well as other older writers, do not mention these prayers, but pass from the Offertory to the Secret. Still, because they contain nothing that offends, little by little they were all received.

But certain minor objections must be answered, which the Lutheran George Major vomits against these prayers. *Firstly*, he objects, why should it be called a salutary chalice, in which there is nothing but wine?

I respond: We do not call it a salutary chalice, but the chalice of salvation, for that chalice of wine is the chalice of salvation, i.e. of Christ, because Christ the savior instituted that chalice to be offered and consecrated. Besides, we could also rightly call the chalice salutary, that chalice of wine both because it is going to bring salvation after the consecration, and because the wine itself, by signifying and representing that salvation, is presented in the way the words of God are called salutary because they save by signifying and rousing faith.

He objects *secondly:* Why does the priest pray on behalf of the chalice, and not rather for himself.

I respond: The priest does not pray for the chalice, but for himself and the whole world when he asks that the oblation would ascend to God with the odor of sweetness, for he adds next, "For our salvation and that of the whole world." And even if this is not expressed, it could be understood *per se*, for God receives the oblation, it is not useful for the oblation, but *for us*.

He objects *thirdly*: Why, in the prayer "In the spirit of humility" does the priest ask that the oblation might be pleasing after he has offered it? It is a sign that he is uncertain whether it is pleasing, and hence he sinned in offering it without faith.

I respond: The priest is not uncertain that the sacrifice of the Mass is pleasing to God of itself, or from the institution of Christ, and so he offers the most pleasing sacrifice to God with certain faith; but he is uncertain on *his own disposition*, and for that reason he asks for himself the spirit of humility, and contrition to so carry out the inchoate sacrifice, that he might please God on his side; nor does he sin by offering without certain faith in his own dignity, because he is not held to have that certitude, rather, he is only held to not be conscious of sin, since Paul says in 1 Cor. 11:28, "Let a man prove himself, etc."

He objects *fourthly*: Why is it said in that prayer, *Come O Sanctifier*, etc., that the sacrifice be prepared when it has already been offered?

I respond: That earlier oblation was a preparation to the second oblation, in which the sacrifice properly consists, hence the sacrifice is rightly said to have been prepared when the matter has been consecrated to God, and dedicated through a certain oblation.

On the Preface

Once the Offertory has been finished, and the matter of the sacrifice prepared, and he washes his hands and the oblation has been commended to God through the prayers of the Secret Collects, the Preface is said, which receives its name because it is a preparation and an incitement to the people toward that action in which the sacrifice properly consists. And first the words: *Per omnia saecula saeculorum*[24] pertain to the previous prayers recited in silence, but that conclusion is said aloud so that the people can respond, *Amen*; and in that word confirm the previous prayers (Micrologus, *loc. cit.* c. 7).

Then, the Preface begins with *Dominus vobiscum*; and that, even to the words *Vere dignum et justum est*[25] is found in the most ancient Greek and Latin authors. For, that I might omit the Liturgies, none of which lack this Preface, Clement mentions these words (*Constit.* 8, 16);

---

24 For ever and ever, which is customarily rendered into English as "world without end."
25 Truly it is right and just.

Cyprian (*De Oratione Dominica*, serm. 6); Cyril of Jerusalem (*Catechesi* 5); Chrysostom in many places, such as in his *Homily on the Eucharist*, where he says: "What do you do, O Man? Did you not promise the priest, when he said: 'Lift up your hears,' and you said, 'We have to the Lord'?" See also *Homil. 4 de Natura Dei*, and Augustine, no less frequently such as in *Epist. 57 ad Dardanum*, and 120 *ad Honoratum*, and 156 *ad Probam*, *de Spiritu et Litera*, c. 11, and *de bono perseverantiae*, 2, 13.

The rest of the words, even to the *Sanctus* are not the same in the Greek and Latin Liturgies; nevertheless, those which are in ours, that is the liturgy of the Roman Church is certain and most ancient. For a thousand years ago, Pope Pelagius II was asked by the Bishops of Germany and France what were the authentic Prefaces and how many; he answered that there were nine. The *first*, of Christmas; the *second*, for the Epiphany; *the third*, for Lent; The *fourth*, of the Cross; the *fifth*, of Easter; the *sixth*, of the Ascension; the *seventh*, for Pentecost, the *eighth*, of the Trinity; the *ninth*, for the Apostles. See the epistle of Pelagius, and Gratian (can. *Invenimus, de consecrate.* Dist. 1). Urban II added the *tenth* Preface, which is of the Blessed Virgin in the Council of Placencia, around the year 1080, as Gratian witnesses, can. *Sanctorum*, dist. 70.

The Sanctus

After the preface has been finished the chant *Sanctus, Sanctus, Sanctus*, etc. is sung, which is partly taken from the hymn of the Angels which Isaiah heard (Isaiah 6:3), and partly from the song which the Jews sang to Christ when he entered Jerusalem on Palm Sunday (Matt. 21:15) and it is found in the ancient Liturgies, those of James, Basil and Chrysostom; and there is a specific canon on it extent in the Council of Vaison, can. 4/6.

CHAPTER XVIII
On the word "Canon"

Now we undertake to defend the Roman Canon from the bites of the impious Lutherans. Indeed, the heretics of this time slander with such incredible fury what Catholics have always retained with supreme veneration.

Luther, in his book *On the Abrogation of Private Mass*, by speaking in this way, shows he sins from malice and not ignorance: "Though I had anything that I might say on behalf of the right sense of the Canon, as I have done previously, still, now I will not dignify it with such honor." And in the same place he throws in jeers and impious jokes as well as blasphemies against that sacred mystery. But he argues more seriously by far in his book *On the abomination of the Canon*, where he so explains the matter that he would have it that after men have heard the word "Canon" they should flee as if the devil met them.

Martin Chemnitz (*Examination of the Council of Trent*, 2 part. p. 825 et *seqq.*) argues on the Canon, and there are four things that he especially condemns. Firstly, that we make that the rite of celebrating the Canon of the Mass a fixed and stable rule, whereas he would have it that one should be free to use this or that prayer. *Secondly*, the Council of Trent makes the author of the Canon partly Christ, partly the Apostles, and partly the ancient Roman Pontiffs, whereas he shows the author was a certain Scholasticus, by the witness of St. Gregory. *Thirdly*, that we affirm it is ancient. He says: "These are smoke and trifles, stories they make up on the antiquity of the Canon." *Fourthly*, that we pronounce the fact that no error is found in the whole Canon, whereas he says there are seventeen errors.

George Major, Zwingli, Illyricus and others also write many things against the Canon. As a result, we will first argue on the word "Canon". Then, on the author. Then its antiquity. Lastly, on the truth of the same as we will explain each of its parts.

What pertains to the first: This word is extant in this signification in St. Gregory (*Epistles* 7, 63) where he gives the reason why, after the Canon, he wished the Lord's prayer to be recited. It is found in Ambrose, or whoever was the author of the *Commentary on 1 Tim. 2*, where the Ecclesiastical Rule is called that which every priest uses. It is found in

Optatus of Miletus, the equal of Ambrose (*Contra Parmenianum*) where it is called *Legitimum*: "For who doubts that you cannot pass over the *legitimum* in the mystery of the Sacraments? You say that you offer to God for the Church, which is one, etc." where he calls the word *legitimum* an established and certain order of prayers, which we use in consecrating the Eucharist, in the beginning of such an order we say that we offer for the Church. Isidor (*de officiis divinis* 1, 15) describes the Order of prayer, in which sacrifices that have been offered to God are consecrated. Strabo (c. 22) calls it both the Action and Canon, and those two terms all later authors use. Moreover, that part of the Mass is called the Action because in it the action of sacrifice is celebrated; for the rest are words rather than actions. Hence, the words *Canon, Regula, Legitimum, Ordo* show sufficiently enough, that among the ancient authors the order of celebrating was not arbitrary, as Chemnitz would have it, rather, the Church so prescribed that anyone who did otherwise would plainly be judged to have transgressed the law.

But Chemnitz objects (*loc. cit.* p. 835) with two arguments. One from the African Council (can. 70) and the Council of Miletus (can. 12) where it is prescribed that in Mass the prayers are not said unless they have been conferred first with more prudent men, or approved by the Council, lest perhaps they might contain something contrary to faith. Thereby it is gathered that a certain Canon of prayers was not prescribed in ancient times, which would obligate all, rather it was permitted for anyone to compose prayers provided these were the analogy of faith. He takes the second argument from the diversity of the Liturgies, of Basil, Chrysostom, Ambrose, Gregory and Isidor.

But these arguments conclude nothing. In the first place, the canons of the Councils he has cited do not speak about the Canon of the Mass, but about the Collects which were always manifold and different. We have already heard Optatus, the bishop of Miletus, speaking of the legitimate prayer that cannot be omitted.

Nor do we deny that there were different words of the Canon, and even today among the Greeks and certain Churches of the Latins; nor does the Roman Church think, as Chemnitz lies (p. 836) that everyone should preserve the Canon of the Roman Mass as altogether necessary to consecrate the Eucharist. Even in Rome itself, and other places throughout Italy, we see, with the consent of the Roman Pontiff, the Liturgy of St. Basil or Chrysostom is retained, and in Milan of St. Ambrose, and in Toledo and Spain, that which they call Mozarabic. But what we assert is the order of celebrating the sacrifice is rightly called the Canon because it should be certain and directed by those who legitimately preside in the Church, not, however, placed in the choice of anyone you like. This is why we rightly rebuke Luther, Calvin and those like them who dared, on their own authority (when they are really private men) to change the order instituted by the Supreme Pontiffs, and preserved in the Churches of Germany and France for at least 800 years.

CHAPTER XIX
On the Author of the Canon

IN REGARD to what pertains to the author: The whole Canon of the Roman Mass is not of one author, but, as the Council of Trent rightly teaches (Sess. 22, cap. 4), it consists partly in the words of the Lord, partly in the Apostolic Tradition, and partly the institution of holy Popes.

First, it was St. Peter who gave some form of celebrating the sacrifice to the Roman Church, by joining certain prayers and rites to the words of the Lord, as Isidore witnesses (*de officiis* 1, 15), but later, different Popes added different prayers, even to the time of Gregory I, who was the last of those who added something to the Canon, as can be gathered from Strabo (*De Observationibus Ecclesiasticis*, c. 22).

After that, we must also observe that although certain liturgies are called "of Basil, another "of Chrysostom", another "of Ambrose", another of "Gelasius," or "of Gregory", namely our Roman, and another of Isidore; still, these authors did not compose the entire Liturgy, but only that which was in use in their time to render a better form by removing that which had crept in which was less suitable, or by adding something for the difference of the times, or lastly, on account of avoiding exhaustion by removing something; still, so that the substantial parts of the Liturgy instituted by the Apostles would remain intact. For St. Gregory abridged the codex of Gelasius, as John the Deacon writes (*Vita Gregorii*, 2, 17) and he himself asserts it (*Epistles* 73, 7). He also restored ancient customs in the Mass and removed certain things which crept in later; therefore, he was not the author of the institution, but the *reformer* of the Liturgy. Likewise, Gregory VII again emended the Ecclesiastical Office, but (as he witnesses, can. *In Die, de consecrate.*, dist. 5) he did not institute something new, but *restored what was ancient*: even Pius V did this in our times in his restoration of the Breviary and the Missal, which is why it is called the Missal of Pius V, or the new Missal, although still it is not completely new, but an amendment and restitution of the ancient.

But in what we have said about the author, Chemnitz condemns us *firstly*, because we hold the Canon was composed by many authors.

But this rebuke is utterly empty. For even the Apostles Creed is one simple confession of faith, and still it was composed by the twelve Apostles, each adding their own teaching, as St. Leo writes (*Epist. 13 ad*

Book II, Ch. XIX: On the Author of the Canon 263

Pulcheriam), and before Leo, Ruffinus in his explanation of the Creed, not to mention Augustine (*Serm. 115 de tempore*). Next, the same Creed was increased, or explained in the Councils of Nicaea and Constantinople, from where, at length, that creed was brought out more fully, which is properly called the Nicene-Constantinoplan Creed. Likewise, the book of Psalms has many authors, if we believe St. Jerome (*Epist. Ad Sophronium*), and in a time when it was thought to be a singular book. Lastly, it is especially to be admired and commended that the Canon of the Mass was composed by many authors and still, all the parts are so joined and adhere to each other, that they seem to be of one author.

Secondly, Chemnitz objects with the testimony of St. Gregory (*Epist.* 7, 63) where he writes two things that seem to be contrary to our teaching. One is that the Apostles customarily consecrated the Eucharist by the Lord's prayer alone, whereby what we teach, that the author of our Canon was St. Peter and many things are found in it from Apostolic tradition, would seem to be refuted. The second is, the Canon was composed by a certain Scholasticus; Scholasticus, however is the proper name of some man, and Chemnitz shows it from the same Gregory (*Epistles* 2, 54 and 9, 14). But if Scholasticus was the author of the Canon, then as a result, what we said with the Council of Trent is false, namely that the Canon was partly composed by Christ and the Apostles, and partly by holy Popes, for there was no Apostle or Pope who was properly called by that name.

Chemnitz receives nearly the whole argument from Blessed Rhenanus, in his annotations to Tertullian's *De Corona Militis*; but it will not be difficult to answer this. *Firstly*, those who deny the Apostles ever celebrated the mystery of the Eucharist according to the Lord's prayer alone are not lacking. For it seems Gregory received it from Jerome in his book *Contra Pelagianos*; but Jerome says the Apostles, by Christ's command, added the Lord's prayer to the celebration of the Eucharist, he did not, however say they *only* used the Lord's prayer.

Whatever is the case on this (for we must not easily repudiate what St. Gregory wrote, nor does it have the appearance of truth that he is the only man not to have noticed what Jerome had already written), I make this response: Above we taught more than once that in the beginning, Apostles customarily added only the Lord's prayer to the words of consecration in the mystery of the Eucharist. Nevertheless, later the same Apostles added many other things: for certainly, the prayer for the dead in the sacrifice of the Mass comes down from Apostolic tradition, as

Chrysostom constantly teaches (*Hom. 3 in Philippians*, and other places).

What Gregory writes on this Scholasticus, however, does not oppose our teaching. For in the first place, it is not certain that this "Scholasticus" is a proper name. Thus, in the time of Gregory men were not called *Scholasticus* as a proper name, whereby, wherever this name is found it must be received as if it was the proper name of somebody: rather, it is by far more probable that through *Scholasticus*, in that place he understands a man known for his erudition and eloquence. Jerome writes this way (*de Scriptoribus, in Serapione*) when he says Serapion, a most learned man had gained the last name *Scholasticus* due to his elegant genius. St. Gregory (*Epistles* 10, 2) calls a Matthew, a famous man *Scholasticus*; and Gennadius (*Catalogus Scriptorum*), describes Prosper by the word *Scholasticus*, i.e. excellent in his eloquence and erudition. Honorius (*Catalogus Scriptorum*) calls Alcuin *Scholasticus* by his office. St. Augustine receives *Scholasticus* in the same sense (*Tract. Supre Psal. 44*). Very learned priests like this, who were formerly put in charge of Christian schools to instruct the unlearned who came to the Church from the Jews or the gentiles, were men like Pantenus, Clement of Alexandria, Origen and others. Lastly, even today in certain Churches, both the name and the dignity of a *Scholasticus* perseveres, although that function has altogether ceased.

Now, if the name *Scholasticus* as it is found in Gregory were to be received for a very learned man, we could admit in the whole business, the whole Canon, with the exception of the Lord's words, was composed by a *Scholasticus*, namely St. Peter, and the other holy Popes may be called *scholastici*. Nor is this foreign to the mind of Gregory, for he does not speak on Scholasticus contemptuously, rather he opposed him to Christ as a man to God, in other words: If the prayer recited over the oblation were composed by a man, how much more ought a prayer composed by God himself be recited?

But if Gregory understands by *Scholasticus* some specific man, who lived in his age, as our adversaries contend; then we are compelled to answer that St. Gregory does not speak about the canon of the Mass, or certainly not on the whole canon, when he says the prayer of Scholasticus is recited over the oblation, but on some other extraordinary prayer; there are three of this kind which are said before Communion, after the *Agnus Dei*, which, as Micrologus writes (c. 18), are not from the Canon, nor prescribed by the ordinary, but are recited from the custom of religious. Moreover, that this is so is certain because the prayers which are in the

Book II, Ch. XIX: On the Author of the Canon

Canon are, for the most part, found in St. Ambrose, as we will show a little later, and hence it could not be the case that they were composed in the time of Gregory, who was two hundred years later than Ambrose.

This explanation is not inconsistent with the words of St. Gregory; for he writes that he was accused of commanding the Lord's prayer to be recited after the Canon, and he answers that he thought it was unbecoming that the prayer composed by Scholasticus is said over the oblation and the very prayer of Christ is not said over his body. By such words, Gregory shows he was not arguing about the Canon, but on prayers which are said after the Canon. And indeed, before his times it seems to have been the practice after the Canon but before Communion, that some prayer composed by Scholasticus was said; moreover, the Lord's prayer, was either said after Communion, after the oblation was consumed, or not at all. But Gregory changed this order, and willed that the Lord's prayer should be said soon after the Canon, while the Lord's body was still present on the altar, but the prayer of Scholasticus followed. From these two opinions both are probable, and neither is against us.

CHAPTER XX
On the Antiquity of the Canon

Now it remains that we speak on the antiquity of the Canon. First, the levity of Chemnitz seems laughable; for on pg. 828, he calls what the Council wrote nonsense and smoke, namely that the Canon was instituted many centuries ago, and still on pg. 826, the same Chemnitz affirms that the Canon was fully developed within the first 600 years from the birth of Christ. Again, on page 872, he writes that the author of the Canon lived around the year 590 A.D., which he also repeats on pg. 828, where he makes Gregory the last author of the Canon in the year 590. For, if the Canon was fully developed in the year 590 A.D., who does not see it was instituted a thousand years ago, and hence what the Council says is very true? Especially when Chemnitz contradicts himself on the same page! Then, we should ask from those who deny the antiquity of our Canon that they show the antiquity of theirs. What could that be, seeing that they scorn our Canon as a novelty which they affirm was brought forth a thousand years ago, when they have a Canon, if it merits being called that, brought forth in this very century?

Now that we have passed over these matters, let us show the antiquity of our Canon. *First*, it is certain that the complete Canon, as we have it now in the Missal, was in the use of the Church before the year 800 A.D. For it is extent in the Roman Ordinal, which Alcuin cites as the *Ordinem*, as well as Amalarius, who lived in the times of Charlemagne. Next, Alcuin (*de officiis Ecclesiast.*, c. *de Celebratione Missae*), explains the whole Canon word by word, and after him the same Canon is explained by all others, such as Amalarius, Hugh, Rupert, Innocent and the rest. Hence, the Roman Ordinal did not institute the Canon, but it relates that it was a normal and frequent thing in the Church. This is why it is necessarily the case that the Canon is still older than the Roman Ordinal.

Although it does not seem that an earlier copy of the Roman Ordinal is extent which contains the whole Canon, still, much more ancient books are extent where parts of the Canon are found, from which we can make a conjecture about the rest.

First, part of the Canon is found in Ambrose (*De Sacramentis*, 4, 5-6) with the words hardly changed: *Quam oblationem tu Deus in omnibus quaesumus, benedictam, adscriptam, ratam, etc.* And: *Qui pride quam*

Book II, Ch. XX: On the Antiquity of the Canon

pateretur, etc., and: *Unde et memores*, etc., and *Supra quae propitio*, etc. These are the four chief parts of the whole Canon; two are right before the consecration, two are right after. And because St. Ambrose was not the first to institute these parts of the Canon, but admits these are from the ancient rite of the Church, as a confirmation of what he is discussing, namely on the truth of the Lord's body in the Eucharist, it necessarily follows that the institution of these preceded the age of Ambrose, hence they were in use 1200 years ago. The same Ambrose (*De Sacramentis*, 4, 4) clearly calls to mind the first prayer of the Canon, where the prayer is made for the Church and for the King, although he does not put it into words. Optatus mentions the same thing (*Contra Parmenianum*) where he says, the *Legitimum* is to offer for the Catholic Church. Moreover, Augustine mentions the prayer where the saints are named and invoked as well as that where prayer is made for the dead (*Tract. In Joannem*, 84), nay more many Fathers mention these prayers, which we adduced in the proper places above. Therefore, that whole part of the Canon, partly insofar as a sentence, partly insofar as words, is found in authors who lived 1100 or 1200 years ago.

Now we add a few manifest conjectures to prove the antiquity of the Canon. The *first* conjecture is that in the whole Canon no mention is made of confessors, or Virgins that were not martyrs, but only of martyrs, whether men or women; Augustine notes this fact in his book *On Holy Virginity*, c. 45. The reason for this, however, is none other than what Innocent III gives (*De Mysteriis Missae* 3, 10), because in the time that the Canon was composed, holy confessors had not yet begun to be publicly venerated in the Church. Accordingly, it is certain, that martyrs began to be publicly invoked and their names venerated on feast days, as well as Churches raised to them from the beginning of the Church. Yet, confessors merited honor in the Church much later. It is certain from the Council of Mainz, celebrated under Charlemagne (can. 36) that the feasts of confessors had already come into practice by the year 800. Accordingly, in the Catalogue of feast days the feasts of St. Martin and St. Remigius are placed, consequently, it necessarily follows that the Canon was composed before the year 800.

The *second* conjecture is, that the ancients diligently annotate a few words which some Popes added to the Canon. The author of the *Pontificalis* writes on the life of Leo I that he added this prayer to the Canon: *Sanctum sacrificium, immaculatam hostiam*; Strabo also notes this (c. 22) as it is very notable, as well as the rest of the authors who write on the Mass. Gregory I added these few words to the Canon: *Diesque nostros in tua pace dispones*, etc., as not only Strabo and other authors record (*loc. cit.*) but even Bede notes it in *hist. Anglicanae* (2, 1), as well as John the deacon in the *Life of Gregory* (2, 17). Moreover, this is a most certain argument that the Canon is more ancient than Leo and Gregory, and was always held in the greatest veneration. Otherwise, why would the historians record that Leo or Gregory added one or another word if the Canon were recent and instituted by some private man named Scholasticus?

The *third* conjecture is the very ignorance of the author of particular parts of the Canon. For those prayers which Ambrose mentions: *Quam oblationem* and the *Unde et Memores*, and the rest, if they were composed by some Roman Pontiff, certainly some historian would have recorded it; if they do not fail to mention who added some particular prayers, how much more would those who write the lives of the Popes, have omitted the very Pope who composed nearly the whole Canon? Therefore, it remains that the Canon is older than memory, and from the Apostles, just as many other things that come down to us through the hands of tradition. Nor is it opposed that the Canon mentions the Apostles and Martyrs who lived in the first three hundred years; there can be no doubt that these names were added little by little.

The *fourth* conjecture is of Strabo (c. 22) who thereby gathers the Canon is ancient because while the Apostles are enumerated, the order, which was corrected by Jerome in the Gospels is not preserved. That is in the argument, that part of the Canon was composed before Jerome corrected the codices of the Latin Gospels according to the old Greek manuscripts; for Jerome himself, in the preface to the Gospels written to Damasus, witnesses there was a great confusion in the older Latin codices.

CHAPTER XXI
On the Truth of the First Prayer of the Canon

Now, at length, we must prove the truth of the Canon, which will be easy to do if we respond to the things which our adversaries object to each of its prayers.

Therefore, the first prayer of the Canon, which begins, *Te igitur clementissime Pater*, is extended even to that: *Hanc igitur oblationem*. For the prayer *Memento Domine*, and *Communicantes, et memoriam venerantes*, are not different prayers, but parts of the first prayer, as is gathered both from the conclusion, *Per eundem Dominum nostrum*, which is placed in the end of all these prayers, and also because the *Communicantes* does not make any sense unless it were a continuation of the preceding words. Therefore, the first prayer of the Canon contains the names of those for whom it is offered, and in whose honor the sacrifice is offered, i.e. for the living in the Church militant, and also the saints who reign with Christ in heaven. And *first* the Church is named. *Secondly*, the Pope. *Thirdly*, the Bishop of the place. *Fourthly*, the king in certain Churches. *Fifthly*, all orthodox believers in general. *Sixthly*, particular persons, but in secret. *Seventhly*, and lastly, the holy Apostles and martyrs.

Now we must observe that the prayer for the Church is contained in all Liturgies, and as we showed above, namely that it is noted by Optatus of Milevis (*Contra Parmenianum*, 2), so also prayer for the Bishop of the place is contained in all the liturgies.

The prayer for the Pope is not found in the ancient Greek Liturgies, but in the Liturgy of Chrysostom translated into Latin by Leo Tuscus, the name of Pope Nicholas is found, from which we understand that even the Greeks customarily added to it in later times. Among the Latins it seems to be a very ancient custom; for not only Alcuin, 800 years ago (*loc. cit.*) when explaining the Mass mentions this thing, giving the reasons why the name of the Pope is added after the Church, but even the Council of Vaison celebrated 1100 years ago (can. 4/6) decreed that in the French Churches the name of the Pope of the city of Rome be recited in all Masses.

The name of the King is also rightly added in those places which are under the rule of kings, for both Innocent III and St. Bonaventure, in their explanation of the Canon, acknowledge this word, and all the ancient Liturgies preserve it, and Ambrose (*de Sacramentis* 4, 4), and Augustine (*Epist.* 59 ad Paulinum) gather it from the Apostle in 1 Tim. 2:2.

On what follows: *Pro omnibus Orthodoxis*, Micrologus (c. 13) writes it is superfluous and not found in more correct books; nevertheless, it is found in Alcuin (*loc. cit.*) who lived 300 years before Micrologus, and among Innocent III and all others. For this reason, it obtains authority in the very use and should not be omitted. Moreover, here we understand through all orthodox believers, as St. Bonaventure explains, not those who are altogether faithful, for then it truly would be a small part, seeing that it is the same to offer for the whole Church and all orthodox believers. Rather, all other apart from the Pope, the local Bishop and one's king, as if we were to say: We offer firstly for all the Church throughout the world, then in particular for the Pope, for the Bishop, for the King and all the other faithful, whether rulers or private men.

1) The *first* objection against this prayer is of Luther in his book *On the Abrogation of Private Mass*, "Who does not see that the Canon was composed by someone very wordy, and hardly spiritual? For what does so superfluous a thing pertain to the words: *Haec dona, haec munera, haec sancta sacrificia?*" He has a similar objection in his book *Against the abomination of the Canon*, where he attacks the prayer, "*Omnibus Orthodoxis, atque Catholicae, et Apostolicae cultoribus*" for it seems the same to him to pray for the orthodox believers and for worshipers of the Catholic faith.

I respond: It appears sufficiently enough that Luther only makes this objection because he is eager to find fault with everything. Otherwise, he could not be unaware that many repetitions of the same thing are made to explain the sense, especially in different words. Certainly, the Liturgies of Basil, and Chrysostom are full of repetitions of this sort; likewise, the Confessions of Augustine, which are directed chiefly to inspire emotion, everywhere reinforces the same thing with many words. The canticles of the Scriptures, and the Psalms, hardly ever pronounce something once, which they do not repeat again in other words, such as in Psalm 91:10: "For behold your enemies, O Lord, behold your enemies shall perish," and in Psalm 115:6, "I am your servant, I am your servant, and the son of your handmaid." Nay more, Psalm 118, which is the longest of all, repeats the same thing in nearly every verse. In Luke 18:34, when it is told how the Lord foretold to the Apostles that his death approached, he adds, "And

Book II, Ch. XXI: The First Prayer of the Cannon

they understood none of these things, and this word was hidden from them, and they did not understand the things that were said." If Luther would consult Luke, he would call him wordy and hardly spiritual. But he multiplied his words at the direction of the Holy Spirit, so that we would understand that in that time that the thought of Christ's death was far from the minds of the Apostles. Even Paul, in 2 Cor. 11:22, when he says: "They are Hebrews, so am I, they are Israelites, and so am I, they are the seed of Abraham, and so am I," he repeats the same thing three times, and still not in vain because that repetition has great emphasis.

2) The *second* objection is of the same Luther (*ibid.*). Before the consecration bread and wine are called holy and spotless sacrifices, which seems absurd because if they are holy, why do we ask God in the same prayer to bless them? If they are sacrifices, then we sacrifice bread and wine to God.

I respond: Bread and wine can rightly be called holy and spotless sacrifices before the consecration. They are truly sacrifices because they are the matter of sacrifice, and have already been dedicated and prepared, that the sacrifice be made from them. For, even in the Old Law sheep are always called sacrifices while they are alive, when clearly, they were being led to be immolated; for this reason, Cyprian says in his *Sermon on Almsgiving*: "Why do you come to the Lord rich and opulent without sacrifice?" Moreover, they are rightly called holy and spotless because they have already been dedicated and consecrated to divine use through the earlier oblation, and also, because they are offered by the Church with a pure and holy intention. But whatever is holy in that manner, nevertheless should become more holy through the change into the body and blood of Christ, and so we rightly ask that God would bless them and sanctify them, namely, that in this way they may become for us the body and blood of Christ, as we ask later in another prayer.

3) The *third* objection (*ibid*): In the Canon it is said: *Quae tibi offerimus, inprimis pro Ecclesia tua.* But these sacrifices consist merely in bread and wine, therefore we offer bread and wine to God on behalf of the Church. Nor can the response be made that "we offer" is received for the future and must be referred to the consecrated host, as if the sense were: "We offer i.e. we will soon offer; for this answer would be opposed by the demonstrative pronoun in : *Haec dona, haec munera,* etc., for we say we offer those gifts which then are shown according to the sense.

I respond: The trifling of the heretics is truly marvelous. The same Luther, who in his book *On the Abomination of the Canon*, gathers from the canon as if it were an absurd thing that we seem to offer bread to God, not Christ; but he also argues in his book *On the Babylonian Captivity*, on the Eucharist, that Catholics think they offer Christ to the Father, and in the same book he advises priests that they should direct their intention to offer the bread, not the Eucharist: "Let priests, who offer the sacrifice observe, in this dangerous and most perilous age, that they direct the words of the greater and lesser canon with the collects, which clearly and especially speak of sacrifice, not to the sacrament, but to the bread and wine that are going to be consecrated; for the bread and wine were already offered to be blessed, but after they have been blessed and consecrated, they should not be offered."

Now, to respond to his argument: The bread is rightly offered for the Church, not because that oblation is properly a propitiatory sacrifice, but because it is a dedication of the matter, whereby it becomes a propitiatory sacrifice; just as a little while ago we were speaking on the word sacrifice, which is attributed to the bread, because it is the matter of the sacrifice. This is why, when we say that we offer the bread to God for the Church, the sense is: we offer to God the bread that is going to be consecrated, and from which through the consecration a true sacrifice has been immolated to God for the Church. This is not foreign to the manner of speech used in the divine Scripture. In Leviticus 4:14, 5:6, 6:6 and other places, every one of the people are commanded to offer a lamb, or something of this sort in sacrifice for sin, and still not any of the people properly sacrificed, for that was the office of the priest alone, but they were said to offer the sacrifice for sin, because they offered the matter whereby it was going to become a sacrifice for sin.

4) The fourth objection of Luther (*ibid*): In the first prayer of the Canon it is said: *Quae tibi offerimus, vel qui tibi offerunt pro redemptione animarum suarum*. And in the same place it is said in regard to the same ones who are offering: *Quorum tibi fides cognita est, et nota devotion*. So, if these are faithful and devout, certainly they are redeemed; if they have been redeemed, to what end do they offer for the redemption of their souls? Is it not the same thing, as if they were to say we that have been redeemed in the blood of Christ are not truly redeemed, or need to be redeemed again by one morsel of bread?

I respond: In regard to what pertains to the piece of bread, we already said that bread is not offered as if it were a propitiatory sacrifice, but that it would be the *matter of the propitiatory sacrifice*. As far as the redemption of the faithful and the devout, among the Lutherans no one

Book II, Ch. XXI: The First Prayer of the Cannon

is considered faithful and devout who is not at the same time just and hence redeemed insofar as the soul; among Catholics, nevertheless, who understand that there can be faith without charity, many faithful and even pious are not doubted to be of a certain imperfect contrition, who still are not justified and through this are not redeemed in the mode which we will soon explain. These are the sort who begin to do penance and desire to be converted to God, and pray for it, as well as devoutly request Masses, although they have not yet obtained perfect contrition. So, the words of the canon can suitably be received in regard to these.

Besides, as the Lutherans understand it, it is not absurd if those that have been redeemed are said to need some redemption, we must advert that in Scripture redemption is received in five ways, and hence they can, who have been redeemed in one way, have need that they be redeemed in the other ways. The *first* mode is said to be redemption from every evil of sin and punishment through the payment of the sufficient price; and in this way all men have altogether been redeemed by the cross of Christ, according to what the Apostle says in 1 Tim. 2:6, "Who gave himself as a redemption for all."

The *second* is redemption from the evil of sin by the application of that price paid on the cross; and this redemption is justification itself: "being justified freely by his grace, through the redemption that is in Christ Jesus," (Romans 3:24), and a great many need this redemption even though they were redeemed in the first mode.

The *third* is from the debt of punishment which often remains after the sin has been forgiven, according to that of Proverbs 13:8, "The redemption of a man's life are his riches," for the riches, when they have been paid out to the poor, free men from punishment; and those who are redeemed in the first and second way often need this redemption.

The *fourth* way redemption is spoken of is in regard to future sin; for God is said to redeem those whom he preserves from a sin, which others committed. "The Lord will redeem the souls of his servants, and all those who hope in him will not err." (Psalm 33:23)

The *fifth* way redemption is spoken of is from the corruption and toil of this life, which will finally take place in the final resurrection, "Lift up your heads, because your redemption is at hand." (Luke 21:28). Just as in the previous way, all will have need of this redemption, even the most holy.

Hence, the first form of redemption is not obtained through the Mass, because it was carried out on the cross, still, *it is represented and applied* in the Mass. The Mass contributes in no small way to obtain all the rest, and therefore, it is no wonder if it is said to be offered for the redemption of the faithful and the pious.

5) The *fifth* objection is also from Luther (*ibid.*), who finds fault with: *Communicantes, et memoriam venerantes*. Christ instituted the Supper to be a communion of the living; the author of the Canon makes even the dead communicants.

I respond: the word *Communicantes* is explained in two ways by the ancient writers. Alcuin, Amalarius, and others relate that it is in regard to the communion with the saints, so the sense would be: We offer this sacrifice having communion with the memories of the saints, and venerating the same saints; where no mention is made of communion through eating the Eucharist, which is not suitable for the dead. Rather, it speaks of the communion through society, and *the union in the mystical body of Christ*. Others, among whom are Micrologus (c. 12) and Hugh of St. Victor (*de Officiis* 2, 29), would have it that *communicantes* refers to those offering among themselves, not with the saints, so that the sense would be: We offer, having communion, i.e. united among ourselves, and joined as is fitting for members of the same body, and besides, venerating the memory of the saints. Micrologus proves it with the best reasoning: On Christmas, Epiphany, Easter, Ascension and Pentecost, after the word *Communicantes*, it is added: *et diem sacratissimum celebrantes, etc.* and a little after, *sed et memoriam venerantes, etc.*, where we clearly see the word *communicantes* is not joined with the memory of the saints, but remains *per se* and must be referring only to those offering.

6) The *sixth* objection is of George Major, who finds fault with the order of the words: *Ut accepta habeas, et benedicas haec dona*; for they should be blessed before they are received by God.

But the answer is easy. For, as this oblation is twofold (which we said above), one of the thing that is going to be consecrated, the second of the thing that has been consecrated, so its reception is twofold: the blessing, however, and the sanctification follows one of these oblations and receptions, the other precedes. This is why, just as in this place, where it is a question of the first reception and the blessing is placed after; so a little after in that prayer, *Quam oblationem tu Deus, in omnibus benedictam, adscriptam, ratam, acceptabilem facere digneris*, where it is a question on the second reception, the blessing is placed before.

7) The *seventh* objection is of Zwingli, who does not approve of: *Memento Domine famulorum, etc.*, for, as he says, "We seem afraid that

Book II, Ch. XXI: The First Prayer of the Cannon 275

God might be oblivious, and therefore, wish to remind him as though he were forgetful."

But it seems Zwingli is rather more forgetful of the sayings of the Scriptures, or certainly, if he did remember them, he would be sure to correct the Holy Spirit! Otherwise, why does it happen more frequently in the Scriptures that someone says, remember O Lord? See Exodus 32:13, Deuteronomy 9:27; Judges 16:28; 4 Kings 20;3; 2 Ezra 5:19; Psalm 131 [132]:1; Luke 23:42, and other places. Not only do we read "remember O Lord" everywhere in the Scripture, but even what seems more marvelous: "Do not forget," or "Why do you forget?" as we see in Psalm 9:32; Psalm 12:2; Psalm 41 [42]:50, and other places, chiefly in the Psalms. Moreover, God is said to forget by a metaphor, when he does not help and on the other hand, remembers when he begins to help.

8) The *eighth* objection is also of George Major, who judges the words: *Pro quibus tibi offerimus, vel qui tibi offerunt:*, and says that the correction: *vel qui tibi offerunt* clearly shows that the Canon speaks about almsgiving which the people offered at the altar for the poor; hence it is not rightly twisted toward the sacrifice of the Eucharist.

The first objection of Chemnitz (from the seventeen which he makes against the Canon in *Exam.* 2 part. P. 839) also pertains to this point. For the first objection holds that once, these words of the canon were merely directed to the customary blessings and commending of almsgiving, but now they are dragged to a hostile representation of sacrifice, and besides, bread is not rightly offered to God on behalf of the Church. The first part of the objection has been taken from the argument of Major which we already refuted, the second part from the argument of Luther which we answered a little before.

I respond: It is not a correction, but a disjunctive sentence, on account of the two orders of those which the priest commended to God; some, for whom it is offered, are absent, and do not offer in act; some are present, who offer at the same time with the priest by their presence and consent. Therefore, this is the sense of the words: Be mindful, O Lord, of this or that man who is absent, and also of all those who are present, for all of whom we offer, namely for those who are now absent from this Church, or even who are together with us in desire, and offer by consent. Moreover, no prayers of the Canon pertain to commend almsgiving, which Major and Chemnitz falsely assume, and that can be known from the whole context of the Canon. In the first place, these gifts which are named in the Canon are said to be offered to God for the Church, for the

Pope, for the king, for all the orthodox faithful; but almsgiving is not usually offered to anyone except for those who gave alms. Next, on the same oblation, which has been named in the beginning of the Canon, but which our adversaries would have it pertain to almsgiving, it is added a little later: *Hanc igitur oblationem servitutis nostrae*, etc., where clearly it is shown that oblation is properly a sacrifice, certainly which is offered to the Lord through the ministry of the priests, and a little later it is said: *Quam oblationem tu Deus in omnibus, quaesumus, benedictam, ... ut nobis corpus, et sanguis fiat dilectissimi Filii tui,*, etc., where we manifestly see that in the whole Canon that oblation is mentioned which becomes the body and blood of the Lord through consecration. Lastly, all the expositors of the Liturgy, both Greek (such as Germanus and Cabasilas), and Latin (such as Alcuin, Amalarius and the rest) explain the whole Canon on the Eucharist.

9) The *ninth* objection is of Chemnitz, which he places as his second: he considers the sentence: *Pro quibus tibi offerimus, vel qui tibi offerunt hoc sacrificium laudis*; and he would have it that the canon, according to the ancient rite, argues in this place on a spiritual sacrifice, which consists in the praise of God and thanksgiving for the redemption he acquired on the cross. Then, after he has posited this foundation, he rebukes Catholics both because they change a sacrifice of praise into the mumbling of a silent priest, and because they twist this sacrifice of praise acquired on the cross for redemption to a representation of a sacrificing priest to obtain and merit the redemption of souls.

I respond: This objection, as the last, and so many that follow, are not against the Canon, but against *the intention of the priests who recite the Canon*; accordingly, the words of the canon themselves can be received in regard to a sacrifice of praise, or almsgiving, etc. Hence, these objections do not really bear on the matter. Accordingly, Chemnitz proposed to demonstrate that there are many errors found in the Canon itself, as is clear from p. 839 where he speaks in this way: "We will propose to show on a chart, as it were, what errors and vices the popish Canon contains." Thus he. But where he begins to enumerate those very errors, he does not so much find fault with the words of the Canon as with the priests who either recite it in a quiet voice, or twist it to a representation.

Next, the things which Chemnitz assumes and does not prove (as is his custom), are false. *First*, it is false that through sacrifice of praise, which is mentioned in the Canon, it should be received as a spiritual sacrifice which consists in praise and thanksgiving; for the sacrifice

Book II, Ch. XXI: The First Prayer of the Cannon

of the true body of the Lord is signified by that word, which is called a sacrifice of praise because through it, God is exceedingly praised and thanks are given to him for his supreme benefits in us, whereby it is rightly called the Eucharistic sacrifice. This is the case: *a)* from the Canon itself; for when the Church is speaking on this sacrifice of praise a little later, it asks from God that he would deign to bless this oblation and cause the body of his most beloved Son to come about. *b)* It is clear from Augustine, who calls the Eucharist a sacrifice of praise more than once: in *Contra Advers. Leg. et Prophet.* (1, 20), where two or three times he calls it a sacrifice of praise, because we offer according to the order of Melchisedech, confected from bread and wine. But if the sacrifice of praise is not the praises which are recited orally, but rather is the very oblation of the Lord's body, then what Chemnitz says, that we transformed a sacrifice of praise into a silent murmur is inane and false; for this sacrifice does not consist in an expression, but *in an action*. And what he adds lastly is also false, that we twisted the sacrifice of praise to a miming representation, since the sacrifice which we properly immolate in the Church is not a representation of a past thing, but a true and real oblation in the present of the Lord's body and blood.

10) The *tenth* objection, which is the third of Chemnitz, is against the words of the Canon: *Reddunt tibi vota sua aeterno Deo, vivo et vero*. For Chemnitz says that formerly it was in use in the Church that, according to the words of Psalm 115 [116]:8, *Vota mea Domino reddam*,[26] thanks was given to God for benefits; but now, seeing that the ancient rite has been abolished, these words of the Canon of the Mass refer to votive Masses, which are commanded to be celebrated once money has been given.

I respond: These are all calumnies and lies, for the Canon does not understand votive Masses for *vota*, rather a pious desire and the oblation of the people who are present; for these words are said in every Mass, not only in votive Masses, and by those who never receive money as well as those who receive it for the celebration of Mass. Rather, Chemnitz should prove what he so boldly upholds with some testimony.

11) The *eleventh* objection, which is the fourth of Chemnitz, is against the words, *Et memoriam venerantes*; for Chemnitz objects that formerly it was in use in the Church to preach the memorials and struggles of the Martyrs, as well as their victories; but now the Canon of the Mass only prescribes the memory by the recitation of names, and in a quiet voice.

---

26 I shall fulfill my vows to the Lord.

But in this objection, we find nothing apart from calumnies and lies. For the ancient writers did not preach the martyrs in the Liturgy, but in sermons and readings, which we do both in sermons to the people and in the readings which are regularly sung in the Canonical hours. Otherwise, let him advance from the Liturgy of Basil, or Chrysostom, or any liturgy you like, that use of preaching the deeds of the Martyrs. It is certainly found in none of them, apart from their names, as we see in our Liturgy.

12) The *twelfth* objection, which is the fifth of Chemnitz, opposes the invocation which is connected to the memory of the saints. But he advances nothing new apart from those which we refuted above when we argued on Masses in honor of the saints in chapter 8.

CHAPTER XXII
On the Truth of the Second Prayer of the Canon

THE SECOND PRAYER of the canon begins with the words: *Hanc igitur oblationem servitutis nostrae*, etc., in which four petitions are contained. *First*, that God would be well-disposed to receive our oblation; *second*, that he might arrange our days with peace; *third*, that he would deliver us from eternal damnation; *fourth*, that he would number us in the company of the elect.

1) The *first* objection is of Luther, who says, "Here again, they offer bread and wine to free the faithful from eternal damnation. They attribute such efficacy to the bread and the wine, for the death and passion of the Son of God is of no importance for this redemption."

I respond: Luther objects with calumnies, not arguments, for the priest does not pray that through the oblation of bread and wine we might be freed from eternal damnation, rather he prays to God that he would receive the very oblation of bread and wine as *the material of the future sacrifice*, and to bless and sanctify it. Lastly, he adds three other petitions over what we have already enumerated, and he does not pray for them to be fulfilled by the oblation of bread and wine, but through *the same Christ our Lord*.

2) The *second* objection is of Chemnitz (which he places as his sixth): "The old Church offered to God in the celebration of the Eucharist, prayers for the impetration of temporal and eternal benefits through Christ, these words could be suitably attributed to this sacrifice of prayers: *Hanc oblationem placates accipias*, etc. But the Papist Canon transfers this to the miming representation of a sacrificing priest offering bread that has not yet been consecrated and prays that God would so receive it that on account of that he might arrange our days in peace, and deliver us from eternal damnation."

I respond: The fact that the old Church offered to God prayers to obtain benefits through Christ is most true; and our Church does the same in this very prayer of the Canon. It is a manifest lie of Chemnitz and Luther, that here we ask benefits on account of the oblation of bread; for that prayer is not obscure nor ambiguous, nor does it contain anything but four petitions, made *through Christ our Lord*.

Now, when Chemnitz says that *hanc oblationem* can suitably be referred to the sacrifice of prayers, he is both against himself and the truth.

It is against Chemnitz himself because in the first objection he related the words of the first prayer, *Haec dona, haec munera, etc.* to almsgiving. But the Canon speaks on the same oblation in the first and second prayer, as is clear from the adverb *Igitur* (therefore), so we see *Hanc igitur obalationem*, etc. This is why, if it is a question of almsgiving in the first prayer, then in the second it must be a question of almsgiving; hence Chemnitz opposes himself. Nevertheless, the whole argument is against the truth because in the first, second and third prayer of the Canon it is a question of the same oblation. It will clearly be shown in the third, that through oblation, the oblation of the bread which is going to be consecrated should be understood, since it is expressly said: "that it would become for us the body and blood, etc." As a result, whatever is said in these prayers does not concern almsgiving or prayer, but *the sacrifice of the Eucharist*.

CHAPTER XXIII
On the Truth of the Third Prayer of the Canon

THE THIRD PRAYER of the Canon begins from the words: *Quam oblationem tu Deus in omnibus*, and it is continued even to the end of the consecration.

The first objection is of Luther (*loc. cit.*) who objects that here we pray for Christ, and the mediators we place between Christ and the Father, to ask God to bless and sanctify the body and blood of Christ.

But Luther does not seem to have remembered the words of the Canon when he wrote these things; for we do not pray for the consecrated Eucharist, but for *the bread and wine that are going to be consecrated*; nor do we ask that God would bless and sanctify the body and blood of Christ, rather that he would bless and sanctify *the bread and wine*, that through that blessing and sanctification they would become the body and blood of the Lord.

The *second* objection is of the same Luther (*ibid.*) against the words: *Benedictam, adscriptam, ratam, rationabilem, acceptabilemque facere digneris:* "What these words portend, neither I nor the fool who wrote them understand."

But these same words are found in Ambrose (*de Sacramentis*, 4, 5), and are elegantly explained by many and in different ways, such as Alcuin, Amalarius, Rupert, Hugh, Innocent, Bonaventure and others. The literal explanation, as we gather it from Alcuin, Hugh and also Innocent III, seems to be the following. We ask from God that he would effect that, by consecrating our oblation, it becomes blessed from the profane; the same by approving, he would make it approved, i.e. he would approve and number it among the gifts which he approves; by confirming he causes it to be ratified, that is stable and firm, that he should relate the certain and perpetual fruit to us; he also makes them reasonable that we would not only offer what is good, but also offer them well, reasonably and prudently, and that our obedience would be reasonable, according to the Apostle in Romans 12:1. Lastly, that he would make them acceptable, i.e. so on every side they are well regarded, not only on the side of the gift, but also on the side of the minister offering, that what God receives would be worthy. See more things brought out by the authors.

3) The *third* objection is of Chemnitz (which is his seventh). He writes that this prayer is found in Ambrose (*loc. cit.* 4, 5) and Augustine

(as Gratian references in can. *Utrum, de consecrate.*, dist. 2) but these words have another sense in the works of those authors than what is found among the Papists; among the former it refers to the reception of the Sacrament, among the latter the representation.

But Chemnitz errs in many ways. *Firstly*, he does not prove that which he sets out to prove. He would have it, as we remarked above, to show the errors of the Canon, but now what he advances does not oppose the Canon, but the sense in which the Papists receive it.

Secondly, he wrongly suborns Augustine, since these words are not extant in Augustine, but partly in Ambrose (*loc. cit.*) and partly in Paschasius (*de Corpore Christi*, c. 4), although in this matter Gratian also seems to have been deceived.

Thirdly, Chemnitz is clearly mistaken when he writes that Augustine interpreted the words *Benedictam, adscriptam, ratam, rationabilem*, etc. on the reception of the Eucharist, as if Augustine thought according to the error of the Lutherans, that in the reception alone the bread becomes the body of Christ, whereby we are blessed and approved in heaven, etc. For Augustine, as I have said, holds nothing of the sort; Ambrose, however, from whom Paschius and Gratian receive the words, does not explain them on the reception, but on the *consecration*, as is clear from a reading of *On the Sacraments*, 4, 5. Nor are the words of the same Ambrose apposed, which Chemnitz incorrectly attributed to Augustine: "Because in baptism we receive the similitude of the death of Christ, we also receive the similitude of his flesh and blood." For these are said by Ambrose in another place (*loc. cit.*, 4, 4) and for a different purpose.

Fourthly, Chemnitz lies when he says the Popes have twisted the word oblation in this prayer of the Canon: *Quam oblationem tu Deus, etc.* to the action of the sacrificing priest, when really it is said in regard to the *bread and wine*. For nobody was ever so absurd or stupid, that he would not see the word oblation in this place can be referred to the bread and wine, not to the action; accordingly, we ask from God to so bless this oblation that it would become for us the body and blood of Christ. Who would say, even in a dream, that the action should become the body of Christ? When Chemnitz contrives these lies about Catholics, he did well to cite nothing or even name any book, lest the lie should be discovered right away.

CHAPTER XXIV
On the Truth of the Fourth Part of the Canon

The fourth prayer is that which is right after the consecration, and is contained in the words: *Unde et memores Domine*, etc., and extends even to: *Memento etiam Domine*, for before the *Memento*, the conclusion *Through Christ our Lord* is placed.

The first objection against this prayer is from Luther, who again argues on the verbosity, on account of the multiplication of the adjoined words: *Hostiam puram, hostiam sanctam, hostiam immaculatam*.

But similar words are found in Ambrose (*de Sacramentis* 4, 6), and Paul wrote in the same spirit in Romans 12:1, "A living sacrifice [hostia], holy, pleasing unto God, your reasonable service."

The *second* objection is also from Luther, and all others who calumniate the words: *Supra quae propitio, ac sereno vultu respicere digneris*; for they say that here we pray for Christ because we wish to reconcile the Son to the Father. Certain of them also suspect that these words were once before the consecration, but what we have now were placed by some unlearned collector of the Canon after the consecration.

But the response to this is easy: in the first place, these words are found in Ambrose after the consecration (*de Sacramentis*, 4, 6). Likewise, all the Greek Liturgies place the prayer for the precious and sanctified gifts after the consecration. This is why it is not new, rather an ancient rite of prayer for the oblation that has already been consecrated. Moreover, in no way is this to pray for the reconciliation of Christ with the Father, but rather more for *our infirmity*; even if the oblation that has already been consecrated would always please God on the side of the thing which is offered, and on the side of Christ the principal one offering, nevertheless, on the side of the minister, or the people present who also offer it at the same time, it cannot please. Therefore, the thing which we ask is that God would kindly regard this offering as it is offered *by us*. The same thing can be discerned in the sacrifices of the ancient Jews; for they humbly asked that God would mercifully look upon the sacrifices of sheep and oxen, but they did not pray properly for the sheep and the oxen; nor did they constitute themselves mediators between the sheep and God, nor reconcile cattle to God; rather they prayed for themselves and desired their service in offering those things to be pleasing to God.

The *third* objection is also of Luther, when he condemns the words: *Sicut accepta habere dignatus es munera pueri tui justi Abel, et sacrificium Patriarchae nostri Abrahae.* For, we appear in this place to attribute no more efficacy to Christ who immolated himself for us than for irrational cattle.

I respond: These are also found in Ambrose (*loc. cit.* 4, 6). Moreover, the comparison is not made absolutely between our sacrifice and the sacrifice of Abel and Abraham, but only by the notion *of faith and devotion of those offering it.* For we desire that God would give us to offer the sacrifice with the same faith and devotion as that which with Abel and Abraham offered, and hence, that on the side of the minister who offers, our sacrifice would be no less pleasing to God than theirs. Moreover, the fact that the comparison is made between their sacrifice and ours by the notion of faith and devotion, and not absolutely, is clear from the fact that the sacrifices of sheep and oxen absolutely and per se have nothing whereby they could please God and render him well disposed. This is why St. Paul does not say in Hebrews 11:4 that the sacrifice of Abel was absolutely pleasing, but on account of faith: "By faith Abel offered to God a sacrifice exceeding that of Cain." And in Genesis 4:4, Moses says, "And the Lord regarded Abel and his offerings."

The *fourth* objection of Luther is against that which follows: *Et quod tibi obtulit summus sacerdos tuus Melchisedech.* Here, Luther charges the Canon with a lie: "They lie in the fact that they assert Melchisedech sacrificed bread and wine."

I respond: The Canon of the Mass does not hold that Melchisedech sacrificed bread and wine, but only that he offered some sacrifice. The fact is, the one who says it is a lie makes the Holy Spirit a liar, who through the mouth of Paul witnesses that Melchisedech was a priest (Hebrews 5:6, 6:20 and 7:1), and through the same Paul (Hebrews 5:1, and 8:3) teaches that every priest should have something to offer. Additionally, the fact that Melchisedech sacrificed bread and wine has been sufficiently proven in the previous book. Lastly, add the fact that not only does Ambrose (*loc. cit.* 4, 6), acknowledge this part of the Canon where Melchisedech is called the supreme priest, but even the author of the *Questions of the old and New Testament,* cited by Augustine (tom. 4, q. 109). That author, however, lived in the same time as Ambrose, as is manifestly gathered from the same questions.

The *fifth* objection is also of Luther, against the words: *Jube haec perferri per manus sancti Angeli tui in sublime altare tuum;* for it seemed

Book II, Ch. XXIV: The Fourth Prayer of the Cannon

to him absurd that the priest would ask it to be taken to heaven, when he is going to consume it soon after. It seems no less absurd that some altar is thought to exist in heaven.

I respond: It must not be understood so crassly, as if we thought some physical and sensible altar were raised in heaven, and that it would be fitting for the Sacrament of the Lord's body to really and corporally be carried there by the hands of an angel, nevertheless, some altar, namely a spiritual one, is in heaven, just as there is also a [spiritual] tabernacle, a throne, incense, trumpets, crowns, palms, and other things of this sort, which no man can deny unless he would deny the Scriptures. Accordingly, in Apocalypse 6:9, 8:3, 9:13, and 14:18, it is often read that there is a golden altar in heaven in the sight of God; in Apocalypse 4:1 thrones, trumpets, and crowns are read to be in heaven; in Apocalypse 7:9 palms in the hands of the saints are seen; in Apocalypse 8:5 a thurible and incense is read; in Apocalypse 21:3, a tabernacle is read; even Christ calls to mind this heavenly tabernacle in Luke 16:9, and Paul in Hebrews 8;2, and 9:11. Irenaeus mentions the same altar placed in heaven (4, 34) as well as Augustine (on Psalm 25) on the words, "I will wash my hands among the innocent", therefore it is not some dream of Catholics, but the divine Scripture itself that constitutes an altar in heaven.

Moreover, that heavenly altar, either signifies Christ himself, through whom our prayers and oblations ascend to God, or certainly because the sacrifices which are immolated to the true God on earth are received in heaven. Moreover, for our sacrifices to be taken to God through the hands of an angel is nothing other than to be helped by the intercession of the angels and for our service and worship to be commended to God, which we desire to show him by immolating. It is also not unlike what we read in Tobit 12:12, and Apocalypse 8:4, that our prayers are taken to God by the angels; for the voices of the angels and our corporal words are taken up, but our devotions and desires for their intercession are commended to God. Therefore, Luther argues ineptly and in vain, that the sacrifice cannot be taken up when the whole thing is consummated on earth.

The *sixth* objection is of Luther against the words: *Ut quotquot ex hac altaris participatione sumpserimus*; for Luther finds fault with the fact that the priest speaks as if it were about many communicants, when he alone is going to communicate.

I respond: He does not speak absolutely on many, or on one; rather he prays that whatsoever they receive, whether one or many, they may receive usefully. But on this matter, we also said something above, when we argued on private Mass.

The *seventh* objection is of George Major, who finds fault with the words: *Panem sanctum vitae aeternae et calicem salutis perpetuae*; he suspects that such words were added by some unlearned and superstitious man, who was persuaded that Christ is offered in Mass to God the Father. Moreover, he shows that when a little before in the same prayer it is said: *Offerimus de tuis donis ac datis*, which without a doubt refers to the alms which are offered by the people, someone could not be anything other than unlearned, to transfer forthwith to Christ a discourse instituted on almsgiving.

I respond: The words which Major suspects were added by some unlearned man are also found in Ambrose (*ibid.*), as though they were customary and received in the whole Church; and something similar is also found in the Greek Liturgies of James, Basil, Chrysostom, as well as in Clement (*Constitutionum Apost.* 8, 17). They also do not badly adhere with the words: *De tuis donis ac datis*; for they can be referred to the bread and wine which became the Eucharist, so the sense would be: we offer to you a pure host, holy bread and the wine of salvation, which we have given from your creation by you, namely from bread and wine through the consecration; Innocent III explains it in this way (*de mysteriis Missae* 5, 3). All of these words can also be referred to the Eucharist itself, or Christ as he exists in the Eucharist, for Christ is rightly said to be given by God. So, Isaiah speaks (9:6), "A son has been given to us." And Christ himself in John 3:16, "God so loved the world that he gave his only begotten son." Are not the sacrament and sacrifice themselves the truest gifts of God?

The *eighth* objection is of Chemnitz, who affirms the prayer *Unde et memores* is taken from ancient writers; but he says among them it was customarily recited out loud, since Cyril says it was an annunciation, and Dionysius uses the word ὑμνεῖν; but in the popish Canon they take pains that it is read in a quiet voice.

I respond: This objection does not show any error in the Canon, or any vice to be present, which our adversary nevertheless proposed. For the *Unde et memores* is read after the words of consecration in secret not only among the Latins, but even among the Greeks; for in the Mass of Basil it is noted that in secret it must be said, and when that prayer has been finished, he says in a loud voice "Offering you your own, from your own." Likewise, we read about this change of the voice at the end of a

Book II, Ch. XXIV: The Fourth Prayer of the Cannon 287

prayer in the Mass of Chrysostom. Hence, Cyril (*Catechesi* 5), where he explains the liturgy, does not mention this prayer, nor does he explain everything, and that is why Chemnitz saw what he did in Cyril. But we do not deny that in the Mass the Lord's death is announced according to the Apostle in 1 Cor. 11:25, rather, as we have said more than once, from Augustine (*Contra Faustum* 20, 18) that it is not done so much in the words, as in *the oblation and participation of the body of the Lord*. Dionysius (*de Eccles. Hier.* 3), where he describes the rite of the Liturgy, calls to mind the hymns whereby the work of Christ is praised, but he places them before the words of consecration, and even in the end when thanksgiving is made to God after Communion; hence Dionysius does not speak on this prayer: *Unde et memores*. But Chemnitz is allowed to play with the Fathers and conclude whatever he likes from any voice he likes.

The *ninth* objection is of the same Chemnitz: "In ancient times, what was sanctified by the word of Christ was taken from the oblations given by the people, so that the Eucharist of the body and blood of the Lord would take place, and this reception and sanctification was called the oblation. But now, seeing that this custom is no longer preserved, the words are transferred to the representation of the sacrificing priest."

I respond: And this is what our adversary takes up to oppose the words of the Canon? Is it not an obvious lie, that Catholics transfer the words to the representation of a sacrificing priest? For all Catholics relate the words: *Offerimus praeclarae Majestati tuae*, which our adversary is speaking about, to the very pure and holy host, confected through the consecration from the gifts of God, as the very words of the Canon declare, not to some representation. It is impertinent, however, whether bread and wine, whereby the Eucharist comes about, are given by the people, or offered by the priest: from wherever they come, they are rightly named gifts of God, and can be the material of the Eucharist.

The *tenth* objection is also from Chemnitz. He finds fault with the words: *Supra quae propitio, ac sereno vultu, etc.*, where he shudders at the comparison that is made between Christ and the brute animals that were immolated in ancient times. And he adds that this prayer which is extant in Basil's liturgy, before the consecration, where the comparison is made of the sacrifice of Abel, Noah, Abraham, and other ancients, with the oblations of bread and wine which are brought by the people; but due to the inexperience of the author of the Canon, they are placed after the consecration, and thence it came to pass, that it contains an intolerable error.

I respond: What pertains to the comparison of Christ with the brute animals, was already answered in the third objection which was from Luther. Moreover, what pertains to the transposition is false, that this prayer was transposed: it is certain from Ambrose (*de Sacramentis*, 4, 6) that it was after the consecration, even in the time of Basil; for Ambrose, who read it after the consecration, lived at the same time as Basil. Nor is it opposed, that in Basil a similar prayer is found before the consecration, for in each place this prayer is rightly imposed. Wherefore, in our Missal a certain similar prayer is found before the consecration, as the same Chemnitz remarked, in the secret Collect for the Seventh Sunday after Pentecost; and still again it is found after the consecration in the place on which we are not treating.

The *eleventh* objection is of the same, against those words: *Jube haec perferri*, etc. For in the first place, Chemnitz shows it is most absurd that we now ask an angel to take the body of Christ into heaven, seeing that the Apostle says (Hebrews 9:12), that Christ has already entered heaven. Then, he affirms these words should be read before the consecration, and referred both to prayers and almsgiving. He proves it both from Irenaeus, who (4, 34) says the prayers and almsgiving are taken to the altar which is in heaven, and from Augustine (can. *Utrum de consecrate*. Dist. 2), as well as Tobit 12, and Apocalypse 5, where prayers are said to be taken into heaven by an angel.

I respond: We affirm that for an angel to *corporally* take the body of Christ into heaven would be most absurd; but no Catholic thinks or speaks in this fashion. For, as we just explained, we only teach the oblation of the body of Christ is taken into heaven insofar as the angels *commend our service to God by their prayer*; which is the same thing Chemnitz is compelled to say about prayers and almsgiving, which the angels take into heaven, which is taught by Tobit, John and Irenaeus. He will certainly not say that almsgiving is really and corporally taken into heaven; for would almsgiving really benefit the poor, if it were taken into heaven? Or how could it be taken into heaven if it is consumed by the poor? Therefore, it is not absurd, as he says he is horrified by it, that the sacrifice of the Eucharist is taken into heaven by the angel, if it is done spiritually, as it is rightly understood.

What pertains to the second part of the objection: it is false that these words were formerly placed in the Canon before the consecration. Ambrose read them after the consecration (*ibid.*), and so also the

Book II, Ch. XXIV: The Fourth Prayer of the Cannon

Liturgies of James and Clement (*Constit.* 8), Basil and Chrysostom. Clearly, the boldness of these innovators is a marvel, who on account of petty syllogisms judge on those matters which they are altogether ignorant. For the passages of Tobit, and the Apocalypse do nothing against our teaching, but rather explain and confirm it. The passage of Irenaeus which he adduced has been distorted, for he does not speak on almsgiving, but on *the Eucharist*, as we showed above (book 1, c. 8), and even if Irenaeus spoke on almsgiving, what would Chemnitz profit from it? Because Irenaeus wrote about almsgiving in some place, that it is customarily taken to the heavenly altar, so this prayer of the Canon must be understood on almsgiving, when Irenaeus does not even name this prayer?

Moreover, what he adduces from Augustine, as we said above, is not a testimony of Augustine, but a rhapsody of fragments from Ambrose, Paschasius, and others, in which rhapsody the order of the Liturgy is not preserved. Firstly, that author mentions the consecration, whereby the bread is turned into the flesh and the wine is turned into the blood; then he lays before us these words: *Jube haec perferri*, etc., and then adds: *hanc oblationem benedictam, ratam,* etc. So, just as Chemnitz contends that *Jube haec perferri* was formerly before the consecration, because these words are placed by the author of the Canon before *Hanc oblationem benedictam, ratam*, etc., so we show the contrary, that they were after the consecration, because they are placed after the consecration itself by the same author; but the truth is, the order of the liturgy is not preserved by that author.

Now, in this place it is hardly to be passed over that in this testimony there are two things against Chemnitz. *Firstly*, in this testimony, the words *Jube haec perferri* are explained on the *consecrated* bread, as we suppose, or certainly on what is going to be consecrated, as Chemnitz would have it; therefore they should not be understood on almsgiving, as the same Chemnitz intends; hence Chemnitz advances this testimony against himself. *Secondly*, in this testimony we clearly read: "By the power of the Holy Spirit from bread it becomes the flesh and the wine becomes the blood," which is against all Lutherans who deny transubstantiation.

CHAPTER XXV
On the Truth of the Fifth Prayer of the Canon

THE *FIFTH* PRAYER is: *Memento etiam Domine*, etc., in which the memory of the dead takes place.

The *first* objection is of Luther, who asserts that he opposes and destroys this very prayer. For here we pray for those who sleep in the sleep of peace, and who rest in Christ, and nevertheless we pray for them a place of rest, light and peace. If they sleep and are at rest, what rest do we ask for? If they have peace, why do we ask that they have peace?

I respond: They have a certain peace and rest, because they are certain and secure in regard to the reward of eternal happiness, and because they are free from the war of temptations, concupiscence, and from every evil work; but they do not yet have peace and rest from torments and from the longing for the sight of the divine. Nor could this prayer have been more suitably composed that it would suit those alone who abide in Purgatory. For those who are in hell, they have no peace and rest; those who are in heaven, possess every peace and rest; they are only administered to those who are in Purgatory, who so rest in the sleep of peace, but still need rest and peace.

The *second* objection is the twelfth of Chemnitz, who boldly affirms that once only the memory of the dead was customarily made, namely to the imitation and testimony to the fact that the dead live with God, as Dionysius witnesses; later that memory also received the prayers for the dead; lastly, the sacrifice itself began to be offered for the dead, so namely, little by little, the ancient institution degenerated into superstitions.

I respond: We have already said many things on this in chapter 7, where we also showed from the ancient author Tertullian that the use of offering for the dead could not be a lie, as Chemnitz writes here, when he says what was instituted by the ancients little by little degenerated into abuse. In this place I shall only proffer the testimony of Dionysius to make Chemnitz blush, if he has any face. In *Ecclesiast. Hierarch.*, part 3 chapter 7, he says: "The hierarch, advancing, offers a sacred prayer over the deceased. After the prayer, both the hierarch himself salutes him, and next, all who are present. As for the prayer, it beseeches the supremely Divine Goodness to remit to the deceased all the failings committed through human infirmity, and to place him in the light and land of the living, etc."

CHAPTER XXVI
On the Sixth Prayer of the Canon

THE *SIXTH* PRAYER, which is the last in the Canon, properly speaking, begins with the words, *Nobis quoque peccatoribus*, and is extended even to *Per omnia saecula saeculorum*, before the Lord's prayer; for the whole Canon is concluded in a loud voice through the latter words, that the whole people would confirm it by responding, *Amen*. This is why, on Good Friday, because the whole canon, which pertains to the consecration, is omitted, none of these six prayers are read, nor is it said, *Per omnia saecula saeculorum*; but immediately after the washing of hands, it passes to the Lord's prayer.

In this prayer, the priest prays for himself and the extension from his merits, he prays for divine mercy to be shown to him, as well as fellowship with the holy Apostles and martyrs. Here we must remark, in the first place John is mentioned; secondly Stephen; thirdly Matthias. Many are uncertain why only John is repeated here from those who are named before the consecration; and why Stephen the deacon is given preference to Mathias the Apostle, and why Matthias was not named in the first rank. And indeed, Innocent and some others answer that John is named twice because he was an Apostle and virgin, and therefore, he is also joined with Stephen who seems to have excelled by his gift of continence, since he was put before a widower. But the opinion of Strabo (c. 22) seems more true to me, who in this place says not the Evangelist, but John the Baptist is named, who was also a martyr of the Lord, and in some manner an Apostle; according to that of John 1:6, "There was a man sent from God, etc."

This is also why Stephen is placed before Matthias, the true reason is because in this place the Church preserves the order of passion, not the dignity; thus, John suffered earlier than Stephen, and Stephen earlier than Matthias.

But why also is Matthias not mentioned in the Canon before the consecration with the other Apostles? I think the reasoning is twofold: One, that there would be some Apostle from the twelve in this second rank, and it could truly be said: "With your Apostles and Martyrs". Secondly, because Mathias was not an Apostle before the Lord's passion, nor is he read in the order of the Apostles in the Gospels. Now, it is not opposed to us that Paul was also not an Apostle before the Lord's passion and is not named in the Gospel, but still is recited in the earlier order, for it is a privilege of Paul to always be joined with Peter.

Now, the *first* objection against this prayer is of Luther, who finds fault with the priest because the priest does not pray in this place to be admitted to the fellowship of Christ, as if he does not need it, but only to the fellowship of the saints; and again because he only asks a share with the saints, although Christ is not prepared to give a share, but his whole treasury.

I respond: These are mere calumnies. For the fellowship of the saints is *the fellowship of Christ*; for we ask that we might have fellowship of the saints in the kingdom of Christ, not the fellowship of the impious in the kingdom of the devil. What pertains to the word *share*, that is taken up from Scripture, which describes every good and happiness with the saints through the word "share". In Colossians 1:12, "Giving thanks to God the Father, who hath made us worthy of a share of the lot of the saints in light." And John 13:8, the Lord says, "If I do not wash you, you shall have no share with me." Add, that this part of the prayer, which Luther finds fault with and mocks, is on the other hand vehemently praised by Chemnitz (*loc. cit.* p. 843). "In the other commemoration of the saints in the canon the words are very beautiful, namely, 'To us sinners also, your servants, etc.' This formula is without a doubt an ancient commemoration of the saints." So, you see kind reader, how well the disciple of Luther agrees with his teacher.

The *second objection* is of Luther against the words, *Per quem haec omnia semper bona creas.* He objects that we think Christ creates us. To this point the thirteenth objection of Chemnitz pertains, who contends in his fashion these were once customarily said before the consecration to commend almsgiving to the people.

I respond: These words were at no time found in the Liturgies or their expositors, placed before the consecration; they are found after the consecration in Alcuin and Amalarius (*de officiis Ecclesiast.*, 3, 26) and among all later authors, which is why the conjecture of Chemnitz is inane.

These words, however, contain nothing absurd, but rather more are suited to the conclusion of the Canon; for they briefly commemorate all the divine benefits in regard to this sacrament, from the first inchoate production from prime matter, from where it is confected. Therefore, we say this sacrament is from God through Christ, by the notion of the matter: *Firstly,* to be created when the bread is created; *secondly* to be sanctified when it is dedicated through the first oblation to confect the sacrament; *thirdly*, to be vivified when the mystery of life is effected, both in the true body of the Lord, and in Christ himself, who is our life, when it is converted through the consecration; *fourthly*, it is blessed since everyone receives the effect of the blessing, namely that he might unite the head with the members by the sacramental efficacy; *fifthly*, and lastly, it is furnished to us to receive so that we might draw life. So, Alcuin explained this whole place, and after him Hugh of St. Victor (*de Officiis Divinis*, 2, 36).

CHAPTER XXVII
On the Lord's Prayer, and the Following Prayers

THE LORD's prayer follows after the canon, and certain other prayers whereby we are prepared to communion; and here the fourth part of the Mass begins. Although Innocent III, and other more recent authors include the Lord's prayer and some others within the Canon, nevertheless, Gregory (*Epistles* 7, 63), and Strabo (c. 22) write the Lord's prayer is read after the Canon. Moreover, the Lord's prayer is found in every Liturgy, and besides it must be read at Mass is clear from Cyril (*loc. cit.*) and Ambrose (*loc. cit.* 5, 4), as well as Jerome (*Contra Pelagianos*, 3), from Augustine (*epist. Ad Paulinum*, epistle 59), and from Gregory (*loc. cit.*), and from the fourth Council of Toledo (can. 17). After that prayer, a certain prayer is added, which begins: *libera nos quaesumus Domine, ab omnibus malis*, etc., which Chemnitz finds fault with in his fourteenth objection, because in it mention is made of the intercession of the saints; but we have already said many things on this matter in chapter 8. Add, that this prayer is found in Alcuin and other ancient authors, hence it is ancient.

Next, another prayer follows, while the host is broken and the body of the Lord is mingled with the blood: *Pax Domini sit semper vobiscum*, and *Haec commixtio et consecratio Corporis et Sanguinis Domini nostril Jesu Christi fiat accipientibus nobis in vitam aeternam.*[27] Now, the *Pax Domini* does not displease Luther or Chemnitz, but the *Haec commixtio* does.

So, Luther *first* objects, that here it is speaking on the mingling of the body of Christ with the blood, when Christ is one and indivisible.

I respond: Catholics do not understand the body and blood to be mingled in their proper species; for they know it cannot happen unless Christ were again wounded; rather, in the species *of bread and wine*. In the same way, by the notion of the species, it can be said to be mingled.

He objects *secondly*, that it is absurd that it says when this mingling is done that it is a consecration, since the consecration already happened by the words of the Lord.

I respond: That word *consecration* is not found in Amalarius (3, 31) and Innocent III (*loc. cit.*, 5), but only: *Fiat commixtio corporis, etc.*, for

---

[27] May the peace of the Lord be with you always; May this mingling and consecration of the body and blood of our Lord Jesus Christ become eternal life for us who receive it.

Book II, Ch. XXVII: The Concluding Prayers

which reason some believe it is superfluous. But the Roman Ordinal distinctly has: *Commixtio et consecratio.* And Micrologus (c. 18) reads it in the same way; the author of the Roman Ordinal was older than Amalarius, and Micrologus is older than Innocent. Nor does this word hold something unsuitable, if it is rightly understood. We do not ask that it should be consecrated now, but rather, that the consecration *which already took place* would be for us salutary unto eternal life. For one could, perhaps, suitably make the response that in this place it is on a question on some new consecration, which now arises from the mingling. For in the Liturgy of James, where the ceremony of the mingling takes place, these words are read: "It is united and sanctified." Hence, this consecration is nothing other than some new sacramental signification, as it is said to be consecrated, which acquires a sacramental signification; so also, it is said to be again consecrated, because it acquires another sacramental signification. Moreover, the Lord's resurrection is signified by that mingling, as Amalarius (3, 31) and all others write; for in the resurrection the Lord's flesh was again united with his blood. Therefore, in that mingling, there is a new consecration, while those species, which represent the death of Christ when they are divided, are now again joined among themselves, the resurrection of the Lord.

Thirdly, the same Luther objects that the force of conveying eternal life is not rightly attributed to that mingling, since the mingling is our work, if it has the force of conveying salvation, certainly we obtain salvation by our own work.

I respond: It is not absurd if we were to say by our work, proceeding from the aid of divine grace, we gain our salvation, for Paul holds: "...with fear and trembling work out your salvation." (Philip. 2:12), and "...with the mouth, confession is made unto salvation." (Rom. 10:10). But in this place, still we do not properly speak of salvation acquired through the mingling and consecration, as if these were our works. For the mingling and consecration are said to take place for our salvation, not because of the very action of mingling and consecration saves us, but because *the things themselves* that are mixed and consecrated, while we piously receive them, are of much benefit to salvation, wherefore, here we say: "May it be to us who receive it unto eternal life."

Fourthly, Chemnitz objects (and it is his fourteenth objection), the Canon of the Mass, when this mingling takes place, commands not only to disagree with Scripture and the Fathers, but also with the ancient Roman Pontiffs, for there is extant a prohibition of Pope Julius, cited by

Gratian, can. *Cum omne, de consecration,* distinc. 2.

I respond: Pope Julius does not forbid the mingling which takes place in the Mass, but that which a few were doing, when they wished to offer the sacrament of the Eucharist to the people. This is why Micrologus (c. 18) describes the mingling which is in the Mass, as the most ancient and legitimate, then in c. 19 he finds fault with that mingling which Julius rebuked. The 4th Council of Toledo (can. 17) calls to mind the mingling which is in the Mass, and proves it; the third Council of Braga (can. 1), however, forbids the mingling which Julius forbids. It does not have the appearance of truth that in the same country (Spain), in the same time, two contrary decrees would come about; for it is certain that those Councils were celebrated around the same time, namely in 650 A.D. Lastly, the mingling which is in the chalice is held in all the Greek liturgies as well as in the Roman Ordinal, still among Alcuin, Amalarius, and all others. Moreover, who would believe either that Julius condemned the use of every Church, or that all the Churches, even the Roman, refused to comply with Julius in the first place?

Next, the prayer *Agnus Dei*, etc. follows, which was instituted by Pope Sergius 900 years ago, as Strabo (c. 22) and Micrologus (c. 18) relate, as well as all others. And this prayer does not displease our adversaries.

Then three prayers follow before communion, which (as we noted above from Micrologus, c. 18), the ordo of the ancient Mass does not prescribe, rather the devotion of religious persons brought in. Luther finds fault with the first of these, on account of the words, *Non respicias peccata mea, sed fidem Ecclesiae tuae.*[28] For he says, with these words, that priests damn themselves because they affirm they are without faith, unworthy, a jackal by nature, to handle this sacrament, and from here it comes to pass that papists think this sacrifice pleases God *ex opere operato*, without the good impulse of the one making use of it.

But here Luther errs in three ways. *First*, he does not say that he does not have faith, but only that he has *sins*. Moreover, someone can not only have faith, but even charity and still acknowledge he is a sinner, otherwise no just man could say in the Lord's prayer, "Forgive us our trespasses." Therefore, the priest affirms he is a sinner, and does not have such faith, insofar as this mystery requires it, wherefore he says a little later, "O Lord, I am not worthy;" and so prefers that God would look to the faith *of the Church*, than to his own. For we distinguish a twofold dignity in regard to this sacrament. One, which the sacrament necessarily requires,

[28] Do not look upon my sins but on the faith of your Church.

Book II, Ch. XXVII: The Concluding Prayers

and this consists in the fact that a man must not be conscious of a mortal sin, and those who do are said to be unworthy (1 Cor. 11:27), and when the latter approach, they sin grievously. The second dignity is what the sacrament requires, if we regard not our imbecility, but its excellence, and this is placed also in the fact that, were we more pure than the rays of the sun and the angels themselves, still the priests speak in regard to this sacrament, when they affirm that they are unworthy.

Next, it is false that Catholics think this sacrifice is pleasing to God without a good activity of the one making use of it. For even if the minister that offers was perhaps bad himself, and lacked a good impulse, still, Christ is the principle one offering, and he does not lack a good impulse, nay more, here we pray that God would regard faith, i.e. the good impulse *of the Church*, because we think without the good impulse of someone offering the sacrifice God will hardly be pleased. But if, perhaps, Luther argues on the good impulse of the man, for whom the sacrifice is offered, a distinction must be made on the immediate effect of the sacrifice, which is to please God, and on the mediate, which is to justify man. If it is a question of the first, it is not absurd that the sacrifice is beneficial without the good impulse of the man for whom it is beneficial. Just the same, we can pray for those who are asleep, or impious, or even impenitent, so also offer the sacrifice. Even as a prayer, the sacrifice is also beneficial for him in this way, although he does not know what is done. But if it is a question of the second, it is false that the sacrifice is beneficial without the good impulse of man, since the sacrifice is chiefly offered that God, being pleased by this sacrifice, would inspire a good impulse in him, i.e. conversion.

Lastly, Luther is deceived when he opposes what takes place *ex opere operato* in the judgment of Catholics, to the good impulse, as if it were the same thing that the sacrifice is beneficial *ex opere operato*, and beneficial without the good impulse of the one using it. For, all Catholics teach the sacraments have force *ex opere operato*, and nevertheless, require a good impulse, i.e. faith and penitence, on the side of the one receiving them.

Then this prayer follows: *Quod ore sumpsimus*, etc. And that: *Corpus tuum Domine, quod sumpsi*, which Luther also approves in his *Formula of the Mass*; rather he only finds fault with the Collects, and the mention of sacrifice that is in them, but enough has been said on this matter.

Then it follows: *Ite Missa est*; the Greeks use such a dismissal, but with the words: "Let us go in the peace of Christ," to which the people respond: "In the name of the Lord", as is clear from the Liturgies of James,

Basil and Chrysostom. Hence, *Ite Missa est*, as Alcuin rightly teaches, means nothing other than "Go, you are allowed to leave;" but we already treated on this in first book, chapter one. This is why in certain Masses *Ite Missa est* is not said, rather *Benedicamus Domino*; and Micrologus (c. 64) gives the reason: in festival Masses the people always come to the Masses, and so, at the end the dismissal is announced publicly, while on ferial days, not very many come except for clergy and monks, for whom it is not said "Go", rather they are invited to remain in the praises of God, since their office is in prayer and the praises of the Lord. Still, there are certain solemn Masses, which the people go to, and still *Ite Missa est* is not said, but *Benedicamus Domino*, as in the Sundays of Advent and Lent. But this is to show only the penitential season; I do not know why it is penitential if the public dismissal is not announced, but each one leaves of his own accord.

Lastly, the *Placeat tibi sancta Trinitas follows*. Luther argues against such a prayer, because in it we pray for Christ; but this was answered above in the second objection of Luther, against the fourth prayer of the Canon.

Chemnitz condemns the same prayer in his sixteenth objection, where he says the representation of the priest is proposed to God for the propitiatory sacrifice. But Chemnitz always sings the same tune; for we do not commend our representation, but the sacrifice of the *Lord's Body* that has really been offered, that he would mercifully receive it, and concede propitiation to us.

Then the Blessing follows: *Benedicat vos, etc.*, which is clearly very ancient, both in the Greek Liturgies, and the Council of Agde (can. 47), where the people are commanded that on Sundays they are to be present for the celebration of the Mass, nor leave before the blessing of the priest. On this blessing, see Micrologus (cap. 21) where he shows it is not only lawful for bishops, but even priests to bless the people after Mass, and in can. 44 of the Council of Agde, where it seems to have been forbidden to priests, he answers that the decrees either needed to be understood on the blessing of a priest while the Bishop was present, or certainly it was abrogated by use. Thus, we have said enough on this sacrifice.

FINIS

AD HONOREM DEI

APPENDIX A

The Text of the Canon

Te ígitur, clementíssime Pater, per Jesum Christum Fílium tuum, Dóminumnostrum, súpplices rogámus, ac pétimus uti accépta hábeas, et benedícas, hæc dona, hæc múnera, hæc sancta sacrifícia illibáta, in primis, quæ tibi offérimus pro Ecclésia tua sancta cathólica: quam pacificáre, custodíre, adunáre, et régere dignéris toto orbe terrárum: una cum fámulo tuo Papa nostro N., et Antístite nostro N.,et ómnibus orthodóxis, atque cathólicæ et apostólicæ fidei cultóribus.

Meménto, Dómine, famulórum, famularúmque tuárum N., et N., et ómnium circumstántium, quorum tibi fides cógnita est, et nota devótio, pro quibus tibi offérimus: vel qui tibi ófferunt hoc sacrifícium laudis, pro se, suísque ómnibus: pro redemptióne animárum suárum, pro spe salútis et incolumitátis suæ: tibíque reddunt vota sua ætérno Deo, vivo et vero.

Communicántes, et memóriam venerántes, in primis gloriósæ semper Vírginis Maríæ, Genitrícis Dei et Dómini nostri Jesu Christi: sed et beáti Joseph, ejúsdem Vírginis Sponsi, et beatórum Apostolórum ac Mártyrum tuórum, Petri et Pauli, Andréæ, Jacóbi, Joánnis, Thomæ, Jacóbi, Philíppi, Bartholomǽi, Matthǽi, Simónis, et Thaddǽi: Lini, Cleti, Cleméntis, Xysti, Cornélii, Cypriáni, Lauréntii, Chrysógoni, Joánnis et Pauli, Cosmæ et Damiáni, et ómnium Sanctórum tuórum; quorum méritis precibúsque concédas, ut in ómnibus protectiónis tuæ muniámur auxílio. Per eúndem Christum Dóminum nostrum. Amen.

Therefore, most merciful Father, we humbly pray and entreat you, through Jesus Christ, your Son, Our Lord, that you would accept and bless these gifts, these offerings, these holy and spotless sacrifices, which, in the first place, we offer you for your holy Catholic Church: deign to pacify, to guard, to unite, and to govern her throughout the world, together with your servant N., our Pope, and N., our Bishop; and all orthodox believers of the catholic and apostolic faith.

Be mindful, O Lord, of your servants and handmaids N. and N., and of all here present, whose faith and devotion are known to you, for whom we offer, or who offer to you, this sacrifice of praise for themselves, and for all their own, for the redemption of their souls, for their hope of salvation and safety; and who pay their vows to you, the everlasting, living, and true God.

United among ourselves, as well as venerating first of all the memory of the glorious and ever Virgin Mary, Mother of our God and Lord Jesus Christ; and also of blessed Joseph, Spouse of the same Virgin, and of your blessed Apostles and Martyrs, Peter and Paul, Andrew, James, John, Thomas, James, Philip, Bartholomew, Matthew, Simon and Thaddeus; of Linus, Cletus, Clement, Sixtus, Cornelius, Cyprian, Lawrence, Chrysogonus, John and Paul, Cosmas and Damian, and all your Saints, by whose merits and prayers, grant that in all things we may be defended by the help of your protection. Through the same Christ, our Lord. Amen.

Appendix A

Hanc ígitur oblatiónem servitútis nostræ, sed et cunctæ famíliæ tuæ, quǽsumus, Dómine, ut placátus accípias: diésque nostros in tua pace dispónas, atque ab ætérna damnatiónenos éripi, et in electórum tuórum júbeasgrege numerári. Per Christum Dóminum nostrum. Amen.

We therefore beseech Thee, O Lord, to graciously accept this oblation of our service, as also of Thy entire family; dispose our days in Thy peace, save us from eternal damnation, and command that we be numbered in the flock of Thine elect. Through Christ our Lord. Amen.

Quam oblatiónem tu, Deus, in ómnibus, quǽsumus, benedíctam, adscríptam, ratam, rationábilem, acceptabilémque fácere dignéris: ut nobis Corpus, et Sanguis fiat dilectíssimi Fílii tui Dómini nostri Jesu Christi.

We beseech You, O God, that you would deign to make such an oblation, blessed, approved, ratified, reasonable and acceptable, so that it may become for us the Body and Blood of Your most beloved Son, our Lord, Jesus Christ.

Qui prídie quam paterétur, accépit panem in sanctas, ac venerábiles manus suas, et elevátis óculis in cælum ad te Deum Patrem suum omnipoténtem, tibi grátias agens, benedíxit, fregit, dedítque discípulis suis, dicens:Accípite, et manducáte ex hoc omnes,

Who, the day before He suffered, took bread into His holy and venerable hands, and with His eyes raised to you in heaven, O God, His almighty Father, giving thanks to You, blessed it, broke it, and gave it to His disciples saying: Take, all of you, and eat of this:

HOC EST ENIM CORPUS MEUM.

FOR THIS IS MY BODY

Símili modo postquam cænátum est,accípiens et hunc præclárum Cálicem in sanctas ac venerábiles manus suas:item tibi grátias agens, benedíxit, dedítque discípulis suis, dicens:Accípite, et bíbite ex eo omnes,

In like manner, after He had supped, taking also this excellent chalice into His holy and venerable hands, and giving thanks to You, He blessed it, and gave it to His disciples, saying: Take, all of you, and drink of this:

HIC EST ENIM CALIX SÁNGUINIS MEI, NOVI ET AETÉRNI TESTAMÉNTI: MYSTÉRIUM FÍDEI: QUI PRO VOBIS ET PRO MULTIS EFFUNDÉTUR IN REMISSIÓNEM PECCATÓRUM.

FOR THIS IS THE CHALICE OF MY BLOOD OF THE NEW AND ETERNAL TESTAMENT: THE MYSTERY OF FAITH: WHICH SHALL BE POURED OUT FOR YOU AND FOR MANY UNTO THE REMISSION OF SINS.

Hæc quotiescúmque fecéritis, in mei memóriam faciétis.

As often as you shall do these things, you do them in memory of Me.

Unde et mémores, Dómine, nos servi tui, sed et plebs tua sancta, ejúsdem Christi Fílii tui Dómini nostri tam beátæ passiónis, nec non et ab ínferis resurrectiónis, sed et in cælos gloriósæ ascensiónis: offérimus præcláræ majestáti tuæ de tuis donis, ac datis, hóstiam puram, hóstiam sanctam, hóstiam immaculátam, Panem sanctum vitæ ætérnæ, et Cálicem salútis perpétuæ.

Wherefore, Lord, we, Your servants, but also Your holy people, mindful of the same Christ, Your Son, our Lord, of His blessed passion, and of His resurrection from the dead, and of His glorious ascension into heaven, offer unto Your most excellent majesty of Your own gifts, bestowed upon us, a pure victim, a holy victim, an unspotted victim, the holy Bread of eternal life and the Chalice of everlasting salvation.

Supra quæ propítio ac seréno vultu respícere dignéris; etaccépta habére, sícuti accépta habére dignátus es múnera púeri tui justi Abel, et sacrifícium Patriárchæ nostri Ábrahæ: et quod tibi óbtulit summus sacérdos tuus Melchísedech, sanctum sacrifícium, immaculátam hóstiam.

Deign to regard them with a gracious and serene countenance, and to accept them, as You deigned to accept the gifts of Your just servant Abel, and the sacrifice of Abraham our Patriarch, and that which Your chief priest Melchisedech offered to You, a holy sacrifice, an unspotted victim.

Súpplices te rogámus, omnípotens Deus: jube hæc perférri per manus sancti Ángeli tui in sublíme altáre tuum, in conspéctu divínæ majestátis tuæ: ut quotquot, ex hac altáris participatióne sacrosánctum Fílii tui, Corpus, et Sánguinem sumpsérimus, omni benedictióne cælésti et grátia repleámur. Per eúndem Christum Dóminum nostrum. Amen.

Humbly we ask You, almighty God: command these offerings to be borne by the hands of Your holy Angel to Your altar on high, in the sight of Your divine majesty, so that as many of us as shall, by partaking from this altar, consume the most holy Body and Blood of Your Son, may be filled with every heavenly grace and blessing. Through the same Christ our Lord. Amen.

Meménto étiam, Dómine, famulórum, famularúmque tuarum N. et N. qui nos præcessérunt cum signo fídei, et dórmiunt in somno pacis. Ipsis, Dómine, et ómnibus in Christo quiescéntibus, locum refrigérii, lucis et pacis, ut indúlgeas, deprecámur. Per eúndem Christum Dóminum nostrum. Amen.

Be mindful also, O Lord, of your servants and handmaids N. and N. who have gone before us with the sign of faith and rest in the sleep of peace. To these, O Lord, and to all who rest in Christ, we plead that you grant a place of comfort, light, and peace. Through the same Christ our Lord. Amen.

Nobis quoque peccatóribus fámulis tuis, de multitúdine miseratiónum tuárum sperántibus, partem áliquam, etsocietátem donáre dignéris, cum tuis sanctis Apóstolis et Martýribus: cum Joánne, Stéphano, Matthía, Bárnaba, Ignátio, Alexándro, Marcellíno, Petro, Felicitáte, Perpétua, Ágatha, Lúcia, Agnéte, Cæcília, Anastásia, et ómnibusSanctis tuis: intra quorum nos consórtium, non æstimátor mériti, sed véniæ, quǽsumus, largítor admítte. Per Christum Dóminum nostrum.	To us sinners also, your servants, trusting in the multitude of your mercies, deign to grant some part and fellowship with your holy Apostles and Martyrs, with John, Stephen, Matthias, Barnabas, Ignatius, Alexander, Marcellinus, Peter, Felicitas, Perpetua, Agatha, Lucy, Agnes, Cecilia, Anastasia, and with all your Saints, into whose company, we beseech you, not as appraiser of merit but as bestower of pardon, to admit us. Through Christ our Lord.
Per quem hæc ómnia, Dómine, semper bona creas, sanctíficas, vivíficas, benedícis, et præstas nobis. Per ipsum, et cum ipso, et in ipso, est tibi Deo Patri omnipoténti, in unitáte Spíritus Sancti, omnis honor, et glória. Per ómnia sǽcula sæculórum.	Through whom, O Lord, you always create, sanctify, vivify, bless and bestow upon us all good things. Through Him and with Him and in Him is to you, God the Father almighty, in the unity of the Holy Spirit, all honor and glory, Through all ages of ages. (Forever and ever)

On the Controversies of the Christian Faith

By St. Robert Bellarmine

*Italic Text means forthcoming from Mediatrix Press

Tomus I
On The Word of God
On Christ
On the Roman Pontiff

Tomus II
On Councils
On the Church Militant
On the Marks of the Church

Tomus III
On Clergy
On Monks
On Laity

Tomus IV
On Purgatory
On Canonization of the Saints
On Relics and Images
On the design of Churches

Tomus V
On the Sacraments in General
On Baptism and Confirmation

Tomus VI
On the Most Holy Eucharist
On the Most Holy Sacrifice of the Mass

Tomus VII
On The Sacrament of Penance
On Indulgences

Tomus VIII
On the Sacrament of Order
On the Sacrament of Matrimony

Tomus IX
On Grace
On Good Works
On Justification

www.ingramcontent.com/pod-product-compliance
Lightning Source LLC
Chambersburg PA
CBHW011405070526
44577CB00004B/403